FINDING THE LAW

Tenth Edition

By

Robert C. Berring
Librarian and Professor of Law
School of Law (Boalt Hall)
University of California, Berkeley

AMERICAN CASEBOOK SERIES®

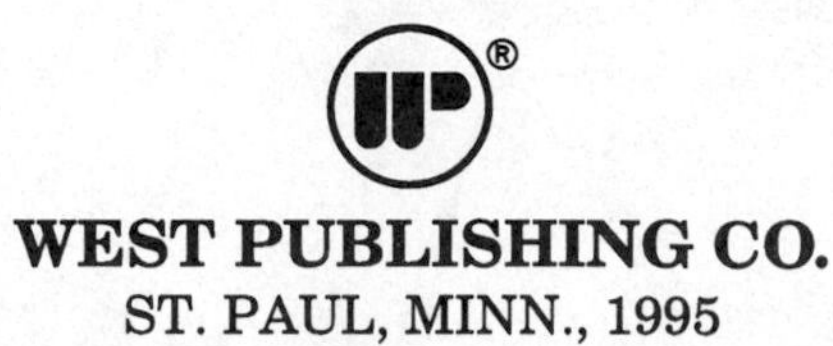

WEST PUBLISHING CO.
ST. PAUL, MINN., 1995

610 Opperman Drive
P.O. Box 64526
St. Paul, MN 55164–0526
1–800–328–9352

Printed in the United States of America

Library of Congress Cataloging-in-Publication Data

Berring, Robert C.
Finding the law / Robert C. Berring. — An abridged ed. of "How to Find the Law, 10th ed."
p. cm. — (American casebook series)
Includes index.
ISBN 0–314–06084–7
1. Legal research—United States. I. Title. II. Series.
KF240.B45 1995
340'.072073—dc20 95–264
CIP

ISBN 0–314–06084–7

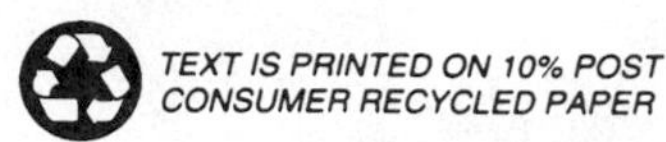

Foreword

Writing a textbook for use in legal research training is a daunting task. The field of legal research has never known a time so fluid as the 1990s. Pushed by burgeoning technology, legal information is changing, and the legal researcher must meet a host of new challenges to complete a successful search. The old research methods alone just will not do the job for the next generation, but the old methods are still important. Today's research text not only carries the traditional burden of conveying information on a difficult topic, it must convince computer lovers to master books and convince booklovers to learn new technology. Equally challenging are the changes on the publishing scene. The world of legal research once was built upon a few known companies like West and Lawyer's Co-operative. Now a spate of mergers and buy-outs have introduced two very large new players—Thompson and Reed–Elsevier, and the strategies of these companies is not yet clear. It is a time of change.

It is also a time of change for this book. **How To Find The Law** has sailed through eight editions as one of the flagship books launched from the bibliographic method of teaching research. It has provided a comprehensive treatment of the materials of legal research, taking them seriously and evaluating them with care. **Finding The Law** began as a paperback Abridgement of the Seventh Edition of **How To Find The Law,** and was meant to offer a less comprehensive alternative for use as a text in research courses. Being an Abridgement, it was a subset of the larger book, a republishing of approximately three quarters of the chapters of the larger book. That pattern of abridgement continued through the Eighth Edition. But this volume of **Finding The Law** is different. It is *not* an abridgement of **How To Find The Law,** it is a distillation of that text. By this we mean that **Finding The Law** now stands on its own. It will contain much information that appears in **How To Find The Law,** but it is designed more as a teaching tool than as a bibliographic resource. It is pared down in the hope that it will be of use in each of the variety of formats covered by legal research courses. For example, rather than treating the large array of secondary sources separately, as **How To Find The Law** will continue to do, it puts them all into one chapter. Most basic legal research courses do not have the time to examine each of the secondary sources in detail, but they do need to be mentioned. Thus **Finding The Law** will compress that discussion. It also will adopt a more informal tone. The book concentrates on the basic elements of legal research that most law school courses cover and will be independent of **How To Find The Law**. Since **Finding The Law** now stands on its own, the decision was made to proceed with its publication separately.

Such a change in **Finding The Law** did not help in solving the problem of how to deal with the moving target of electronic information. Law students today are studying legal research when it is in a time of profound change. It is not at all clear what the new world of legal research will look like when the dust has settled. Will everything and everyone be electric? Will there be different tiers of research according to wealth? Will new publishers reconfigure what has been a stable legal information universe? When law publishers are being sold for prices in the billions, and very large new players are entering the scene just as new information formats are gaining acceptance, everything is up for grabs. We elected to try to incorporate the newest formats and information innovations into the discussion of each type of information as it arises, but it is clear that no definitive description of each new product could be provided. We reason that information in electronic form is functionally no different than information printed on paper, even if the strategies for search may differ. With things changing so rapidly the best service that we can perform is to make students aware of how information works and to prepare them to evaluate intelligently and critically the inevitable barrage of new legal information products that they will encounter. We try to touch upon all new concepts and products, but in the current environment, there is not much more of use that can be done. The plan will be to update **Finding The Law** frequently. Now that it is freed from its umbilical link to **How To Find The Law,** that should be possible, and frequent updating may be the only answer.

How To Find The Law will remain the comprehensive treatment of legal information, but we hope that the new form of **Finding The Law** will be of service to those who labor in the vineyard of legal research training. Because the schedule for revision will be frequent, comments and criticisms are especially welcome.

ROBERT C. BERRING

Acknowledgments

Reaching the end of the process of redrafting and revision is humbling. Looking at the final manuscript one thinks of all that has gone into getting to this last stage. This book of course carries special debts. Although it is a new cut at Finding The Law, and is no longer just an abridgement of How To Find The Law, much of the old text carries forward. Certainly the ideas and energy of Morris Cohen and Kent Olson remain on every page. They bear no responsibility for errors or choices now, though, so send all corrections and complaints to me.

Special thanks are due to Vivian Distler, Esq. who provided invaluable assistance in putting it all together. She was indefatigable in checking sources, playing with data bases and coming up with new ideas. She also proved a researcher can work anywhere as she meandered across the country, laptop in hand. A tip of the hat to the folks at the University of Utah Law Library who were her most frequent host.

Leslie Farrer, Registrar at Boalt Hall, read the manuscript for style and comprehensibility. Bringing a professional editor's touch, she labored long to shorten my sentences. The parts that bog down are probably where I did not take her advice.

Ginny Irving, Senior Reference Librarian at Boalt Hall, read a number of chapters for content and provided invaluable help. Michael Levy and Rick Schultz saved my life a few times online, as I tried producing this with my own fingers.

Finally, I have to thank Kathleen Vanden Heuvel, Deputy Director and Lecturer in Law here at Boalt. Since we have taught Advanced Legal Research together for almost ten years, her ideas have profoundly influenced me. Not that she agrees with a lot of what I say, but she always makes it better.

*

Summary of Contents

*

Summary of Contents

*

Table of Contents

APPENDICES

*

FINDING THE LAW

Tenth Edition

*

Chapter 1

THE CONTEXT OF LEGAL RESEARCH

A. INTRODUCTION

Legal research is a complex enterprise. The typical first year law student might expect that the study of how to use legal materials, how to find particular cases, statutes and regulations, would be central to legal education. In fact, most of the first year of law school is spent reading and analyzing excerpts of cases as presented in casebooks. Casebooks are collections of severely edited cases that have been chosen by the casebook editors (these books are invariably done by law professors who teach in the field and are usually done as team efforts) to illustrate points of law or to raise legal issues. Unlike the original versions of casebooks, which consisted of nothing but cases, the modern casebook contains additional materials and commentary, but the edited cases remain the core of the casebook and the staple of the law school diet.

The resulting volume is usually a rather desiccated collection of the salient parts of a number of judicial opinions. The casebook is by its nature a hothouse text—the material is all there, preassembled and arranged. Rarely does a casebook require the student to read external materials, and when the students in a first year law school class are assigned "outside" reading, it is usually put on reserve in the law library. Thus it is possible for a first year law student to navigate through the common law courses that make up the first year of law school without doing any real research at all.

Of course most law schools have a moot court experience at some point in the first year of law school. The moot court exercise will require students to argue an appellate case by first preparing a brief and then carrying through an oral argument. Some real research may be involved here, but once again, the materials may be pre-assembled. There are frequently large numbers of students working on the same problem making the research process into more of a scavenger hunt than a real research experience. Moot court students may be directed to the materials that they need, and certain materials may even be designated as out of bounds. This hothouse variety research could hardly be deemed a "real" research situation, to say nothing of the fact that most lawyers do not do the specialized style of research that is typical of appellate practice.

Thus there is very little context in which to place any research training that the first year of law school might offer. One of the ideas that this book will build upon is that of **context**. To master research one must understand the context of a research problem, one must see it in a real world setting. This seldom happens in the first year of law school. Typical first year law students are busy with casebooks, not carrying out legal research. Rather than appearing as a natural part of the lawyering process, combined with legal analysis and reasoning, legal writing and other clinical skills, legal research training is presented to most law school students as a separate set of skills. One doesn't need research skills to read a casebook and there is no venue for using any newly acquired research skills in the normal first year program. Learning research in such splendid isolation is rather like learning to ride a bicycle by reading a book. The directions make little sense, the information seems boring and hard to retain, and when the time comes to actually ride a bicycle, one has to start over. It is no wonder that most first year research programs at American law schools are constantly under review; they are trying to accomplish the impossible.

It is therefore ironic that a major premise of modern American legal education is that the process of legal research—the finding, reading and analyzing of legal information—is central to the law school process. Christopher Columbus Langdell himself, the architect of modern legal education, uttered the following quotation in 1887

> We have ... constantly inculcated the idea that the library is the proper workshop of professors and students alike; that it is to us all that the laboratories of the university are to the chemists and

physicists, the museum of natural history to the zoologists, the botanical garden to the botanists.[1]

Langdell saw the library as a workshop, the place where the real learning was to go on. As in a workshop, it becomes essential to learn how to use the tools. (Of course Dean Langdell was also the man who developed the first casebook, which meant that law students had less need to go into the library to do any research, so don't be surprised if this all gets even stranger.)

What Langdell really meant was that students should read cases. Langdell believed that law was a science. If you read enough cases, especially the right ones, truth would begin to emerge. Langdell probably did not think that the process of legal research, which for him would be the process of finding cases, was very difficult. In the context of where and when Langdell lived, i.e. Cambridge, Massachusetts in 1870, he was right. In 1870 there were only a few thousand cases to be found. As a part of his everyday routine, a good legal scholar in 1870 was probably reading every case published by the United States Supreme Court, every decision from the lower federal courts, every case published in his own state, as well as cases from other important state courts, and quite likely cases from England as well. Most important cases were probably stored in his memory, supplemented by his notes. Legal research was one integrated process for legal scholars in the time of Langdell.

The real problem for someone in the age of Langdell was access to the cases in the first place. As Chapter 2 will relate, publication of cases in 1870 was unsystematic and slow. Once someone like Langdell did find cases though, he would read them all. One may have needed training in how to know which of the highly subjective and idiosyncratic early case reporters was reliable, but the techniques of searching were elementary. Volumes of case reporters were few and far between, and often expensive. These legal researchers had a data base problem; just getting their hands on the data was hard.

Further, in 1870, there was relatively little statutory law to be examined, only a trace of administrative material, and a very small body of secondary sources. It was a manageable and comfortable universe of legal information. Every relevant book would easily have fit in the reading room of today's typical law school law library. There was no need to learn search strategy; the legal research process came simply and naturally to one who read lots of cases.

No amount of imagination could have prepared Christopher Columbus Langdell for the world of legal information presented to the law student in the twenty first century. There are an estimated 3,000,000 cases now available, with another 100,000 being added each year. Rivers of statutes and administrative regulations are pouring forth from the state and federal governments. Municipalities, counties and other units

1. Langdell, "The Harvard Law School", 3 Law Q. Rev. 123, 124 (1887).

of local government are publishing law. A fixed constellation of traditional legal publishers is being augmented by dozens of new publishers entering the field. There are large numbers of secondary sources ranging from practice-related materials to scholarly commentaries. And the material is produced in a dizzying array of formats. Books, periodicals, newsletters, compact discs, on-line data bases, microform, and audio visual materials are in the mix, and the potential of technology is not exhausted yet. The legal researcher in 1995 is not sitting down in the quiet, book-lined study that Langdell knew at the Harvard Law Library in Cambridge in 1870 (the researcher is certainly not sitting down there if she is a woman since women had to wait another 80 years to be admitted to Harvard Law School). The legal researcher in 1995 is thrust into a maelstrom of information, more like a Stephen Spielberg movie than a scholarly afternoon.

Yet legal education has not adjusted for all of this change. Legal research is still taught in much the same way as it was fifty years ago. Therefore this book, and you as the person using it, face some serious challenges. Four are worth setting forth at the start of the process.

1. RESEARCH IN TWO WORLDS

First, the legal researcher of 1995 must live in two worlds: paper and electronic. Over the past one hundred years legal publishers developed an intricate set of printed materials which controlled the flow of legal information. Most of this apparatus was built around cases. Elaborate systems of reporting, digesting, tracing and evaluating cases developed. Mastering these systems was the core of legal research courses until very recently. The lawyer graduating from law school in 1970 had to know much more than someone like Langdell, because the use of the traditional paper- based, case-centered tools had grown more complex. But it was still a system built on the old paradigm. This is old style, traditional research, and it is the only kind of research that some senior lawyers, judges and law professors accept as legitimate. That will change in the course of the next generation, but it hasn't changed yet. Many of those in decision-making roles are part of the world of paper information.

The new world of legal research is rooted in electronic information. In the past twenty years the variety of electronic data bases has grown, and the information which they store and the search methods for using them have improved enormously. Two of the systems, WESTLAW and LEXIS now play a major role in the research process, and will be an important part of today's law school experience. The vendors of these systems invest considerable sums in providing training, materials and low cost usage of their systems to law students. Compact disk-based systems (CD–ROMS) are already making inroads in many states, assuming central roles in some of them. The internet is carrying a wide array of legal information. Some law firms are totally networked and are led by true cyberspace cowboys who are on the cutting edge of the information revolution. Some courts are similarly advanced. But such organizations are the pioneers. The large mass of the legal community is still in the midst of change.

It is inevitable that in the use of electric research sources lies the future of law, but the future is not quite here. Many sources currently appear in both paper and electronic form. Law students must learn how to use both. This will appear irrational at times since for all but the computerphobe life will be so much easier on-line. It is important to keep in mind that this current ease of use depends on the fact that the vendors of on-line data bases supply their products to law schools at a deep discount. There is no cost to most law students who use the data bases. The vendors of the systems are willing to underwrite the law students' initial forays into electronic research in hope of gaining future users. The pay-off for the vendors comes after law school. Once out of the cocoon of legal education, the researcher's world will change and on-line usage will be billed to one's employer. Some employers may not have on-line systems or may severely restrict the use of such systems. The researcher may have to rely heavily on a combination of paper and electronic sources, or on paper alone. Those who work in small practices or public interest organizations will face even more challenging budgetary constraints. Intelligent choices about format and resource allocation will have to be made. These are questions that no one had to consider in 1960. Today's intelligent researcher must know how to use both kinds of material.

2. RESEARCH AS A NEW SKILL

Second, the process of finding information has grown much more complex. Intuitive methods based on the case system and grounded in the old Digest System, (a marvelously complex method of sorting cases that will be explored at length in Chapter 4), are no longer enough. Where research was once fairly straightforward, it is now filled with choices and alternatives. In the old world of legal research everything started and ended with cases. Langdell's world consisted largely of cases, and tools that sorted and updated them. These days are also gone. Research in legislation and administrative law are much more central to the work of many of today's lawyers. Indeed, some lawyers spend much of their research time on non-legal research. For example, if one's client owns a coal mine one will do a great deal of research in the area of coal and its extraction. Such research does not fit into the old model of legal research, but it may be crucial to the success of one's practice. Legal research is growing much more sophisticated.

For all of these purposes the old tools and methods are inadequate. One still must find cases, but one needs a much wider range of skills and familiarity with special tools and special search techniques. Using some tools will call for special skills, and only the foolhardy will venture into this jungle without training.

3. THE ECONOMICS OF RESEARCH

When legal information consisted of the traditional sets of books that reported cases and statutes, the idea of thinking of legal research in economic terms would have seemed bizarre. Although the sets did cost money, it was easy to think of them as sunk costs, after all every law library had to have them. And the use of these books was more informal; sloppy research was more likely to be tolerated as a young lawyer learned the ropes.

That world is gone. Legal information, like other forms of information, is now presented as a commodity. It is priced by the unit, in different pricing schemes and different combinations. The lawyers may pay for electronic information in any of a variety of ways, but all will reflect in the eventual charge. Today's legal researcher must factor in how much the research will cost. It may be that a faster or more complete way of gathering data or solving a problem exists, but that cost will force a slower or less complete method to be used. As one senior partner put it, "It is just as foolish to do $2,000 worth of research on a $300 problem as it is to do $300 worth of research on a $2,000 problem."

The time of the researcher is also a cost factor. As attorneys in private practice and in some public sectors as well are forced to account for their time in 6 minute increments, the pressure to accomplish tasks quickly grows apace. A premium will be put on efficiency, and sloppiness or wastefulness will be disastrous.

To operate in this new world, the researcher must know what information costs, and what levels of performance the particular problem requires. This reinforces the need to understand all forms of information from the oldest to the newest, and it introduces a new level of calculation to the research process.

4. LEARNING ABOUT LEGAL RESEARCH

The great challenge for any research text is to balance the need to communicate the excitement of legal research with the tedium of detail inherent in discussing individual research tools. No book can hope to describe it all, and no book can hope to accurately detail the latest advances in technology. Technology will not hold still. This book strives towards two goals. It will attempt to provide the student with a firm grounding in how the tools of legal research **function**. This should prepare one for legal information in any form. It should prepare one to use traditional tools or the newest that technology offers. Second, it will attempt to provide a comprehensive discussion of each of the tools that one might encounter. By using both a macro and micro approach, this book should become a resource. At some point in the future when the student is asked to prepare a legislative history, this text should be of help. No one, not even the author, aged and wise as he is, knows all of this material by heart. Learn the patterns, the way things work, and then look up specific information when it's needed. If one understands the functioning of the tools, one will always be able to fall back on the text for details.

B. CHARACTERISTICS OF LAW

There are some general characteristics of American law that will help in understanding the materials. In general these characteristics are as true of electronic information as they are of paper. Understanding them provides a template for all that follows. Some of them touch on quite fundamental issues where this text can not offer much detail, still it will help to understand the lay of the land.

1. THE UNITED STATES AS A FEDERAL SYSTEM

The United States is a federal system. When the Constitution was adopted, it represented the agreement of thirteen colonies, each of which wished to retain as much independence as possible. Though times have changed the balance of federal and state power, each state retains law making power in some areas. In other areas, the federal government holds sway. Inevitably, some areas are ambiguous. There will be entire courses, and parts of other courses, in the law school curriculum devoted to various aspects of the balance of these powers. For purposes of legal research, however, the salient point is that there will be a profusion of materials to deal with in doing research. Each state and the federal government has its own court system, its own legislature and its own group of administrative agencies. Each of these bodies will publish its own materials. Each is important. No one can master the idiosyncracies of the legal system of each state, and even the seasoned researcher is sometimes surprised by what they find.

This book will attempt to introduce patterns of publication that aid in understanding the common features among all of these materials. Most of them do follow fairly predictable lines, but the profusion of materials is an intimidating distraction. The need to provide bibliographic detail is unavoidable, and this is another area where this book will try to be resource to the user. In addition, Appendix A lists guides that have been prepared for the researcher working in one specific state jurisdiction. These are good sources that treat state publications in the depth of detail that a practitioner will need in order to work in that particular jurisdiction.

2. THE UNITED STATES AS A COMMON LAW SYSTEM

The United States is a common law country. The roots of the common law lie in English history and the way in which the United States has evolved its common law has been full of twists and turns. For the purposes of legal research several facts are clear.

A. Judicial Decisions and Precedent. Court decisions and the doctrine of precedent play an especially important role in American legal research. The common law was based on the belief that there was a set of customs, a way of doing things, that was common to the English people. This set of customs was unwritten, but it was very real. When judges rendered opinions they were to draw on the "common law" for legal principles. Judges did not "make" the law, a judge instead was to draw upon the common law for the relevant principle. Once a judge enunciated a common law legal principle, especially once the opinions of such judges were written down, then that principle was frozen. Then it was published and others could refer to it. Even if the facts in a subsequent case differed, the same legal principle could be applied. This is the concept of precedent. Once a judicial opinion on an issue of law was settled, then it is settled for all time and can be referred to by other courts and judges. This process of referring to fixed precedent was called "stare decisis." Thus it became important to find earlier cases that might be relevant to the legal questions raised in any legal research problem.

One unfamiliar with this system might ask about the role of legislation. Shouldn't the elected legislators of the relevant jurisdiction be making the law? That seems obvious today, but in the days in which the system of English common law was developing the legislature had almost no role. A very small amount of legislation was passed, and it was seen as filling in the missing spots of the common law. Great legal writers like William Blackstone, who wrote his Commentaries at the end of the 18th Century, mistrusted the actions of the legislature and preferred the perceived elegance of the common law.

American legislatures today pass thousands of laws each year touching on any subject they please, and the myth of a perfect overarching common law has been abandoned. But the holdover of the common law heritage is that American judges can "make" law when necessary. In fact although most judicial opinions today interpret statutes or administrative rules, American judges still have great power. Reconciling this power in a democratic society, how judges who are often not elected can be given such power, is the frequent subject of scholarly analysis. Here it is only necessary to note that appellate court decisions still have precedential value, and finding a case on point is a major goal of research. Jurisdiction is crucial here. Only the court in one's jurisdiction has legal authority. A court in another jurisdiction does not hold power outside its jurisdictional boundaries.

B. Is the Precedent Still Good Law? There is a judicial hierarchy within each jurisdiction. A court higher on the ladder can always reverse or revise one lower down if a case is appealed and considered. There is also a time factor here. A court may change its mind and reverse itself on an issue later in time when a subsequent case raises the same issue. A flat-out reversal is a rather rare occurrence, however, since it puts incredible strain on the common law tradition. The court is contradicting itself, and that can quickly create problems. The ultimate expression of the cynicism that this can produce was the late Justice William O. Douglas's statement that constitutional law is whatever five Justices on the United States Supreme Court think it is. This cynical statement has been much criticized but it points to a real problem. Reversals do occur and it will be vital to the researcher that he unearth them.

If one finds a case that one wished to rely on, it will be important to find out not just if it has been overruled, but how it has been treated. Courts sometimes criticize or limit past opinions rather than overturning them. The researcher will need to know if that has happened. Cases are organic, they grow or wither. There is a universe of tools that the researcher will need to master in order to succeed at this. Such mastery is an essential part of the research process.

3. THE OBSESSIVE/COMPULSIVE NATURE OF LEGAL RESEARCH

One of the most distinctive and difficult features of American legal research is the obsession that many American legal researchers have with finding every relevant case. Since an American law student is immersed in the system it seems only natural, but research need not be done in this manner. The English, from whom we inherit the common law system, have never believed in publishing every possible case. The drive to publish and to retrieve every case is a peculiarly American phenomenon. It traces back to some decisions made in the 19th Century by American lawyers and by the legal information market.

English legal publishers and reporters selected cases for their value, focusing on those which made new or useful points or were otherwise likely to be important to lawyers and judges. From the earliest of American publications, however, most of the reporters sought comprehensive rather than selective coverage. Although not always achieved, this was a goal through the 19th century. But efforts at reporting remained unsystematic. This system grew chaotic as the 19th Century progressed. American law was growing, the number of jurisdictions was increasing and the volume of caselaw was becoming unmanageable. Lawyers were crying out for more cases. Into this breach stepped John B. West.

Mr. West was not a judge, lawyer or librarian, he was a salesman. He saw that lawyers wanted cases and wanted them quickly. To meet that need he founded the West Publishing Company and decided that the best approach would be to publish every appellate decision from every jurisdiction in a standard format. Rather than having editors choose what cases were useful, West published them all, and published them quickly and cheaply and let the researcher decide which cases were useful. The result was the National Reporter System, a set of case reporters which will be discussed in the chapters immediately following this one. West's National Reporter System drove almost all competitors out of the market. Coupled with the American Digest System, a method West developed to classify all of the cases by subject, it came to dominate American law.

Publishing all of the cases and allowing the lawyer to sort out what was important allowed obsessive research to flourish. The reporter volumes on the shelf are filled with many trivial, repetitive cases, but there might be a gem hidden in the compost heap, and the researcher felt compelled to check.

This obsessiveness was capped by the development of the Shepards citation system. Frank Shepard designed a system of tables that allowed one to take the citation to a case in which one is interested and find every subsequent mention of that case by later courts. Once again the mention might be trivial or repetitive, but if a subsequent opinion mentioned that citation, it would be listed in Shepards. Shepards performs other functions of course. It tells the researcher if the case has been overruled or modified, for example. But at its heart is the listing of every subsequent mention of the case. Looking up a case like **Roe v. Wade** in Shepards is an awe inspiring act. There are thousands of listings. This text will devote a chapter to using citators, and will describe how on-line systems are affecting this use. For the purposes of traditional legal research, however, we can note that by 1910 the perfect paper tools for obsessive research were in place. West was reporting virtually every appellate decision, then classifying it into its digest system, and the Shepards Company was listing every subsequent citation of the case.

This obsessive/compulsive research style has carried over into other sources as well. The standard operating procedure for American legal publishers has been to provide everything and more. Legal information consumers are thus presented with a myriad of tools that contain staggering amounts of information. It has lead to data base overload. One of the most basic principles of information theory is that the larger a data base is, the more difficult it is to work with. Law is a collection of mega-data bases. This may be the biggest challenge facing the researcher.

4. LEGAL JARGON

Studying law involves learning a new language. Every field has its own set of terms and special usage, but law not only creates but is also shaped by its language to a very high degree. The traditional adage that law school teaches one to "think like a lawyer" refers in part to one's ability to use legal terminology effectively. There is no simple way to accomplish this. Much of it will come via osmosis during law school.

One problem in doing legal research is that subject access to materials depends so heavily on jargon. Legal materials like cases and statutes have always been published in chronological and jurisdictional order instead of in a subject arrangement. A volume of the West National Reporter System will have a case on criminal law sitting next to a case on real estate which is next to a case on copyright etc. The primary statutory volumes operate the same way. This makes the tools that allow subject access to these materials essential. And it is not just a matter of the index to each individual case reporter or statutory publication. As later chapters will explain, these books are issued in lengthy series, comprising dozens or hundreds of volumes. Tools are needed that offer access to the whole set.

The grandparent of such tools is the American Digest System from the West Publishing Company. Since it has been used for one hundred years to organize the points of law in all published cases, it has become a part of the deep structure of American law, and many other tools are built around it. But there are other indexes and abstracting systems that will be important to the researcher, and each will be built around legal jargon. This is why legal materials are often difficult for non-specialists. Anyone can understand how to work an index, but one has to know what entries to check under.

This is one area where the advent of electronic research has not yet changed things. Both the Boolean searching method, and the WIN and Freestyle systems, both of which will be discussed later in detail are dependent on the specific language used by judges, legislators, administrative personnel and commentators.

There is no simple solution here. One must be especially careful and make liberal use of legal dictionaries. When doing legal research, be especially careful to check the meaning of words. Some quite common expressions, for example "liability" or "reasonable" have quite different meanings when used in a legal context. Learning these usages and other aspects of legal meaning will be a major part of legal education for most students. It is a learning process which should never stop.

C. LEGAL AUTHORITY

Traditionally, legal research texts divided all legal sources into primary and secondary authority. Primary authority is authority which is a statement of the law itself. It is not commentary on the law or description of the law, it **is** the law. Finding primary authority has long been the focus of most legal research.

In a common law jurisdiction like the United States, there are two basic sources of primary authority: appellate decisions and statutes. The relation of cases to precedent has already been discussed. It is important to note as well that not all parts of a judicial opinion are primary source material. Only when a judge is resolving an issue of law is the opinion primary source material. Judges often write quite discursive opinions. A judge may lament the decline of Western civilization, discuss the cinema or ramble as he or she pleases, but that part is nothing but "dicta". "Dicta" is a term that means any words in the appellate opinion that do not relate to resolving an issue of law. Only when the judge resolves an issue of law does primary authority appear. Nor does the written resolution of an issue of law that appears in a concurring opinion or in a dissenting opinion count as primary authority. If one is reading an opinion written by a court that has more than one judge and there are several opinions, the primary source lies only in the majority opinion of the court.

Statutes and administrative materials are primary sources, but sorting them out can be tricky. Enactments of the legislative body in a jurisdiction are clearly primary sources of law. Constitutions and treaties also fall under this rubric as statutory in nature. The delicate part arises in the matter of administrative law. Technically administrative agencies are created by legislative enactment, and their law-making power is delegated to them by their authorizing statute. Therefore all administrative rules and regulations are subject to legislation. The enormously complex entities that federal and state agencies become are often systems unto themselves and one is sometimes hard pressed to think of them as simple creatures of a legislative act, but they are. Because of the pervasiveness of administrative law in today's legal system, and the complexity of materials that comprise administrative publications, most commentators now list administrative materials as a distinct and separate source of primary authority.

In the end it is probably only of importance in textbooks like this one how one classifies the materials. The important point is that administrative materials are vital to legal research in the real world. The fact that many law school curricula will never call on the student to actually use these materials make the treatment of them in Chapter 8 even more important.

Complicating the notion of primary authority is the fact that the three types of materials intersect at many points. Cases frequently interpret statutes or regulations, statutes or regulations may be passed in reaction to a particular decision or a line of cases or a particular administrative rule, and administrative rules may implement cases or statutes. The legal researcher must be adept at navigating between these shoals.

Quite simply, secondary sources consist of everything else. Even information that looks as official as the headnotes in a reported decision or the annotations to a statute are secondary. They are written by editors who work with the publishers, not by the lawmaker. Someone has intervened between the researcher and the primary source. In research one has to rely on such interpretive aids, and in some cases they will take on decisive importance, but they are not primary. Several chapters will be devoted to types of finding aids and advising on when and how to best use them.

D. CONCLUSION

Legal research is a body of skills which require an appreciation of traditional sources and an understanding of the new world of legal information. If approached functionally, concentrating on how tools work and why they work in that particular way, the great body of information will yield it secrets. Memorizing the names of all the sets of materials in this book is less important than understanding how they work. If one can accomplish that one can have a bit of Langdell's world and the newest in computer technology and make them work together.

Chapter 2

COURT REPORTS

A. Introduction.
B. The Hierarchy of Court Systems.
C. The Distinction Between Holding and Dictum.
D. Publication of Cases.
E. Forms of Published Decisions.
F. Components of a Decision.
   1. Caption.
   2. Docket Number.
   3. Citation.
   4. Syllabus and Headnotes.
   5. Attorneys.
   6. Opinion.
G. Supreme Court of the United States.
   1. *United States Reports.*
   2. *United States Supreme Court Reports, Lawyers' Edition.*
   3. West's *Supreme Court Reporter.*
   4. Looseleaf Services.
   5. WESTLAW and LEXIS.
   6. Other Electronic Sources.
   7. Newspaper Accounts.
H. Lower Federal Courts.
   1. *Federal Cases.*
   2. *Federal Reporter* and *Federal Supplement.*
   3. Specialized West Reporters.
   4. Looseleaf Services and Topical Reporters.
   5. WESTLAW and LEXIS.
   6. New Electronic Sources.
I. State Courts.
   1. Official Reports.
   2. West's National Reporter System.
   3. Looseleaf Services and Topical Reporters.
   4. WESTLAW and LEXIS.
   5. Compact Disks.
J. Summary.
K. Additional Reading.

A. INTRODUCTION

American law, both in its popular manifestations and in the minds of many of its practitioners, focuses upon "case law." Law students are educated by the case method, lawyers portrayed in the media are almost always working on litigation, and the American legal system, along with the common law system generally, is most easily distinguished from other legal systems by its heavy reliance on the precedential value of judicial opinions. Traditionally, legal research courses and texts have given considerable attention to cases, their forms of publication, and their finding tools. This emphasis was perhaps justified by the complicated modern systems of case publication and digesting, but it was also a result of the commonly shared assumption that mastering case law research was the most important and the necessary first step in legal research.

Today, most commentators acknowledge that statutory law plays a far more important role than case law in the day-to-day life of individuals in the United States, and the influence of administrative law is similarly pervasive. While the significance of case law in everyday life may be somewhat reduced, its vitality in legal thinking, and therefore in legal research, is unchallenged. It is impossible to conduct systematic research without a complete understanding of cases, their components, their systems of publication, and the means of access to them. The next three chapters will concentrate on these questions.

B. THE HIERARCHY OF COURT SYSTEMS

"Case law" generally refers to the written opinions of appellate courts on specific issues raised in litigated disputes. Only a tiny fraction of court cases result in such opinions. To understand this, one must have a sense of the basic structure of American judicial systems. In every jurisdiction, federal and state, there is a hierarchy of at least two and often three levels of courts.

The *trial court* level is the first level in the court system. In operation it may have numerous subdivisions and special branches (e.g., probate, family court, small claims court, etc.), but every jurisdiction has a trial court of general jurisdiction at which most disputes, both civil and criminal, are initially adjudicated. Here persons who wish to litigate a civil matter can bring before a trier of fact (a judge or jury) the issues in their case. Most criminal cases are brought to trial at this level.

It is in the trial court that issues of fact are determined. In an automobile accident case, for example, the trier of fact must decide such matters as the color of a traffic light or the relative speed of two vehicles. Either a jury or a judge will answer these factual questions, and those answers will be fixed for the balance of the litigation, unless some irregularity of procedure or bias can be shown in the fact-finding process. That is to say once the trial court determines the light was red for oncoming traffic, that fact is determined and cannot be appealed.

There is, however, another kind of issue that can arise at the trial court level—an issue of "law." The plaintiff, for example, might attempt to introduce testimony from a witness who claims to have heard the defendant's mother say that the defendant admitted he had been speeding at the time of the accident. Defense counsel might object that such testimony should not be admitted into evidence because of the *hearsay rule,* which governs what secondhand testimony is admissible at trial. A question concerning the admissibility of evidence is an issue of law and must be determined by the judge, even in a jury trial. If the trial judge issues a written opinion on the decision of that issue, it may be published and included within our notion of "case law."

The trial judge's ruling on an issue of law *can* be appealed to a higher court. The next level in most jurisdictions, including the federal court system, is the *intermediate appellate court.* If there was a valid evidentiary question posed, and if it was an issue that was appealable under the rules of the court system, then the appellate court would decide whether or not the trial court was correct in its ruling on the admission of evidence. If this occurs, the attorneys for each party file and exchange written briefs setting forth their respective positions, and an oral argument may be held. An appellate court usually consists of three or more judges, who confer and vote on the determination of the issue. One of the judges usually writes an opinion summarizing the question, stating the determination (or holding), and setting forth the reasoning behind it. The written resolution of such issues of law constitute the decision of the case. "Cases," as we will use the term in this text, represent those decisions, or the written determination of issues of law.

If the losing party in the appellate court continues to believe that his or her position is legally correct, the decision of that court can frequently be appealed to a *higher* court. The highest court in each jurisdiction, the *court of last resort,* is known as the Supreme Court in most states and in the federal system. (A few states have no intermediate appellate court, and appeals go directly from the trial court to the supreme court.) The court of last resort's pronouncements are binding on all trial and intermediate appellate courts in its jurisdiction.

Because judicial decisions resolve issues of law, most are generated from the upper two levels of the court systems. The United States District Courts (the trial courts of the federal system) do produce a substantial number of opinions, but very few states publish any decisions from their trial court level. Those that do, publish only a small fraction of the opinions written. Most trial court actions do not produce a written opinion at all. They do generate a record, as trial transcripts and pre-trial proceedings are filed with the clerk of the court, but such materials are rarely published. The absence of a written or published opinion often confuses novice researchers who expect to find a report of every "case." One may read in the newspaper about an important new case but find no published opinion, for the simple reason that no judicial opinion was written.[1]

Not all appellate decisions are published, since the sets of published cases for intermediate appellate courts are selective, like those for trial courts. On the other hand, virtually all decisions of the courts of last resort for every state and for the federal system are reported in full. Often, however, a court of last resort will simply reject an appeal from the lower court or affirm its holding by order without writing an opinion. When the Supreme Court of the United States refuses to hear a case, its action is known as *denying a petition for writ of certiorari,* or "cert. denied." A court of last resort may determine the outcome of a case by refusing to hear an appeal and thereby letting a lower court decision stand. Frequently newspapers carry articles about such "decisions" of a court, where no opinion was actually written and consequently no report of the case produced.

C. THE DISTINCTION BETWEEN HOLDING AND DICTUM

Under the doctrine of *stare decisis,* a case's holding will govern other cases in the same jurisdiction in which the facts and issues are substantially similar to those of the case which generated the rule of law. The holding, or *ratio decidendi,* of a case can usually be summed up in a single declaratory sentence. Everything else in the court's opinion is *dicta,* or *obiter dicta,* something "said by the way." Judges may comment in their opinions on any number of extraneous issues, or enlarge on their reasoning, or speculate about possibilities which are not material to the resolution of the immediate controversy.

The importance of the distinction between holding and dictum is that only the holding of the court is authoritative and binding in like cases under the doctrine of precedent. The reason for the distinction lies in the adversary system which is central to our legal process. That system assumes that both parties to a legal controversy will be represented by competent counsel, that counsel will each produce the best possible arguments for the resolution of disputed issues in his or her favor, that lapses in the legal reasoning espoused by either party will become apparent, and a right result will be reached. Whatever the validity of these assumptions, the consequence is that a court is considered competent to decide only those issues which were in dispute and which were therefore argued before it. The issues in dispute, of course, are the issues the court is required to resolve in order to decide the controversy between the parties. The holding is limited to the decision and the significant or material facts upon which the court necessarily

1. Information on trial verdicts and damage awards, primarily for different types of tort litigation, is available in services known as *verdict reporters.* The best known of these publications is *Personal Injury Valuation Handbooks* (Jury Verdict Research, looseleaf); others include *Jury Verdicts Weekly* and *Verdicts, Settlements & Tactics* (Shepard's/McGraw–Hill, monthly).

relied in arriving at its determination. Everything else is dicta and therefore not binding.

The language employed by the court in explaining and clarifying its decision helps one ascertain the court's intention regarding the narrowness or breadth of its decision, so no competent lawyer ever totally ignores dictum. A later court, however, is not bound by that dictum and may not be receptive to its rationale. While dictum cannot be ignored, then, it cannot be relied upon as precedent and cannot be cited as authority for a proposition, without explanation. It should be noted, however, that a court may clarify its views on an important legal question not necessarily before it in a case, in anticipation that the question will arise in the future. A well-reasoned dictum may be more persuasive—and therefore more significant—than an outworn holding.

D. PUBLICATION OF CASES

From its earliest beginnings in antiquity, the reporting of cases helped to achieve certainty in the law, by providing written records for later tribunals faced with similar issues and thereby reducing further disputes. The earliest evidence of recorded judicial decisions in England dates from the 11th century. Two hundred years later a series of case reports, known as the Year Books, began providing notes of debates between judges and counsel on the points in issue in cases. While not containing actual reports of decisions, the Year Books were used to guide pleaders in subsequent cases. Although manuscripts of reported cases exist from as early as the 13th century, the first printed versions appeared in about 1481 or 1482, and the Year Books continued until 1535.[2] The Year Books were replaced by *nominative* reporters, that is, reports named for the person who recorded or edited them. The first nominative reporter was prepared by Edmund Plowden and published in 1571. It was followed by numerous volumes by dozens of jurists and lawyers, of varying accuracy and authority.[3]

The decisions of American courts, on the other hand, were not published at all during the colonial period and the early years of independence. American lawyers and judges relied for precedent on the decisions of the English courts, even though only a limited number of those volumes were available here. The first volumes of American court decisions were not published until 1789, thirteen years after independence. Publication of domestic reports developed slowly, and the courts of some states operated for decades without published decisions.

The movement for publication grew, however, spurred by several concerns. There was the patriotic feeling that it was important to

2. Percy H. Winfield, *The Chief Sources of English Legal History* (Harvard University Press 1925), chapter VII.

3. For an excellent history of early English reports after the Year Books, see L.W. Abbott, *Law Reporting in England 1485–1585* (Athlone Press 1973). For a more extensive survey of the nominative reporters, see John W. Wallace, *The Reporters, Arranged and Characterized with Incidental Remarks* (reprint 1959) (Soule & Bugbee 1882).

construct an American system of jurisprudence. Now that the country had freed itself from English rule, it should no longer be subject to English case law.[4] Yet the doctrine of precedent created a need for the publication of decisions. If American judges rendered decisions which created new rights and responsibilities and changed the common law, those decisions should be recorded and made available to the public. Moreover, revolutionary times produced a general distrust of judges. Wary of unrepresentative authority, the citizens of the new republic felt that judges should be accountable for the decisions they made. Written decisions and their publication would facilitate that accountability.

Ephraim Kirby's *Reports of Cases Adjudged in the Superior Court of the State of Connecticut from the Year 1785 to May 1788* (Collier & Adam, 1789) is generally regarded as the first American reporter volume.[5] In a preface Kirby discusses the concerns which led to the publication of his reports, including the inapplicability of English law in the new country and the need to create a permanent body of American common law.

The early volumes of privately published court decisions differ markedly from the sophisticated case reporters of today. The individual reporter compiled the decisions (often from his own observation and notes, rather than from texts submitted by the judges), summarized the oral arguments, and often added his own analysis. Many of the early reports were quite unsystematic—they sometimes contained decisions from several courts, and sometimes even from several jurisdictions. Alexander Dallas' first volume of the *United States Reports* contains only Pennsylvania decisions, and none from the U.S. Supreme Court. His second and third volumes contain cases from both Pennsylvania and the U.S. Supreme Court, and his fourth volume adds decisions from Delaware and New Hampshire.

Systematic official publication of judicial decisions was needed to bring order to reporting, but state appointment of reporters and officially sanctioned publication of decisions developed slowly. The first statute for this purpose was passed in Massachusetts in 1804,[6] and some other states soon followed. The Supreme Court of the United States had no official reporter until 1817,[7] and Pennsylvania had none until 1845.[8] Gradually the nominative reporters gave way to officially published sets of sequentially numbered reports. Some states subsequently renumber-

4. This is apparent from the "reception" statutes passed by many state legislatures, which accepted English common law but limited the "reception" to those cases which were not repugnant to the law of the newly independent state, and often further limited those to cases decided before the date of independence. *See, e.g.,* Act of January 28, 1777, §§ 2 to 3, 1 *Smith's Pa.Laws* 429 (current version at 1 Pa.Cons.Stat. § 1503).

5. Francis Hopkinson's *Judgements in the Admiralty of Pennsylvania* was also published in 1789, in Philadelphia by Dobson & Lang. Although some later reports include cases decided earlier than those in Kirby and Hopkinson, they were the first to be published.

6. Act of March 8, 1804, ch. 133, 1803 Mass. Acts 449.

7. Act of March 3, 1817, ch. 63, 3 Stat. 376.

8. Act of April 11, 1845, ch. 250, 1845 Pa. Laws 374.

ed their reports, incorporating the volumes of the nominative reporters as the first numbered volumes in the official set. Other states, particularly those which were among the early colonies, have many nominative volumes without an overall numbering sequence. To determine where particular citations can be found, researchers need to use tables of reports or dictionaries of legal abbreviations.

The development of official reports represented only the second phase of American case reporting. In the 19th century, as the population grew and the country expanded and became industrialized, the volume of litigation increased rapidly and the official reporting system became overburdened with the proliferation of judicial decisions. Furthermore, the reporter in many states became a political position and publication was subject to the uncertainties of legislative appropriation, so the reports were often inaccurate and frequently slow in appearing. In 1876, in response to the need for improved and more rapid publication, an entrepreneur in Minnesota, John B. West, started a private reporting system, beginning with selected decisions of the Minnesota Supreme Court in an eight-page weekly leaflet called the *Syllabi.*[9] Coverage gradually expanded, adding decisions from Minnesota federal and lower state courts, and abstracts of decisions from other states. The venture proved so successful that in 1879, West incorporated full decisions from five surrounding states in a new publication, the *North Western Reporter.*

By grouping states, the West Publishing Company was able to publish cases far more frequently than official reports could. Of more significance for legal research, West added to each case editorial material which allowed comprehensive and uniform subject access to the cases of different jurisdictions. Every decision was given numbered headnotes summarizing its points of law, and every headnote was designated by its legal topic and a number indicating a particular subdivision of that topic. This scheme, known as the *key number system,* remains one of the most important means of finding cases and will be discussed at length in Chapter 4.

West's thriving business quickly drew competition from other publishers beginning their own series of regional reporters, with the result

9. When West began his first publications, another commercial approach to reporting was already underway. This was the selective publication of a limited number of important decisions of general interest from the courts in many states, annotated with notes to reflect the state of the law throughout the country. Begun in 1871 by the Bancroft-Whitney Company, the first three of these reporters became known as the "Trinity Series": *American Decisions* (covering from the colonial period to 1868), *American Reports* (covering 1871 to 1887), and *American State Reports* (covering 1887 to 1911). In 1906 the Edward Thompson Company began the rival *American and English Annotated Cases,* which merged with Bancroft-Whitney's series to form *American Annotated Cases* in 1912. Meanwhile the Lawyers' Co-operative Publishing Company had since 1888 been publishing *Lawyers' Reports Annotated,* which entered its third series in 1914. All three publishers joined forces in 1918 to begin a new series, *American Law Reports Annotated.* This set, known as *ALR,* continues to this day as the modern successor to the annotated reports, but its annotations are far more important than the cases it still reprints. *ALR* and its federal counterpart, *ALR Federal,* will be discussed more fully in Chapter 4.

that some states were covered by two or three rival schemes.[10] West responded to the growing competition by establishing a national system, publishing all the states' decisions in seven regional reporters. Its comprehensive reporting and accuracy made it the dominant publisher of law reports within a few years. Some of the rival publications folded. Others were absorbed by West into its National Reporter System, which by 1887 covered every state and the federal system. West's unofficial publication of state court decisions has proven so effective that over one-third of the states have discontinued their official publications. In most states, however, cases appear in both official and unofficial editions.

Another unofficial version of some decisions may be published as part of the coverage of topical looseleaf services or specialized reporters. These research tools focus on specific areas of law such as antitrust or labor relations and often provide the full text of judicial decisions. Many cases in topical reporters also appear in official or West series, but some are not published elsewhere.

The next stage in American case reporting was the development of full-text online computer systems that put every word of every case into electronic form. Two privately produced systems have performed this function since the 1970's. WESTLAW, owned by the West Publishing Company, and LEXIS, owned by Reed Elsevier, an English/Dutch information conglomerate, provide access to the full text of federal and state cases. This electronic information is not constrained by the limits of being in paper form, which requires it to be arranged in a certain way with its indexing keyed to that one specific arrangement. Instead, the online searcher can create her own database of cases by using various available tags or "fields" (e.g, date, court, judge). The electronic form also allows the searcher to use either Boolean search strategies or new associative retrieval systems; this benefit will be discussed when questions of case finding are addressed in Chapter 4. Because of the substantial investment that LEXIS and WESTLAW have made in training law students in the use of their systems, and the 24 hour access numbers given to American law students, these two systems have become accepted in the legal community. Law is the first profession or discipline to have truly moved to online full-text research. It was the availability of cases on WESTLAW and LEXIS that led the way.

The newest forms of case publication are on compact disk and on the Internet. Compact disks can contain huge amounts of information and can be used with search software that looks much like that on LEXIS and WESTLAW, forms that are familiar to every American law student and recent graduate. In some states, official versions of the state reports now appear in disk form. Large companies like West and Thompson Publishing are creating compact disks of cases on a national level, while smaller companies like LOIS, in Arkansas, are producing sets that have met with great local acceptance. This situation is fluid, so the

10. "The New 'Reporters'," 19 *Am. L. Rev.* 930, 932 (1885).

researcher can expect to find more and more cases available on compact disk.

The Internet, an amorphous information entity that links computer networks from around the world, contains an increasing amount of legal information, including cases. Some courts, including the United States Supreme Court and other federal courts, now post copies of new decisions on electronic bulletin boards; anyone with the correct equipment and the requisite technical skills can access them and download them to her computer. It is questionable, however, whether the Internet will long survive in its current form, and it is impossible to predict what data will stay on it. James Milles' *Internet Handbook for Law Librarians* (Glanville, 1993) is the best current guide to legal resources, but the fate of cases on the information superhighway will outrun any attempt to describe it on paper.

Just as the West system has not supplanted official reports, the electronic case databases have not eliminated the need for published reports with expert editorial treatment. Full-text searching will retrieve cases in which the court's language meets the specifications of the request. Some legal research can best be conducted in such a manner, while some topics will continue to be most fruitfully approached through use of an editorial index or another search tool. In most research situations, the two methods complement each other. Moreover, the published versions of cases provide precise, standard citations allowing a reader convenient access to cited references, a feature not yet well developed in computer databases.

E. FORMS OF PUBLISHED DECISIONS

When published in paper form, judicial decisions appear in a succession of three different formats. The first appearance of most decisions is as an official *slip opinion*. The slip opinion is issued by the court itself, in the form of a separate pamphlet publication of a single opinion (or opinions, if there are concurring or dissenting judges) in one case. It is individually paginated and contains the full text of the court's decision, sometimes with an official syllabus, or summary. Some slip opinions are simply copies of the original typescript decision, but in some jurisdictions they are printed and distributed on a subscription basis. Lawyers rarely subscribe to the slip opinions, however, because of their expense, their slow distribution, and the difficulty of organizing them for retrieval by subject.

Some courts now post copies of judicial opinions on electronic bulletin boards that are accessible via the Internet. The cases thus posted are really versions of slip opinions. They may lack much in the way of organization, and the use of them may call for either considerable skill with computer technology or sophisticated local software, but the information will be available fast. It is difficult to predict how widespread this version of electronic slip opinion publication will become.

The first form of publication that is distributed widely is the *advance sheet,* a pamphlet which contains the full text of a number of the court's decisions, arranged chronologically, and paginated in a continuous sequence. The advance sheet usually contains the syllabus, headnotes, digests, index and tables which appear in the permanent form of publication, the bound volume. However, advance sheets are preliminary in form, and judges may revise the text of their opinions between that publication and its final form in the bound volume. Most advance sheets contain the pagination that will appear in the bound volume, but occasionally there are minor variations. If the advance sheet does feature the same pagination as the eventual bound volume, citation is made much simpler. Advance sheets are published for most official reporters, for all West reporters, and for some other unofficial reporters. Advance sheets often contain information other than judicial opinions. Some contain court rules, notations on petitions for rehearing or tables of overruled cases. Each advance sheet should be viewed as an important information source.

The third stage of publication is the bound case reporter volume. The bound volumes consolidate several advance sheets and contain a large number of decisions arranged chronologically in the same sequence as they appeared in the advance sheets. They usually contain subject indexes, alphabetical lists of the cases reported therein, and often lists of words defined, statutes construed, and earlier cases cited. The volumes are numbered in a consecutive series. Some reporters have begun second, third and even fourth series, each time beginning the new series with volume one again. The creation of a new series is not related to legal doctrine, it normally is done at an arbitrary time convenient for publication or sales purposes. A new series of a reporter does not replace the prior series, but merely continues it with a new numbering sequence. The notation that a series is other than the first must always be included in the citation to a case.

F. COMPONENTS OF A DECISION

The features of published decisions vary somewhat between publishers and series, but several components are standard and important for case research. References in this section are keyed to the pages that comprise Illustration A, the official report of a decision of the Supreme Court of the United States.

Illustration A–1

Opening page of a decision in the official *United States Reports*

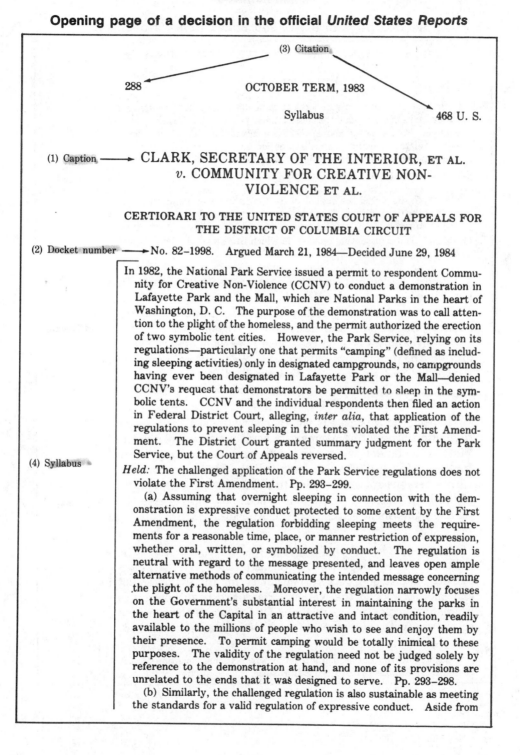

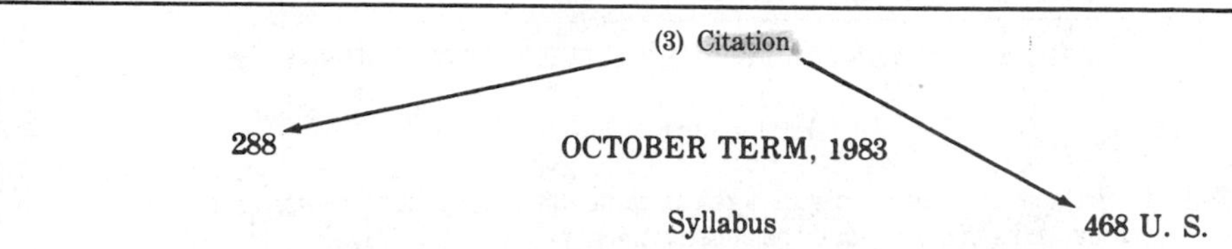

(1) Caption → CLARK, SECRETARY OF THE INTERIOR, ET AL. *v.* COMMUNITY FOR CREATIVE NON-VIOLENCE ET AL.

CERTIORARI TO THE UNITED STATES COURT OF APPEALS FOR THE DISTRICT OF COLUMBIA CIRCUIT

(2) Docket number → No. 82–1998. Argued March 21, 1984—Decided June 29, 1984

(4) Syllabus

In 1982, the National Park Service issued a permit to respondent Community for Creative Non-Violence (CCNV) to conduct a demonstration in Lafayette Park and the Mall, which are National Parks in the heart of Washington, D. C. The purpose of the demonstration was to call attention to the plight of the homeless, and the permit authorized the erection of two symbolic tent cities. However, the Park Service, relying on its regulations—particularly one that permits "camping" (defined as including sleeping activities) only in designated campgrounds, no campgrounds having ever been designated in Lafayette Park or the Mall—denied CCNV's request that demonstrators be permitted to sleep in the symbolic tents. CCNV and the individual respondents then filed an action in Federal District Court, alleging, *inter alia,* that application of the regulations to prevent sleeping in the tents violated the First Amendment. The District Court granted summary judgment for the Park Service, but the Court of Appeals reversed.

Held: The challenged application of the Park Service regulations does not violate the First Amendment. Pp. 293–299.

(a) Assuming that overnight sleeping in connection with the demonstration is expressive conduct protected to some extent by the First Amendment, the regulation forbidding sleeping meets the requirements for a reasonable time, place, or manner restriction of expression, whether oral, written, or symbolized by conduct. The regulation is neutral with regard to the message presented, and leaves open ample alternative methods of communicating the intended message concerning the plight of the homeless. Moreover, the regulation narrowly focuses on the Government's substantial interest in maintaining the parks in the heart of the Capital in an attractive and intact condition, readily available to the millions of people who wish to see and enjoy them by their presence. To permit camping would be totally inimical to these purposes. The validity of the regulation need not be judged solely by reference to the demonstration at hand, and none of its provisions are unrelated to the ends that it was designed to serve. Pp. 293–298.

(b) Similarly, the challenged regulation is also sustainable as meeting the standards for a valid regulation of expressive conduct. Aside from

Illustration A–2

Second page of the *United States Reports* decision

CLARK *v.* COMMUNITY FOR CREATIVE NON-VIOLENCE 289

288 Opinion of the Court

its impact on speech, a rule against camping or overnight sleeping in public parks is not beyond the constitutional power of the Government to enforce. And as noted above, there is a substantial Government interest, unrelated to suppression of expression, in conserving park property that is served by the proscription of sleeping. Pp. 298–299.

227 U. S. App. D. C. 19, 703 F. 2d 586, reversed. (4) Syllabus

WHITE, J., delivered the opinion of the Court, in which BURGER, C. J., and BLACKMUN, POWELL, REHNQUIST, STEVENS, and O'CONNOR, JJ., joined. BURGER, C. J., filed a concurring opinion, *post*, p. 300. MARSHALL, J., filed a dissenting opinion, in which BRENNAN, J., joined, *post*, p. 301.

Deputy Solicitor General Bator argued the cause for petitioners. With him on the briefs were *Solicitor General Lee, Assistant Attorney General McGrath, Alan I. Horowitz, Leonard Schaitman*, and *Katherine S. Gruenheck*. (5) Attorneys

Burt Neuborne argued the cause for respondents. With him on the brief were *Charles S. Sims, Laura Macklin, Arthur B. Spitzer*, and *Elizabeth Symonds*.*

JUSTICE WHITE delivered the opinion of the Court.

The issue in this case is whether a National Park Service regulation prohibiting camping in certain parks violates the First Amendment when applied to prohibit demonstrators from sleeping in Lafayette Park and the Mall in connection with a demonstration intended to call attention to the plight of the homeless. We hold that it does not and reverse the contrary judgment of the Court of Appeals. (6) Opinion

I

The Interior Department, through the National Park Service, is charged with responsibility for the management and maintenance of the National Parks and is authorized to promulgate rules and regulations for the use of the parks in accordance with the purposes for which they were established.

**Ogden Northrop Lewis* filed a brief for the National Coalition for the Homeless as *amicus curiae* urging affirmance.

1. CAPTION

The *caption* (or *name* or *style*) of a case sets forth the names of the parties involved. The normal form is *X v. Y.* Note that the caption of the case beginning in Illustration A–1 is *Clark v. Community for Creative Non–Violence.* The party which appears first in the caption is usually the plaintiff, or the party bringing suit, and the second party is usually the defendant. There are other names by which these parties can be designated. If it is a case on appeal, as is often the situation, the first party will often be the appellant or petitioner and the second party the appellee or respondent, no matter which was the original plaintiff. In some matters concerning the disposition of an estate or litigation over a particular piece of property, the caption *In re* may be used, followed by the name of the person or estate, or a description of the property which is the subject of the action. In a criminal prosecution, since the State brings the action, the first party will often be the jurisdiction itself, e.g., *United States,* or *Commonwealth of Massachusetts,* or *People of the State of New York.*

As a case goes through the levels of a court system, the parties may change places in the caption, and the defendant at the trial level becomes the petitioner at an appellate level. Thus it is important to check for a party's name in either position when searching for a case. Most digests have both a Table of Cases (listing cases under the first parties' names) and a Defendant–Plaintiff Table (providing cross-reference from the second parties' names) to facilitate searching for decisions by case name.

2. DOCKET NUMBER

The docket number, or record number, is assigned by the court clerk to the case when it is filed initially for the court's consideration. It is the number the court then uses to keep track of the documents and briefs filed in the case. In the case shown in Illustration A, the docket number is No. 82–1998.

The docket number is useful in following the case on the court's calendar before it is decided. Decisions which have not been published but are available in slip opinion form are usually filed and cited by docket number. Even long after the decision in a case has been published, its appeal record and briefs, increasingly valuable sources of information on important and complex decisions, are generally filed by docket number.

As the discussion in the next section makes clear, some schemes for changing the current system of case citation may rely heavily on the docket number as a general case tracer.

3. CITATION

While slip opinions are generally cited by docket number, published opinions are cited by the reporter volume in which they appear and the page number on which the caption appears. The citation does not always appear at the beginning of an opinion, but can readily be determined if the volume is in hand. In Illustration A, the volume number (468 U.S.) is indicated at the top right and the page number (288) at the top left. Citations normally include the year of decision, making the citation for this case 468 U.S. 288 (1984).

Reporters, particularly those published commercially, will often also include other citations of the case either above or below the caption. West's regional reporters provide the official citation if it is available when the West publication is issued. Reporters of Supreme Court cases published by West and Lawyers Co-op both provide citations to the official *United States Reports* and to the competition.

There is a movement toward creating a new system of citation for cases that is both format and vendor neutral. The traditional method of citing cases is tied to the paper sets in which they were reported. As the on-line systems, compact disks, and the Internet versions of cases discussed above have grown, some have called for a new citation format that is created by the court at the time the opinion is issued. This citation may be keyed to a court-created number, like the docket number of the case, with each paragraph of the decision numbered. This proposed system avoids the reliance on paper, but poses many problems. There will likely be a long battle over its future. Issues of reliability and the development of too many separate, incongruous citation forms will need to be addressed. Already, states like Louisiana, Colorado, and Wisconsin are experimenting with different variations on the theme, and others probably will follow. There are almost one million lawyers currently trained in the old system who will need to be educated anew. This could be one of the biggest changes in the history of legal research, but even if a change is made prospectively, one will still have to master the old system to find cases from the time before any change is made.

4. SYLLABUS AND HEADNOTES

Below the docket number in the illustration is the *syllabus,* a summary of the case's facts and the court's holding. In the official reports of some jurisdictions, the syllabus is prepared by the court itself. Many actions contain more than one question of law, and a court may dispose of two, three or more individual legal questions in a single opinion. It is also common for the reporter to prepare separate *headnotes* describing the various points decided by the court.

Although the official reporter is appointed by the court, the syllabus and headnotes are not an "official" part of the decision. The opinion itself gives the holding, although it is often not expressly designated as such. If the syllabus or headnotes are inconsistent with the court's opinion, the opinion governs.[11] The syllabus may still serve as a useful

11. Every U.S. Supreme Court slip opinion carries a warning that the syllabus "constitutes no part of the opinion of the Court and has been prepared by the Reporter of Decisions for the convenience of the reader," citing *United States v. Detroit Timber & Lumber Co.,* 200 U.S. 321, 337 (1906).

Ohio is unusual in providing that the syllabus be prepared by its Supreme Court

guide to what is discussed in the case. Many official reporters prepare only the briefest of summaries, however, and there may be none officially prepared in those states that have discontinued their official reports.[12]

The commercial publishers of case reports assign their editors to read and digest each decision which they print. These editors prepare their own headnotes, which are usually more extensive than those of the official reporter. They are specifically designed to aid the researcher in locating relevant material in the opinion, and are usually part of a larger system of digesting and case finding. In using unofficial reports, it is essential to remember that the headnotes are not prepared by the court or the official reporter, but by an editor working for a commercial publisher. The headnotes are thus merely finding aids and should not be cited or relied upon as authoritative.

5. ATTORNEYS

The names of the lawyers who represented the parties to an action usually appear after the syllabus and before the opinion of the court. Identifying the attorneys can be helpful because they may provide further information about the litigation or its outcome. They may be able to furnish copies of briefs they submitted. At one time reports regularly carried excerpts or summaries of the arguments of counsel, but this information is no longer provided in most reports.

6. OPINION

The name of the judge writing the opinion appears at the beginning of the opinion. At the appellate levels of a court system, it is likely that more than one judge will hear a case. In the court of last resort, there is usually a bench of five, seven or nine judges, while at the intermediate appellate level three or five judges are common. The decision thus may be the product of discussion and compromise among several judges. When it is impossible to achieve unanimity among them, more than one opinion may result. The opinion of the court, reflecting at least a majority of the vote, almost always appears first.[13] It can be assumed that all other judges subscribe to the first opinion, unless they have written or expressly joined in either a concurring or dissenting opinion.

A concurring opinion is written when one or more judges agree with the result reached by the majority of the court, but do not agree with the

as the official statement of the law of the case. Ohio Rev.Stat. § 2503.20. The syllabus governs if there is any inconsistency between it and the opinion.

12. Official reports are published for the Georgia Supreme Court and Court of Appeals, but no syllabi or headnotes accompany the cases. The statutory mandate requires only that the volumes contain the decisions and an index. Ga. Code Ann. § 50–18–26.

13. Occasionally there is no line of reasoning agreed upon by a majority, and a plurality opinion is printed first. Another type of opinion which should be noted is the *per curiam* opinion, which represents the court without authorship attributed to any individual judge. *Per curiam* opinions are generally short, and either cover points of law the court feels are too obvious to merit elaboration or represent sensitive issues the court does not want to treat at length. They do, however, carry the weight of precedent.

reasoning used to reach that result or with the opinion written for the majority. Because it is the reasoning of the majority opinion that will be used as precedent in the future, a judge may wish to explicitly disassociate herself from the reasoning of the majority while agreeing with the opinion. In some decisions, there is more than one concurring opinion.

Following the majority opinion and any concurrences, there may be one or more dissenting opinions. Dissenting opinions reflect the views of judges who do not agree with the result reached by the majority of the court. Sometimes judges will simply note their dissent, but often they set forth their reasons. Although dissenting opinions carry no force as precedent, they may have persuasive authority and can be cited if clearly labelled as dissents. Dissents in some areas have been used as persuasive authority and have led to changes in the law. Some opinions will feature a dizzying array of concurrences and dissents, and some judges may concur in part and dissent in part. This atomization of opinion is not uncommon among the justices of the Supreme Court of the United States.[14]

G. SUPREME COURT OF THE UNITED STATES

The rest of this chapter describes the existing sets of reported decisions which the researcher will encounter in working with American case materials. Because of the preeminent role of the United States Supreme Court, in both practical and jurisprudential terms, its decisions will be discussed first and in some detail. Explanation of reporters covering lower federal courts and state courts will follow in subsequent sections.

The Supreme Court is the court of last resort in any federal dispute and has the final word on federal issues raised in state courts. In most situations, however, it has discretion to decline to review lower court decisions and disposes of most matters by denying petitions for *certiorari* or dismissing appeals. Only a small percentage of the cases appealed to the Supreme Court are accepted for consideration. There are some situations in which the Court *must* hear an appeal, and even cases in which the Court serves as the first forum for a dispute.[15] In the end, however, the Court typically writes opinions in fewer than 125 cases each year and the number has been shrinking.

14. The Pentagon Papers case, *New York Times Co. v. United States,* 403 U.S. 713 (1971), had ten opinions: the Court's judgment announced in a brief *per curiam* opinion, plus six concurrences and three dissents.

15. Jurisdiction of the Supreme Court is determined by Congress pursuant to Article III, § 2 of the United States Constitution, and is prescribed in 28 U.S.C. §§ 1251 to 1259. The right to file an appeal rather than petition for discretionary review is generally limited to situations that threaten the balance of power between federal and state governments, such as when a state statute is found unconstitutional by a federal court (§ 1254) or a federal statute is held invalid by a state court (§ 1257). The Supreme Court has original jurisdiction in all controversies between two or more states (§ 1251).

Today the decisions of the Supreme Court are available in a variety of formats, including three permanent, bound reporters, two looseleaf services, two electronic databases, CD–ROM, and the Internet. Its early cases were not so widely reported. The history of their publication corresponds to the brief history of American law reporting already described. The first reports were compiled by individuals and were known as "nominative" reporters. Even after the federal government began to officially sanction the reports, they were still private ventures of the individual reporters. Later sets, including current reprints, have incorporated the nominatives into the general numbering scheme of the *United States Reports* but retained the reporters' names. Thus the first ninety volumes of *U.S. Reports* are still cited by the name of the individual reporter.[16] The early reporters, their nominative and *U.S. Reports* citations, and dates of coverage are as follows:

Reporter	Nominative Citation	U.S. Reports Citation	Terms
A.J. Dallas	1–4 Dall.	1–4 U.S.	1790–1800
William Cranch	1–9 Cranch	5–13 U.S.	1801–1815
Henry Wheaton	1–12 Wheat.	14–25 U.S.	1816–1827
Richard Peters	1–16 Pet.	26–41 U.S.	1828–1842
Benjamin C. Howard	1–24 How.	42–65 U.S.	1843–1860
J.S. Black	1–2 Black	66–67 U.S.	1861–1862
John William Wallace	1–23 Wall.	68–90 U.S.	1863–1874

Thus the case in which the Supreme Court held that the reporter had no copyright in the text of the decisions is cited as *Wheaton v. Peters,* 33 U.S. (8 Pet.) 591 (1834), meaning that the case originally appeared in volume eight of *Peters' Reports* and is now in volume 33 of the renumbered set. The financial impact of that decision led ultimately to the demise of official reporting by private individuals and to the beginning of the modern series of officially published *U.S. Reports.*[17]

1. UNITED STATES REPORTS

The official reporter for the Supreme Court of the United States is the *United States Reports* (abbreviated in citations as U.S.). Although there are still individual reporters preparing the current volumes, they are now employees of the Court and their names are no longer used to designate their volumes.

The Supreme Court's annual term runs from October to July, and several volumes of *U.S. Reports* are added every year. Following the

16. Those working with older collections may find mixed into their sets some of the various recompilations that attempted to reprint earlier cases in smaller and less expensive editions. Perhaps the best known are those of Richard Peters (*Peters' Condensed Reports,* covering 1 to 25 U.S., 1790–1827, in four volumes) and Benjamin Curtis (*Curtis' Reports of Decisions,* covering 2 to 58 U.S., 1790–1854, in 22 volumes). These reprints are no longer used much, but are still found on the shelves of many law libraries and are occasionally needed to trace citations to them in older works.

17. A history of the case and its impact on Supreme Court reporting can be found in Craig Joyce, "Wheaton v. Peters: The Untold Story of the Early Reporters," 1985 *Sup. Ct. Hist. Soc'y Y.B.* 35.

general pattern of publication, the decisions appear first in slip opinion form, followed by an official advance sheet (called the "preliminary print"), and finally appear in the bound *U.S. Reports* volume. Illustration A, earlier in this chapter, presents the beginning pages of a case in the *U.S. Reports.* Note that the official court reporter has prefaced the text of the decision with a *syllabus,* preliminary paragraphs summarizing the case and indicating what the Court has held.

The *U.S. Reports* is an accurate, well-indexed compilation of the full official text of all decisions of the Supreme Court of the United States. At first glance it might seem that it should provide quite adequately for the needs of researchers. Unfortunately, as with many official publications, the advance sheets and volumes of the *U.S. Reports* tend to appear quite slowly. Currently, almost three years pass between the announcement of a decision and its appearance in the advance sheet, and another year before its inclusion in a bound volume. Because of the importance of Supreme Court opinions, this glacial pace of reporting is inadequate for practicing attorneys. In response to the need for more timely publication, commercial publishers produce a variety of unofficial reporters which are distributed much more quickly than the official set.

2. UNITED STATES SUPREME COURT REPORTS, LAWYERS' EDITION

There are two commercial sets of Supreme Court decisions which not only publish cases sooner than the official reports but also provide special editorial features for the legal researcher. Both sets are very useful even after the appearance of a case in *U.S. Reports* and therefore are published in both advance sheets and permanent bound volumes. Both have been in existence since 1882.

United States Supreme Court Reports, Lawyers' Edition is published by the Lawyers Co-operative Publishing Company, or Lawyers Co-op. Popularly known as *Lawyers' Edition* (and cited as L.Ed.), the set began by reprinting all the earlier Supreme Court decisions in smaller type and fewer volumes than the official reports. Upon the completion of retrospective coverage, Lawyers Co-op continued publishing the Court's decisions as they were issued. After reaching one hundred volumes in 1956 (covering through volume 351 of *U.S. Reports*), it began a second series, known as *Lawyers' Edition 2d* (L.Ed.2d), which continues today.

Unlike the official set, *Lawyers' Edition* issues advance sheets which put decisions in researchers' hands in a matter of weeks rather than months. In addition to printing the official reporter's syllabus and the opinion, the editors at Lawyers Co-op prepare both a "summary" of each case and their own headnotes. They also provide cross-references to treatments of the case's subject in other Lawyers Co-op publications. These features are shown in Illustrations B–1 and B–2, the opening pages of the *Lawyers' Edition* version of *Clark v. Community for Creative Non–Violence,* the same case shown in its *U.S. Reports* version in Illustration A.

Illustration B-1

The first page of a decision in *Lawyers' Edition*, showing publisher's summary and references to annotations and briefs

[468 US 288]

WILLIAM P. CLARK, Secretary of the Interior, et al., Petitioners

v

COMMUNITY FOR CREATIVE NON-VIOLENCE et al.

468 US 288, 82 L Ed 2d 221, 104 S Ct 3065

[No. 82–1998]

Argued March 21, 1984. Decided June 29, 1984.

Decision: National Park Service anti-camping regulation held constitutionally applied to Washington, D.C., demonstrators.

SUMMARY

The Community for Creative Non-Violence and several individuals brought suit in the United States District Court for the District of Columbia to prevent the application of a National Park Service regulation, prohibiting camping in national parks except in designated campgrounds, to a proposed demonstration in Lafayette Park and the Mall, in the heart of Washington, D.C., in which demonstrators would sleep in symbolic tents to demonstrate the plight of the homeless. The District Court granted summary judgment in favor of the Park Service. The United States Court of Appeals for the District of Columbia Circuit reversed on the ground that the application of the regulation so as to prevent sleeping in the tents would infringe the demonstrators' First Amendment right of free expression (703 F2d 586).

On certiorari, the United States Supreme Court reversed. In an opinion by WHITE, J., expressing the views of BURGER, Ch. J., and BLACKMUN, POWELL, REHNQUIST, STEVENS, and O'CONNOR, JJ., it was held that the Park Service regulation did not violate the First Amendment when applied to the demonstrators because the regulation was justified without reference to the content of the regulated speech, was narrowly tailored to serve a significant governmental interest, and left open ample alternative channels for communication of the information.

BURGER, Ch. J., while concurring fully in the court's opinion, filed a concurring opinion stating that the camping was conduct and not speech.

MARSHALL, J., joined by BRENNAN, J., dissented on the ground that the

SUBJECT OF ANNOTATION

Beginning on page 958, infra

Restriction of use of public parks as violating freedom of speech or press under First Amendment of Federal Constitution

Briefs of Counsel, p 956, infra.

Illustration B–2

The second page of a *Lawyers' Edition* decision, showing headnotes and cross-references

demonstrators' sleep was symbolic speech and that the regulation of it was not reasonable.

HEADNOTES

Classified to U.S. Supreme Court Digest, Lawyers' Edition

Constitutional Law § 960 — demonstration — camping

1a–1c. A National Park Service regulation prohibiting camping in national parks except in campgrounds designated for that purpose does not violate the First Amendment when applied to prohibit demonstrators from sleeping in Lafayette Park and the Mall, in the heart of Washington, D. C., in connection with a demonstration intended to call attention to the plight of the homeless. (Marshall and Brennan, JJ, dissented from this holding.)

[See annotation p 958, infra]

Parks, Squares, and Commons § 2 — camping

2a, 2b. Sleeping in tents for the purpose of expressing the plight of the homeless falls within the definition of "camping" in a National Park Service regulation defining camping as the use of park land for living accommodation purposes such as sleeping activities, or making preparations to sleep (including the laying down of bedding for the purpose of sleeping), or storing personal belongings, or making any fire, or using any tents or other structure for sleeping or doing any digging or earth breaking or carrying on cooking activities when it appears, in light of all the circumstances, that the participants, in conducting these activities, are in fact using the area as a living accommodation regardless of the intent of the participants or the nature of any other activities in which they may also be engaging.

Evidence § 102 — First Amendment — application

3a, 3b. Although it is common to place the burden on the government to justify impingements on First Amendment interests, it is the obligation of the person desiring to engage in assertedly expressive conduct to demonstrate that the First Amendment even applies.

Constitutional Law § 934 — expression — restriction

TOTAL CLIENT-SERVICE LIBRARY® REFERENCES

59 Am Jur 2d, Parks, Squares, and Playgrounds § 33
USCS, Constitution, 1st Amendment
US L Ed Digest, Constitutional Law §§ 934, 960
L Ed Index to Annos, Parks
ALR Quick Index, Parks and Playgrounds
Federal Quick Index, National Parks; Parks
Auto-Cite®: Any case citation herein can be checked for form, parallel references, later history and annotation references through the Auto-Cite computer research system.

ANNOTATION REFERENCE

Restriction of use of public parks as violating freedom of speech or press under First Amendment of Federal Constitution. 82 L Ed 2d 958.

Each headnote in *Lawyers' Edition* is assigned a topic and section number by the editors. These headnotes are then reprinted, arranged by topic, in the companion set to the reports, *United States Supreme Court Digest, Lawyers' Edition.* The digest allows retrieval of other cases in the same subject area, and will be more fully described in Chapter 4, Case Finding. A table in each advance sheet and volume of *Lawyers' Edition* lists the digest topics and numbers appearing in that volume.

By the time a bound volume of *Lawyers' Edition* is ready for publication, the editors have added other useful features. First, they provide short summaries of the briefs of counsel. (Such summaries were a common feature of early reports, but now appear only in *Lawyers' Edition* and *New York Reports.*) Second, the editors prepare *annotations* on a few of the more important cases in each volume. These annotations analyze in considerable detail one or more of the points of law covered in the case and present other primary authorities on the same topic. Since 1957 these annotations have been regularly supplemented. References to briefs and annotations, both printed elsewhere in the volume, appear at the bottom of the page in Illustration B–1. Each volume also includes a table of cases reported, an index, a table of cross-references from official *U.S. Reports* citations, and a table of federal laws cited or construed in the volume.

Lawyers' Edition is part of the "Total Client–Service Library," a trademark name for the research system developed by the publisher to link its various publications. This "library" includes a wide range of primary and secondary sources such as statutory codes, annotations, and legal encyclopedias. Each Lawyers Co-op publication refers the researcher to other Co-op products that deal with the same issue.

3. WEST'S SUPREME COURT REPORTER

As part of its burgeoning National Reporter System, the West Publishing Company began coverage of the Supreme Court in the October 1882 term. Unlike Lawyers Co-op, it did not attempt a retrospective recompilation, and the first volume of the *Supreme Court Reporter* contains cases reported in volumes 106 and 107 of the *U.S. Reports.* West has published one numbered volume of the *Supreme Court Reporter* (cited as S.Ct.) each year. The volumes grew larger with time, until two physical volumes were needed for the 1959 term's decisions; by 1989, three physical volumes were required for each term's decisions. Since then, West has published each year the numbered volume and two supplements designated "A" and "B" (e.g., volumes 110, 110A, and 110B cover the October 1989 term).

Like *Lawyers' Edition,* the *Supreme Court Reporter* appears much more quickly than the official reports, reaching researchers in advance sheet form within weeks of decisions. It also includes tables of cases reported and of statutes construed in each advance sheet and volume, as well as a table of words and phrases judicially defined. Like Lawyers Co-op, West prepares its own summary, which it calls a *synopsis,* and headnotes for each case. These features are shown in Illustration C, the first page of the *Supreme Court Reporter* edition of *Clark v. Community for Creative Non–Violence.*

It is West's headnotes that make the *Supreme Court Reporter* an invaluable research tool. As in *Lawyers' Edition,* each headnote is assigned to a general topic and to a numbered subdivision within the topic. Subject access to the headnotes is provided in the *United States Supreme Court Digest,* a companion set to the reporter. Unlike the *Lawyers' Edition* classifications, however, West's "key number" classification system is used not only for Supreme Court decisions but for court decisions throughout its National Reporter System. Thus the same point of law discussed in a Supreme Court case can be researched in all reported federal and state court cases through West's comprehensive subject digest system, which will be discussed at length in Chapter 4, Case Finding.

In comparing the editorial treatments in Illustrations B and C, note that the publishers have assigned different topics to the same judicial text. The fact that the editors of the two commercial publications formulate different statements of the points of law in a case demonstrates the subjectivity of legal research. It also underscores the fact that headnotes are merely finding aids, guiding the reader to the actual words of the decision. In each reporter the numbers of the headnotes are inserted in brackets into the text of the majority opinion, so that the researcher can go directly to a particular point in the opinion.

Another useful feature of both commercial editions is the inclusion in the final, bound volumes of cross-references to the location of the same decision in the competing reporter and in the *United States Reports.* Moreover, each includes within the text of opinions a device known as *star paging,* indicating the beginnings of pages in the official edition. This enables the researcher to read the more useful commercial version but have available the precise official citations to the case and to any page within the case.

Star paging is not available until the final bound volumes of *Lawyers' Edition* and the *Supreme Court Reporter,* since the commercial publishers must wait for the government to issue the "preliminary print" pamphlets for the *U.S. Reports.* The long delay in publication means that the commercial advance sheets are heavily used, and in 1986 West began publishing an "interim edition" of the *Supreme Court Reporter.* The "interim edition" consists of two or three bound volumes, like the permanent edition, so that it can withstand wear and tear better than unbound pamphlets. It lacks parallel references to *U.S. Reports* and the official reports' final text corrections, however, and is printed on less expensive paper.

Illustration C

The first page of a decision in West's *Supreme Court Reporter*, showing the synopsis and headnotes

468 U.S. 288, 82 L.Ed.2d 221

|288 **William P. CLARK, Secretary of the Interior, et al., Petitioners**

v.

COMMUNITY FOR CREATIVE NON-VIOLENCE et al.

No. 82–1998.

Argued March 21, 1984.

Decided June 29, 1984.

Demonstrators permitted to participate in round-the-clock demonstration on the Mall and in Lafayette Park in Washington, D.C., brought action challenging the United States Park Service's denial of permission to sleep in temporary structures permitted to be erected as part of the demonstration. The United States District Court for the District of Columbia granted the government's motion for summary judgment, but the Court of Appeals, District of Columbia Circuit, reversed, 703 F.2d 586. Motion to vacate the order staying the mandate of the United States Court of Appeals for the District of Columbia Circuit was denied, 104 S.Ct. 478. Certiorari was granted, and the Supreme Court, Justice White, held that a National Park Service regulation prohibiting camping in certain parks did not violate the First Amendment though applied to prohibit demonstrators from sleeping in Lafayette Park and the Mall in connection with the demonstration, which was intended to call attention to the plight of the homeless.

Judgment of the Court of Appeals reversed.

Chief Justice Burger filed concurring opinion.

Justice Marshall dissented and filed opinion in which Justice Brennan joined.

1. United States ⟹57

Sleeping in tents for purpose of expressing plight of homeless falls within definition of "camping" in National Park Service regulation. U.S.C.A. Const.Amend. 1; 16 U.S.C.A. §§ 1, 1a–1, 3.

See publication Words and Phrases for other judicial constructions and definitions.

2. Constitutional Law ⟹90(1)

Although it is common to place burden upon government to justify impingements on First Amendment interests, it is obligation of person desiring to engage in assertedly expressive conduct to demonstrate that First Amendment even applies. U.S.C.A. Const.Amend. 1.

3. Constitutional Law ⟹90(3)

Expression, whether oral or written or symbolized by conduct, is subject to reasonable time, place and manner restrictions. U.S.C.A. Const.Amend. 1.

4. Constitutional Law ⟹90(3)

Message may be delivered by conduct that is intended to be communicative and that, in context, would reasonably be understood by viewer to be communicative, and symbolic expression of this kind may be forbidden or regulated if conduct itself may constitutionally be regulated, providing regulation is narrowly drawn to further substantial governmental interest and providing the interest is unrelated to suppression of free speech. U.S.C.A. Const. Amend. 1; 16 U.S.C.A. §§ 1, 1a–1, 3.

5. United States ⟹57

National Park Service regulation forbidding sleeping in certain areas was defensible either as time, place or manner restriction or as regulation of symbolic conduct. U.S.C.A. Const.Amend. 1; 16 U.S.C.A. §§ 1, 1a–1, 3.

6. United States ⟹57

Fact that sleeping, arguendo, may be expressive conduct, rather than oral or written expression, did not render prohibition against sleeping in certain areas of national parks any less an acceptable time, place or manner regulation. U.S.C.A. Const.Amend. 1; 16 U.S.C.A. §§ 1, 1a–1, 3.

4. LOOSELEAF SERVICES

The three standard print versions of United States Supreme Court decisions just described are well-established forms of legal publication, but they are not the only print products that publish the full text of each case. Two looseleaf services—*The United States Law Week* from the Bureau of National Affairs, and Commerce Clearing House's *U.S. Supreme Court Bulletin*—meet the need of lawyers, and others interested in national policy or current affairs, to have access to Supreme Court decisions much sooner than the fastest advance sheet of *Lawyers' Edition* or the *Supreme Court Reporter* is available. Because both services reproduce the full text of each slip opinion in a looseleaf binder format, releases containing all of the new cases can be mailed out several times a week, and can be added directly into the binder sets. During the Supreme Court's term, from October to July, the sets stay just about as up to date as a print tool can.

Both sets have simple indexing and cumulate into large binders at the end of the year. Each has added features, like summaries of pending cases and information about the Court's docket, but the main function of these looseleaf services is to provide a faster print version of each new Supreme Court case. Since they publish the cases before other citations are available, each set has its own citation system, which is acceptable to use in research work until one of the three traditional print tools is available.[18]

U.S. Law Week and *Supreme Court Bulletin* are widely used sets, but the role that they play has diminished in recent years. Before the advent of electronic systems, getting access to the full text of a new Supreme Court case within a few days was quite impressive. Now, online research tools like WESTLAW and LEXIS are supplanting these looseleaf services.

5. WESTLAW AND LEXIS

Computerized access to the text of decisions of the Supreme Court is available through the online databases, WESTLAW and LEXIS. The databases contain the text of opinions not only well before the publication of advance sheets but also sooner than either *U.S. Law Week* or the *Supreme Court Bulletin* can print and mail them. Getting United States Supreme Court opinions on-line fast is an intelligent good will move by the two vendors, so each concentrates on doing it quickly. The race varies, but both WESTLAW and LEXIS generally allow access to most Supreme Court decisions within hours of when they are announced. As the first available source of United States Supreme Court opinions, the databases are widely consulted by lawyers needing immediate access to decisions. Most large research law libraries and many law firms have

18. A citation to *U.S. Law Week* (abbreviated U.S.L.W.) is recognized as the standard means of identifying Supreme Court opinions until they appear in the standard reporters. A citation to the *Supreme Court Reporter* is preferred once a case is published in its advance sheets, and then after a long delay a case finally receives its official *U.S. Reports* citation.

terminals for one or both of these computer systems. Illustrations D and E present printouts of screens from the WESTLAW and LEXIS displays of the case shown earlier in its printed forms.

Illustration D

Printout of three screens from the WESTLAW display of a case

```
Citation                Rank(R)          Page(P)          Database        Mode
104 S.Ct. 3065          R 1 OF 1         P 1 OF 58        SCT             Term
 82 L.Ed.2d 221
(Cite as: 468 U.S. 288,  104 S.Ct. 3065)
        William P. CLARK, Secretary of the Interior, et al., Petitioners
                                  v.
                   COMMUNITY FOR CREATIVE NON-VIOLENCE et al.
                              No. 82-1998.
                         Argued March 21, 1984.
                         Decided June 29, 1984.
 Demonstrators permitted to participate in round-the-clock demonstration on the
Mall and in Lafayette Park in Washington, D.C., brought action challenging the
United States Park Service's denial of permission to sleep in temporary
structures permitted to be erected as part of the demonstration.  The United
States District Court for the District of Columbia granted the government's
motion for summary judgment, but the Court of Appeals, District of Columbia
Circuit, reversed, 703 F.2d 586.  Motion to vacate the order staying the
mandate of the United States Court of Appeals for the District of Columbia
Circuit was denied, 104 S.Ct. 478.  Certiorari was granted, and the Supreme
Court, Justice White, held that a National Park Service regulation prohibiting
camping in certain parks did not violate the First Amendment though applied to
prohibit demonstrators from sleeping in Lafayette Park and the Mall in
connection with the demonstration, which was intended to call attention to the
                        Copr. (C) West 1995 No claim to orig. U.S. govt. works
```

[G20,031]

```
104 S.Ct. 3065          R 1 OF 1         P 4 OF 58          SCT           Page
(Cite as: 468 U.S. 288,  104 S.Ct. 3065)
 Clark v. Community for Creative Non-Violence
 [2]
 92       CONSTITUTIONAL LAW
 92V        Personal, Civil and Political Rights
 92k90        Freedom of Speech and of the Press

 92k90(1)  k. In general.
 U.S.Dist.Col.,1984.
 Although it is common to place burden upon government to justify impingements
 on First Amendment interests, it is obligation of person desiring to engage in
 assertedly expressive conduct to demonstrate that First Amendment even
 applies.  U.S.C.A. Const.Amend. 1.
                        Copr. (C) West 1995 No claim to orig. U.S. govt. works
```

[G20,032]

```
104 S.Ct. 3065          R 1 OF 1         P 15 OF 58         SCT           Page
(Cite as: 468 U.S. 288, *289,  104 S.Ct. 3065, **3067)
 suppression of expression, in conserving park property that is served by the
 proscription of sleeping.  Pp. 3071-3072.
  227 U.S.App.D.C. 19, 703 F.2d 586 (1983), reversed.
  Deputy Solicitor General Bator argued the cause for petitioners.  With him on
 the briefs were Solicitor General Lee, Assistant Attorney General McGrath, Alan
 I. Horowitz, Leonard Schaitman, and Katherine S. Gruenheck.
  Burt Neuborne argued the cause for respondents.  With him on the brief were
 Charles S. Sims, Laura Macklin, Arthur B. Spitzer, and Elizabeth Symonds.*
  * Ogden Northrop Lewis filed a brief for the National Coalition for the
 Homeless as amicus curiae urging affirmance.

  Justice WHITE delivered the opinion of the Court.
  The issue in this case is whether a National Park Service regulation
 prohibiting camping in certain parks violates the First Amendment when applied
 to prohibit demonstrators from sleeping in Lafayette Park and the Mall in
 connection with a demonstration intended to call attention to the plight of the
 homeless.  We hold that it does not and reverse the contrary judgment of the
 Court of Appeals.
                                   I
  The Interior Department, through the National Park Service, is charged with
 responsibility for the management and maintenance of the National Parks and is
                        Copr. (C) West 1995 No claim to orig. U.S. govt. works
```

[G20,033]

Illustration E

Printout of three screens from the LEXIS display of a case

LEVEL 1 - 1 OF 1 CASE

CLARK, SECRETARY OF THE INTERIOR, ET AL. v. COMMUNITY FOR CREATIVE NON-VIOLENCE ET AL.

CLARK v. COMMUNITY

No. 82-1998

SUPREME COURT OF THE UNITED STATES

468 U.S. 288; 104 S. Ct. 3065; 1984 U.S. LEXIS 136; 82 L. Ed. 2d 221; 52 U.S.L.W. 4986

March 21, 1984, Argued
June 29, 1984, Decided

PRIOR HISTORY: [***1]

CERTIORARI TO THE UNITED STATES COURT OF APPEALS FOR THE DISTRICT OF COLUMBIA CIRCUIT.

[G20,038]

---

468 U.S. 288, *; 104 S. Ct. 3065, **;
1984 U.S. LEXIS 136, ***1; 82 L. Ed. 2d 221

DISPOSITION: <=1> 227 U. S. App. D. C. 19, 703 F.2d 586, reversed.

SYLLABUS: In 1982, the National Park Service issued a permit to respondent Community for Creative Non-Violence (CCNV) to conduct a demonstration in Lafayette Park and the Mall, which are National Parks in the heart of Washington, D. C. The purpose of the demonstration was to call attention to the plight of the homeless, and the permit authorized the erection of two symbolic tent cities. However, the Park Service, relying on its regulations -- particularly one that permits "camping" (defined as including sleeping activities) only in designated campgrounds, no campgrounds having ever been designated in Lafayette Park or the Mall -- denied CCNV's request that demonstrators be permitted to sleep in the symbolic tents. CCNV and the individual respondents then filed an action in Federal District Court, alleging, inter alia, that application of the regulations to prevent sleeping in the tents violated the First Amendment. The District Court granted summary judgment for the Park Service, but the Court of Appeals reversed.

Held [***2] : The challenged application of the Park Service regulations does not violate the First Amendment. Pp. 293-299.

(a) Assuming that overnight sleeping in connection with the demonstration is expressive conduct protected to some extent by the First Amendment, the

[G20,039]

---

468 U.S. 288, *; 104 S. Ct. 3065, **;
1984 U.S. LEXIS 136, ***3; 82 L. Ed. 2d 221

COUNSEL: Deputy Solicitor General Bator argued the cause for petitioners. With him on the briefs were Solicitor General Lee, Assistant Attorney General McGrath, Alan I. Horowitz, Leonard Schaitman, and Katherine S. Gruenheck.

Burt Neuborne argued the cause for respondents. With him on the brief were Charles S. Sims, Laura Macklin, Arthur B. Spitzer, and Elizabeth Symonds. *

* Ogden Northrop Lewis filed a brief for the National Coalition for the Homeless as amicus curiae urging affirmance.

JUDGES: WHITE, J., delivered the opinion of the Court, in which BURGER, C. J., and BLACKMUN, POWELL, REHNQUIST, STEVENS, and O'CONNOR, JJ., joined. BURGER, C. J., filed a concurring opinion, post, p. 300. MARSHALL, J., filed a dissenting opinion, in which BRENNAN, J., joined, [***4] post, p. 301.

OPINIONBY: WHITE

OPINION: [*289] [**3067] JUSTICE WHITE delivered the opinion of the Court.

The issue in this case is whether a National Park Service regulation prohibiting camping in certain parks violates the First Amendment when applied

[G20,040]

In Illustrations D and E, note that WESTLAW and LEXIS [19] include star paging similar to that found in *Lawyers' Edition* and the *Supreme Court Reporter*. This feature provides references to the exact pages in the *U.S. Reports* and the *Supreme Court Reporter* of material shown on the screen. It allows one to cite material directly from the database without going to the printed versions to find page references, and also makes it much easier to find particular passages upon turning to those versions for further reading. Star paging may become obsolete if proposals to create a format- and vendor-neutral citation system take hold.

Both systems provide complete historical coverage of the Supreme Court since its first term in 1790.[20] Every case ever decided by the Supreme Court can be searched for particular terms or combinations of terms and concepts. The sophisticated retrieval capabilities of WESTLAW and LEXIS will be discussed in Chapter 4, Case Finding.

6. OTHER ELECTRONIC SOURCES

When the United States Supreme Court releases an opinion, a version of it is placed on a bulletin board on the Internet. This form of publication of Supreme Court cases is part of an effort called Project Hermes, a collaboration of private publishers and the federal government designed to experiment with public access via Internet technology. Access to the bulletin board is free to anyone who wishes to use it, so one can download the cases into a local system and create one's own database, if desired. To this point, only a handful of the technologically gifted have made use of the information (some small publishers use it to produce their own products), but Project Hermes represents the edge of the future.

West Publishing and Lawyers Co-op produce compact disk versions of the *Supreme Court Reporter* and *Lawyers' Edition*, respectively. Also available now is at least one CD–ROM product featuring Supreme Court slip opinions, with coverage beginning in 1990. Given the relatively low cost of producing CD–ROMs of Supreme Court opinions—one can get the data for free from Project Hermes—it is likely that a series of new ones will appear. Check with a reference librarian for which are available in your library.

7. NEWSPAPER ACCOUNTS

Copies of decisions, as they are issued, are distributed to the press and any other interested persons at the Supreme Court in Washington,

19. LEXIS did not begin to feature star paging until 1989, following a settlement between West and Mead Data Central (which then owned LEXIS) of litigation over the copyright status of star paging references. "West and Mead Data Settle Copyright Dispute," *Nat'l L.J.*, Aug. 1, 1988, at 6; *see West Publishing Co. v. Mead Data Central, Inc.*, 799 F.2d 1219 (8th Cir. 1986), *cert. denied*, 479 U.S. 1070 (1987).

20. Coverage in both systems begins, as it does in the *United States Reports*, with a summary of a case before the Supreme Court of Pennsylvania in its September 1754 term. The case, *Anonymous*, 1 U.S. (1 Dall.) 1 (Pa.1754), held that the Statute of Frauds and Perjuries did not extend to the province.

D.C. National newspapers, such as the *New York Times* and the *Washington Post,* assign reporters to the Supreme Court to follow and report on its activities. The day after most important decisions are rendered, articles in these and other papers discuss the decisions, and a side bar on an inside page summarizes actions of the Court. While newspapers rarely provide any material that would be cited in a legal brief, they inform lawyers and researchers of major developments. On occasion newspaper accounts even include docket numbers, a valuable aid in finding the opinions in the more traditional legal sources. Many newspapers, including those mentioned above, feature excerpts from the opinions themselves in cases of major national impact.

Local legal newspapers often print full-text copies of recent opinions as a supplement. Coverage of local courts may vary, but they almost always include all Supreme Court cases. This is often the first appearance in print that a decision will make in today's library. The pagination will be from the slip opinion state of the case.

H. LOWER FEDERAL COURTS

Below the Supreme Court in the federal court system are both intermediate appellate courts and trial courts. Congress was given the power to create the lower federal courts by Article III of the Constitution, which vests the judicial power of the United States "in one supreme Court, and in such inferior Courts as the Congress may from time to time ordain and establish." The Judiciary Act of 1789, which established the federal court system, created thirteen District Courts, one for each of the eleven states that had ratified the Constitution as well as for the Districts of Kentucky and Maine, and three Circuit Courts.[21] Both District and Circuit Courts served as trial courts, with the Circuit Courts having appellate jurisdiction in limited areas. Over the next hundred years, the structure of the federal court system changed several times. In 1891 Congress created the Circuit Courts of Appeals to serve as intermediate appellate courts,[22] and twenty years later it abolished the old Circuit Courts.[23] The Circuit Courts of Appeals were renamed the United States Courts of Appeals in 1948.[24]

There are now thirteen United States Courts of Appeals, consisting of the First through Eleventh Circuits, each covering three or more states; the District of Columbia Circuit; and the Federal Circuit.[25]

21. Judiciary Act of 1789, ch. 20, §§ 2 to 4, 1 Stat. 73.

22. Act of March 3, 1891, ch. 517, 26 Stat. 826.

23. Act of March 3, 1911, ch. 231, § 289, 36 Stat. 1087, 1167.

24. Act of June 25, 1948, ch. 646, § 2(b), 62 Stat. 869, 985.

25. The Courts of Appeals for the District of Columbia Circuit and the Federal Circuit are both in Washington. The D.C. Circuit has a general appellate jurisdiction like the other circuits, but is kept busy by the presence in Washington of federal agencies. The Federal Circuit was created in 1982 with a specialized subject jurisdiction, and hears appeals from throughout the country on such matters as customs, patents and public contracts. See 28 U.S.C. § 1295 for an account of the Federal Circuit's jurisdiction.

Each Court of Appeals hears cases from the trial courts within its circuit, and its decisions have binding authority over those trial courts. The map in Illustration F shows the geographic jurisdiction of the numbered circuits.

The trial courts in the federal system are the United States District Courts. The geographic jurisdiction of the district courts is generally based on state boundaries, with each state having one or more districts. California, New York, and Texas are each divided into four districts, while twenty-six of the states have just one district apiece.

It is a surprising fact that no official case reporter publishes the decisions of these lower federal courts. Although records for each case are kept on file with the clerk of the individual court, there are no official publications of the decisions of these courts other than their slip opinions.[26] The slip opinions are not widely distributed, and the decisions can be obtained effectively only through unofficial reporters or online through WESTLAW or LEXIS.

Until the advent of computerized research, however, the only comprehensive source of decisions of the lower federal courts was in the publications of the West Publishing Company. These publications continue to be essential but selective reporters of lower federal court decisions.

1. FEDERAL CASES

During the 19th century a number of individual "nominative" reporters published decisions of the many lower federal courts. Over sixty separate reporters, most covering but a single court, published cases of the circuit and district courts, and scattered decisions appeared in more than a hundred other publications.[27] Chaos attended any attempt to retrieve federal cases, and in a few instances different reporters presented varying texts of the same decision. Only a few libraries throughout the country could have a comprehensive collection of federal case law.

This troublesome situation was resolved by the West Publishing Company, which collected the decisions from all of the various reporters and compiled them into a single closed set entitled *Federal Cases* (and cited as F.Cas.). West arranged the more than 20,000 cases in alphabetical order by case name and assigned a number to each. The resulting thirty-volume set, published from 1894 to 1897, contains all available lower federal court case law up to 1880. If the only available citation is

26. The Court of Appeals for the Federal Circuit does have an official reporter for the customs cases it decides, continuing the official reports of the former U.S. Court of Customs and Patent Appeals. Official reports are also published for specialized federal tribunals such as the U.S. Court of International Trade and the U.S. Tax Court.

27. Lists of the nominative reporters, by circuits and districts, and of all the various publications printing cases appear in the first volume of West's *Federal Cases*, at pages xxxvii and xxxix. The prefaces and biographical notes written by the nominative reporters are reprinted in volume thirty, beginning at page 1261.

Illustration F

Map from *Federal Reporter* volume, showing jurisdiction of U.S. Courts of Appeal

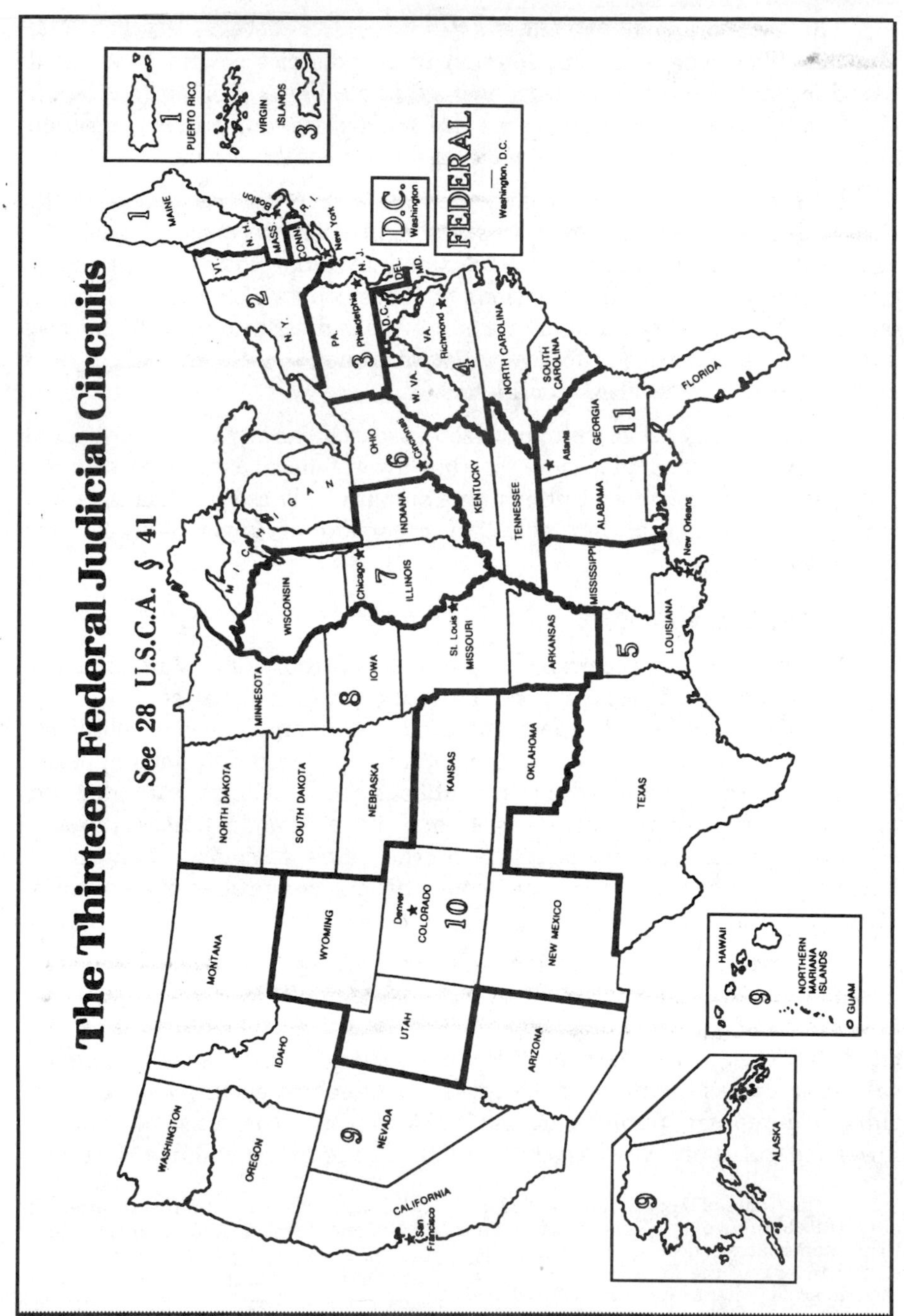

from one of the original nominative reporters, the researcher can consult the digest volume accompanying the set, which includes a table with cross-references from the various reporters to the case's location in *Federal Cases.* The alphabetical arrangement, however, means that the name of a case usually provides quick and easy access. Any published lower federal court case decided before 1880 can thus be found in *Federal Cases* by (1) names of the parties, (2) nominative reporter citation through the conversion table, or (3) the case number assigned by the West Publishing Company.

2. FEDERAL REPORTER AND FEDERAL SUPPLEMENT

Well before it compiled the historical *Federal Cases,* the West Publishing Company began in 1880 a set called the *Federal Reporter* to cover current decisions of the lower federal courts. *Federal Reporter* (cited as F., or in some older cases as Fed.) systematically published decisions from both Circuit and District Courts, as well as the new Circuit Courts of Appeals following the reorganization of the federal judiciary system in 1891.[28] The dramatic increase in federal litigation in the early part of this century caused the series to grow quickly. When the set reached 300 volumes in 1924, the publisher introduced a larger, double-column format and began the *Federal Reporter, Second Series* (cited F.2d). When that set reached 999 volumes in 1993, West inaugurated the *Federal Reporter, Third Series.*

The scope of the *Federal Reporter* was gradually expanded to include decisions of various specialized federal courts created by Congress. Opinions of the U.S. Commerce Court appeared during its short life from 1910 to 1913; the Court of Customs and Patent Appeals was added in 1929 and the Court of Claims in 1930. In 1932 West divided the *Federal Reporter* into two parts and began publishing a new reporter, *Federal Supplement* (F.Supp.), for the decisions of the United States District Courts and the Court of Claims. The *Federal Reporter* continued to publish the decisions of the appellate courts, adding the Emergency Court of Appeals from 1942 to 1961 and the Temporary Emergency Court of Appeals since 1972. Coverage of the Court of Claims returned to the *Federal Reporter* from 1960 until that court and the Court of Customs and Patent Appeals were abolished in 1982. *Federal Supplement* included decisions beginning in 1956 of the United States Customs Court, which was replaced by the United States Court of International Trade in 1980. Current *Federal Supplement* coverage consists of the District Courts, the Court of International Trade, the Special Court

28. The creation of the Circuit Courts of Appeals prompted the publication of two commercial reporters limited, unlike the *Federal Reporter,* to the appellate decisions. Banks & Brothers published *Blatchford's United States Courts of Appeals Reports* (U.S.App.) from 1893 to 1899; each of the first 54 volumes contained only one circuit's decisions, but this method was abandoned in 1898 for the final nine volumes of the set. The West Publishing Company launched *United States Circuit Courts of Appeals Reports* (C.C.A.) in 1892 as an annotated reporter to compete with its own *Federal Reporter.* Publication of the series was taken over by Lawyers Co-op in 1899 and returned to West in 1910. The annotations disappeared in 1916, and the series itself ceased in 1920 after 171 volumes.

under the Regional Rail Reorganization Act of 1973, and the Judicial Panel on Multidistrict Litigation.

Many researchers labor under the mistaken assumption that *all* cases considered by the federal courts are represented by decisions published in one of the reporter series. In fact, only a small percentage of the matters that come before the courts even result in written opinions. Initially, all opinions issued by the U.S. Circuit Courts of Appeals appeared in the *Federal Reporter,* but even from the beginning only a selection of U.S. District Court opinions were published.

The explosive growth in the number of cases being decided by the federal courts in the 1960's caused increasing concern that *too many* cases were being published. The cost of maintaining the reporters and the burden of researching innumerable routine and repetitive decisions led the Judicial Conference of the United States in 1972 to request that each circuit determine criteria to limit publication. An advisory council created by the Federal Judicial Center drafted recommendations that publication be limited to opinions (1) laying down a new rule of law or altering an existing rule, (2) involving a legal issue of continuing public interest, (3) criticizing existing law, or (4) resolving an apparent conflict of authority.[29] Each of the U.S. Court of Appeals established publication rules, and fewer than half of federal appellate decisions are now published.[30] Despite efforts to stem the tide of published cases, however, both the *Federal Reporter* and *Federal Supplement* continue to grow at staggering rates. In 1993, a total of 61 volumes were added to the two reporter series.[31]

3. SPECIALIZED WEST REPORTERS

One solution attempted by West to slow the growth of the *Federal Reporter* and *Federal Supplement* has been the creation of topical reporters offering decisions in certain specialized fields separately to researchers primarily interested in those subjects. The first and most important of this breed is *Federal Rules Decisions* (cited F.R.D.), which began in 1940. It contains selected opinions of the United States District Courts on matters related to the Federal Rules of Civil Procedure and the Federal Rules of Criminal Procedure. In addition to the text of decisions, the reporter includes proceedings of judicial conferences, speeches,

29. Advisory Council on Appellate Justice, *Standards for Publication of Judicial Opinions* 15–17 (Federal Judicial Center and National Center for State Courts, 1973).

30. The history of this process is explained and analyzed in William L. Reynolds & William M. Richman, "The Non–Precedential Precedent—Limited Publication and No–Citation Rules in the United States Courts of Appeals," 78 *Colum. L. Rev.* 1167 (1978), and William L. Reynolds & William M. Richman, "An Evaluation of Limited Publication in the United States Courts of Appeals: The Price of Reform," 48 *U. Chi. L. Rev.* 573 (1981). For a more critical view of limited publication, see Daniel N. Hoffman, "Nonpublication of Federal Appellate Court Opinions," 6 *Just. Sys. J.* 405 (1981).

31. A few years ago, Federal Circuit Judge Philip Nichols, Jr. wrote of "[t]he bloating of the current volumes of *Federal Reporter* and their rabbit-like multiplication on library shelves." Philip Nichols, Jr., "Selective Publication of Opinions: One Judge's View," 35 *Am. U. L. Rev.* 909 (1986).

and articles on federal procedural law. *Federal Rules Decisions* does not contain *all* District Court procedural decisions; many cases involving interpretation of court rules continue to appear in *Federal Supplement,* and opinions in one reporter are generally not reprinted in the other.

In recent years, West has responded to congressional restructuring of the specialized federal judiciary by creating new topical reporters rather than adding courts to *Federal Reporter* or *Federal Supplement.* In 1980, *West's Bankruptcy Reporter* began publication to cover proceedings under the bankruptcy reforms enacted in 1978.[32] Most of each *Bankruptcy Reporter* consists of Bankruptcy Court decisions, but some District Court opinions appear here instead of in *Federal Supplement.* The reporter also includes bankruptcy opinions from the Supreme Court and Courts of Appeals, but these are simply reprinted from the *Supreme Court Reporter* and *Federal Reporter* with their original page numbers.

Similarly, when Congress abolished the Court of Claims in 1982 and established the United States Claims Court to assume its trial jurisdiction,[33] West created the *United States Claims Court Reporter.* The new reporter includes the trial court decisions of the Claims Court and appellate decisions from the Court of Appeals for the Federal Circuit and the Supreme Court. The appellate decisions, however, are merely reprints like those in the *Bankruptcy Reporter.*

West again created a new publication when Congress established the United States Court of Veterans Appeals in 1988.[34] The *Veterans Appeals Reporter* includes the full text of decisions issued by the U.S. Court of Veterans Appeals and appellate decisions from the United States Court of Appeals for the Federal Circuit and the Supreme Court. It also features a section of judicial highlights, featuring summaries of current state and federal decisions of special interest.

Since 1978 West has also published the decisions of the United States Court of Military Appeals, and selected decisions of the Courts of Military Review, in *West's Military Justice Reporter.* This series has not affected the volume of other West reporters, since it simply replaced *Court-Martial Reports,* published from 1951 to 1975 by Lawyers Co-op.

Also worth noting are two subject reporters consisting of cases reprinted from West's federal and state reporter series: *West's Education Law Reporter,* begun in 1982, and *West's Social Security Reporting Service,* begun in 1983. Both reproduce cases as they originally appear, without new page numbers, but each contains articles and other materials of interest to practitioners in the field. Each of these subject-oriented reporters contains the standard West research aids, including the key-number digesting system, and represents a response to the flood of case law and the need of specialists to have affordable access to primary materials in their fields.

32. Bankruptcy Reform Act of 1978, Pub.L. No. 95–598, 92 Stat. 2549.

33. Federal Courts Improvement Act of 1982, Pub.L. No. 97–164, 96 Stat. 25.

34. Veterans' Judicial Review Act, Pub. L. No. 100–687 § 4051, 102 Stat. 4105, 4113 (1988).

The growing influence of on-line data bases will retard the development of more specialty reporters in print. The same function is performed by the specialized files in both WESTLAW and LEXIS that group judicial opinions, statutes and other materials by subject.

4. LOOSELEAF SERVICES AND TOPICAL REPORTERS

Looseleaf services typically bring together all of the major types of legal publications on one subject, frequently with weekly supplementation, several indexing approaches, and explanatory text material. A very comprehensive looseleaf service may include federal and state court decisions, federal and state statutes, and federal and state administrative regulations and rulings, all in the particular subject field of the service. Sometimes the decisions appear only as abstracts, but most of the major services provide the full text of decisions, including many lower federal court cases which do not appear in the West reporters described above.

The three largest publishers of looseleaf services, Commerce Clearing House, Prentice Hall, and Bureau of National Affairs, also issue bound volume series of the full text of court decisions in their selected subject areas. These topical reporters give a more permanent form to decisions which have already appeared in the looseleaf service and which may not be included in *Federal Reporter* or *Federal Supplement.*

The series that focus specifically on *federal* court decisions include those in the areas of copyright (*Copyright Law Decisions,* published by CCH); international trade (*International Trade Reporter Decisions,* BNA); patents (*United States Patents Quarterly,* BNA); securities (*Federal Securities Law Reports,* CCH); and taxation (*American Federal Tax Reports, Second Series,* Prentice Hall, and *U.S. Tax Cases,* CCH). Series in the fields of environmental law (*Environment Reporter Cases,* BNA) and labor relations (such as *Labor Cases* and *Employment Practices Decisions,* CCH, or *Labor Relations Reference Manual* and *Fair Employment Practice Cases,* BNA) also consist predominantly of federal decisions. Most of these series also include reports of agency adjudications as well as state court decisions.

Other reporters, not issued in conjunction with the major looseleaf services, also specialize in the publication of federal court decisions. Since 1939 Callaghan & Company has published *Federal Rules Service,* which is now in its third series. The Callaghan service prints decisions from all levels of the federal court system concerning the Federal Rules of Civil Procedure and the Federal Rules of Appellate Procedure. Most but not all of its decisions also appear in West reporters. In 1979, Callaghan began a new series, called the *Federal Rules of Evidence Service,* to cover cases construing the Federal Rules of Evidence. Both Callaghan services are accompanied by digests which arrange the case headnotes by rule number. The Lawyers Co-operative Publishing Company has since 1969 been publishing *ALR Federal* as a component of its annotated reporter system, with about two dozen decisions printed in each volume. *ALR Federal* will be discussed further in Chapter 4.

Finally, federal court decisions also appear in other, specialized topical reporters. Those in the fields of admiralty (*American Maritime Cases,* published by American Maritime Cases, Inc.) and bankruptcy (*Bankruptcy Court Decisions,* CRR Publishing, and *Collier Bankruptcy Cases 2d,* Matthew Bender) deal with distinctly federal issues. Several other reporters print both federal and state cases, often including administrative agency decisions as well.

5. WESTLAW AND LEXIS

Another important source of federal decisions is the two computerized legal research services, WESTLAW and LEXIS. They provide full-text coverage of all federal court cases that appear in print in the various West reporters, back to the earliest decisions in *Federal Cases.* Access to the decisions is provided through databases of varying size, scope and cost; one can search all federal cases of the past several decades or limit oneself to a particular court.

New decisions are usually available via the computer terminals before they appear in advance sheets. The West Publishing Company, for example, adds a new case to its WESTLAW system as soon as it receives the slip opinion from the court. It inserts its headnotes, any necessary typographical or editorial changes, and star paging references to the *Federal Reporter* later when the case is ready to be published. After minimal editorial checking, LEXIS also adds decisions to the data base immediately upon receipt. As with current Supreme Court decisions, the fastest way for someone not at the courthouse to see an important new opinion is by computer, online.

Both systems include decisions which appear in the looseleaf or topical reporters but which may not be published in a West reporter. Both WESTLAW and LEXIS also include the text of many slip opinions that are never published at all. WESTLAW, for example, has the full text for table decisions from all federal circuits except the 2nd, 3rd, 5th & 11th. Although most court rules limiting the number of published decisions provide that "unreported" decisions cannot be cited as precedent, some courts permit citations to such decisions if a copy is served on all parties and the court.

The availability of computerized databases creates a disadvantage for the practitioner who does not have access to computerized research tools, and who must compete with government agencies and law firms that have such terminals at their disposal. This inequity is not being alleviated by the limited number of public or shared terminals available. The situation is not essentially different than the problem of inequality in access to research facilities between large firms and single practitioners or between urban and rural practitioners, and the differences in representation for the rich and poor generally in our society, but the computer certainly increases these inequities. This problem in legal research must be faced by the courts, the legal profession, and society as a whole.

6. NEW ELECTRONIC SOURCES

For generations, the West National Reporter System was the only source for comprehensive coverage of lower federal court decisions. LEXIS and WESTLAW provided full-text online coverage of the same material, but at a substantial cost. In the mid–1990's, a wide variety of other approaches are being tried. These efforts range from computer bulletin boards created by appellate courts to post new opinions publicly, to on-demand publishers like Barclays providing full coverage of the opinions of the United States Courts of Appeal, to various ventures (including West Publishing) that put decisions on compact disk. It is impossible to predict if any of these formats will provide the complete, reliable coverage offered by the National Reporter System or even LEXIS or WESTLAW. They will continue to proliferate, and some will succeed, but reliability and comprehensiveness will be the tests of such systems.

A number of Federal Circuits are creating their own electronic bulletin boards for publication of the text of decisions. Questions of access to such material as well as the possibility of charging for its use are yet to be worked out. Other case-related information, e.g. docketing information, is available via experiments like the PACER project. Events are moving rapidly in this area. The researcher is best advised to check with a local law librarian about available materials.

I. STATE COURTS

The decisions of the courts of the fifty states have traditionally been published in both official and unofficial reporters, but West's unofficial publication of state court decisions has proven so effective that over one-third of the states have discontinued their own official series. For the states which still publish their own reporters, that publication is the authoritative text of decisions and must be cited in briefs, arguments and memoranda to the courts. Most professional research, however, is actually conducted in an unofficial reporter covering decisions of that state—usually one of the reporters in West's comprehensive National Reporter System. There are several other unofficial sources for state decisions, including the two computer research systems (WESTLAW and LEXIS), the looseleaf services in some subject fields, and specialized topical reporters issued by a number of different publishers.

1. OFFICIAL REPORTS

The most striking features of the official reports today are almost all negative—the trend of discontinuance; the long delays in publication; the relative lack of auxiliary research aids in most of them (as compared to their commercial counterparts); and the failure of many to provide preliminary access to decisions by advance sheets. Their positive aspects should in fairness be stated: many are still well prepared and a few offer useful research features like headnotes, summaries, tables, extensive indexing, and texts of new court rules. Some official reports are exemplary, useful research tools, and a few publish decisions as quickly as

West does. It is sad to note, however, that the long and often distinguished history of official reporting, which succeeded the early nominative reporting, is now waning.[35]

Most of the surviving official state reports include *only* the decisions of the highest court in the state, usually called the Supreme Court. More than a dozen of the more populous (and hence more litigious) states publish more than one official report, the second set usually reporting decisions from the intermediate appellate court. New York is one of the few states to issue three official reporters (*New York Reports* for its highest court, the Court of Appeals; *Appellate Division Reports* for the Appellate Division of its Supreme Court; and *Miscellaneous Reports,* containing a selection of lower court decisions).

Slip opinions in individual cases are issued by at least the highest court in most states, but these are usually not widely distributed. Advance sheets, although not always as prompt as their West counterparts, are available in well over half of the states that publish official reports.

In several states West is now publisher of the official reports, continuing the state's numbered report series but adding its own editorial headnotes. In several other states, including such large jurisdictions as California and New York, the state has an official report, but it is printed by companies owned by Thomson International. Wherever there is an official state report, it is possible to have a state-specific case-finding digest. Illustration G shows the first page of a case from *California Official Reports,* the advance sheet service for both *California Reports* and *California Appellate Reports,* which are published by the Bancroft–Whitney Company, a Thomson subsidiary.

Most of the states which have discontinued their official reports have designated a West reporter as the official reporter for the state. This is either the regional reporter covering the state, or an "offprint" reporter which reproduces the state's decisions from the West regional reporter in separate volumes but maintains the same regional page numbers.

In states with official reports, those reports are the authoritative source for the decisions and must be cited in briefs and other court papers. It is customary in most legal writing to add the unofficial regional reporter citation of the text, so that readers can easily find a case no matter which version they have available. Many reporter series, including West's regional reporters, indicate the other citation at the beginning of a case, *if* another citation exists when the case is printed. Due to the slower publication of most official reports, however, the unofficial citation is frequently the only one available for recent cases.

35. It is just as sad to see the physical deterioration of the books themselves due to the high acid content of book paper since the industrial revolution. An increasing number of these early reports, however, have been filmed and are available in microform.

Illustration G

Advance sheet opinion in *California Official Reports*

[No. D004711. Fourth Dist., Div. One. Mar. 10, 1987.]

JOYCE NELSON et al., Plaintiffs and Appellants, v.
BOARD OF SUPERVISORS OF SAN DIEGO COUNTY et al.,
Defendants and Respondents.

SUMMARY

The superior court, in an action for mandate, injunction, and declaratory relief brought against a county by homeless indigent county residents to challenge the statutory and constitutional validity of certain county regulations, entered a judgment of dismissal after sustaining the county's general demurrer to the complaint without leave to amend. The residents brought the action after they were denied general assistance benefits pursuant to county regulations which authorized termination of such benefits to recipients who failed to establish a "valid address" within 60 days. The residents alleged that the regulations violated the county's mandatory duty, pursuant to Welf. & Inst. Code, § 17000, to provide general relief to indigent county residents. In addition, they alleged that the regulations created a classification which unconstitutionally discriminated against indigent county residents without "valid addresses." (Superior Court of San Diego County, No. 552669, Mack P. Lovett, Judge.)

The Court of Appeal reversed. It held that the residents' allegations were sufficient to proceed on both the statutory and the constitutional claims. (Opinion by Kremer, P. J., with Wiener and Lewis, JJ., concurring.)

HEADNOTES

Classified to California Digest of Official Reports, 3d Series

(1) **Public Aid and Welfare § 4—County Assistance—General Relief.**—Welf. & Inst. Code, § 17000, imposes a mandatory duty on counties and cities to provide general relief to indigent residents. The term "general relief" refers to the residual funds by which indigents who

[E7377]

A researcher with a citation to one source for a state decision can find its *parallel citation* through various tables and other resources to be described in the next chapter.

2. WEST'S NATIONAL REPORTER SYSTEM

The West Publishing Company's development of the National Reporter System in the 1880's was a turning point in access to legal information. Its nationwide coverage and distribution allowed researchers to read cases from every state, and its systematic editorial treatment allowed them to find relevant cases from any jurisdiction.

The National Reporter System began with the publication of the *North Western Reporter* (cited as N.W.) in 1879. The years 1884 to 1887 saw cases from the appellate courts of every other state added to West's system in five additional reporters named after regions of the country: *Atlantic* (A.), *North Eastern* (N.E.), *Pacific* (P.), *South Eastern* (S.E.), *South Western* (S.W.), and *Southern* (So.). The grouping of states in each reporter remains unchanged (except for the addition of newly admitted states to the *Pacific Reporter*), and is shown in map form in Illustration H. The naming of the regions and the allocation of the states reflect the perspective of a 19th century Minnesota publisher (Kansas is in the *Pacific Reporter,* Kentucky in the *South Western*), but the regions are simply convenient groupings so that decisions of several states can be published promptly and conveniently.

In 1928 the *South Western Reporter* reached 300 volumes and, like the *Federal Reporter* before it, began a second series. By 1942, after either 200 or 300 volumes, the other reporters followed suit. Each continues today in its second series, adding a "2d" to each citation: A.2d, N.E.2d, N.W.2d, P.2d, S.E.2d, S.W.2d, and So.2d. The reporters include the opinions of both courts of last resort and intermediate appellate courts, where such exist.

Even in the 1880's, New York was a heavily populated, litigious state with an extensive court system. Its intermediate appellate decisions would have swamped the *North Eastern Reporter,* so in 1888 West established a separate reporter for the state, the *New York Supplement* (N.Y.S.). The decisions of the New York Court of Appeals appear in both the *North Eastern Reporter* and the *New York Supplement.* Lower court decisions are only in the *Supplement,* which is in its second series and cited as N.Y.S.2d.

As the population and court system of California grew in this century, its reported decisions occupied more and more space in the *Pacific Reporter.* In 1960, West launched a new *California Reporter* (Cal.Rptr.), now in its second series, for its cases. The decisions of the court of last resort, the California Supreme Court, are printed in both the regional and the state reporter, while intermediate appellate decisions no longer appear in the *Pacific Reporter.*

Illustration H

Map of West's regional reporters and their coverage

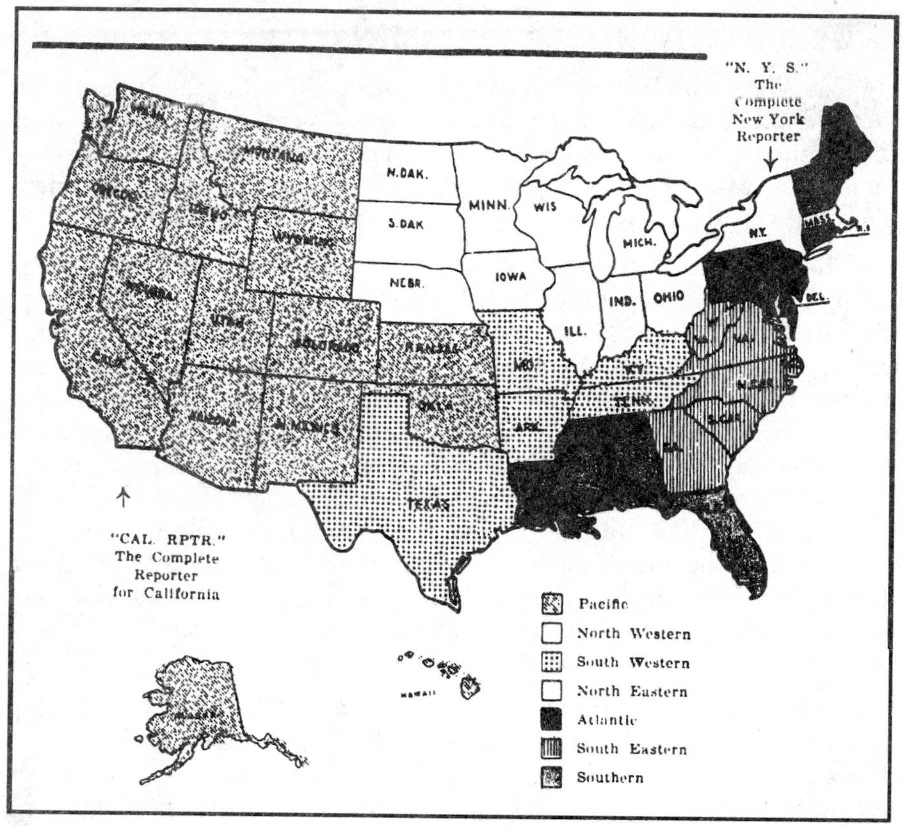

Because the New York and California reporters contain appellate decisions that do not appear in a multistate regional reporter, they are considered integral parts of the National Reporter System. West also publishes reporter series that are limited to the decisions of other states, but the cases also appear in the regional reporter that covers the state. One of these reporters, *West's Illinois Decisions,* gives cases its own page numbers, but all the others merely reprint selected contents from one of the regional reporters. There are over thirty of these "offprint" reporters, published for practitioners in the state who wish to purchase their state's decisions but rarely need cases from other states.

All these reporters are linked by West's systematic editorial control. Every case has a synopsis and headnotes prepared by a West editor, similar to those shown in Illustration C from the *Supreme Court Reporter.* These headnotes are arranged by subject in *digests,* tools for finding cases which will be discussed in Chapter 4. West publishes digests that cover all fifty states and the federal court system, digests just for the states within some of the regional reporters, and digests limited to the cases of individual states.

Each reporter volume and advance sheet contains other helpful features, including a digest of its contents and tables of cases reported, of statutes and rules considered, and of words and phrases defined. Regional reporter advance sheets also carry other material for current awareness, such as summaries of recent developments and texts of newly promulgated court rules.

3. LOOSELEAF SERVICES AND TOPICAL REPORTERS

Almost all of the looseleaf services and topical reporters described in the "Lower Federal Courts" section contain state court decisions. Even legal issues that are distinctly federal can arise in state court, so some state cases appear even in patent or federal tax services. Other series, such as *Media Law Reporter* (published by BNA) and *Trade Cases* (CCH), include a representative selection of state cases.

Public Utilities Reports (published by Public Utilities Reports, Inc., and in its fourth series) and *Uniform Commercial Code Reporting Service* (published by Callaghan & Co., and in its second series) are worth noting not only because they focus on issues commonly litigated in state courts, but because each series is accompanied by its own digesting system. Both sets have tables of cases as part of their digests, although neither lists cases separately by jurisdiction.

There are also the topical reporters published by West and already mentioned for their inclusion of federal court decisions: *West's Education Law Reporter,* which includes a great number of state cases reprinted from the regional reporters; and *West's Social Security Reporting Service,* which is limited mostly to federal cases but does contain a few reprinted state cases.

Finally, a few of the legal newspapers published in large cities report lower court decisions which do not appear in the standard state court reports or the regional reporters. These elusive opinions are generally accessible only through the indexes included periodically in some of the newspapers. New York, however, has a digest specifically designed for this purpose: the *New York Law Journal Digest–Annotator,* covering decisions published in the *New York Law Journal.*

4. WESTLAW AND LEXIS

The online database systems, WESTLAW and LEXIS, are important and increasingly comprehensive sources for state court decisions. New decisions from all state appellate courts are added to the databases, usually before they are available in published form, and retrospective coverage of case law is an ongoing project for both systems. Decisions of every state are available online from at least 1945, and each system has cases dating back to the 19th century for a growing number of states. WESTLAW also provides star paging references to West's regional reporters.

In both systems, state cases are available either in databases for the individual states or in multistate databases. Using comprehensive databases covering all fifty states and the District of Columbia, lawyers can search for specific legal concepts or particular words in the appellate opinions of the entire country. In addition, WESTLAW offers topical databases for each state in areas such as corporations or family law, allowing specialists to limit their research to cases in their fields.

5. COMPACT DISKS

Case law in all fifty states is now available on compact disk from West Publishing; in most states, West competes for a share of the market with a variety of other CD–ROM producers. In some states, like California and New York, disks are produced by the Thomson Company in an arrangement with the state, whereby the disks, along with printed reporters also prepared by Thomson, are considered official reports. In other states, a local publisher will create an unofficial state disk; one example that is meeting with approval is a system in Arkansas called LOIS, which produces a local product containing all relevant cases. These CD–ROM products are making headway, especially with smaller firms, because they are cheaper. They also represent a fixed cost, the subscription price is the same no matter how much one searches. Since the same Boolean search operators are available, they provide inexpensive electronic searching of cases. This development will have to be monitored closely by researchers.

J. SUMMARY

This chapter has described the publication of court decisions, one of the central sources of American law and one of the most important and interesting forms of legal publication. Although often criticized as an overused and outdated method of learning, the analysis of cases continues to play an essential role in legal education. Case law also has a key role in legal research, not as a pedagogical device but as a vital resource. The central role of court reports in legal research may become increasingly apparent as the discussion returns to them again and again throughout this book.

The variety and overwhelming detail of the published reports should not obscure the literary quality and the multifaceted significance of the decisions they contain. The style of judicial opinions ranges from mundane prose and legalese to the clear, sharp texts of masters like Learned Hand and Oliver Wendell Holmes and the sometimes poetic humanism of Benjamin Nathan Cardozo. One can be moved by the human drama reflected in opinions which struggle to resolve the disputes arising between ordinary people, which reveal the tensions and conflicts besetting groups in society, or which judge the individual who has broken the law. The published cases also reflect the social, economic and political changes which have affected our world. We usually confront these movements as impersonal, abstract forces, but in the microcosm of the law reports they can be seen more vividly. One can trace in decisions on the law of property, for example, the evolution from feudalism to mercantilism to capitalism, and then through the industrial revolution, the welfare state, and the modern post-industrial society. There are more than headnotes, citations, and holdings in these volumes.

K. ADDITIONAL READING

M. Ethan Katsh, *The Electronic Media and the Transformation of Law* (Oxford University Press, 1989).

M. Ethan Katsch, *Law in a Digital World* (Oxford University Press, 1995).

Karl N. Llewellyn, *The Common Law Tradition: Deciding Appeals* (Little, Brown 1960). A classic jurisprudential study of appellate law. It is very dated, but still of interest.

Erwin C. Surrency, *A History of American Legal Publishing* (Oceana, 1987). A detailed treatment of early publishing.

Thomas A. Woxland, " 'Forever Associated with the Practice of Law': The Early Years of the West Publishing Company," *Legal Reference Services Q.*, Spring 1985, at 115.

T.J. Young, Jr., "A Look at American Law Reporting in the 19th Century," 68 *Law Libr. J.* 294 (1975). Another historical view.

Chapter 3

CASE VERIFICATION AND UPDATING

A. INTRODUCTION

Under the doctrine of precedent, or *stare decisis,* the holdings of governing cases determine the resolution of issues in subsequent controversies. Authoritative decisions continue to have binding effect regardless of their age. Yet the mere fact that a case once held something does not make that the law for all time. The standing and authority of a case are always subject to either sudden change or gradual erosion. A decision may be reversed on appeal to a higher court or may be overruled years later by a decision of the same court. Later courts also may criticize or question the reasoning of a decision, or may limit its holding to a specific factual situation. Any of these circumstances may diminish or negate the authority of the case so as to render its citation useless or even counter-productive. Judicial decisions are organic; they can wax and wane in authority as time passes. Because constant change is a basic characteristic of the legal system, the researcher must always determine the *current* status of any case which appears to be relevant to an issue at hand.

This function is usually performed by an ingenious series of research tools called *Shepard's Citations,* which consist of lists of citations indicating every time a published decision is cited in, and perhaps affected by, a subsequent decision. In 1873, Frank Shepard began printing lists of citations to Illinois Supreme Court cases on gummed paper for attorneys to stick in the margins of their bound reporters. Before long he began publishing his citation lists in book form, and coverage expanded gradually to include every state and the federal courts.

The idea of using one of the Shepard's citators to check up one's case became so much a part of the fabric of the practice of law that Frank Shepard's name became a verb. Each day thousands of lawyers are asked "to shepardize" a case. Indeed, learning to use Shepard's products became one of the great hazing experiences of American law school.

Shepard's federal and state case *citators* are now available in published volumes with regular supplements, in electronic form on CD–ROM, and online through the WESTLAW and LEXIS computerized research systems.

The scope of *Shepard's Citations* extends beyond cases to include treatment of statutes, administrative documents, and some secondary material, as will be revealed in relevant sections of this book. Shepard's/McGraw–Hill, Inc. also publishes a variety of other legal research materials, but its case citators are its great innovation and are among the most essential tools in legal research. *Shepard's Citations* are such basic tools that the process of searching the history of a decision is commonly called *Shepardizing* a case.

Before a case can be relied upon in court as authoritative, its continuing validity must be determined. Shepardizing is an essential part of the research process. A lawyer who neglects this step may base arguments on cases subsequently reversed or limited in scope, thereby practicing law incompetently *and* risking embarrassment. In one federal case, defense counsel failed to inform the court that a case on which it relied had been specifically overruled and was "admonished that diligent research, which includes Shepardizing cases, is a professional responsibility." [1]

The use of Shepard's in its paper form has been a staple of learning legal research for decades. The LEXIS and WESTLAW versions of Shepard's discussed later in this chapter are often easier and quicker to use. The two on-line case verification systems; Auto–Cite on LEXIS and Insta–Cite on WESTLAW, will seem far simpler and more complete.

1. *Cimino v. Yale University,* 638 F.Supp. 952, 959 n. 7 (D.Conn.1986).

Some students may bridle at having to master the older, more difficult paper process. But remember that law school is not the real world. Many research environments continue to **require** the use of the print versions of Shepard's. It is imperative that the novice researcher master the paper system. Be strong.

B. THE FEATURES OF SHEPARD'S CITATIONS

A Shepard's entry may look strange and impenetrable at first, but Shepard's is really a fairly simple tool to use once its format is understood. The functional underpinning of Shepard's citators is very straightforward. Using the same form of comprehensive obsessiveness that John West employed in creating the National Reporter System, Frank Shepard determined that his books would allow the researcher to see **every** subsequent mention of a case that interested him. If a researcher found a case that was on point, Shepard's citators would show him every subsequent mention of that case. This would catch any important comments on one's case, but it would also catch every trivial mention as well. The point is that it would catch everything. It is up to the researcher to sift it out. As this chapter will show, Shepard's citators perform many other functions for a researcher, but the heart was total retrieval of relevant information. Shepard's citators did this so well that they came to be accepted and trusted universally. Lawyers have believed in Shepard's citators for a long time.

Shepard's citators facilitate the verification of authority through a system of concise abbreviations consisting almost exclusively of volume and page citations combined with one- or two-letter symbols. Under the citation of a published decision, a list of *citing references* indicates every subsequent mention of that decision. If the citing court took some specific action with regard to the earlier case (e.g., affirmed or overruled it) or indicated some specific attitude (e.g., followed it or distinguished its facts), that action or attitude is noted by an alphabetical symbol preceding the volume number of the citing case. The subsequent action must be very explicit to merit comment. The Shepard's editorial staff has always been conservative. They do not infer, they only note action that is explicitly taken. One cannot go out on a limb and retain universal credibility.

Any case can be located in Shepard's according to the publication in which it is reported, the appropriate volume number, and the specific page on which the opinion begins. The publication name and the volume number of the cited authority appear in the top margin of the Shepard's citator. A boxed, bold-faced number designates the beginning of a new volume, while the smaller bold numbers between dashes indicate the page number of each cited case. Recently, Shepard's has begun to include the case name and date of decision following the page number reference. In Illustration A, a page from *Shepard's New Jersey Citations,* the coverage includes cases in volumes 102 and 103 of *New*

Jersey Reports. The citation for *Midland Insurance Co. v. Colatrella* is 102 N.J. 612 (1986).

Illustration A

***Shepard's New Jersey Citations,* Case Edition, Part One, 1994, showing (1) parallel citation, (2) case history, (3) treatment and related cases, and (4) secondary material and annotations**

Vol. 102 NEW JERSEY REPORTS

226NJS553
231NJS[7]380
233NJS[9]395
233NJS[7]396
236NJS[9]477
242NJS[2]365
253NJS70
e 253NJS72
253NJS[1]79
253NJS[2]224
253NJS[11]226
253NJS662
f 253NJS[4]662
f 253NJS[17]662
f 253NJS[8]663
255NJS612
Cir. 3
897F2d[2]698
954F2d145
685FS[2]94
706FS320
706FS[14]324
707FS171
708FS643
712FS[1]459
712FS[2]459
f 712FS[14]460
722FS[2]1164
726FS[1]110
736FS[2]1301
736FS[8]1302
736FS[9]1302
f 805FS[2]1181
f 805FS[9]1181
805FS[7]1183
805FS[11]1187
42RLR1171
17SeH524
17SeH700
23SeH513

—485—
Monmouth Chrysler-Plymouth Inc. v Chrysler Corp. 1986
(509A2d161)
s 102NJ336
s 203NJS281
103NJ97
17SeH174
82AL664n

—504—
In the Matter of Johnson 1986
(509A2d171)
(61AL1207)
105NJ248
107NJ170
107NJ181

115NJ[1]519
d 118NJ[1]168
124NJ[1]279
224NJS[1]228

—512—
In the Matter of Brown 1986
(509A2d176)
104NJ[1]350
f 104NJ[1]489
105NJ[1]248
105NJ[1]259
108NJ[1]521
109NJ[1]141
114NJ[1]13
114NJ[1]222
f 115NJ[1]501
d 117NJ[1]491
d 126NJ[1]230
d 131NJ[1]168

—518—
In the Matter of Lennan 1986
(509A2d179)
j 104NJ336
f 104NJ489
105NJ248
106NJ533
109NJ[1]141
114NJ[1]13
114NJ221

—526—
Continental Trailways Inc. v Director Division of Motor Vehicles 1986
(509A2d769)
US cert dis
in 481US1001
in 107SC1636
s 201NJS71
s 201NJS257
s 6NJT42
j 108NJ308
111NJ[3]217
212NJS174
221NJS[5]95
f 221NJS[6]97
259NJS[7]154
9NJT[7]270
9NJT[7]484
9NJT632
d 9NJT[7]633
f 9NJT[7]657
12NJT65

—559—
Entwistle v Draves 1986
(510A2d1)
s 102NJ310
s 194NJS571
s 200NJS1
cc 102NJ564
102NJ[1]579
104NJ[1]4
j 122NJ82
212NJS[1]255
217NJS[1]460
218NJS[1]578
227NJS[1]479

—564—
Mahoney v Carus Chemical Company Inc. 1986
(510A2d4)
(62AL703) ①
s 96NJ314
cc 102NJ[2]559 ①
102NJ593
e 102NJ[2]596
j 102NJ597
j 103NJ680
104NJ[1]4
104NJ[2]278
d 122NJ[2]72
j 122NJ78
212NJS[1]255
212NJS[3]259
212NJS[2]261
213NJS607 ④
214NJS[2]373
224NJS[5]444
230NJS[2]120
230NJS[5]125
e 232NJS[5]236
232NJS[2]241
247NJS537
260NJS[2]321 ②
260NJS[2]321
265NJS[1]99
266NJS609
Cir. 3
e 667FS[2]161
780FS256
Cir. 4
769FS950
Cir. 11
f 971F2d[4]687
648FS[2]471
18RLJ261
17SeH858
78AL2594s
11AL597s
30AL81s
③

—591—
Wietecha v Peoronard 1986
(510A2d19)
s 97NJ690
104NJ[1]4 ③
122NJ[2]75
j 122NJ78
212NJS[1]255
212NJS[2]255
224NJS[2]444
232NJS[2]236
258NJS[2]435
f 258NJS[3]436

—598—
Christy v Newark 1986
(510A2d22)
s 96NJ262
104NJ[4]4
d 114NJ[1]142
119NJ[1]411
f 218NJS329
218NJS[3]331
223NJS198
225NJS614
227NJS[1]154
e 227NJS[3]155
228NJS[4]433
232NJS[1]403
234NJS464
d 237NJS[2]470
237NJS[4]478
249NJS[2]93
250NJS[1]541
250NJS[2]543
f 251NJS[1]375
255NJS[4]176
264NJS[3]256
24AL31369s

—612—
Midland Insurance Co. v Colatrella 1986
① (510A2d30)
s 101NJ278
s 200NJS101
f 102NJ[3]610
104NJ[3]4
107NJ27
108NJ499
108NJ[2]504
110NJ[1]144
113NJ[1]617
114NJ145
L 127NJ188
220NJS297
d 220NJS299
f 220NJS[1]299
e 227NJS[2]156
232NJS[3]310
236NJS[1]215
237NJS468
237NJS[2]470
249NJS[3]92
c 249NJS94
250NJS[2]543
e 255NJS[2]178
e 255NJS[3]178
f 263NJS439
263NJS[2]439
263NJS[3]439
Cir. 3
826F2d1344
18RLJ711

—622—
In the Matter of Maurello 1986
(510A2d36)
121NJ469
96AL2823s
66AL380n
67AL476n
68AL764n
70AL791n
70AL814n

—635—
In the Matter of Hazelwood 1986
(510A2d276)
132NJ6
132NJ44
e 209NJS109
215NJS185
215NJS[8]186
215NJS[20]186
e 215NJS[21]190
222NJS[12]136
222NJS160
224NJS459
225NJS[1]526
232NJS[10]190
232NJS[15]207
233NJS8
242NJS[4]80
242NJS[5]80
242NJS[24]221
242NJS[1]224
243NJS[5]163
243NJS[6]166
244NJS[4]443
e 247NJS[18]155
247NJS[10]171
247NJS191
247NJS[19]196
257NJS365
264NJS340
265NJS481
Cir. 3
951F2d569
641FS775
645FS719
41RLR1198
16SeH595
18SeH30
22SeH1244
23SeH15
90CR55
50LCP(1)160
87AL302n
87AL316n
1AL5733n

Vol. 103

—1—
Hills Development Co. v Bernards 1986
(510A2d621)
s 209NJS393
s 228NJS635
s 229NJS318
cc 220NJS388
cc 222NJS482
105NJ174
j 108NJ393
111NJ17
115NJ541
116NJ[9]222
120NJ238
120NJ[17]245
121NJ[2]556
125NJ103
125NJ[4]108
125NJ[9]111

—75—
In the Matter of Gipson 1986
(510A2d660)

—79—
Desai v St. Barnabas Medical Center 1986
(510A2d662)
s 99NJ216
d 103NJ101
103NJ[7]107
103NJ[13]114
107NJ[9]248
e 107NJ[8]249
212NJS90
d 213NJS[10]348

922 [G20,0011]

One aspect of Shepard's which often confuses researchers at first is its idiosyncratic abbreviations. To fit citations in limited spaces Shepard's uses very concise abbreviations, many of which appear in no other publications. *West's California Reporter,* for example, is uniformly cited elsewhere as "Cal.Rptr.," but appears in Shepard's listings as "CaR." However, a table of the reporter abbreviations used appears at the beginning of each Shepard's volume, so it is easy to dispel alarm caused by an unfamiliar abbreviation. The researcher need not memorize a whole new set of abbreviations, she just needs to check in the front of the book.

Although their underlying purpose is to indicate the current status and treatment of primary sources, entries in *Shepard's Citations* provide a variety of other important information. The various features are indicated in Illustration A with numbers corresponding to the following sections.

1. PARALLEL CITATIONS

Many cases are published in more than one report series. For example, decisions of the Supreme Court of the United States appear in the *United States Reports, Lawyers' Edition,* and *Supreme Court Reporter,* and most state cases are printed in both official reports and one of the regional reporters of West's National Reporter System. Often researchers have a citation to one version of a case but need to find a different report of that case. A lawyer who has read the unofficial edition of a case may need its official citation to cite in a brief, while a researcher may know only the official citation but wish to use the editorial headnotes available in a commercial version. Different citations to the same judicial decision are referred to as *parallel citations.*[2]

Shepard's Citations provide one of the easiest ways to find parallel citations. The first entry for most cited cases, in parentheses, is the parallel citation to another series of reports. Illustration A shows that the parallel *Atlantic Reporter* citation for the *Midland* case is 510 A.2d 30.

Since Shepard's has citators for both official state reports and regional reporters, it is possible to find an official citation listed under a regional reporter citation and to find a regional reporter citation using an official citation. Similarly, Shepard's has lists for all three editions of U.S. Supreme Court opinions, each with parallel citations to the other two.[3] If a state has discontinued its official reports and the National Reporter System is the only source of its recent decisions, no parallel citation is listed. On the other hand, if a case is reprinted in one of the

2. The concept of parallel citations is currently premised on existing paper sets of case reporters. The revolution in electronic information may bring about major changes, at least prospectively.

3. As part of its *United States Citations* unit, discussed in section C.1 below, Shepard's publishes a Parallel Reference Table volume that provides an easy, alternative method of finding parallel citations of U.S. Supreme Court cases.

annotated or topical reporters as well as in official and regional reporters, more than one parallel citation may be listed. For example, the case that appears at 102 N.J. 564 in Illustration A has parallel citations in the regional reporter and in *American Law Reports, 4th Series.*

Parallel citations appear the first time a Shepard's volume or pamphlet includes a case, and are not repeated in later supplements. Sometimes a parallel citation is not available at the time the case is initially listed in Shepard's, as when a *Supreme Court Reporter* case is cited by other courts long before the official *U.S. Reports* version appears. In such instances the parallel citation is provided in the first volume published after it becomes available.

Other resources to be discussed later in this chapter also can be used to find parallel citations, but are often not as convenient as Shepard's. Some are only updated annually, far less frequently than *Shepard's Citations.* Others are not published at all, and are available only through online computer systems.

2. CASE HISTORY

Case history citations, those indicating prior or subsequent proceedings in the *same* case, follow the parallel citation. The most significant history citations for determining a case's validity are subsequent decisions by a higher appellate court. The citation for the higher court's decision is always preceded by a letter indicating if the cited case is affirmed, modified, or reversed on appeal. These identifying abbreviations, assigned by Shepard's editors, are explained in a table found in the front of each Shepard's volume. The table in *Shepard's New Jersey Citations* is reproduced here in the top portion of Illustration B, under the "History of Case" heading. These same abbreviations are used in the citator for every jurisdiction, although some state Shepard's include additional abbreviations for other actions of their courts.

In Illustration A, the case history portion of the Shepard's display for 102 N.J. 526 indicates that the U.S. Supreme Court denied *certiorari* at 481 U.S. 1001. Decisions relating to the same case also appeared at 201 N.J.Supp. 71, 201 N.J.Supp. 257, and 6 N.J. Tax 42.

The use of the notations preceding the listed citations is the first step in determining whether or not the case being Shepardized is still good authority. If a case was reversed on appeal, it cannot be cited *as authority.* Even a reversed case, of course, may contain passages worth reading or reasoning worth considering. Such a case *can* be cited in a brief, as long as it is clearly noted that it is not binding precedent. It is even possible that a higher court decision listed with an "r" in Shepard's did not reverse the judgment on the specific issue being researched. Only by reading and analyzing the citing decision can a researcher determine its precise effect. The abbreviations in *Shepard's Citations* assist in case analysis but are no substitute for reading the decisions themselves.

Illustration B

Shepard's New Jersey Citations, history and treatment abbreviations

ABBREVIATIONS—ANALYSIS

CASES

History of Case

a	(affirmed)	Same case affirmed on appeal.
cc	(connected case)	Different case from case cited but arising out of same subject matter or intimately connected therewith.
D	(dismissed)	Appeal from same case dismissed.
m	(modified)	Same case modified on appeal.
r	(reversed)	Same case reversed on appeal.
s	(same case)	Same case as case cited.
S	(superseded)	Substitution for former opinion.
v	(vacated)	Same case vacated.
Cert	den	Petition for certification denied.
Cert	gra	Petition for certification granted.
US	cert den	Certiorari denied by U. S. Supreme Court.
US	cert dis	Certiorari dismissed by U. S. Supreme Court.
US	reh den	Rehearing denied by U. S. Supreme Court.
US	reh dis	Rehearing dismissed by U. S. Supreme Court.
US	app pndg	Appeal pending before the U. S. Supreme Court.

Treatment of Case

c	(criticized)	Soundness of decision or reasoning in cited case criticized for reasons given.
d	(distinguished)	Case at bar different either in law or fact from case cited for reasons given.
e	(explained)	Statement of import of decision in cited case. Not merely a restatement of the facts.
f	(followed)	Cited as controlling.
h	(harmonized)	Apparent inconsistency explained and shown not to exist.
j	(dissenting opinion)	Citation in dissenting opinion.
L	(limited)	Refusal to extend decision of cited case beyond precise issues involved.
o	(overruled)	Ruling in cited case expressly overruled.
p	(parallel)	Citing case substantially alike or on all fours with cited case in its law or facts.
q	(questioned)	Soundness of decision or reasoning in cited case questioned.

ABBREVIATIONS—COURTS

Cir. DC–U. S. Court of Appeals, District of Columbia Circuit
Cir. (number)–U. S. Court of Appeals Circuit (number)
Cir. Fed.–U. S. Court of Appeals, Federal Circuit
CCPA–Court of Customs and Patent Appeals
CIT–United States Court of International Trade
ClCt–Claims Court (U. S.)
CtCl–Court of Claims (U. S.)
CuCt–Customs Court
ECA–Temporary Emergency Court of Appeals
ML–Judicial Panel on Multidistrict Litigation
RRR–Special Court Regional Rail Reorganization Act of 1973

[G20,002] xv

Only decisions which directly affect the result in the case being Shepardized are considered part of its "case history." A decision need not be reversed or modified by a higher court, however, to have its status as authority diminished or erased. Subsequent unrelated decisions, by overruling the case or limiting its holding, may yet have an important impact on its status as precedent.

3. TREATMENT AND RELATED CASES

Shepardizing a case almost always will yield a list of subsequent cases which have cited the decision. In a Shepard's display, these citing references immediately follow any parallel citations and case history citations. Shepard's provides several ways of indicating what attitudes toward the case are expressed by later courts or what aspects of the cited case are discussed. The *treatment* of a case by later decisions may have just as important an effect on its precedential value as a direct reversal or affirmance. Courts do not like to reverse themselves for a variety of reasons, so they may seek other means to weaken a precedent by limiting its application to very restricted circumstances. Or a lower court that is faced with a distasteful decision from a higher court may seek to maneuver around it distinguishing it from the case at hand by one means or another. Such treatment can kill the power of a precedent with a thousand small cuts. The researcher needs to know about such treatment.

In the parallel citation and case history sections of a Shepard's listing, the references are to the beginning page (or *citation*) of the relevant case. In the treatment section, on the other hand, each reference is to the exact page within a decision on which the Shepardized case is cited. Some of the citations in the "treatment" section of a Shepard's listing are assigned abbreviation symbols to indicate the attitude or effect stated by the citing court. These symbols are explained in the *bottom* portion of Illustration B, under the heading "Treatment of Case." It is important to note that in assigning these notational symbols, the Shepard's editors rely largely upon the specific language of the citing court. Hence they will not indicate, for example, that a case has been overruled if such effect is not expressly stated in the later decision, no matter how contrary the holding.[4] Other symbols, such as "d" for "distinguished" or "q" for "questioned," may be just as important as an overruling in determining the precedential value of a decision.[5]

4. For over thirty years, *Shepard's United States Citations* indicated that the separate-but-equal doctrine of *Plessy v. Ferguson,* 163 U.S. 537 (1896), was questioned in *Brown v. Board of Education,* 347 U.S. 483 (1954), rather than overruled by *Brown.* Only when Judge John R. Brown noted this fact in a recent opinion, *United States v. Holmes,* 822 F.2d 481, 503 n. 2 (5th Cir.1987) (Brown, J., concurring and dissenting), did Shepard's add a belated "overruled" notation in its *Plessy* entry. Although Shepard's follows the express words of opinions, it can occasionally be swayed by later criticism.

5. In *Glassalum Engineering Corp. v. 392208 Ontario Ltd.,* 487 So.2d 87 (Fla.App. 1986), the appellee relied on a case, *Gonzalez v. Ryder Systems, Inc.,* 327 So.2d 826 (Fla.App.1976), the holding of which had been abrogated by an amendment to the

The citations in the treatment section of a Shepard's listing are arranged by court. Decisions of that jurisdiction's courts are listed first. If cases from the court of last resort and from an intermediate appellate court are published in separate reporters, the high court's decisions precede those of the appellate court. Within the listing for each reporter, however, citations are listed chronologically. There is no ranking by importance or effect on the cited case. A citation to an overruling case may appear towards the end of a long list of other cases. In Illustration A, the *Midland* case at 102 N.J. 612 was cited in several subsequent cases in *New Jersey Reports* before being *limited* to its specific facts at 127 N.J. 188. Depending on the Shepard's unit, citing references in federal cases and decisions from other jurisdictions follow the list of citations from the cited source's jurisdiction.[6]

Shepard's employs another notational system to aid researchers interested in particular points of law in the cited case. Small raised numbers to the left of the page numbers of the citing references indicate the headnote number of the cited case corresponding to the specific issue being discussed. If a case addresses several issues but only one aspect is relevant to a particular research problem, one simply determines which headnote or syllabus paragraph addresses the issue and scans the Shepard's listing for that number. Several subsequent cases discuss the point of law abstracted in headnote three of Illustration A's *Midland* case. For example, it is addressed on page four of volume 104, *New Jersey Reports*, and in volume 263 of the *New Jersey Supplement,* on page 439. Note that the latter citing reference also considers the subject matter of *Midland* 's second headnote.

When researching a case that appears in more than one publication, it is important to understand that while the different Shepard's listings for an opinion cover the same judicial decision, each is keyed to that publication's particular editorial treatment.[7] This means that the small raised numbers indicating which headnote issue is being discussed refer to the headnote numbers in that particular version of the case. A frequent mistake researchers make is to look for headnote numbers from

Florida Rules of Civil Procedure. As the court noted:

> By Shepardizing the *Gonzalez* case, one would have been alerted that its soundness or reasoning had been questioned in a later case; and by reading that later case, *Rivera v. A.M.I.F., Inc.,* 417 So.2d 304, one would have discovered that *Gonzalez* is no longer the law....
>
> If counsel did not observe Shepard's "questioned" signal (designated by a "q") and read *Rivera,* then they, at the least, performed inadequately: appellant's counsel (now the beneficiary of this court's own research) lost the opportunity to argue the controlling *Rivera* case; appellee's counsel, the opportunity to attempt to convince this court why we should not, as we do, find *Rivera* dispositive. Without belaboring the point, we remind the bar that, as this case so dramatically shows, cases must be Shepardized and that when Shepardizing, counsel must mind the "p's" and "q's." 487 So.2d at 88 (footnotes omitted).

6. Although the scope of coverage of the various Shepard's citators will be discussed more fully later in this chapter, generally cases from other states appear only in the Shepard's units for regional reporters and not those for state reports.

7. For an example of this feature of Shepard's, see Illustration C and the accompanying discussion in Section C.1.

one edition while scanning the Shepard's listing under a different version.

Since the citing references found in Shepard's presumably touch upon some or all of the legal issues involved in the original case, Shepard's can function as a tool for finding related cases. However, many of the later cases listed may prove to make only passing reference to the cited case, particularly if the citation does not include a raised headnote number indicating a specific point under discussion. Moreover, later cases which deal with similar issues but do not expressly cite the original case will not be found through Shepardizing. For these reasons Shepard's is just one of several tools used for finding cases on a particular topic.

For some cases there are few or no citing references in Shepard's. Note in Illustration A that the only reference to 102 N.J. 635 is its parallel *Atlantic Reporter* citation. In such situations Shepard's is of little help in a search for related cases. The fact that no citations can be found, however, may itself have some meaning. Several court decisions have mentioned the lack of citations in Shepard's as an indication that earlier decisions are of limited merit or scope.[8]

4. SECONDARY MATERIAL AND ANNOTATIONS

Finally, after the references to citing cases, Shepard's listings include citations indicating when a decision has been mentioned in secondary sources and annotations. Shepard's state citators include citing references in nineteen leading national law reviews, as well as those in bar journals and law reviews published in the particular state. Note in Illustration A that the case at 103 N.J. 1 has been cited in the *Rutgers Law Review* (RLR) and *Seton Hall Law Review* (SeH), as well as in *Columbia Law Review* (CR) and *Law and Contemporary Problems* (LCP). As with citing cases, these references are to the exact page on which the cited case is mentioned. Every state Shepard's, except those for Delaware, Hawaii and Rhode Island, includes at least one law review or bar journal from that state, allowing lawyers in a state to find references to cases in those periodicals which most closely monitor developments in that state's courts. Several Shepard's units, including those for the three largest states, also include references to state attorneys general opinions which discuss a cited case.

Federal citators generally do not include periodical citations.[9] Instead, a separate publication, *Shepard's Federal Law Citations in Select-*

8. In *Meadow Brook National Bank v. Recile,* 302 F.Supp. 62, 82 (E.D.La.1969), the federal district court in applying Louisiana law noted that an 1865 Louisiana Supreme Court case relied upon by the plaintiff was "clearly a maverick decision ... totally ignored by every subsequent decision on the subject."

The courts in *Jeffres v. Countryside Homes of Lincoln, Inc.,* 333 N.W.2d 754, 764 (Neb.1983), and *Amalgamated Casualty Insurance Co. v. Helms,* 212 A.2d 311, 319 (Md.1965), used the absence of citations to denigrate decisions from other states which they did not care to follow.

9. Law review citations to Supreme Court decisions were added to *Shepard's United States Citations* in 1988, but coverage includes citations only since 1973. Old-

ed Law Reviews, is used for locating citing references in the nineteen leading law reviews covered in each of the state citators. Shepard's federal units do list citations from the Opinions of the Attorneys General of the United States.

Annotations in *American Law Reports (ALR)* or *Lawyers' Edition* are included among citing references in both state and federal Shepard's units. The case at 103 N.J. 1 in Illustration A, for example, is cited three times in *ALR*. All annotation references in Shepard's include a suffix symbol indicating the nature of the source. In this example, the three *ALR* citations are followed by an "n," which means simply that the citing source is an annotation. Note that the case at 102 N.J. 564 also is cited in *ALR*; the letter "s" following these citations indicate that the references appear in a supplement to an annotation.

Last and least, a Shepard's listing may also include reference to one or more of the many legal treatises published by Shepard's/McGraw–Hill, Inc. The abbreviations used for these works are included in the list at the front of each volume. Obviously, they are included not for their scholarly or practical value but merely because they are issued by the same publisher.

C. THE COVERAGE OF SHEPARD'S CASE CITATORS

The process of Shepardizing is essentially a simple one: using the proper unit of Shepard's, the researcher locates the citation for a particular case and finds a list of references to parallel citations, earlier or later proceedings in the same case, decisions in other cases, and various other documents. Determining the proper Shepard's unit to use is a necessary first step. Shepard's does not merely publish citators for the cases of every jurisdiction, it publishes citators for every set of official and unofficial reports and every unit of West's National Reporter System. A case with more than one citation can be Shepardized in more than one citator. While the coverage of Shepard's units overlaps considerably, it is important to know what information is available in each.

1. UNITED STATES CITATIONS

Decisions of the Supreme Court of the United States are covered in twenty-three volumes of *Shepard's United States Citations, Case Edition.* Because many Supreme Court decisions are frequently cited in subsequent opinions from federal and state courts, this recently republished bound set is updated regularly by several supplements.

A Supreme Court case may be Shepardized under its official *United States Reports* citation or its citation in either of the permanent unofficial reporters. Volumes 1.1–1.8 of *Shepard's U.S. Citations* contain

er law review citations to Supreme Court decisions appear in *Shepard's Federal Law Citations in Selected Law Reviews.*

United States Reports citations, while volumes 2.1–2.8 and 3.1–3.7 cover *Lawyers' Edition* and *Supreme Court Reporter* citations, respectively. Until recently, the coverage of citing sources differed between the listings for the official citations and those of the unofficial citations. With the 1994 edition of *Shepard's U.S. Citations*, however, the coverage is substantially the same. Under each of a case's three parallel citations, citing references in subsequent Supreme Court decisions, lower federal court cases, and state court decisions are listed. If a state court decision is published in both official and regional reporters, both citations are included in the Shepard's listing. Each parallel citation now also provides citing references in secondary materials, including opinions of the United States Attorneys General, several federal administrative agency reports, nineteen major law reviews, and annotations in *ALR* and *Lawyers' Edition*.

Although the coverage of citing sources is now uniform in all three parts of *U.S. Citations*, a Shepard's listing under a case's *Lawyers' Edition* or *Supreme Court Reporter* citation may provide valuable information that the *U.S. Reports* listing might not. These parallel citations are essential for finding references to recent Supreme Court cases, since the official citation is not available for up to three years after the date of decision. During the interim, cases and secondary sources will have cited to the unofficial reporters. Until the official citation and its accompanying Shepard's listing become available, these citing references will be found only in Shepard's *Lawyers' Edition* and *Supreme Court Reporter* volumes. In the past, when a secondary source only cited to one of the three versions of a Supreme Court case, the citing reference was listed under that particular citation and not the others. Shepard's recently changed this practice, but it remains important to check all three citations for older citing references.

Illustration C shows the listings under the three versions of the well-known civil procedure case, *Burnham v. Superior Court of California,* 495 U.S. 604 (1990). Note that each provides a parallel reference to the other two. Although all three include citations from subsequent federal and state court decisions, as well as from secondary sources, the listings are not identical. For example, none of the decisions citing *Burnham* in the First Circuit of the United States Court of Appeals are displayed under the case's *U.S. Reports* citation. A researcher who fails to Shepardize *Burnham* using its parallel citations would not find these potentially valuable citing references.

Illustration C

Comparison of three listings for same case in *Shepard's United States Citations*

UNITED STATES REPORTS	UNITED STATES SUPREME COURT REPORTS, LAWYERS' EDITION, 2d EDITION	SUPREME COURT REPORT
—604—	—631—	—2105—
Burnham v Superior Court of California County of Marin 1990	Burnham v Superior Court of California County of Marin 1990	Burnham v Superior Court of California County of Marin 1990
(109LE631)	(495US604)	(495US604)
(110SC2105)	(110SC2105)	(109LE631)
150FRD227	s 107LE16	s 110SC47
Cir. 2	111LE71	110SC2741
f 789FS580	j 111LE81	j 110SC2749
792FS224	113LE20	133FRD73
825FS516	113LE32	Cir. 1
Cir. 3	j 113LE47	940F2d23
805FS1182	133FRD73	942F2d^{1}40
806FS58	Cir. 1	742FS^{4}721
825FS1208	940F2d23	754FS^{8}254
834FS679	942F2d40	Cir. 2
Cir. 5	742FS^{1}721	744FS1221
d 966F2d182	754FS254	f 789FS580
11F3d1258	Cir. 2	792FS^{2}224
829FS846	744FS1221	825FS^{5}516
829FS886	f 789FS580	Cir. 3
Cir. 6	792FS^{1}224	805FS^{4}1182
789FS903	825FS516	806FS^{2}58
Cir. 7		825FS1208
8F3d452		834FS679

The *Lawyers' Edition* and *Supreme Court Reporter* volumes of *Shepard's U.S. Citations* also allow a researcher to take advantage of each publication's particular editorial treatment of a case. These commercial versions of Supreme Court opinions often will have a different number of headnotes, or will assign headnotes to different parts of the opinion. As a result, the same citing reference may appear in both Shepard's listings with a different raised number in each. It is important to remember not to look for headnote numbers from one edition while scanning the Shepard's listings under the other edition. You cannot use a *Supreme Court Reporter* headnote number to limit a search for cases listed under the *Lawyers' Edition*, but must examine that version of the case to determine which of *its* headnote paragraphs summarizes the point of law in issue.

In Illustration C, the point of law in *Burnham* discussed in a Second Circuit case, at 792 F.Supp. 224, has been assigned headnote number one in *Lawyers' Edition,* and number two in the *Supreme Court Reporter.* Note that no raised number appears next to the same citing reference listed under the *U.S. Reports.* Shepard's recently discontinued its practice of keying these listings to the official syllabus paragraphs.

Shepard's supplemental coverage includes cases published as *slip opinions.* Shepard's editors examine slip opinions from the Supreme Court and from a majority of the United States Courts of Appeals, and include citing references in those opinions in their listings. Because a slip opinion by definition has no citation, the reference Shepard's provides is a docket number, such as 93–5256 or 94–1269. The docket number is preceded by an abbreviation indicating the deciding court, such as "USDk" for the Supreme Court or "DkDC" for the District of Columbia Circuit. The inclusion of docket numbers in Shepard's makes its coverage more current, although in most libraries the citing opinions are rarely available except through an online database.

Coverage of Supreme Court decisions is just one part of *Shepard's United States Citations.* As it does for each jurisdiction, Shepard's provides citations to both cases *and* statutes. *Shepard's United States Citations, Statute Edition* is used to find citations to either legislative or judicial treatments of federal statutes, and includes coverage of other material such as the United States Constitution, treaties, and federal court rules. Shepard's treatment of statutes and related materials will be discussed in Chapter 5, and is an important part of each jurisdictional Shepard's unit.

To confuse the uninitiated researcher, two other Shepard's units also bear the label *Shepard's United States Citations* on the spines of their volumes. *Shepard's United States Administrative Citations* provides citations to the decisions and orders of various federal administrative agencies, commissions and courts, and will be discussed in Chapter 8. *Shepard's United States Citations: Patents and Trademarks* provides citations to patents (listed numerically) and to copyrights and trademarks (listed alphabetically) as well as to relevant decisions of the courts and the Commissioner of Patents.

2. FEDERAL CITATIONS

Citations to the decisions of the lower federal courts can be found in *Shepard's Federal Citations,* a voluminous set divided into two parts. Generally, Part 1 covers the United States Courts of Appeals and Part 2 the United States District Courts and the United States Claims Court. The publications which can be Shepardized in Part 1 are the *Federal Reporter* and *Federal Cases;* those covered in Part 2 are the *Federal Supplement, Federal Rules Decisions, Court of Claims Reports,* and *Claims Court Reporter.*

Both parts of *Federal Citations* refer to the same citing sources. Coverage incorporates all levels of the federal system, including opinions of the U.S. Attorneys General and slip opinions from the Supreme Court and several of the Courts of Appeals, as well as state cases in both official and National Reporter System citations. At this time, the only periodical cited is the *American Bar Association Journal,* with treatment in the law reviews relegated to *Shepard's Federal Law Citations in Selected Law Reviews.*

3. SHEPARD'S STATE CITATORS

A separate unit of *Shepard's Citations* is published for each of the fifty states, for the District of Columbia, and for Puerto Rico. In addition to cases, each of these units typically covers citations to the state's constitution, statutes, attorney general opinions, and municipal charters and ordinances. However, since the scope of coverage varies somewhat between states, it is wise for a lawyer to be familiar with the contents of the particular Shepard's for the state in which he or she practices.

The "Cases" portion of a state Shepard's unit contains separate sections listing citations to the official reports of the jurisdiction and to the regional reporter covering that state. The former section provides lists of subsequent citing cases in the state's official reports, followed by citations in federal cases, law review articles, and annotations. The official reports section of *Shepard's New Jersey Citations* has already been shown in Illustration A, and its features discussed.

Using its parallel (regional reporter) citation, a case also can be Shepardized in the regional reporter section of the state citator. This section of a state Shepard's unit generally provides fewer secondary authorities as citing references, but does list the regional reporter citations of subsequent citing cases from that state, as well as federal cases. Thus, cases which have a precedential impact on the decision being Shepardized *would* appear here. Law review articles and annotations that have mentioned only the regional reporter citation may be listed here and not in the official reports section.

Illustration D shows the *Atlantic Reporter, 2d Series* section of *Shepard's New Jersey Citations*. Parallel citations to *New Jersey Reports* are provided, followed only by citing references in subsequent New Jersey cases (as published in the *Atlantic Reporter*), and federal cases. Note that the *Midland* case at 510 A.2d 30, examined earlier in its *New Jersey Reports* form, was limited at 603 A.2d 512.

While the regional section of a state Shepard's unit has fewer citing sources, it may be a convenient tool if the regional reporter is the only version of the state's cases at hand and the volumes for Shepard's regional citator are unavailable. Moreover, if the official reports are published more slowly than the regional reporter, as is usually the case, new citations will appear in the official reports section only when page numbers have been assigned. They will be listed under the regional citations much earlier, so a recent important case could be listed *only* here for several months or longer. To be up to date, therefore, it is important to check under both citations.

If official reports are no longer published for a state, then there are no parallel citations and the regional reporter version of a case is the only one available. Its citation is also then the only one used in the state Shepard's unit, and citations in law reviews and *ALR* annotations are listed under the regional reporter citation.

Neither the official reports section nor the regional reporter section of a state Shepard's unit include any citations from courts in other

Illustration D

Shepard's New Jersey Citations, Case Edition, Part Six, 1994

Vol. 510 ATLANTIC REPORTER, 2d SERIES (New Jersey Cases)

557A2d[1]337
560A2d1319
d 568A2d[2]133
568A2d[4]138
575A2d[1]421
592A2d[2]18
595A2d[1]566
595A2d[2]567
f 598A2d[1]253
624A2d[3]602

—30—
Midland Insurance Co. v Colatrella
1986
(102NJ612)
s 490A2d366
s 501A2d942
f 510A2d[3]29
514A2d[3]833
526A2d123
531A2d720
531A2d[2]722
531A2d1362
d 531A2d1363
f 531A2d[1]1363
539A2d[1]1219
e 545A2d[2]851
549A2d[1]907
552A2d[1]152
553A2d18
556A2d[3]1303
565A2d[1]416
568A2d132
568A2d[2]133
592A2d[3]18
c 592A2d19
595A2d[2]567
L 603A2d512
623A2d[2]254
623A2d[3]254
f 623A2d255
Cir. 3
826F2d1344

—36—
In the Matter of Maurello
1986
(102NJ622)
582A2d623

—42—
South Harrison v Gloucester
1986
(210NJS370)
s 516A2d1140
530A2d333
d 576A2d932

—47—
New Jersey v Cartier
1986
(210NJS379)
538A2d[2]1234
539A2d[1]754
545A2d[1]209
576A2d[1]951
576A2d[2]951

—49—
New Jersey v Porter
1986
(210NJS383)
s 523A2d191
f 511A2d[3]1225
521A2d369
528A2d[12]935
534A2d753
534A2d[12]754
544A2d[12]410
550A2d[12]1249
551A2d547
567A2d[3]294
577A2d[12]860
589A2d181
599A2d[12]547
607A2d1314
q 609A2d406
f 618A2d385
f 618A2d[7]386
f 618A2d[8]386
Cir. 3
990F2d758

—56—
Bernick v Frost
1986
(210NJS397)
s 523A2d158
547A2d[1]1174
593A2d374
612A2d388
612A2d391
Cir. 3
795FS[1]683

—62—
South Orange Village v Hunt
1986
(210NJS407)
d 539A2d[9]1284
547A2d[2]333
f 560A2d742
566A2d832
576A2d[6]33
576A2d[7]33
576A2d[1]34
576A2d[3]34
576A2d[4]34

—68—
Overlook Terrace Corp. v Excel Properties Corp.
1986
(210NJS420)
609A2d8

—72—
New Jersey v Chung
1986
(210NJS427)
519A2d[3]344
j 527A2d441
575A2d[1]514
575A2d[5]514
582A2d[2]633

—80—
New Jersey v Breakiron
1986
(210NJS442)
m 532A2d199
s 523A2d166
515A2d[1]1232
517A2d[5]511
538A2d1259
562A2d[6]1332
e 563A2d461
q 579A2d[5]839
603A2d935

—95—
McGowan v Barry
1986
(210NJS469)
527A2d[4]81
543A2d[1]1036

—98—
Fidelity Union Bank v Trim
1986
(210NJS476)
s 499A2d245
518A2d528
587A2d1270
592A2d1245
592A2d[2]1248

—101—
Brick v Block 48-7 Lots 34 35 36
1986
(210NJS481)
US cert den
in 481US1049
in 107SC2181
Cert den
in 526A2d151
s 494A2d829
532A2d[1]742

—103—
613 Corp. v New Jersey
1986
(210NJS485)
522A2d[8]444
540A2d[6]1341
567A2d[4]285
580A2d283
591A2d1018
592A2d257
f 607A2d1026

—117—
In the Matter of J.P.M.
1985
(210NJS512)
524A2d1263
565A2d[1]715
576A2d[9]269

—123—
Pozzi v Pozzi
1986
(210NJS522)
518A2d[4]785

—125—
In the Matter of Visbeck
1986
(210NJS527)
514A2d1346
517A2d[1]888
524A2d[3]452

—133—
In the Matter of Jobes
1986
(210NJS543)
m 529A2d434
s 523A2d173
d 517A2d893

—136—
In the Matter of Clark
1986
(210NJS548)
cc 515A2d276

—276—
In the Matter of Hazelwood
1986
(102NJ635)

—278—
New Jersey v Hancock
1985
(210NJS568)
s 506A2d855
e 521A2d[1]1313
535A2d[1]972
537A2d755
537A2d[1]1326
f 559A2d[1]1385
562A2d[1]268
586A2d[1]1346
587A2d[1]264
589A2d[1]192
599A2d[1]904

—279—
Brancasons v New Jersey
1986
(210NJS570)

—281—
Fuchilla v Layman
1986
(210NJS574)
US cert den
in 488US826
a 537A2d652
s 523A2d196
555A2d761
487US[7]155
101LE[7]148
108SC[7]2315
56USLW4696
Cir. 3
682FS[4]254

—286—
Levine v Levine
1986
(210NJS585)
c 541A2d[1]1124
569A2d[1]853

—288—
Union County Savings Bank v Johnson
1986
(210NJS589)
Cir. 3
82BRW18
86BRW[4]372

—295—
Contento v Contento
1986
(210NJS601)
548A2d[4]245
598A2d[4]960

—300—
Private Truck Council of America Inc. v New Jersey
1985
(210NJS611)
r 534A2d13
s 544A2d33

—308—
Ocean Cablevision Associates v Hovbilt Inc.
1986
(210NJS626)
572A2d[2]1195
Cir. 11
835F2d[1]1364

—314—
Blair v Anik Liquors
1986
(210NJS636)
Cir. 3
668FS[1]401

846 [G20,004]

states. Since Shepardizing a case in the state citator, using either its official or regional citation, will yield references to all home jurisdiction or federal cases that have affected its authority in any way, some researchers stop Shepardizing when they have completed their search in the appropriate state unit. One can expand a search, however, by tracing the treatment of a state decision in the courts of every other state, using the appropriate Shepard's regional reporter unit.

4. REGIONAL SHEPARD'S UNITS

Shepard's publishes a separate unit for each series in the National Reporter System, including the *New York Supplement* and *California Reporter*. Like the regional reporter section of a state unit, these lists provide citing references in subsequent home state cases (as reported in the regional reporter) and federal cases. The advantage the regional reporter units offer over the state units, however, is the inclusion of citing references from other states (again, as reported in the appropriate regional reporter). Although decisions from other state courts are not binding on the courts of the home jurisdiction, they are often useful as persuasive authority, particularly if no relevant decisions within the home state can be found. The regional citators also contain citing references in annotations, but the law review citations found in the state units are not supplied. Because of the difference in coverage, it is always important to examine both state and regional units when using Shepard's for finding related material.

Illustration E shows the *Midland* case, discussed above, as listed in *Shepard's Atlantic Reporter Citations* at 510 A.2d 30. Note that the same New Jersey and federal cases appear first, followed by citing references from Delaware, Iowa, and Wisconsin.

The citing cases from other states are listed separately by state, in two sequences. First are cases from states in the same regional reporter as the case being Shepardized, arranged alphabetically by state. Then, in a second alphabetical arrangement, are cases from states covered in the other regional reporters. In Illustration E, for the case appearing at 510 A.2d 22, the citing references from three states in the *Atlantic Reporter*, including Pennsylvania, precede the references from Massachusetts, Missouri, and South Carolina.

For cited cases published since the inception of the National Reporter System in the late 19th century, the regional Shepard's unit is the only place to find citing cases from other states. Since earlier cases do not have regional reporter citations, however, they cannot be Shepardized in those units. Shepard's coverage under the official citations of the earliest cases, therefore, includes citations from the courts of other states as published in the regional reporters. The only citing cases not included are decisions from other states published before the National Reporter System began.[10] The scope of Shepard's coverage is vast but not universal.

10. "One problem for legal historians is that ante-bellum cases cannot be Shepardized between states. Thus, the only way to determine if a case has been cited by other

Illustration E

Shepard's Atlantic Reporter Citations, Part Eight, 1994

Vol. 510 ATLANTIC REPORTER, 2d SERIES

648FS[2]471
Del
562A2d[2]597
D C
569A2d[1]1177
569A2d[2]1177
R I
556A2d[4]41
Haw
811P2d825
Idaho
777P2d728
Ill
519NE492
Ind
590NE143
N Y
619NE377
548NYS2d380
580NYS2d607
Va
436SE606
Wis
467NW512
78AL2594s
11AL4597s
30AL481s

—19—

Wietecha v
Peoronard
1986

(102NJ591)
s 483A2d202
514A2d[1]833
514A2d[1]867
514A2d[2]867
540A2d[2]921
556A2d[2]1264
583A2d[2]1134
j 583A2d1135
609A2d[2]1318
f 609A2d[3]1319
Mo
787SW711

—22—

Christy v
Newark
1986

(102NJ598)
s 475A2d567
514A2d[4]833
f 527A2d912
527A2d[3]913
538A2d426
543A2d115
545A2d[1]850
e 545A2d[3]851
f 549A2d[1]906
f 549A2d[3]907
549A2d[4]1278
d 553A2d[1]17
557A2d[1]337

560A2d1319
d 568A2d[2]133
568A2d[4]138
575A2d[1]421
592A2d[2]18
595A2d[1]566
595A2d[2]567
f 598A2d[1]253
624A2d[3]602
633A2d978
Conn
e 595A2d[1]889
595A2d[2]889
595A2d[3]889
610A2d[2]1253
j 610A2d1256
N H
d 589A2d1018
Pa
538A2d[2]868
Mass
624NE949
Mo
755SW333
S C
419SE221
24AL31369s

—30—

Midland
Insurance Co. v
Colatrella
1986

(102NJ612)
s 490A2d366
s 501A2d942
f 510A2d[3]29
514A2d[3]833
526A2d123
531A2d720
531A2d[2]722
531A2d1362
d 531A2d1363
f 531A2d[1]1363
539A2d[1]1219
e 545A2d[2]851
549A2d[1]907
552A2d[1]152
553A2d18
556A2d[3]1303
565A2d[1]416
568A2d132
568A2d[2]133
592A2d[3]18
c 592A2d19
595A2d[2]567
L 603A2d512
623A2d[2]254
623A2d[3]254
f 623A2d255
Cir. 3
826F2d1344
Del
575A2d1107
Iowa
465NW854

Wis
469NW177

—36—

In the Matter
of Maurello
1986

(102NJ622)
582A2d623
96AL2823s
66AL4380n
67AL4476n
68AL4764n
70AL4791n
70AL4814n

—42—

South Harrison
v Gloucester
1986

(210NJS370)
s 516A2d1140
530A2d333
d 576A2d932
Ind
553NE1389
38AL31070s

—47—

New Jersey
v Cartier
1986

(210NJS379)
538A2d[2]1234
539A2d[1]754
545A2d[1]209
576A2d[1]951
576A2d[2]951

—49—

New Jersey
v Porter
1986

(210NJS383)
s 523A2d191
f 511A2d[3]1225
521A2d369
528A2d[12]935
534A2d753
534A2d[12]754
544A2d[12]410
550A2d[12]1249
551A2d547
567A2d[3]294
577A2d[12]860
589A2d181
599A2d[12]547
607A2d1314
q 609A2d406
f 618A2d385
f 618A2d[7]386

f 618A2d[8]386
634A2d[11]107
Cir. 3
990F2d758
N Y
519NYS2d616

—56—

Bernick v Frost
1986

(210NJS397)
s 523A2d158
547A2d[1]1174
593A2d374
612A2d388
612A2d391
Cir. 3
795FS[1]683

—62—

South Orange
Village v Hunt
1986

(210NJS407)
d 539A2d[9]1284
547A2d[2]333
f 560A2d742
566A2d832
576A2d[6]33
576A2d[7]33
576A2d[1]34
576A2d[3]34
576A2d[4]34
86AL4667n

—68—

Overlook
Terrace
Corp. v Excel
Properties
Corp.
1986

(210NJS420)
609A2d8
Calif
245CaR885

—72—

New Jersey
v Chung
1986

(210NJS427)
519A2d[3]344
j 527A2d441
575A2d[1]514
575A2d[5]514
582A2d[2]633
Pa
f 555A2d[5]94
Ariz
766P2d111

Colo
746P2d526
746P2d531
Fla
504So2d456
Ill
502NE1186
Mich
425NW786
Wash
750P2d646
Wis
401NW858
65AL4723n

—80—

New Jersey
v Breakiron
1986

(210NJS442)
m 532A2d199
s 523A2d166
515A2d[1]1232
517A2d[5]511
538A2d1259
562A2d[8]1332
e 563A2d461
q 579A2d[5]839
603A2d935
50AL2176s
17AL3146s
22AL31228s

—95—

McGowan
v Barry
1986

(210NJS469)
527A2d[4]81
543A2d[1]1036

—98—

Fidelity Union
Bank v Trim
1986

(210NJS476)
s 499A2d245
518A2d528
587A2d1270
592A2d1245
592A2d[2]1248

—101—

Brick v Block
48-7 Lots
34 35 36
1986

(210NJS481)
US cert den
in 481US1049
in 107SC2181

Cert den
in 526A2d151
s 494A2d829
532A2d[1]742

—103—

613 Corp. v
New Jersey
1986

(210NJS485)
522A2d[8]444
540A2d[6]1341
567A2d[4]285
580A2d283
591A2d1018
592A2d257
f 607A2d1026
Md
575A2d328
Haw
828P2d804

—117—

In the Matter
of J.P.M.
1985

(210NJS512)
524A2d1263
565A2d[1]715
576A2d[9]269
53AL3605s

—123—

Pozzi v Pozzi
1986

(210NJS522)
518A2d[4]785
Mo
734SW277
96AL3968s
5AL5860n
6AL538n

—125—

In the Matter
of Visbeck
1986

(210NJS527)
514A2d1346
517A2d[1]888
524A2d[3]452
Mich
491NW636
Mo
760SW413

290

5. TOPICAL SHEPARD'S UNITS

In addition to the jurisdictional citators, Shepard's publishes a variety of specialized topical citators, most of which include citing

courts is to read the decisions of the other courts." Paul Finkelman, "Exploring Southern Legal History," 64 *N.C.L.Rev.* 77, 95 n. 105 (1985).

references to cases in their subject area. While the topical units are less comprehensive than the standard jurisdictional Shepard's units, their advantage is that they include citing material not covered in the regular units. *Shepard's Federal Energy Law Citations,* for example, includes citations to federal court cases by Federal Energy Regulatory Commission decisions. Many of the specialized units also feature as *cited* material administrative decisions and regulations in the area, and they will be discussed further in Chapter 8. The following topical citators include analysis of court cases in their fields:

Shepard's Bankruptcy Citations

Shepard's Corporation Law Citations

Shepard's Criminal Justice Citations

Shepard's Employment Law Citations

Shepard's Evidence Citations

Shepard's Federal Energy Law Citations

Shepard's Federal Labor Law Citations

Shepard's Federal Occupational Safety and Health Citations

Shepard's Federal Tax Citations

Shepard's Immigration and Naturalization Citations

Shepard's Insurance Law Citations

Shepard's Labor Arbitration Citations

Shepard's Medical Malpractice Citations

Shepard's Military Justice Citations

Shepard's Partnership Law Citations

Shepard's Products Liability Citations

Shepard's Professional and Judicial Conduct Citations

Shepard's Uniform Commercial Code Case Citations

The publisher has in recent years continued to add new specialized citators, so others may soon exist. This list does not include those specialized citators (such as *Shepard's Code of Federal Regulations Citations* or *Shepard's Law Review Citations*) which do not provide citing references to court cases.

D. THE FORMATS OF SHEPARD'S CITATIONS

Deciding upon which Shepard's unit to use is but the first step in properly Shepardizing a case. Whether using Shepard's to determine a legal authority's current status or to find other helpful research material, a search must be as up-to-date as possible. Shepard's editorial staff comprehensively monitors new court decisions and regularly updates its bound volumes through paperback supplements. A single volume or pamphlet rarely contains all of the citations to a particular case. Depending on the age of a decision, a researcher may have to consult more than one bound volume, each covering a different span of years, and up to three supplementary pamphlets. A common error made by novice researchers when Shepardizing is to look in the most recent supplement and think that they have checked everything relevant. The most recent supplement will only cover what happened in the most recent three or six month period. If the case that one is checking on was decided in 1988, one must check coverage back that far. It could have been overruled in 1990 and that information would not appear in the latest supplement.

In an effort to simplify access to its material Shepard's has recently recompiled and reissued many of its citator units, reducing the number of volumes in which a researcher must look. To provide the latest information on the status of cases, however, Shepard's must supplement the citators promptly and frequently. Each Shepard's unit usually consists of one or more bound volumes and one or more paperback supplements. All Shepard's units are supplemented every month or two, depending on the jurisdiction, with red-covered, cumulative pamphlets. Some citators also have gold-covered, annual or semi-annual cumulative supplements. Many units are further updated between publication of the supplements by newsprint advance sheets.

In an ongoing effort to improve the currency of its product, Shepard's now supplements *United States Citations* and *Federal Citations* twice a month with blue-covered pamphlets; other units soon may be updated with the same frequency. *Shepard's Daily Express*, a facsimile transmission service available for about twenty jurisdictions, provides the researcher with a list of cases that have been cited since the most recent soft-covered supplement in some significant way (i.e., to which the Shepard's editors have assigned a letter indicating its treatment) by the United States Supreme Court or any of the United States Courts of Appeals.

To insure that the researcher has at hand all the necessary parts, Shepard's prints on the cover of each pamphlet a list, "What Your Library Should Contain," indicating which issues are current and may be needed for a complete search in that citator. Checking the list on the cover of the most recent supplement will ensure that no essential components are missing or have been overlooked. The cover of a *Shepard's New Jersey Citations, Advance Sheet*, with its "What Your Library Should Contain" feature, appears in Illustration F.

The tables of abbreviations for reporters and for Shepard's treatment symbols, provided in the front of each bound volume, are also included at the beginning of each soft-covered supplement, but do not appear in the uncovered interim advance sheets. It cannot be overemphasized that these convenient tables are essential for turning Shepard's from an indecipherable jumble into a simple and effective research tool.

Illustration F

***Shepard's New Jersey Citations*, advance sheet**

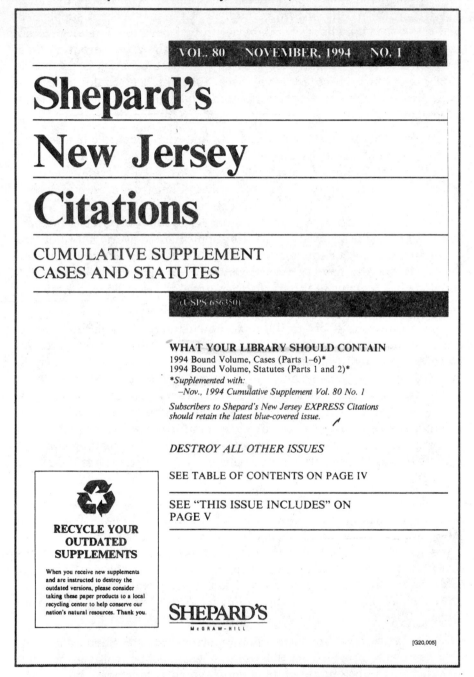

VOL. 80 NOVEMBER, 1994 NO. 1

Shepard's New Jersey Citations

CUMULATIVE SUPPLEMENT
CASES AND STATUTES

(USPS 656350)

WHAT YOUR LIBRARY SHOULD CONTAIN

1994 Bound Volume, Cases (Parts 1–6)*
1994 Bound Volume, Statutes (Parts 1 and 2)*
**Supplemented with:*
–Nov., 1994 Cumulative Supplement Vol. 80 No. 1

Subscribers to Shepard's New Jersey EXPRESS Citations should retain the latest blue-covered issue.

DESTROY ALL OTHER ISSUES

RECYCLE YOUR OUTDATED SUPPLEMENTS

When you receive new supplements and are instructed to destroy the outdated versions, please consider taking these paper products to a local recycling center to help conserve our nation's natural resources. Thank you.

SEE TABLE OF CONTENTS ON PAGE IV

SEE "THIS ISSUE INCLUDES" ON PAGE V

[G20,005]

Once you have mastered Shepardizing a case in print, doing it in electronic media will be even easier.

Shepard's case citators are also available online through the WESTLAW and LEXIS database systems. One great advantage of the online versions of Shepard's is that all citing entries are cumulated in one listing, eliminating the need to search through several volumes and pamphlets. Moreover, the systems allow the researcher to go directly to a Shepard's display for any case being viewed, and then from Shepard's to the text of a citing case. This allows Shepardizing to be a more integral part of the process of finding and reading cases, rather than an afterthought that might be neglected.

Perhaps the most important advantage offered by online Shepard's retrieval, however, is that the computer can scan the listing and limit a display to particular requests. A researcher interested only in a particular point of law, as indicated in Shepard's by a certain headnote number, need not read carefully through several columns of irrelevant cases but can automatically retrieve only those citing cases on point. A display can also be limited to those cases with particular history or treatment symbols, so that one can retrieve, for example, only those cases that distinguish or limit the holding of the cited decision.

Unfortunately, the online versions of Shepard's are no more current than the soft-covered supplements.[11] Shepard's adds material to its databases at the same time the print version goes to press, but often the published version is available in libraries first. The publisher may have valid commercial reasons for delaying online access to its product, but its protectionist approach negates the vast improvement in retrieval time possible through computerized access.

Shepard's online coverage is fully retrospective, duplicating everything in the "Cases" sections of its published volumes. For reference, both WESTLAW and LEXIS Shepard's displays indicate the scope of coverage at the top of the first screen, but WESTLAW users must enter a "scope" command to determine any limitations in the database in use.

Illustration G shows a LEXIS Shepard's display for 510 A.2d 30, restricted to those cases referring to the point of law summarized in headnote 3. Note the scope of coverage explained at the top of the screen, which indicates that this second of two documents is from the Atlantic Reporter, 2d Series division of *Shepard's New Jersey Citations*. The numbers in the lefthand column can be used to view the citing cases.

Several citator units, including *U.S. Citations, Federal Citations*, and those of the largest state jurisdictions, are now available on CD–ROM. A Shepard's citator on CD–ROM is updated with the same frequency as the print version. As with the online databases, this medium cumulates citing references, eliminating the need to search through several volumes and pamphlets. In addition to this conve-

11. In WESTLAW, a related service called Shepard's PreView provides citing references from the National Reporter System before they are available in the online version of *Shepard's Citations*.

Illustration G

A LEXIS Shepard's printout, restricted to headnote 3

(c) 1994 McGraw-Hill, Inc. - DOCUMENT 2 (OF 2)

CITATIONS TO: 510 A.2d 30
SERIES: Shepard's New Jersey Citations
DIVISION: Atlantic Reporter, 2d Series (New Jersey Cases)
COVERAGE: All Shepard's Citations Through 12/94 Supplement.

RESTRICTIONS: 3

NUMBER	ANALYSIS	CITING REFERENCE	SYLLABUS/HEADNOTE
1	parallel citation	(102 N.J. 612)	
4	followed	510 A.2d 29	3
5		514 A.2d 833	3
17		556 A.2d 1303	3
21		592 A.2d 18	3
26		623 A.2d 254	3

nience, CD–ROM enables the user to track a research trail and the amount of time spent. Some of the citators offer the unique feature of providing explanatory summaries of the citing references to which Shepard's editors have assigned a treatment letter. CD–ROM technology allows Shepard's to adapt these products to local conditions; when networked in any number of configurations, Shepard's on CD–ROM will appear to the user to be much like the online versions.

E. OTHER VERIFICATION AND UPDATING TOOLS

Shepard's Citations is the preeminent resource in the field of case verification, an essential component of American legal research for over a century. No publication or service attempts to duplicate Shepard's work of listing every subsequent citation to every published decision. In recent years, however, two on-line case verification systems; Insta–Cite and Auto–Cite have appeared. While lacking the comprehensiveness of Shepard's citators, they offer great advantage in speed and ease of use. They still lack the universal acceptance of Shepard's products, and they must be used on WESTLAW and LEXIS, so there are cost issues.

WESTLAW and LEXIS themselves can be used as citators. The pros and cons of such use is set out below.

In addition, some specialized looseleaf services publish sets of citator volumes for cases in their subject area, such as Lawyers Co-op/Bancroft Whitney's *American Law of Products Liability Citator,* Commerce Clearing House's *Standard Federal Tax Reporter Citator,* and Research Institute of America's *Federal Taxes Citator.*[12] For general research, these are materials which serve *some* of the same purposes as *Shepard's Citations.* Each such set stands on its own and it must be evaluated along the lines set out in Chapter 10.

Finally, there are volumes which simply provide parallel citations, allowing one to convert a citation from one set to another. These sets were a staple in previous days, but their function has largely been superceded.

1. AUTO–CITE AND INSTA–CITE

Both LEXIS and WESTLAW have online services designed specifically for the purpose of verifying the accuracy and validity of citations. These services do not provide the breadth of information available in Shepard's, but focus specifically on developments in the same litigation and cases which have a precedential impact on the decision being verified. Called *Auto–Cite* on LEXIS and *Insta–Cite* on WESTLAW, these systems operate similarly to Shepard's online in that the researcher simply types in the citation to a case. The resulting display includes the name of the case, any parallel citations, and the names and citations of relevant cases, with the effect of each subsequent decision noted. Even if there are no subsequent developments in a case or later decisions affecting its authority, Auto–Cite and Insta–Cite are simple and trustworthy means of verifying the accuracy of citations and of finding parallel citations.

In Auto–Cite, the citation verification service of Lawyers Cooperative Publishing, the display first lists the name and citation of the case for which information is sought, followed by subsequent decisions in the same case and any later cases which have explicitly affected its validity. In a second paragraph, any published prior decisions are listed. Finally, Auto–Cite identifies any cases to which the case in question makes negative reference, and also lists any annotations in the *ALR* series or in *Lawyers' Edition* that have cited any of the cases in its display. The first screen of the Auto–Cite display for 102 N.J. 612 is shown in Illustration H.

Insta–Cite is a citation verification and case history service of the West Publishing Company. Unlike Auto–Cite, it lists decisions in chronological order, with an arrow marking the citation transmitted by the researcher. Like Auto–Cite, it verifies citations, provides case names and parallel citations, lists cases in the direct and precedential history of a case, and includes research references (in *Corpus Juris Secundum,* West's legal encyclopedia). Cases in the "direct history" section include

12. The CCH Tax Citator Service is also available in WESTLAW, while RIA's Tax Citator Service is in LEXIS.

Illustration H

An Auto-Cite Display

```
Auto-Cite (R) Citation Service, (c) 1994 Lawyers Cooperative Publishing

102 NJ 612:

CITATION YOU ENTERED:

Midland Ins. Co. v. Colatrella, 102 N.J. 612, 510 A.2d 30 (1986)

PRIOR HISTORY:

Midland Ins. Co. v. Colatrella, 200 N.J. Super. 101, 490 A.2d 366 (1985)

    aff'd, (BY CITATION YOU ENTERED)

CITATION YOU ENTERED MAKES NEGATIVE REFERENCE TO:

Pullen v. Travelers Ins. Co., 206 N.J. Super. 227, 502 A.2d 70 (1985)
                                                              [G20,007]
```

prior and subsequent decisions rendered in the course of the same litigation, while "negative indirect history" involves subsequent decisions that have commented negatively on the authority of the case.[13] The Insta-Cite display for 102 N.J. 612 is shown in Illustration I.

A strong advantage the two systems have over *Shepard's Citations* is speed of updating. New developments are added to the databases as they become available (often within 48 hours), rather than on a monthly or bimonthly publication basis. For recent cases it would be wise to check Auto-Cite or Insta-Cite, if available, for developments since the latest Shepard's supplement.[14]

It is important to understand that the editorial processes behind Insta-Cite and Auto-Cite are separate and distinct from that of Shepard's. As a result, an Insta-Cite "negative indirect history" listing or an Auto-Cite display will not coincide with Shepard's broader editorial analysis of a case's subsequent negative treatment. For example, note that the case listed in Illustration A as limiting the *Midland* decision does not appear in either Illustration H or I. Although Insta-Cite and Auto-Cite are useful for verifying the current status of a case, *Shepard's*

13. Direct history and citation verification are available for any federal case on WESTLAW, and for state cases published since 1879. Negative indirect history is available only for cases affected by decisions published since 1972.

14. The marketing materials of each system claim that it is the faster and more reliable of the two. A more objective viewpoint, with descriptions of the editorial processes involved in creating the databases, appears in Barbara Bintliff, "Auto-Cite and Insta-Cite: The Race to Update Case Histories," 15 *Colo. Law.* 1675 (1986).

Illustration I

An Insta-Cite Display

```
Insta-Cite                                                          PAGE      1
                                                   Date of Printing: DEC 15,94
                                   INSTA-CITE

CITATION: 102 N.J. 612
                                 Direct History

     1  Midland Ins. Co. v. Colatrella, 200 N.J.Super. 101, 490 A.2d 366
             (N.J.Super.A.D., Mar 28, 1985) (NO. A-499-84T3)
             (Additional Negative Indirect History)
          Certification Granted by
     2  Midland Ins. Co. v. Colatrella, 101 N.J. 278, 501 A.2d 942
             (N.J., May 24, 1985)
          AND Judgment Affirmed by
=>   3  Midland Ins. Co. v. Colatrella, 102 N.J. 612, 510 A.2d 30
             (N.J., Jun 11, 1986) (NO. A-52)

                            Negative Indirect History

  Disagreed With by
     4  Schaser v. State Farm Ins. Co., 255 N.J.Super. 169, 604 A.2d 687
             (N.J.Super.L., Feb 19, 1992) (NO. L-001363-90)
             (Additional History)
  Declined to Follow by
     5  March v. Pekin Ins. Co., 465 N.W.2d 852 (Iowa, Feb 20, 1991)
             (NO. 90-95) (Additional History)
  Declined to Extend by
     6  Charnecky v. American Reliance Ins. Co., 249 N.J.Super. 91,
             592 A.2d 17 (N.J.Super.A.D., Jun 21, 1991) (NO. A-852-90T5)
             (Additional History)
  Limitation of Holding Recognized by
     7  Charnecky v. American Reliance Ins. Co., 127 N.J. 188, 603 A.2d 512
             (N.J., Mar 23, 1992) (NO. A-96) (Additional History)

                               Secondary Sources

Corpus Juris Secundum (C.J.S.) References
        101 C.J.S. Workmen's Compensation Sec.1041 Note 6 (Pocket Part)
 (C) Copyright West Publishing Company 1994                        [G20,008]
```

Citations remains the definitive means of determining the strength of its continuing authority.

As legal research becomes increasingly automated, the Auto-Cite and Insta-Cite systems may take over the verification functions traditionally deemed to be Shepard's primary function. *Shepard's Citations* will remain, however, as the basic means of finding all later cases citing a precedent. The credibility of the Shepard's system is likely to last well into the 21st Century.

2. WESTLAW AND LEXIS

The full-text databases of WESTLAW and LEXIS can be used to find subsequent references to a decided case. One can search the case databases for the names of parties or a case citation and retrieve every document in which those terms appear. A search for *all* subsequent cases would merely duplicate the results found in Shepard's, without the aid of editorial information on the citing cases. A search limited to decisions within the past year, however, will often retrieve new cases that have not yet been covered in Shepard's print or online citators.[15] In an area of law that is rapidly developing, it may well be worth the expense to obtain the up-to-the-minute citations available through full-text retrieval.

3. PARALLEL CITATION TABLES

The *National Reporter Blue Book,* published by West and supplemented annually, consists of lists of case citations for every volume of official reports, with cross-references to National Reporter System citations. For example, the listing for volume 102 of *New Jersey Reports* shows that the *Midland* case, 102 N.J. 612, discussed above, is also published at 510 A.2d 30.

For approximately half of the states, West publishes a *Blue and White Book,* which also has parallel citation tables from regional reporter locations to official reports. The blue pages in one of these volumes duplicate the information provided in the *National Reporter Blue Book,* with parallel citations from the official reports to the regional reporter; the white pages provide the opposite references, from the regional reporter to the official reports. A state's *Blue and White Book* is only available in that state.

Parallel citations, of course, can often be found without use of either Shepard's or a book of conversion tables. If an official citation is available at the time the regional reporter goes to press, it is provided at the beginning of the decision. Most of the official reports indicate the National Reporter System locations of their cases, although several follow the lead of the *United States Reports* and do not supply this useful piece of information.

F. SUMMARY

Shepard's Citations will rear its head throughout this volume, not only as a means of checking the status of cases but as a basic tool for finding and analyzing case law. It may appear a strange and uninviting system of notation at first. As with many new things, experience will show not only its value but its simplicity in use.

The current status of primary sources other than cases also needs to be verified. Statutes may be repealed or amended by the legislature, or declared unconstitutional by a court; regulations may be superseded and treaties abrogated. As these primary sources are introduced in later chapters, means for determining their status, including *Shepard's Citations,* will be explained.

15. WESTLAW's now offers a service that automatically performs this function. When a citation is entered, Quick*Cite* retrieves the most recent decisions citing the case. Although the text of the citing case is provided, no editorial enhancements are included.

G. ADDITIONAL READING

Patti Ogden, " 'Mastering the Lawless Science of Our Law': A Story of Legal Citation Indexes," 85 *Law Libr. J.* 1 (1993). A discussion of citation services from before Frank Shepard's time to the present.

Frank Shepard Company, *A Record of Fifty Years of Specializing in a Field that is of First Importance to the Bench and Bar of the United States: An Insight into an Establishment that has Grown from Small Beginnings to the First Rank in the Law Publishing Field* (Frank Shepard Co.1923). Of interest only to bibliographic types, but full of laudatory prose and early photographs of Shepard's staffers at work.

How to Use Shepard's Citations: A Presentation of the Scope and Functions of Shepard's Citation Books and Services with Methods and Techniques to Enhance their Value in Legal Research (Shepard's/McGraw–Hill 1986). A helpful manual, and proof that the publisher still can wield an imposing book title.

Chapter 4

CASE FINDING

A. INTRODUCTION

Having described the way in which the decisions of the courts are reported and verified, we now confront the question of how to locate a particular decision, a process called *case finding*. Though the world may be tilting toward statutes and administrative rules, locating a particular case or finding cases that deal with a particular issue is still at the heart of the research process. Case finding remains an essential legal research skill. The field of case law research spans the entire history of legal publishing. When looking for judicial opinions one will encounter the most traditional and the most modern of research tools.

How to approach the 3,000,000 cases that are already reported, with another 100,000 entering the world each year? How to find the one decision that will answer the needs of a particular research assignment? This chapter first will describe the traditional means of finding cases—the venerable paper-based systems—and then will approach the methods made possible by the new technologies. To sound again a theme set out before, in today's research world one still must understand both ways of carrying out research.

B. TRADITIONAL METHODS OF CASE FINDING

Although computerized research services are becoming the primary case-finder for many researchers, the most well-developed and probably still the most widely used method of case location is the *digest*. A digest is a subject arrangement of the headnote summaries of each point of law treated in the cases that it covers. The summaries are usually grouped under alphabetically arranged topics and then organized by subject within that topic. A digest functions in a manner similar to an index; instead of simple one-line entries, however, it consists of paragraphs describing the legal principles decided.

1. WEST KEY-NUMBER DIGESTS

a. Overview

The first half of the legal information system built by the West Publishing Company, the National Reporter System, was described in Chapter 2. But reporting the opinions of the courts was only the initial step, West also created a set of tools that allowed the researcher to find any case by the legal subjects that it covered. Through a system of case digests, West offered subject access to the full body of American case law.

To do this West first needed a pre-existing set of subject headings. This subject scheme would have to provide a subject location for every possible legal point that might be covered in a judicial opinion. To meet this need they produced the Topic and Key Number system.

The West Topic and Key Number system divides all foreseeable legal situations into seven major categories: Persons, Property, Contracts, Torts, Crimes, Remedies, and Government. These seven areas are subdivided into more than four hundred individual topics, which are then arranged in one alphabetical sequence. Each of the topics is further subdivided in an increasingly narrow refinement, and each of the resulting subtopics is then assigned a classification number, which West calls a "key number." Each topic receives just as many Key Number subdivisions as it needs. Some of the larger and more complex topics have thousands of key numbers, while smaller topics have only a few. This subject framework seeks to provide a particular topic and key number subdivision to cover *every* conceivable legal situation that could be treated in a case. This effort may represent an oversimplification and potential distortion of the legal universe, but it remains an impressive achievement which has had an enormous intellectual impact on American jurisprudence.[1]

Illustration A shows the beginning of the current list of 414 topics now in use; the full list is printed in the front of most digest volumes. The topics vary widely in scope (e.g., from the very broad "Criminal Law" to the relatively narrow "Bounties") and in current importance (from "Blasphemy" to "Civil Rights"). The subject structure created by West around the turn of the century not only survives, but is still relatively effective and widely used today. West periodically adds new subdivisions within a topic, and occasionally adds new topics as needed, but for the most part West's original divisions have been maintained.[2]

The digest system is most easily understood by examining how it is constructed. Every decision West publishes is read by its editorial staff. *Each* of the legal issues treated by a decision is identified abstracted as a headnote. Each headnote is assigned a topic and subtopic key number from the West classification scheme. Some headnotes which cannot be so neatly pigeonholed are assigned more than one key number. But every headnote has at least one assigned location. These summaries or abstracts, with their topic names and key numbers, are then placed in separate headnotes at the beginning of the published opinions. A short decision may have just one headnote, while some long opinions have several dozen or more. Illustration B shows an opinion from the Michigan Court of Appeals, including two headnotes written by West's editors for its *North Western Reporter*. Note that each headnote has a topic and key number assigned to it.

1. For a discussion of the impact of West's digest system on legal thinking, see Robert C. Berring, "Legal Research and Legal Concepts: Where Form Molds Substance," 75 *Calif. L. Rev.* 15, 24–25 (1987).

2. West continues to adapt its scheme to the changing law, although its changes are slow and cautious. Obviously changes cannot be made casually or too frequently in a system so large and complex. Nonetheless, in the past decade West has added new topics, such as "Double Jeopardy" and "Racketeer Influenced and Corrupt Organizations," and eliminated others through new combinations and reorganizations.

Illustration A

Partial list of digest topics in the *Tenth Decennial Digest, Part 1*

DIGEST TOPICS

The topic numbers shown below may be used in WESTLAW searches for cases within the topic and within specified key numbers.

1 Abandoned and Lost Property
2 Abatement and Revival
3 Abduction
4 Abortion and Birth Control
5 Absentees
6 Abstracts of Title
7 Accession
8 Accord and Satisfaction
9 Account
10 Account, Action on
11 Account Stated
11A Accountants
12 Acknowledgment
13 Action
14 Action on the Case
15 Adjoining Landowners
15A Administrative Law and Procedure
16 Admiralty
17 Adoption
18 Adulteration
19 Adultery
20 Adverse Possession
21 Affidavits
22 Affray
23 Agriculture
24 Aliens
25 Alteration of Instruments
26 Ambassadors and Consuls
27 Amicus Curiae
28 Animals
29 Annuities
30 Appeal and Error
31 Appearance
33 Arbitration
34 Armed Services
35 Arrest
36 Arson
37 Assault and Battery
38 Assignments
40 Assistance, Writ of
41 Associations
42 Assumpsit, Action of
43 Asylums
44 Attachment
45 Attorney and Client
46 Attorney General
47 Auctions and Auctioneers
48 Audita Querela
48A Automobiles
48B Aviation
49 Bail
50 Bailment
51 Bankruptcy
52 Banks and Banking
54 Beneficial Associations
55 Bigamy
56 Bills and Notes
57 Blasphemy
58 Bonds
59 Boundaries
60 Bounties
61 Breach of Marriage Promise
62 Breach of the Peace
63 Bribery
64 Bridges
65 Brokers
66 Building and Loan Associations
67 Burglary
68 Canals
69 Cancellation of Instruments
70 Carriers
71 Cemeteries
72 Census
73 Certiorari
74 Champerty and Maintenance
75 Charities
76 Chattel Mortgages
76A Chemical Dependents
76H Children Out-of-Wedlock
77 Citizens
78 Civil Rights
79 Clerks of Courts
80 Clubs
81 Colleges and Universities
82 Collision
83 Commerce
83H Commodity Futures Trading Regulation
84 Common Lands
85 Common Law
86 Common Scold
88 Compounding Offenses
89 Compromise and Settlement
89A Condominium
90 Confusion of Goods
91 Conspiracy
92 Constitutional Law
92B Consumer Credit
92H Consumer Protection
93 Contempt
95 Contracts
96 Contribution
97 Conversion
98 Convicts
99 Copyrights and Intellectual Property
100 Coroners
101 Corporations
102 Costs
103 Counterfeiting
104 Counties
105 Court Commissioners
106 Courts
107 Covenant, Action of
108 Covenants
108A Credit Reporting Agencies
110 Criminal Law
111 Crops
113 Customs and Usages
114 Customs Duties
115 Damages
116 Dead Bodies

[G20,009]

VII

1-1

Illustration B

A decision, with headnotes, in the *North Western Reporter, 2d*

122 Mich.App. 418

William L. FISHER, Plaintiff-Appellant,

v.

Karen LOWE, Larry Moffet and State Farm Mutual Automobile Insurance Company, Defendants-Appellees.

Docket No. 60732.

Court of Appeals of Michigan.

Submitted Nov. 3, 1982.

Decided Jan. 10, 1983.

Released for Publications May 6, 1983.

A wayward Chevy struck a tree
Whose owner sued defendants three.
He sued car's owner, driver too,
And insurer for what was due
For his oak tree that now may bear
A lasting need for tender care.

The Oakland County Circuit Court,
John N. O'Brien, J., set forth
The judgment that defendants sought
And quickly an appeal was brought.

Court of Appeals, J.H. Gillis, J.,
Gave thought and then had this to say:
1) There is no liability
Since No-Fault grants immunity;
2) No jurisdiction can be found
Where process service is unsound;
And thus the judgment, as it's termed,
Is due to be, and is,

Affirmed.

1. Automobiles ⇐251.13

Defendant's Chevy struck a tree—
There was no liability;
The No-Fault Act comes into play
As owner and the driver say;
Barred by the Act's immunity,
No suit in tort will aid the tree;
Although the oak's in disarray,
No court can make defendants pay.
M.C.L.A. § 500.3135.

2. Process ⇐4

No jurisdiction could be found
Where process service was unsound;
In personam jurisdiction
Was not even legal fiction
Where plaintiff failed to well comply
With rules of court that did apply.
GCR 1963, 105.4.

William L. Fisher, Troy, in pro. per.

Romain, Donofrio & Kuck, P.C. by Ernst W. Kuck, Southfield, for defendants-appellees.

Before BRONSON, P.J., and V.J. BRENNAN and J.H. GILLIS, JJ.

J.H. GILLIS, Judge.

[1, 2] We thought that we would never see
A suit to compensate a tree.

A suit whose claim in tort is prest
Upon a mangled tree's behest;

A tree whose battered trunk was prest
Against a Chevy's crumpled crest;

A tree that faces each new day
With bark and limb in disarray;

A tree that may forever bear
A lasting need for tender care.

Flora lovers though we three,
We must uphold the court's decree.

Affirmed.[1]

1. Plaintiff commenced this action in tort against defendants Lowe and Moffet for damage to his "beautiful oak tree" caused when defendant Lowe struck it while operating defendant Moffet's automobile. The trial court granted summary judgment in favor of defendants pursuant to GCR 1963, 117.2(1). In addition, the trial court denied plaintiff's request to enter a default judgment against the insurer of the automobile, defendant State Farm Mutual Automobile Insurance Company. Plaintiff appeals as of right.

The trial court did not err in granting summary judgment in favor of defendants Lowe and Moffet. Defendants were immune from tort liability for damage to the tree pursuant to § 3135 of the no-fault insurance act. M.C.L. § 500.3135; M.S.A. § 24.13135.

The trial court did not err in refusing to enter a default judgment against State Farm. Since it is undisputed that plaintiff did not serve process upon State Farm in accordance with the court rules, the court did not obtain personal jurisdiction over the insurer. GCR 1963, 105.4.

How does West make this subject information available? Each advance sheet published as part of the National Reporter System contains a section entitled "Key Number Digest," which reprints the headnote abstracts of each of the cases included. The headnotes arearranged by the topics and key numbers assigned to them. Each West advance sheet thus contains a mini-digest in which one can find, by topic and key number, the cases published therein covering a particular point of law. The advance sheets are later compiled into bound volume reporters, each of which carries a similar digest section. Of course, only a handful of topics and key numbers appear in any individual advance sheet or volume, but the ones that are there are arranged into the system. Illustration C shows a typical page from the Key Number Digest of a bound volume of the *North Western Reporter 2d,* including the first headnote abstract from the *Fisher v. Lowe* decision in Illustration B.

If digesting extended no further than each individual advance sheet or volume, it would simply function as an index to the cases immediately at hand and would be of limited research value. West, however, takes the same headnotes and publishes them in separate sets covering many volumes of reporters. As will be explained in the following pages, there are digest sets covering individual states, sets covering separate multistate units of the National Reporter System, and a comprehensive set spanning the decisions of each and every jurisdiction.

Illustration D shows the page from *West's Michigan Digest* containing the first headnote from the case in Illustration B. This set covers all published decisions of Michigan appellate courts from 1838 to date in one alphabetical series of volumes. Each volume is updated annually by means of a *pocket part.*

Pocket parts are a common method of updating legal publications, first used in 1916 in *McKinney's Consolidated Laws of New York Annotated.* Changes and new information are printed in a supplement which fits into a pocket flap inside the back cover of the volume. The volume stays up to date without having to be republished. By looking in one *Michigan Digest* volume and its pocket part, a researcher can see headnotes to all the Michigan cases on a topic for over 150 years.

The set is brought further up to date by supplementary pamphlets published between annual pocket parts. Each supplement, whether annual pocket part or interim pamphlet, indicates its scope by listing the most recent reporter volumes it covers. A search can then be brought even more up to date by searching in the Key Number Digests in

Illustration C

Key Number Digest in 333 N.W.2d, showing the first headnote in Illustration B

AUTOMOBILES ⊂⊃297

McKenzie v. Ladd Trucking Co., 333 N.W.2d 402, 214 Neb. 209.

⊂⊃153. Law of road.

Iowa 1983. Driving on the left side of the road in situations other than the exceptions set forth in statute is negligence per se in rural as well as urban areas. I.C.A. § 321.297.—Bannon v. Pfiffner, 333 N.W.2d 464.

⊂⊃159. Acts in emergencies.

Iowa 1983. A driver is excused from violating a statutory rule of the road if he is confronted by an emergency not of his own making and by reason thereof fails to obey the statute.—Bannon v. Pfiffner, 333 N.W.2d 464.

If ice has not formed on the highway so far as the driver reasonably observes, although the weather may be inclement, and driver proceeds in accordance with conditions as they appear, but suddenly encounters an unanticipated patch of ice and slides, the driver may rightly claim an emergency, with the decision of whether the ice was reasonably foreseeable being for the jury to make.—Id.

If a person tortiously brings about an emergency, he cannot rely on it as an excuse for resulting harm under § 296 of the Restatement (Second) of Torts although he conducts himself property in the emergency itself.—Id.

A motorist who is confronted with an emergency which is not of his own making may not be completely absolved from exercise of care under § 296 of the Restatement (Second) of Torts unless motorist conducts himself as a reasonably prudent person in a similar emergency.—Id.

⊂⊃168(3). Nature of highway.

Iowa 1983. If the icy condition of a highway is general, the driver must be taken as being aware of it and, if he proceeds in normal fashion notwithstanding the ice and eventually slides on a patch of it, he cannot set up the icy condition as an emergency, which requires an unforeseen combination of circumstances, including the element of unforeseeability.—Bannon v. Pfiffner, 333 N.W.2d 464.

⊂⊃168(9). Obstruction of view.

Neb. 1983. Conditions blocking visibility impose upon a driver the duty to exercise a degree of care commensurate with the existing conditions, including waiting to proceed until it can be done in safety.—McKenzie v. Ladd Trucking Co., 333 N.W.2d 402, 214 Neb. 209.

⊂⊃208. —— Vehicles crossing.

Neb. 1983. When a motorist, being in a place of safety, sees, or by the exercise of reasonable care could have seen, the approach of moving vehicle and moves from the place of safety into the path of that vehicle and is struck, the motorist's own conduct constitutes negligence more than slight, as a matter of law, and precludes recovery.—McKenzie v. Ladd Trucking Co., 333 N.W.2d 402, 214 Neb. 209.

Where each truck driver was aware of the presence and location of the other's vehicle, where each knew the general custom of usage of the premises on which the vehicles were located, and where each driver proceeded to move into the path of the other at a time when each admitted that his visibility in that direction was blocked, each driver was guilty of contributory negligence which was more than slight, and neither owner could recover.—Id.

(B) ACTIONS.

⊂⊃245(49). Acts in emergencies.

Iowa 1983. If ice has not formed on the highway so far as the driver reasonably observes, although the weather may be inclement, and driver proceeds in accordance with conditions as they appear, but suddenly encounters an unanticipated patch of ice and slides, the driver may rightly claim an emergency, with the decision of whether the ice was reasonably foreseeable being for the jury to make.—Bannon v. Pfiffner, 333 N.W.2d 464.

Whether defendant's decedent, the eastbound motorist, was confronted with a sudden emergency because, although the weather was inclement, ice had not formed so far as she reasonably observed, she proceeded in accordance with conditions as they appeared, and suddenly encountered an unanticipated patch of ice, which caused her vehicle to slide into westbound lane where it collided head-on with vehicle driven by plaintiff's decedent, was a question for jury.—Id.

Question whether defendant's decedent, the eastbound motorist, negligently produced the emergency under § 296 of the Restatement (Second) of Torts when her vehicle encountered an unanticipated patch of ice, causing vehicle to slide into westbound lane and head-on into vehicle of plaintiff's decedent, was question of fact for jury.—Id.

Whether evidence showing that brake lights on eastbound vehicle of defendant's decedent flashed on prior to time vehicle encountered unanticipated ice and slid over into westbound lane and head-on into vehicle of plaintiff's decedent was evidence which showed lack of reasonable care under § 296 of the Restatement (Second) of Torts was question for jury.—Id.

Whether conduct of defendant's decedent in sudden emergency prior to time of fatal collision with vehicle driven by plaintiff's decedent was reasonable under evidence indicating that defendant's decedent had an estimated distance of 100 feet in which to adjust for a newly encountered condition, that her vehicle was traveling 66 feet each second, and that time it took to cover 100 feet was approximately one and one-half seconds was question for jury.—Id.

(D) EFFECT OF NO FAULT STATUTES.

⊂⊃251.13. —— Vehicles, persons, occurrences within restrictions.

Mich.App. 1983.
Defendant's Chevy struck a tree—
There was no liability;
The No-Fault Act comes into play
As owner and the driver say;

Barred by the Act's immunity,
No suit in tort will aid the tree;
Although the oak's in disarray,
No court can make defendants pay,
M.C.L.A. § 500.3135.—Fisher v. Lowe, 333 N.W.2d 67.

VI. INJURIES FROM DEFECTS OR OBSTRUCTIONS IN HIGHWAYS AND OTHER PUBLIC PLACES.

(B) ACTIONS.

⊂⊃297. Parties.

Mich.App. 1983. In view of state's statutory jurisdiction over all state trunkline highways,

(11)

Illustration D

A page from *West's Michigan Digest*, covering part of one key number

⚷251.13 AUTOMOBILES 3 Mich D—118

Mich.App. 1983. Injury to eye, which occurred when pedestrian was splashed by city bus with water, slush, ice, and lye while he was standing at bus stop, was foreseeable injury which arose out of city's use of bus as motor vehicle for purposes of no-fault personal protection benefits, since it was eminently foreseeable that bus, upon encountering pool of water while being operated in normal fashion as motor vehicle, would propel puddle of water containing caustic chemical in direction of nearby pedestrian. M.C.L.A. § 500.3105.—Jones v. Tronex Chemical Corp., 341 N.W.2d 469, 129 Mich.App. 188.

Mich.App. 1983. For purposes of section of no-fault statute precluding recovery of personal protection insurance benefits if a person is the owner of an uninsured motor vehicle "involved" in an accident, a parked uninsured vehicle is not "involved" in the accident unless one of the exceptions to the parked vehicle provision is applicable. M.C.L.A. §§ 500.3106, 500.3113.—Braun v. Citizens Ins. Co., 335 N.W.2d 701, 124 Mich.App. 822.

For purposes of section of no-fault statute precluding recovery of personal protection insurance benefits if the person is the owner of an uninsured motor vehicle "involved" in an accident, a parked vehicle can be "involved" in the accident when the vehicle is parked in such a way as to cause unreasonable risk of the bodily injury which occurred. M.C.L.A. §§ 500.3106, 500.3113.—Id.

In action brought by plaintiff who was injured when he was pinned between an automobile and the tow truck which had pulled his uninsured automobile out of a snow drift, evidence sustained finding that plaintiff's automobile was "involved" in the collision, because the vehicle was parked in such a way as to cause an unreasonable risk of bodily injury which occurred, and therefore, plaintiff's recovery was barred by statute precluding recovery of personal protection insurance benefits if a person is the owner of an uninsured motor vehicle "involved" in an accident. M.C.L.A. § 500.3113.—Id.

Mich.App. 1983. Damage to loader which contractor was transporting on his tractor, caused by striking underside of an overpass, arose out of contractor's use of its tractor as motor vehicle, and thus, under No-Fault Act, contractor was not liable in tort to owner of loader for damage thereto. M.C.L.A. §§ 500.3123(1), 500.3135.—National Ben Franklin Ins. Co. v. Bakhaus Contractors, Inc., 335 N.W.2d 70, 124 Mich.App. 510.

Mich.App. 1983. Uninsured motorist is outside the basic no-fault system of allocating the costs of accidents and remains subject to tort liability. M.C.L.A. § 500.3135(1, 2).—Jones v. Detroit Auto. Inter-Ins. Exchange, 335 N.W.2d 39, 124 Mich. App. 363.

Mich.App. 1983.
Defendant's Chevy struck a tree—
There was no liability;
The No-Fault Act comes into play
As owner and the driver say;

Barred by the Act's immunity,
No suit in tort will aid the tree;
Although the oak's in disarray,
No court can make defendants pay,
M.C.L.A. § 500.3135.—Fisher v. Lowe, 333 N.W.2d 67, 122 Mich.App. 418.

Mich.App. 1982. Statute requires compliance with security requirements of no-fault insurance after 30-day period, 30-day period being intended to protect tourists and other transient nonresidents from criminal sanctions imposed by the Act. M.C.L.A. §§ 500.3102, 500.3135(2).—Berrien County Road Com'n v. Jones, 326 N.W.2d 495, 119 Mich.App. 315.

Defendants, having paid their dues in risk-spreading system by voluntarily acquiring insurance, and being owners or registrants of motor vehicle as defined in statute, though neither plaintiff's nor defendants' vehicle was required to be registered as vehicle within the state and therefore neither was required to be covered by no-fault insurance, were entitled to immunity provided by the no-fault act. M.C.L.A. §§ 500.3101(1, 3, 4), 500.3102, 500.3135(2).—Id.

Mich.App. 1981. Damages awarded to plaintiff for personal injuries sustained as result of negligence of state in failing to maintain roads were not subject to no-fault motor vehicle act since act applied only to accidents caused by motor vehicles and not to those caused by negligent highway maintenance. M.C.L.A. § 500.3135.—Longworth v. Michigan Dept. of Highways and Transp., 315 N.W.2d 135, 110 Mich.App. 771.

Mich.App. 1981. A motorcycle owner may not recover no-fault benefits for damage to his motorcycle unless it was properly parked at time of the accident; like an automobile owner, a motorcycle owner has option of purchasing collision coverage if he wishes to insure his motorcycle against damage resulting from accidents other than those in which the motorcycle is properly parked, notwithstanding definition of "motor vehicle" as a vehicle which has more than two wheels. M.C.L.A. §§ 500.3101 et seq., 500.3101(2), 500.3121, 500.3123; GCR 1963, 515.2.—Burk v. Warren, 307 N.W.2d 89, 105 Mich.App. 556, modified 360 N.W.2d 585, 417 Mich. 959, appeal after remand 359 N.W.2d 541, 137 Mich.App. 715, affirmed DiFranco v. Pickard, 398 N.W.2d 896, 427 Mich. 32.

No-fault law has abolished tort liability with respect to unintentionally occasioned property damage arising from the use, ownership or maintenance of motor vehicles within the state and automobile owner, including a motorcycle owner, who has not obtained his own collision insurance has no recourse to tort when his vehicle is damaged by another insured vehicle. M.C.L.A. § 500.3123(1)(a).—Id.

Mich.App. 1981. In automobile accident case in which owner and manager of shopping center and contractor in charge of parking lot snow removal were named defendants on basis of their alleged failure to remove pile of snow obscuring stop sign, No-Fault Act did not apply to plaintiff's claims against shopping center defendants and she could therefore seek recovery for economic damages caused by alleged failure to maintain safe parking area. M.C.L.A. § 500.3135.—Pustay v. Gentelia, 304 N.W.2d 539, 104 Mich.App. 250.

Mich.App. 1981. While installation of auxiliary gas tank might arguably fall outside strict definition of "maintenance" where truck equipment company was correcting carburetor flooding problem when accident occurred, acts of truck equipment company constituted "maintenance" of vehicle for purposes of determining applicability of no-fault insurance statute. M.C.L.A. §§ 500.3101 et seq., 500.3121.—Liberty Mut. Ins. Co. v. Allied Truck Equipment Co., 302 N.W.2d 588, 103 Mich.App. 33.

Accident must arise out of maintenance of vehicle for No-Fault Insurance Act to apply, and causal connection to be established between the injuries and maintenance of vehicle need not approach proximate cause. M.C.L.A. §§ 500.3101 et seq., 500.3121.—Id.

Where vehicle, at time of fire, was in care and custody of bailee and fire occurred as result of negligent act of bailee in placing exposed light bulb in position where gasoline could fall on it, accident arose out of bailment-for-hire, not out of maintenance of motor vehicle within meaning of No-Fault Insurance Act, and, therefore, Garage Keepers' Liability Act, and not No-Fault Insurance Act, applied. M.C.L.A. §§ 256.541 et seq., 500.3101 et seq.—Id.

volumes and advance sheets published since the latest digest supplement.

West in effect publishes two interlocking, comprehensive services. The first is a system of case reporting which contains the full text of appellate decisions from state and federal courts. The second is a digest structure providing for the classification and retrieval, by subject, of the points of law determined in all judicial decisions reported by West. The editorial staff at West strives to guarantee uniform treatment of issues of law. The goal is to ensure that points of law are always treated in the same manner. Each headnote touching on a particular point will be sent to the same Topic and Key Number location. By providing uniform editorial treatment for each jurisdiction's opinions and having the points of law in each published decision classified into the same subject scheme, a highly effective case finding mechanism is created. When a researcher locates a case in which a relevant point of law is discussed, the West headnotes can be scanned to identify the Topic and Key Numbers assigned to that point of law. These Topics and Key Numbers can then be used as locators in the West digests to find other decisions from all West reporters on the same issues. The system theoretically allows a researcher to find decisions from any time period in any American jurisdiction on any specific topic.

In these days of data bases and machine indexing, it is almost incredible to think that all of this abstracting and indexing is done by human beings. Editors at West are reading and headnoting every case that is published in print. They then place each headnote into the Topic and Key Number structure. It boggles the mind.

It should be emphasized that these digests do not constitute legal authority and contain no substantive narrative text. They are effective for identifying and locating relevant decisions, but those decisions must be read and evaluated (and then Shepardized and evaluated again) before being cited in a brief, argument, or memorandum. Each case is decided on its own facts. Its listing under a particular digest topic and key number may be appropriate and helpful, but its relevance and authority for the researcher's purpose must be determined from the opinion itself.

b. Digests of Federal Court Opinions

Numerous digests are published by West. They parallel the format of the publisher's case reporters outlined in Chapter 2. Just as the discussion in that chapter began with the federal court system, here we will first discuss the digests covering the decisions of the Supreme Court of the United States and the lower federal courts.

(1) *United States Supreme Court Digest*

West's *United States Supreme Court Digest* provides access to decisions of the Supreme Court of the United States, by subject and by case name. Its format is similar to that used in all other West digests:

headnote abstracts (in this case from West's *Supreme Court Reporter*) arranged by West topics and key numbers. Each of the more than 400 topics is included, with an explanation of its scope and an outline of its arrangement of key numbers, even though there have been no Supreme Court headnotes classified under more than thirty of the topics.[3] The topics are arranged in alphabetical order in about two dozen volumes, each supplemented with an annual pocket part. The set has grown gradually as the publisher periodically recompiles the contents of an overcrowded volume and reissues its contents in two separate books, designated with numbers such as "2" and "2A."

The *United States Supreme Court Digest* is totally cumulative, back to the Court's beginning in 1790.[4] Once a researcher has identified a proper topic and key number, all Supreme Court cases on that specific legal issue may be located by looking in one bound volume and its pocket part. A key number search for Supreme Court cases may be further updated by consulting the "Cumulative Key Number Digest" in the advance sheets of West's *Supreme Court Reporter*. Unlike other West reporter advance sheets, the digest in the latest issue of the *Supreme Court Reporter* cumulates all headnote references for the entire Supreme Court term. The headnotes themselves are printed only for cases printed in that one advance sheet, but names and citations are provided for all earlier cases in the term.

Accompanying the digest volumes containing the alphabetically arranged topics are several additional finding aids. A two-volume "Table of Cases" lists each Supreme Court decision under the name of the plaintiff or first party named (in cases before the Supreme Court, usually the petitioner or appellant), and provides citations to the case in all three reporters as well as the key numbers under which its headnotes are classified. A "Defendant–Plaintiff Table" volume lists the cases under defendants' (respondents' or appellees') names, providing citations but not key numbers. A four-volume "Descriptive–Word Index" includes entries for legal and factual issues addressed in the headnotes, and provides references to topics and key numbers. Finally, a "Words and Phrases" volume lists all terms judicially defined by the Supreme Court, with references to case names and citations. The use of the case tables and the subject index will be explained in section B.1.e., "Finding Cases in the West Digests," and the use of "Words and Phrases" will be discussed later in the chapter.

(2) Federal Digests

West also publishes a series of digests covering the decisions of the several levels of the federal court system. These digests cover in one

3. Three topics, "Arson," "Notaries," and "Sodomy," have been in the West system since it began, but did not receive their first Supreme Court headnotes until the 1980's.

4. Coverage actually begins in 1754, with the first case in volume one of *United States Reports*. The only case digested under the topic "Embracery" is a Pennsylvania Supreme Court decision, *Morris's Lessee v. Vanderen*, 1 U.S. 64 (1782).

sequence the U.S. Supreme Court (duplicating coverage of the *United States Supreme Court Digest*), the U.S. Courts of Appeals, the U.S. District Courts, and various specialized federal courts. Under each key number, headnotes from Supreme Court cases are listed first and Court of Appeals cases second, followed by the District Courts and other lower federal courts. Within each hierarchical level, digest entries are alphabetized by the state from which the case originated.

There are five separate digests, but they are simply successive series, each covering a different time period. The unfortunate use of different names for the five digests confuses some researchers. The original set was sensibly called the *Federal Digest,* and covers cases through 1939. When its supplementation grew too unwieldy, West published *Modern Federal Practice Digest* (now covering cases from 1940 to 1960). When this second series also became difficult to use efficiently, *West's Federal Practice Digest 2d* (now covering cases from 1961 to 1975) was published. Because the third series was called "2d," the next series, covering cases from late 1975 to the mid–1980's, was called *West's Federal Practice Digest 3d.* It follows that the fifth series, recently completed in 105 volumes, is called *West's Federal Practice Digest 4th.* The *Federal Practice Digest 4th* covers all cases reported since the mid–1980's. (The dates of coverage between the fourth and fifth series vary by topic, but there is no gap in coverage.) The current volumes are updated by annual pocket parts, which are further supplemented several times each year by pamphlets.

For many searches of current interest, it may be necessary only to consult the most recent digest set and its supplements. For comprehensive research of all federal case law, however, all four series must be used. The same classification system is used in all West digests, so the same topic and key number can be searched in all four series. Each series also contains one or more volumes for each of the basic finding aids described above: Tables of Cases, Defendant–Plaintiff Tables, Descriptive–Word Indexes, and Words and Phrases. The series can be distinguished from each other by the colors of their bindings: *Federal Digest,* red; *Modern Federal Practice Digest,* green; *Federal Practice Digest 2d,* blue; *Federal Practice Digest 3d,* red; and *Federal Practice Digest 4th,* blue.

(3) *Specialized Digests*

Just as West publishes reporters covering the decisions of specialized federal tribunals, it publishes digests for the headnotes from those reporters. The same material appears as well in the *Federal Practice Digest 4th* and its predecessors, but for some research the specialized digests may be a more convenient research tool. Each follows on a smaller scale the pattern of the larger federal digests, with accompanying tables and indexes.

West's Bankruptcy Digest covers all cases reported in *West's Bankruptcy Reporter,* which began publication in 1979. *West's Military Jus-*

tice Digest covers the decisions in *West's Military Justice Reporter* of the United States Court of Military Appeals and the Courts of Military Review for the various service branches. The *United States Claims Court Digest* indexes all cases reported in the *United States Claims Court Reporter,* and decisions of the former United States Court of Claims (published in the *Federal Reporter* or *Federal Supplement*) are covered in the *United States Court of Claims Digest.*

In addition, both *West's Education Law Reporter* and *West's Social Security Reporting Service* include digests for the decisions they reprint. In both sets, however, the digest provides only the National Reporter System citations and does not indicate where in the topical reporter the cases appear. A researcher with access only to the topical set must then look up the cases' names in an accompanying Table of Cases to find their locations.

c. *Digests of State Court Opinions*

Just as the opinions of most state appellate courts are published in both official reports and in West regional reporters, for most states there are two West key number digests covering those decisions: a state digest and a regional digest. It is the scope of coverage and not the digest entries that distinguishes state from regional digests, since the abstracts in both are taken from the headnotes in West's National Reporter System.

(1) State Digests

Forty-six state digests are published by West, including one for the District of Columbia. All but two of the digests cover a single jurisdiction, while the *Dakota Digest* and *Virginia and West Virginia Digest* each cover two states. Only Delaware, Nevada and Utah do not have individual West digests; Delaware decisions, however, are covered in the *Atlantic Digest,* and Nevada and Utah in the *Pacific Digest.*

Most of the state digests are cumulated in one series like the *United States Supreme Court Digest,* so that a researcher need only look in one volume and one pocket part for all of the decisions since the beginning of a state's appellate court system. Volumes are occasionally recompiled and split into two, as required by the quantity of headnotes. More than ten states now have *two* series, with the original set used only for research in older case law. Coverage in the second series begins usually in the 1930's and is updated by pocket parts. New York has *four* series, with the coverage in the latest beginning in 1978. Every state digest is updated between annual pocket parts by one or more interim pamphlets. (These are published several months after pocket parts are issued, however, so there is not always one available.)

In addition to state court cases, West state digests cover the decisions of federal courts sitting in that state, and decisions of the U.S. Court of Appeals and U.S. Supreme Court in cases arising in the state. This sometimes useful feature is often overlooked by researchers. For

New York digests, coverage of federal decisions began only with the third series.

In addition to the alphabetical arrangement of topics, each of the state digests includes the finding tools and indexing features described above in the discussion of the *United States Supreme Court Digest:* Tables of Cases, Defendant–Plaintiff Tables, Descriptive–Word Indexes, and Words and Phrases.

(2) *Regional Digests*

Although West publishes seven regional reporters, it only publishes five regional digests. There is no current regional digest for the cases appearing in the *North Eastern* or *South Western Reporter,* although coverage of the ten states in those reporters is provided by state digests. The *Southern Digest* is complete in one series. The *Atlantic, North Western,* and *South Eastern Digests* are each in a second series beginning in the 1930's. The *Pacific Digest* is in five series, with the current set designated *West's Pacific Digest, Beginning 585 P.2d.* As with the federal digests the divisions are chronological, and a researcher attempting comprehensive coverage must search all components (including the pocket part to the current series, and interim supplementary pamphlet, if any). The regional digests include Tables of Cases (by plaintiff only) and Descriptive–Word Indexes. They do *not* contain Defendant–Plaintiff Tables or Words and Phrases.

The *Pacific, South Eastern,* and *Southern Digests* include indexing of cases published in the region's state reports before the beginning of West's National Reporter System. Coverage is retrospective to the earliest published cases, starting with California cases from 1850 in the *Pacific Digest,* with Virginia cases from 1729 in the *South Eastern Digest,* and with Louisiana cases from 1809 in the *Southern Digest.*

For most states, then, one can search for decisions in either a state digest or a regional digest. If a choice between the two is available, the decision may depend on the time permitted for the research, the number of cases decided in a particular area, or whether authority from other jurisdictions might be persuasive or would simply be irrelevant. Regional digests are of diminishing importance, but remain handy tools if material from other jurisdictions would be useful. State digests, uncluttered by decisions from other jurisdictions or by the commentary found in most other sources, are among the quickest and most convenient ways to determine one state's judgments in a specific area of law.

d. *The Comprehensive American Digest System*

There remains the colossus of West's digesting system, one series including all of the material mentioned to this point. In one massive set appear the headnotes for the courts of every state and federal jurisdiction. The American Digest System is the appropriate tool either if one seeks to find cases from throughout the country or if a specific state's digest is unavailable.

(1) Century Digest and Decennial Digests

The modern era of digesting began with the publication of the *1906 Decennial Edition of the American Digest* by West Publishing. This set contained the headnotes of every case, state and federal, that had been decided for the ten year period from 1897 to 1906. The headnotes were arrayed in Topic and Key Number order. West continued the practice of publishing a ten year, "Decennial" compilation on the sixth year of every decade. (For coverage of cases before 1897, West published the Century Digest, which covered all cases up to that date.)

There are two key points here. First, the Decennials cover every case for a ten year block of time. Second, the Decennials use the same Topic and Key Number arrangement through every edition. If the researcher finds a Topic and Key Number on point, she can review all of the relevant cases back to 1897. Classifications have gradually been refined or changed with developments in the law, but one can convert them through conversion tables in each Decennial. Because the numbers in the *Century Digest* are different from those in later digests, the *First Decennial Digest* includes cross-references providing the *Century* counterparts of modern topics and key numbers.

The decennial system carries on today, but by the *1980s*, the of number of cases being reported had grown to such an extent that no reasonable set could hold ten years worth of headnotes. The Eighth Decennial consisted of 50 volumes. To make subsequent digest units more manageable, West began issuing them in five-year cumulations. The *Tenth Decennial Digest, Part 1* covers cases published from 1986 to 1991, and the *Tenth Decennial Digest, Part 2* will cover 1991 to 1996. The fact that West would retain the name "Decennial" for a set published every five years is a good indication of how innately conservative legal publishing is.

Within a *Decennial Digest* it is likely that almost every topic and most key numbers will be represented by at least one headnote, and some of the more common key numbers may include thousands of digested cases. Each of the over four hundred topics in a *Decennial Digest* begins with a scope note and an outline of its classification, even if there are no cases assigned to it.[5] Under each key number, cases are listed in the following order: first federal decisions in hierarchical order (Supreme Court first), then the courts of each state in alphabetical order. Only very common key numbers, however, will have entries from *every* jurisdiction. Each decision is represented, as it was in the smaller digest units, beginning with the digest section of the reporter advance sheet where the decision appeared, by a reprinting of the original headnote abstract. The headnote is followed by the citation to the decision, so that one may easily locate and read the full text of the case. Illustration E shows the same abstract from the Michigan case *Fisher v.*

5. The topic "Dueling," for example, carried no cases between 1925 and 1977. The topic "Criminal Law," on the other hand, has occupied six or more volumes in each *Decennial* unit since 1966.

Lowe, seen earlier, this time as it appears with abstracts from six other states on a page in the *Ninth Decennial Digest, Part 2.*

Illustration E

A page from the *Ninth Decennial Digest, Part 2*

⚷251.13 AUTOMOBILES 4 9th D Pt 2—246

Vehicle Reparations Act applicable to motor vehicle "user," which is defined in the Act to mean person who resides in household in which any person owns or maintains motor vehicle, which category did not include subject passenger. KRS 304.39–020(15), 304.39–060(1), (2)(c).—Id.

Ky.App. 1983. Automobile accident victim who failed to file rejection of no fault insurance with Department of Insurance presented no proof of rejection, and thus was subject to "no fault" threshold requirements. KRS 304.39–010 et seq, 304.39–060(1), (2)(b), (5)(a).—Thompson v. Piasta, 662 S.W.2d 223.

Md.App. 1985. Under proper circumstances, passengers in taxicabs may seek recovery for injuries caused by uninsured motorists from the Maryland Automobile Insurance Fund. Code 1957, Art. 48A, § 541(c).—Pope v. Sun Cab Co., Inc., 488 A.2d 1009, 62 Md.App. 218, certiorari granted Maryland Auto. Ins. Fund v. Sun Cab Co., 497 A.2d 484, 304 Md. 47, affirmed 506 A.2d 641, 305 Md. 807.

Mich. 1982. Neither motorist nor his no-fault insurer is subject to liability for damage to a moving vehicle, but no-fault insurer is subject to liability for damage to a parked vehicle. M.C.L.A. §§ 500.3121, 500.3123(1)(a), 500.-3135(2)(d).—Heard v. State Farm Mut. Auto. Ins. Co., 324 N.W.2d 1, 414 Mich. 139, 27 A.L.R.4th 163.

Mich. 1981. Tort liability abolished by no-fault act is only such liability as arises out of ownership, maintenance or use of motor vehicle, not liability which arises out of other conduct, such as negligent keeping of cattle. M.C.L.A. § 500.3101 et seq.—Citizens Ins. Co. of America v. Tuttle, 309 N.W.2d 174, 411 Mich. 536.

In context of no-fault act, abolition of tort liability "arising from" ownership, maintenance or use of motor vehicle carries implicit sense of tort liability for injuries or damages caused by ownership, maintenance or use of motor vehicle. M.C.L.A. § 500.3135(2).—Id.

Only persons who own, maintain or use motor vehicles can be subject to tort liability for injuries or damage caused by ownership, maintenance or use of motor vehicle; nonmotorist tort-feasor cannot be subject to tort liability for injuries or damage caused by ownership, maintenance or use of motor vehicle. M.C.L.A. § 500.3135(2).—Id.

Abolition of tort liability for injuries or damage caused by ownership, maintenance or use of motor vehicle does not abolish tort liability of nonmotorist tort-feasor. M.C.L.A. § 500.-3135(2).—Id.

Person is to be relieved of tort liability arising from ownership, maintenance or use of motor vehicle only upon participating, through payment of premiums, in system for spreading costs of compensating vehicular injuries without regard to fault. M.C.L.A. §§ 500.3101 et seq., 500.-3135(2).—Id.

Both nonmotorist tort-feasor and uninsured motorist are outside basic no-fault system of allocating costs of accidents and both remain subject to tort liability. M.C.L.A. § 500.3101 et seq.—Id.

Mich.App. 1986. There is no right to sue for motorcycle damage under the minitort provision of the No-Fault Act. M.C.L.A. §§ 500.-3101(2)(c), 500.3135(2), (2)(d).—Nerat v. Swacker, 388 N.W.2d 305.

Mich.App. 1985. Estate of passenger who was killed when pickup she was riding in collided with uninsured motor vehicle may have common-law cause of action in tort, as the No-Fault Act, M.C.L.A. § 500.3101 et seq., did not abolish the tort liability of uninsured motorists.—Aetna Cas. & Sur. Co. v. Collins, 373 N.W.2d 177, 143 Mich.App. 661.

Mich.App. 1985. Tort liability of an uninsured motorist or liability which does not arise from tort-feasor's ownership or operation of a motor vehicle is not abrogated by No-Fault Act. M.C.L.A. § 500.3116(2).—Ryan v. Ford Motor Co., 368 N.W.2d 266, 141 Mich.App. 762.

Mich.App. 1985. Though garage mechanic was actually working on insured's automobile at the time of the alleged negligence which resulted in insured's being sprayed with radiator fluid and suffering personal injuries, mechanic was, in fact, a nonmotorist tort-feasor, against whom tort action could be maintained; that is, the suit was not one for damages for personal injuries arising out of ownership, maintenance, or use of motor vehicle so as to be barred by the No-Fault Insurance Act. M.C.L.A. § 500.3135.—Coleman v. Franzon, 366 N.W.2d 86, 141 Mich.App. 99.

Mich.App. 1983. Injury to eye, which occurred when pedestrian was splashed by city bus with water, slush, ice, and lye while he was standing at bus stop, was foreseeable injury which arose out of city's use of bus as motor vehicle for purposes of no-fault personal protection benefits, since it was eminently foreseeable that bus, upon encountering pool of water while being operated in normal fashion as motor vehicle, would propel puddle of water containing caustic chemical in direction of nearby pedestrian. M.C.L.A. § 500.3105.—Jones v. Tronex Chemical Corp., 341 N.W.2d 469, 129 Mich.App. 188.

Mich.App. 1983. For purposes of section of no-fault statute precluding recovery of personal protection insurance benefits if a person is the owner of an uninsured motor vehicle "involved" in an accident, a parked uninsured vehicle is not "involved" in the accident unless one of the exceptions to the parked vehicle provision is applicable. M.C.L.A. §§ 500.3106, 500.3113.—Braun v. Citizens Ins. Co., 335 N.W.2d 701, 124 Mich.App. 822.

For purposes of section of no-fault statute precluding recovery of personal protection insurance benefits if the person is the owner of an uninsured motor vehicle "involved" in an accident, a parked vehicle can be "involved" in the accident when the vehicle is parked in such a way as to cause unreasonable risk of the bodily injury which occurred. M.C.L.A. §§ 500.3106, 500.3113.—Id.

In action brought by plaintiff who was injured when he was pinned between an automobile and the tow truck which had pulled his uninsured automobile out of a snow drift, evidence sustained finding that plaintiff's automobile was "involved" in the collision, because the vehicle was parked in such a way as to cause an unreasonable risk of bodily injury which occurred, and therefore, plaintiff's recovery was barred by statute precluding recovery of personal protection insurance benefits if a person is the owner of an uninsured motor vehicle "involved" in an accident. M.C.L.A. § 500.3113.—Id.

Mich.App. 1983. Damage to loader which contractor was transporting on his tractor, caused by striking underside of an overpass, arose out of contractor's use of its tractor as motor vehicle, and thus, under No-Fault Act, contractor was not liable in tort to owner of loader for damage thereto. M.C.L.A. §§ 500.-3123(1), 500.3135.—National Ben Franklin Ins. Co. v. Bakhaus Contractors, Inc., 335 N.W.2d 70, 124 Mich.App. 510.

Mich.App. 1983. Uninsured motorist is outside the basic no-fault system of allocating the costs of accidents and remains subject to tort liability. M.C.L.A. § 500.3135(1, 2).—Jones v. Detroit Auto. Inter-Ins. Exchange, 335 N.W.2d 39, 124 Mich.App. 363.

Mich.App. 1983.
Defendant's Chevy struck a tree—
There was no liability;
The No-Fault Act comes into play
As owner and the driver say;

Barred by the Act's immunity,
No suit in tort will aid the tree;
Although the oak's in disarray,
No court can make defendants pay.

M.C.L.A. § 500.3135.—Fisher v. Lowe, 333 N.W.2d 67, 122 Mich.App. 418.

Mich.App. 1982. Statute requires compliance with security requirements of no-fault insurance after 30-day period, 30-day period being intended to protect tourists and other transient nonresidents from criminal sanctions imposed by the Act. M.C.L.A. §§ 500.3102, 500.3135(2).—Berrien County Road Com'n v. Jones, 326 N.W.2d 495, 119 Mich.App. 315.

Defendants, having paid their dues in risk-spreading system by voluntarily acquiring insurance, and being owners or registrants of motor vehicle as defined in statute, though neither plaintiff's nor defendants' vehicle was required to be registered as vehicle within the state and therefore neither was required to be covered by no-fault insurance, were entitled to immunity provided by the no-fault act. M.C.L.A. §§ 500.-3101(1, 3, 4), 500.3102, 500.3135(2).—Id.

Mich.App. 1981. Damages awarded to plaintiff for personal injuries sustained as result of negligence of state in failing to maintain roads were not subject to no-fault motor vehicle act since act applied only to accidents caused by motor vehicles and not to those caused by negligent highway maintenance. M.C.L.A. § 500.3135.—Longworth v. Michigan Dept. of Highways and Transp., 315 N.W.2d 135, 110 Mich.App. 771.

Minn.App. 1986. No-Fault Act did not bar a governmental agency established under the laws of Quebec, Canada to administer automobile insurance plan covering Quebec citizens from maintaining a subrogation action against driver of automobile involved in Minnesota collision in which Quebec resident met her death; agency paid benefits to surviving husband as result of wife's death and took assignment from heirs and next-of kin of their claims against the other motorist. M.S.A. § 65B.53, subds. 2, 3.—Regie de l'assurance Auto. du Quebec v. Jensen, 389 N.W.2d 537.

N.H. 1983. Tractor with backhoe attachment is "motor vehicle" for purposes of Financial Responsibility Act. RSA 259:61.—Royal Globe Ins. Companies v. Fletcher, 459 A.2d 255, 123 N.H. 189.

N.J.Super.A.D. 1984. Fact that automobile was object of robbery during which plaintiff's decedent was killed did not transform incident into "accident involving an automobile" within meaning of State Automobile Reparation Reform Act. N.J.S.A. 39:6A–1 et seq., 39:6A–4.—Uzcatequi-Gaymon v. New Jersey Mfrs. Ins. Co., 472 A.2d 163, 193 N.J.Super. 71.

N.Y.A.D. 1 Dept. 1983. New York resident who registered vehicle in Connecticut and whose automobile was uninsured in either New York or Connecticut and thus could not qualify as a covered person under New York no-fault law was liable for basic economic loss for damages to himself and could not recover those amounts from third-party tort-feasor. McKinney's Insurance Law § 671, subd. 1.—Wilson v. E. & J. Trucking Corp., 462 N.Y.S.2d 660, 94 A.D.2d 666.

For references to other topics, see Descriptive-Word Index

Each *Decennial Digest* unit contains two finding aids: a Table of Cases, listing alphabetically the name of every case appearing in the unit, and a Descriptive–Word Index, which serves as the basic subject finding tool for all West digests.[6] Until 1976 the *Decennials* included no Defendant–Plaintiff Tables, but beginning with the *Ninth Decennial Digest, Part 1,* there are tables listing cases under both parties' names.

The *Decennial Digests* are massive tools offering subject access to all American jurisdictions for five- or ten-year periods. In one place, headnotes and citations are available from all cases published during the years of coverage and dealing with any specific point of law. While of little practical use for most research problems, they are a valuable archive of information.

(2) General Digest

Unlike the digests for individual jurisdictions or regions, the *Decennial Digests* are not supplemented by pocket parts, and once they are published they are not updated and recompiled. They are published every five or ten years to provide comprehensive coverage of a specific period. A search in the most recent *Decennial* can, however, be updated by using a series of bound volumes known as the *General Digest*. Each new *General Digest* volume contains the latest headnotes in all West reporters, arranged by topic. The entire digest spectrum, from "Abandoned and Lost Property" to "Zoning and Planning," is covered in each *General Digest* volume. In effect, these volumes are "advance sheets" for the next *Decennial Digest,* and once publication of the *Decennial* is completed they are no longer needed.

In recent years, fourteen volumes of the *General Digest* have been published annually. These abstracts are not cumulated again until the publication of the next edition of the *Decennial Digest.* Depending on the date of the most recent *Decennial,* a researcher may need to examine fifty or more *General Digest* volumes to find recent cases. Most key numbers do not appear in every *General Digest* volume, so examining each volume would be fruitless and time-wasting. One can determine which volumes contain a particular key number, however, by consulting a "Table of Key Numbers" included in each volume of the *General Digest.* This table is cumulative in every tenth volume, indicating in one location which of the previous ten volumes contain abstracts for each topic/key number combination. In addition, the most recent table includes references to all volumes published since the latest ten-volume cumulative table. If, for example, there have been sixteen volumes in the current *General Digest* series, one would have to consult tables in volume 10 (for references in volumes 1 through 10) and volume 16 (for references in volumes 11 through 16).

6. The *Century Digest* and the *First Decennial Digest* share a combined Table of Cases, located in volumes 21 to 25 of the *First Decennial;* and combined Descriptive–Word Indexes cover both the *First* and *Second Decennials,* and the *Third* and *Fourth Decennials,* respectively.

In addition to abstracts arranged by topic and key number and the Table of Key Numbers, each *General Digest* volume contains a Descriptive–Word Index, a Table of Cases listing decisions abstracted in that volume, and a "Table of Cases Affirmed, Reversed, etc.," which lists earlier cases affected by that volume's decisions. These indexes and tables cumulate in every tenth volume, like the Table of Key Numbers, but they do *not* cumulate in volumes between the ten-volume cumulations. The latest volumes, therefore, must be searched individually or not at all. Even in the ten-volume cumulations there is no Defendant–Plaintiff Table, so recent cases can be found only under the plaintiffs' names.

The *General Digest* is currently in its eighth series, which began in 1991. If West's format of *Decennial* publication does not change, this series will continue until 1996, at which point it will be entirely superseded by the *Tenth Decennial Digest, Part Two.*

The following table traces in chronological order the present components of the American Digest System:

Years Covered	Digest Unit	Number of Volumes
1658–1896	*Century Digest*	50
1897–1906	*First Decennial Digest*	25
1907–1916	*Second Decennial Digest*	24
1916–1926	*Third Decennial Digest*	29
1926–1936	*Fourth Decennial Digest*	34
1936–1946	*Fifth Decennial Digest*	52
1946–1956	*Sixth Decennial Digest*	36
1956–1966	*Seventh Decennial Digest*	38
1966–1976	*Eighth Decennial Digest*	50
1976–1981	*Ninth Decennial Digest, Part 1*	38
1981–1986	*Ninth Decennial Digest, Part 2*	48
1986–1991	*Tenth Decennial Digest, Part 1*	44
1991–date	*General Digest, Eighth Series*	In progress

With the increasing use of computer services and the availability of more convenient federal and state digests, one may well question the continued utility of this comprehensive and unwieldy set. While older *Decennial* volumes do little but gather dust, however, recently published *Decennials* can be useful compendia of contemporary case law from throughout the country.

e. *Finding Cases in the West Digests*

Having described the structure and forms of publication of the various West digests, we turn now to the actual search procedures employed in their use. How does one find cases in the digests? There are three basic approaches: working from a case, by subject searching in indexes, or by analyzing the classification outline of a particular topic.

(1) Starting With a Case

The simplest and often the most successful means of approaching a digest is with a case already in hand. Half the battle of legal research is won by having "one good case" to serve as a basis for finding other cases and resources. As seen in the last chapter, for example, the Shepard's listing for one case can serve as a springboard to numerous later decisions on the same issues.

When using a digest, starting with a case means that there is no need to search through indexes or figure out the digest's classification system. The appropriate topics and key numbers are already available in the headnotes of the decision in hand. If a headnote has been written for that part of the opinion addressing the issue being researched, the topic and key number assigned to the headnote can be searched in the digests for other relevant cases. Occasionally the key number assigned covers a very broad area, so that the digest includes abstracts of many irrelevant cases, but more often it's an ideal lead and a shortcut through the indexes and finding aids.

To read a decision and examine its headnotes, of course, one must know its citation. Often a researcher has heard of a relevant case but does not know where to find it. A case name may come up in conversation or may be mentioned in nonlegal literature with no reference to its citation. Using the tables in West's digests, however, one can easily use a case name to find its citation. As noted in the discussion of the different digests, every digest has a Table of Cases, an alphabetical listing of all cases covered in the publication. Each jurisdictional digest has a complete listing of published cases from that jurisdiction, updated by pocket parts and further updated by interim pamphlets. For digests in more than one series, each component has a table of the cases for its period. There are, for example, five separate case tables in federal digests, with the most recent (in *West's Federal Practice Digest 4th*) covering cases since the mid–1980's (coverage start dates for this digest vary by topic).

The decisions known most often by name only are those of the Supreme Court of the United States. One can easily find all three citations to famous cases such as *Brown v. Board of Education* or *Roe v. Wade* by using the Table of Cases in the *United States Supreme Court Digest*. This table is cumulative from the beginning of the Court, and was updated and republished in 1986 as volumes 14 and 14A of the set.

Illustration F shows the page of the *Michigan Digest* table of cases listing *Fisher v. Lowe,* the case in Illustration B. Note that following the name of each case are its citations in both official and regional reporters. If a case has been affirmed, reversed or modified on appeal or rehearing, that information is included as well, with a citation to the later decision. (The decision immediately following *Fisher v. Lowe* in the illustration was *reversed* by the Michigan Supreme Court.) Finally, the listing includes the topics and key numbers under which the headnote abstracts can be found in the digest. One can go directly to those key numbers from the Table of Cases. If one has not yet read the case, however, it is usually better to go first to the opinion to determine which headnotes, if any, are indeed relevant to a particular search.

Illustration F

A page from the Table of Cases in *West's Michigan Digest*

References are to Digest Topics and Key Numbers

Fisher v. Johnson Milk Co 383 Mich 158, 174 NW2d 752—Neglig 25, 27; Sales 441(3).
Fisher v. Johnson Milk Co 163 NW2d 652, 13 MichApp 10, rev 383 Mich 158, 174 NW2d 752—Judgm 181(29, 33), 185.3(21); Prod Liab 41.
Fisher v. Kavanagh 100 FSupp 248—Int Rev 764.3.
Fisher v. Lowe, MichApp, 333 NW2d 67, 122 MichApp 418.—Autos 251.13; Proc 4.
Fisher v. Michigan Dept. of Mental Health, MichApp, 339 NW2d 692, 128 MichApp 72, rev 368 NW2d 229, 422 Mich 884, reconsideration den 374 NW2d 418—App & E 175; Judgm 181(11), 185(2), 186, 829(3); Offic 114; Phys 18.40; States 79, 191(2).
Fisher v. Muller 53 MichApp 110, 218 NW2d 821—Const Law 284(2), 285, 309(2); Decl Judgm 345; Estop 62.1, 62.3; Evid 65, 86; Statut 245; Tax 360, 363, 431, 491, 505, 619, 689(2), 818.
Fisher v. Provin 25 Mich 347—Hus & W 14.2(6), 14.4.
Fisher v. Stolaruk Corp., EDMich, 648 FSupp 486.—Labor 1570, 1572.
Fisher v. Stolaruk Corp., EDMich, 110 FRD 74.—Contracts 19, 93(1); Fed Civ Proc 2725.
Fisher v. Sunfield Tp., MichApp, 415 NW2d 297, 163 MichApp 735.—Tax 348(6), 485(3), 493.8, 493.9.
Fisher v. Travelers Indem Co 13 MichApp 208, 163 NW2d 822—Insurance 508.
Fisher v. Volkswagenwerk Aktiengesellschaft, MichApp, 321 NW2d 814, 115 MichApp 781.—Death 11, 39; Ex & Ad 509(1).
Fisher-New Center Co., Appeal of 375 Mich 559, 134 NW2d 758—Tax 493.9.
Fisher-New Center Co v. City of Detroit 38 MichApp 750, 197 NW2d 272—Tax 490, 493.1, 535, 537, 543(1).
Fisher-New Center Co v. Michigan State Tax Commission 381 Mich 713, 167 NW2d 263—Admin Law 462, 788; Tax 452, 485(3), 493.8, 493.9.
Fisher-New Center Co v. Michigan State Tax Commission 380 Mich 380, 157 NW2d 271, reh 381 Mich 713, 167 NW2d 263.
Fisher-New Center Co v. Wayne County 38 MichApp 750, 197 NW2d 272. See Fisher-New Center Co v. City of Detroit.
Fisher Provision Co v. LoPatin 65 MichApp 568, 237 NW2d 562—Corp 340(3).
Fisher's Estate, In re 70 MichApp 117, 245 NW2d 427. See Gruskin v. Fisher.
Fishleigh v. Detroit United Ry, Mich, 171 NW 549, 205 Mich 145.—App & E 1004.1(4).
Fisk, In re, BkrtcyMich, 36 BR 924.—Bankr 2233(1), 2559, 2784; Judgm 828(3.53).
Fisk v. Allis Chalmers Credit Corp., BkrtcyMich, 36 BR 924. See Fisk, In re.
Fisk v. Fisk, Mich, 53 NW2d 356, 333 Mich 513.—App & E 1056.1(4).
Fisk v. Powell 349 Mich 604, 84 NW2d 736—App & E 1008.1(1).
Fister v. Henschel 7 MichApp 590, 152 NW2d 555—App & E 1010.1(7); Brok 9, 11; Damag 22, 40(2), 190.
Fister Realty Co v. Henschel 7 MichApp 590, 152 NW2d 555. See Fister v. Henschel.
Fiszer v. White Pine Copper Co 405 Mich 105, 274 NW2d 411. See Kostamo v. Marquette Iron Mining Co.
Fitch v. Constantine Hydraulic Co, Mich, 6 NW 91, 44 Mich 74.—Arbit 3.2.
Fitch v. Crime Victims' Compensation Bd 99 MichApp 363, 297 NW2d 667—Crim Law 1220.
Fithian v. Papalini, Mich, 378 NW2d 467, 424 Mich 77. See Leggett, Matter of Estates of.
Fittante v. Schultz 383 Mich 722, 179 NW2d 20. See Albert, In re.
Fittante v. Schultz 20 MichApp 259, 174 NW2d 29—Contempt 20, 24.
Fitterer Engineering Associates, Inc., Matter of, BkrtcyMich, 27 BR 878.—Atty & C 175, 182(1); Bankr 2573, 2603; Fed Cts 407.
Fitz v. Board of Educ. of Port Huron Area Schools, EDMich, 662 FSupp 1011, aff 802 F2d 457.—Armed S 114(1), 118(7), 119; Schools 133.9; States 18.15.
Fitzcharles v. Mayer 284 Mich 122, 278 NW 788—Trial 139.3.
Fitzgerald v. Challenge Cook Bros, Inc 80 MichApp 524, 264 NW2d 348—Work Comp 2251.
Fitzgerald v. Detroit United Ry 206 Mich 273, 172 NW 608—App & E 1060.1(1), 1064.1(4); Trial 133.1.
Fitzgerald v. Hubert Herman, Inc 23 MichApp 716, 179 NW2d 252—Contracts 316(1); Trial 139.1(17).
Fitzgerald v. Lozier Motor Co 187 Mich 660, 154 NW 67—Trial 139.1(3).
Fitzke v. Shappell 468 F2d 1072—Civil R 13.12(1, 6); Const Law 272(2); Fed Civ Proc 654, 1788.5, 2539, 2543, 2544.
Fitzpatrick, In re Estate of, MichApp, 406 NW2d 483.—Courts 202(5); Wills 435, 523, 552(1), 552(3).
Fitzpatrick v. Wolfe, MichApp, 406 NW2d 483. See Fitzpatrick, In re Estate of.
Fitzwater v. Fitzwater 97 MichApp 92, 294 NW2d 249—Const Law 305(5); Courts 12(2.35); Divorce 403(7); Parent & C 3.4(2).
511 Detroit Street, Inc. v. Kelley, CA6 (Mich), 807 F2d 1293, cert den 107 SCt 3211, 96 LEd2d 698—Const Law 46(1), 90.1(1), 90.4(1); Crim Law 13.1(1), 986.-2(1); Obscen 2.5.
Fizer v. Onekama Consol Schools 83 MichApp 584, 269 NW2d 234—Mun Corp 869, 907; Schools 97(4).
Fjerstad's Estate, In re 47 MichApp 100, 209 NW2d 302. See Besemer v. Fjerstad's Estate.
F J Siller & Co v. City of Hart 400 Mich 578, 255 NW2d 347—Arbit 2.1, 7.9, 9, 82(1).
F J Siller & Co v. City of Hart 68 MichApp 265, 242 NW2d 547, rev 400 Mich 578, 255 NW2d 347—Arbit 2.1, 7, 82(1).
Flack v. Waite 18 MichApp 339, 170 NW2d 922—Dismissal 81(3, 6).
Flager v. Associated Truck Lines, Inc 52 MichApp 280, 216 NW2d 922—Neglig 93(5, 10).
Flaherty v. Smith 87 MichApp 561, 274 NW2d 72—Parent & C 2(14).
Flaig v. Bendix Corp 488 FSupp 336, aff 701 F2d 177—Civil R 38, 44(1).
Flamini, Matter of, BkrtcyMich, 23 BR 668.—Bankr 3361.
Flamini, Matter of, BkrtcyMich, 19 BR 303, on reh 23 BR 668.—Bankr 2023, 3350; Statut 263, 268, 270.
Flamm v. Scherer 40 MichApp 1, 198 NW2d 702—Contracts 321(1); Evid 442(6); Sales 98, 174, 405, 417.
Flamm Pickle & Packing Co v. Scherer 40 MichApp 1, 198 NW2d 702. See Flamm v. Scherer.
Flanagan v. General Motors Corp 95 MichApp 677, 291 NW2d 166—Costs 105, 172; Judges 49(2); Judgm 181(1, 33).
Flanders Co v. Canners' Exchange Subscribers at Warner Inter-Insurance Bureau 235 Mich 157, 209 NW 113—Insurance 579.1.
Flat Hots Co v. Peschke Packing Co, Mich, 8 NW2d 295, 301 Mich 331.—App & E 1011.1(1), 1012.1(3).
Fleckenstein v. Citizens' Mut Auto Ins Co 326 Mich 591, 40 NW2d 733—Insurance 435.2(4).
Fleischer v. Buccilli 13 MichApp 135, 163 NW2d 637—Costs 173(1); Damag 71, 91(1), 184; Spec Perf 114(1), 129; Ven & Pur 350.
Fleisher v. U S 91 F2d 404—Crim Law 1144.3.
Fleming v. Chrysler Corp 575 F2d 1187—Labor 136, 416.3.
Fleming v. Chrysler Corp., EDMich, 659 FSupp 392.—States 18.45, 18.49.
Fleming v. Chrysler Corp, DCMich, 416 FSupp 1258, aff 575 F2d 1187—Labor 136, 219, 221, 416.3, 759, 777.
Fleming v. Mohawk Wrecking & Lumber Co 67 SCt 1129—Statut 219(6).
Fleming v. Rex Oil & Gas Co 43 FSupp 950—Commerce 62.56.
Flemings v. Jenkins, MichApp, 360 NW2d 298, 138 MichApp 788.—Autos 251.15, 251.19.
Fletcher v. Advo Systems, Inc., DCMich, 616 FSupp 1511.—Fed Civ Proc 202, 203; Fed Cts 286, 289, 303, 306; Rem of C 31.
Fletcher v. Aetna Cas & Sur Co 409 Mich 1, 294 NW2d 141. See Bradley v. Mid-Century Ins Co.
Fletcher v. Aetna Cas & Sur Co 80 MichApp 439, 264 NW2d 19, aff Bradley v. Mid-Century Ins Co, 409 Mich 1, 294 NW2d 141, 20 ALR4th 1069—Damag 89(2); Insurance 4.4, 531.3(2), 602.2(1); Interest 39(1); Statut 263.
Fletcher v. Flynn 368 Mich 328, 118 NW2d 229—App & E 1003(4).
Fletcher v. Ford Motor Co., MichApp, 342 NW2d 285, 128 MichApp 823, appeal den—Evid 363; Prod Liab 96, 98.
Fletcher v. Grinnell Bros 62 FSupp 258—Commerce 62.60.
Fletcher v. Harafajee 100 MichApp 440, 299 NW2d 53—Work Comp 1087, 2168, 2253.
Fletcher v. Kentucky Inns, Inc 88 MichApp 456, 276 NW2d 619—Corp 113.
Fletcher v. State Treasurer 384 Mich 289, 181 NW2d 909—Costs 221; Insurance 72.9.
Fletcher v. State Treasurer 16 MichApp 87, 167 NW2d 594, aff 384 Mich 289, 181 NW2d 909—Costs 221; Insurance 8, 72.9; Statut 181(1).
Fletcher v. Stratton 20 MichApp 540, 174 NW2d 307—Autos 246(9, 38).
Fletcher, Baby Girl, Matter of 79 MichApp 219, 256 NW2d 444. See Baby Girl Fletcher, Matter of.
Flexitype & Douglas Offset Co v. Department of Treasury, Revenue Division 52 MichApp 153, 216 NW2d 609—Tax 1237, 1336.
Flick v. Larue, DCMich, 608 FSupp 1281, aff 821 F2d 649—Civil R 13.1, 13.4(5), 13.8(1), 13.13(1).
Flinn v. Sun Oil Co 96 MichApp 59, 292 NW2d 484—App & E 969; New Tr 29; Sales 427; Trial 295(5); Witn 379(10).
Flint Bd of Ed v. Williams 88 MichApp 8, 276 NW2d 499—Schools 160; Statut 181(1, 2), 223.1, 223.4.
Flint, City of. See City of Flint.

All digest units have tables listing cases by plaintiffs' names. The state and federal digests, but not the regional digests, also have Defendant–Plaintiff Tables providing cross references from the second party's name to the first party's. If only one party to a case is known and nothing is found under the name in the Table of Cases, often a search in the Defendant–Plaintiff Table will turn up the case. This is particularly true for criminal cases, where the jurisdiction bringing the action, the U.S., is always the plaintiff. The Defendant–Plaintiff Tables do not include the case history information or the topics and key numbers that are part of the Tables of Cases listings, but they do contain both official and National Reporter System citations. Defendant–Plaintiff Tables are updated in pocket parts, but not in interim supplementary pamphlets.

If a case is too recent to be included in the latest supplement to the digest but one knows which court wrote the opinion, there is still hope. A search for its name can be brought up to date by looking in the "Cases Reported" tables in reporter bound volumes and advance sheets. National Reporter System bound volumes generally contain two Cases Reported tables. One consists of a single alphabetical list of all cases in the volume, listed under both plaintiffs' and defendants' names. The other, in reporters covering more than one jurisdiction, lists cases separately under each jurisdiction, by plaintiff only. Advance sheets, on the other hand, include only the latter table, listing cases only by plaintiff and separately for each jurisdiction. The tables in advance sheets do, however, cumulate for the contents of each bound volume; instead of looking in every single advance sheet, a person searching for the name of a recent case needs only to look in the last advance sheet for each bound volume number. Since the Cumulative Cases Reported tables in advance sheets cover more than one pamphlet, the names of cases appearing in the issue being examined instead of earlier issues are printed in bold type. In the regional reporters the table also indicates on what pages of the pamphlet cases from each state are printed, so that an attorney wishing to scan a state's latest decisions each week can easily do so.

If one knows the name of a case but not its jurisdiction, the Tables of Cases in the *Decennial* and *General Digests* may be used to find its citation. All cases published before 1907 are contained in one table in volumes 21 to 25 of the *First Decennial Digest,* and each subsequent *Decennial* includes a table of cases for its time period. (The first *Decennial* Defendant–Plaintiff Table, unfortunately, was not published until the *Ninth Decennial, Part 1,* covering 1976 to 1981.) For the period since the most recent *Decennial,* each *General Digest* volume contains a listing of the cases it covers. Starting with the *General Digest, Seventh Series,* which began in 1986, these listings cumulate in every tenth volume. Searching the *Decennial* or *General Digests* for a case by name is not such an onerous task if the date of decision is known or can be estimated. Otherwise it may be necessary to look in over a dozen tables, covering from the 17th century to the current year.

Occasionally a judicial decision is referred to by a "popular name," or a term other than the names of its parties. For example, *Youngstown Sheet & Tube Co. v. Sawyer,* 343 U.S. 579 (1952), is often referred to as the "Steel Seizure Case." The closing pages of *Shepard's Acts and Cases by Popular Names: Federal and State* list many of these names, and provide reporter citations (but neither dates nor parties' names). A few of the designations included are very well-known, but many are quite obscure, "popular" only in the broadest sense of the term. In recent years the use of "popular names" has declined precipitously, and very few new cases are being added to the list.[7]

(2) *Descriptive–Word Indexes*

Each West digest includes a minutely constructed index referring to the specific topics and key numbers under which decisions on that subject have been abstracted in the digest. These "Descriptive–Word Indexes" are simply detailed subject indexes to the contents of the digests. The indexes are usually quite large, occupying three or more volumes in most jurisdictional digests.

There are generally two types of entries in a Descriptive–Word Index. Each West key number is represented in every jurisdictional and regional digest's index, even if no cases are represented, so the Descriptive–Word Index functions in part as a subject index to the key number classifications. Descriptive–Word Indexes for different jurisdictions or regions are quite similar, in that a particular entry will refer in any digest to the same key number. In addition, however, there are entries for specific fact situations represented by individual cases covered in the digest. The Descriptive–Word Index for each jurisdiction therefore contains some entries unique to its jurisprudence.

The *Decennial* and *General Digests* also contain Descriptive–Word Indexes, but these lists no longer attempt to be comprehensive finding tools. The index in the *Ninth Decennial Digest, Part 1,* for example, is less than a quarter of the size of the index for the *Eighth Decennial,* although the digest itself is almost as large. The indexes in *General Digest* volumes are usually only seven or eight pages long. (If they *did* index every case digested, of course, the Descriptive–Word Indexes would be nearly as massive as the digests themselves.) If a jurisdictional or regional digest is available, its comprehensive Descriptive–Word Index is usually a better first place to look for general coverage of a subject. The indexes in recent *Decennial* or *General Digest* volumes, however, can be useful resources for searches concerning currently developing areas of legal doctrine.

7. Similar popular name tables were published in some older West digests, including the first *Federal Digest* and the *Second* through *Sixth Decennials.* These tables have long since been discontinued, but may occasionally be useful for older cases, since the Shepard's and West tables do not duplicate coverage entirely.

Shepard's Acts and Cases by Popular Names serves a far more important function as a finding tool for legislative acts, as will be discussed in Chapter 5.

West suggests that before consulting a Descriptive–Word Index, the researcher analyze the problem to be searched, and determine very specific words or phrases to be used by breaking the problem down into the following elements common to every case:

(1) the *parties* involved;

(2) the *places* where the facts arose, and the *objects* or *things* involved;

(3) the *acts* or *omissions* which form the *basis of action* or *issue* ;

(4) the *defense* to the action or issue; and

(5) the *relief* sought.

In the case of *Fisher v. Lowe,* shown in Illustration B earlier in the chapter, the plaintiff is suing to recover for damage to an oak tree struck by an automobile. The defendants asserted that no-fault insurance granted them immunity from tort liability. The attorneys for the parties could have found relevant case law by looking in a Descriptive–Word Index under such terms as "trees" or "no fault insurance." As a general rule, one should use search terms that are both *specific* and *material.* General terms such as "automobiles" or "negligence" are likely to have too many references covering an enormous number of irrelevant issues and cases. A search term such as "oak" would be very specific, but has no legal importance and does not even appear in the index.

Illustrations G and H reproduce pages from the Descriptive–Word Index in *West's North Western Digest 2d* showing entries under "Trees—automobile collision" and "No fault insurance—limitation of tort remedy." Note that under "Trees" one is directed to a variety of topics and key numbers that might arise in such a case, but not the topic and key number used in *Fisher v. Lowe.* Under "No fault insurance," on the other hand, one is directed to the digest location where the West editors classified the first *Fisher* headnote.

A misleading byproduct of many law school legal research problems is that they encourage the belief that for every hypothetical problem there is a perfectly-designed case abstract waiting to be found. In practice one seldom finds a precedent in which an identical fact situation raises the exact legal issues with which one is confronted. What one realistically hopes to find is a precedent that involves *similar* facts and the same legal issues. One must usually draw analogies from similar situations. Descriptive–Word Indexes can be quite effective in finding precedential cases, if used with an understanding that they may not always contain the precise factual terms one would wish to find.

Illustration G

Entries under "Trees" in a Descriptive–Word Index

Illustration H

A Descriptive–Word Index entry for the classification used in *Fisher v. Lowe*

(3) Topical Analysis

One can also find cases by examining the topic outlines, printed at the beginning of each digest topic in any of the jurisdictional or *Decennial* digests.[8] A researcher who knows which topic is most relevant to an issue, or who can determine which is most appropriate by scanning the list of topics at the beginning of the digest, can focus on that one topic for searching. The topic outlines begin with a general summary of major subdivisions, followed by a detailed outline of all individual key numbers. The researcher finds relevant key numbers and then examines the abstracts listed under those numbers for cases on point. Illustration I shows the page including the key number classification for the first *Fisher v. Lowe* headnote in the "Automobiles" outline, from the *Ninth Decennial Digest, Part 2.* The page shown is part of an eleven-page outline for the topic "Automobiles."

If one knows an area of law well and is able to place a particular problem in its logical location within that area, this approach may not only lead to relevant cases but may clarify one's thinking about the issue by placing it in context. Without a thorough understanding of a body of law, however, this is usually an ineffective means of research. The process of scanning the subdivisions for the relevant key numbers may be very time-consuming and the chances of choosing the appropriate key number limited. Moreover, a researcher unfamiliar with the classification system may not even choose the correct topic. Many contractual issues are found, for example, under "Sales" or "Vendor and Purchaser" rather than under the topic "Contracts." A more prudent use of topic outlines is to refer to them *after* using the Descriptive–Word Index to find the correct topic, if a precise key number in the index is not located.

f. Summary

The comprehensive scope of West digests makes them one of the most important case-finding tools. The key number system spans all federal and state jurisdictions, and *every* point of law treated in a published case fits somewhere and somehow into the classification scheme.

There are, however, several dangers and disadvantages inherent in the use of digests, and these should be recognized by the researcher. Instead of narrative text or explanatory comments, digests frequently consist only of long, undifferentiated series of abstracts which the researcher must plow through and attempt to synthesize. Because digests contain summaries of the points of law in court decisions, there may be the temptation to treat those summaries as primary source material. As noted before, however, a case should *never* be cited merely on the basis of a digest abstract. The point digested may be dictum, or the opinion may clarify it in ways not shown in the headnote. The decision itself must be read and evaluated, and for that reason every digest abstract includes a case citation.

8. The researcher can also consult West's *Analysis of American Law, 1994 ed.*, an annual, soft-cover volume listing the most current topic and key numbers.

Illustration I

Part of a topical outline in the *Ninth Decennial Digest, Part 2*

4 9th D Pt 2—9 **AUTOMOBILES**

V. INJURIES FROM OPERATION, OR USE OF HIGHWAY.—Cont'd

(B) ACTIONS.—Cont'd

⊶246. Instructions.—Cont'd
(19). Lookout, signals, and warnings.
(20). Speed and control.
(21). Acts in emergencies.
(22). Proximate cause of injury.
(23). Contributory negligence.
(24). —— Reliance on care of person causing injury.
(25). —— Vehicles meeting or crossing.
(26). —— Vehicles following, overtaking, or passing.
(27). —— Vehicles at rest or unattended.
(28). —— Collision with bicycle or motorcycle.
(29). —— Owners, riders, or drivers of animals.
(30). —— Persons on foot in general.
(31). —— Persons crossing or walking along highway.
(32). —— Persons moving to or from street cars.
(33). —— Persons standing or sitting in highway or street.
(34). —— Persons under disability in general.
(35). —— Children.
(36). —— Passenger, guest or occupant.
(37). —— Acts in emergencies.
(38). —— Injury avoidable notwithstanding contributory negligence.
(39). Applicability to pleadings and evidence.
(40). —— Violation of statute or ordinance in general.
(41). —— Equipment and lights on vehicles.
(42). —— Identity, status and competency of operator.
(43). —— Signals and warnings.
(44). —— Defects in vehicles.
(45). —— Willful, wanton, or reckless acts or conduct.
(46). —— Vehicles stopping, backing, or turning.
(47). —— Vehicles meeting or crossing.
(48). —— Vehicles following, overtaking, or passing.
(49). —— Persons on foot in general.
(50). —— Persons crossing or walking along highway or street.
(51). —— Children.
(52). —— Persons moving to or from street cars.
(53). —— Persons standing or sitting in highway or street.
(54). —— Passenger, guest or occupant.
(55). —— Vehicles at rest or unattended.
(56). —— Speed and control.
(57). —— Proximate cause of injury.
(58). —— Contributory negligence.
(59). —— Injuring or frightening animals.
(60). Presumptions and burden of proof.
247. Verdict and findings.
248. Judgment and review.
249. Damages.
250. Lien on vehicle for injuries.
251. Costs.

(C) ACCIDENT INDEMNITY FUNDS.

⊶251.1. Uninsured or unknown motorists indemnity funds in general.
251.2. Statutory provisions.
251.3. Persons protected.
251.4. Limitation of liability.
251.5. Proceedings for compensation.
251.6. —— Notice.
251.7. —— Arbitration.
251.8. —— Evidence.

(D) EFFECT OF NO FAULT STATUTES.

⊶251.11. Abolition of tort liability in general.
251.12. —— Constitutional and statutory provisions.
251.13. —— Vehicles, persons, occurrences within restrictions.
251.14. —— "Threshold" requirement in general.
251.15. —— Nature of injury; serious or permanent injury.
251.16. —— Expenses included in threshold computation.
251.17. —— Elements of recovery; economic or non-economic loss.
251.18. —— Procedure peculiar to no fault cases; jurisdiction.
251.19. —— Evidence and fact questions.

VI. INJURIES FROM DEFECTS OR OBSTRUCTIONS IN HIGHWAYS AND OTHER PUBLIC PLACES.

(A) NATURE AND GROUNDS OF LIABILITY.

⊶252. In general.
253. Requirements of statutes and ordinances.
254. Places to which liability extends.
255. Cause of or responsibility for defects, obstructions, or dangerous conditions.
256. Care required as to condition of way in general.
257. Sufficiency and safety of way in general.
258. Nature of defects.
259. Defective plan of construction.
260. Oil or tar on highway.
261. Embankments, excavations, and openings.
262. Water, snow, or ice.
263. Obstructions.
264. —— In general.
265. —— Poles and wires.
266. Failure to prevent or remove defects or obstructions.
267. Smoke or steam obstructing view.
268. Falling objects.
269. Property adjacent to highway.
270. Bridges.
271. Culverts.
272. Notice of defects or obstructions.
273. —— In general.
274. —— Hidden or latent defects.
275. —— To public officers, agents, or private citizens.
276. —— Constructive notice.
277. Precautions against injuries.

The universal nature of the key number system allows it to be used in all jurisdictions, but does so sometimes at the expense of recognizing significant differences between states in approaches to jurisprudential issues. Digest classifications are choices made at the West Publishing Company, not in the courts, and may be misleading or have an unwarranted impact on subsequent interpretation of a holding.[9] The West system of topics and key numbers, however, is not the only way to classify legal situations, and other digesting and indexing systems exist that divide legal subjects in very different ways. An unsuccessful search in the digests does not preclude more favorable results in other systems.[10] Often a textual discussion of an area of law, such as in a legal encyclopedia or a law review article, offers a clearer and more selective introduction to relevant case law.

The greatest strength of the digests, the editorial expertise of its editors, is also one of its weaknesses. Human editors can sort information and help the researcher. At the same time, human editors are subject to errors and inherently conservative about change.

Several other case finding methods will be described in this chapter, but the West key number digest remains an ingenious and essential part of the research apparatus. While a digest may not always be the best place to *begin* a search for relevant decisions, it is often a very effective tool for enlarging a search from the topics and key numbers of a known relevant decision.

2. OTHER DIGESTS

Because the West Publishing Company publishes digests spanning the entire field of American state and federal jurisprudence, its key number classification system is more widely used and better known than any other digesting system. West is not the only publisher of digests, however, and key numbers are not the only means of classification. West is the only publisher of a *comprehensive* set of digests. Other digests are available for specific jurisdictions and specialized areas of research. These digests may prove as useful as West's in particular research situations and may lead to different cases than would be found using the key number system.

9. " 'If they do a headnote wrong,' says Robert Hursh of Lawyers Co-op, 'it's as though a case has been overruled. Anything they omit is not the law.' " Martin Mayer, *The Lawyers* 431 (Harper & Row, 1967).

10. The holding in a New York case was based on an appellate court precedent that neither party had cited. To determine the statute of limitations for bail jumping, the court had to determine whether bail jumping was a "continuous offense." The appellate court had clearly made such a determination in another context, not involving the statute of limitations. The court noted that the controlling case was so difficult to find because the editors at West Publishing Co. indexed it solely as a "habitual offender case" (Criminal Law, West's New York Digest 3d, vol 13, key No. 1202[7]). Its import as a dispositive limitations case for the crime of bail jumping was completely overlooked. The question arises: how can a case which is clearly controlling on a particular issue properly serve as precedent when it is virtually unknown and undiscoverable? This dilemma evokes the age-old query—is there a sound if a tree falls in the forest but nobody hears it?

People v. Barnes, 130 Misc.2d 1058, 1063, 499 N.Y.S.2d 343, 346 (1986).

a. United States Supreme Court Digest, Lawyers' Edition

In Chapter 2 we discussed the two commercial reporters for the opinions of the Supreme Court of the United States, West's *Supreme Court Reporter* and Lawyers Co-operative Publishing Co.'s *United States Supreme Court Reports, Lawyers' Edition.* For both editions the publishers' editorial staffs prepare headnotes to accompany the opinions. Like the headnotes in the *Supreme Court Reporter,* each headnote in *Lawyers' Edition* is assigned to a legal topic and a numbered subdivision of that topic. The Lawyers Co-op classification scheme, like West's, divides the legal issues covered by the decisions of the Supreme Court into some 400 topics and numerous numbered sections of those topics. The two publishers' lists of topics are not the same, however, nor are the subject arrangements of the sections within each topic identical. The two systems may assign the same point of law to two different topics.[11]

The headnotes in *Lawyers' Edition* are compiled and published in a set of volumes entitled *United States Supreme Court Digest, Lawyers' Edition.* The digest is cumulative from the Court's earliest decisions. It is organized like the West digest, in that each topic begins with an outline of its contents and consists of the text of headnotes arranged by section number. Each headnote's topic and section number are indicated in the reporter, so a researcher reading a *Lawyers' Edition* decision can go straight from the opinion to the relevant headnote and then to the digest for other cases on the same topic. In addition to case headnotes, digest entries include references to other Lawyers Co-op research aids such as annotations, in *Lawyers' Edition* itself and in *ALR,* and the publisher's legal encyclopedia, *American Jurisprudence 2d.*

Some claim that the *Lawyers' Edition* digest, designed specifically for Supreme Court decisions, is better adapted to the issues in those decisions than the West system, which has to be general enough to cover *all* jurisdictions. Because the *Lawyers' Edition* classifications are limited to one court, however, they cannot be used to find relevant cases from lower federal courts and from state jurisdictions. Even lawyers arguing before the Supreme Court cannot ignore precedent from lower courts.

The *Lawyers' Edition* digest can be approached through a Word Index and by topical analysis, as well as from the cases' headnotes, the same three basic approaches applicable to West digests. The two-volume Word Index functions in a manner similar to West's Descriptive–Word Indexes, providing references to topics and sections numbers. A five-volume Table of Cases contains entries under both plaintiffs' and defendants' names in one alphabetical listing, as well as some "popular name" listings. Plaintiff entries include all three reporter citations and the digest classifications assigned to the headnotes, but those under defen-

11. Compare the editorial treatments in Illustrations B–2 and C in Chapter 2, on pages ___ and ___. The second headnote in *L.Ed.2d* and the first headnote in *S.Ct.* cover the same issue, whether sleeping in tents for the purpose of expressing the plight of the homeless falls within the National Park Service definition of "camping." Yet Lawyers Co-op editors have assigned the headnote to the topic "Parks, Squares, and Commons," while West editors assigned it to the topic "United States."

dants are mere cross-references to plaintiff listings and do not even contain citations. The set also includes several volumes containing the text of federal court rules and rules of evidence.[12]

Each volume of the digest is updated by an annual pocket part. *Lawyers' Edition* advance sheets contain several tools for finding more recent cases, including a Table of Cases and a subject index containing short summaries of holdings. A Table of Classifications lists any topics and to which headnotes have been assigned. It indicates the beginning page numbers of relevant cases, but does not include abstracts or headnotes. These finding aids cumulate for each volume of *L.Ed.2d*, but not for the entire term. Since the opinions of one term often span five volumes, it may be necessary to examine up to five separate pamphlets (one for each volume) to find a case or topic.

b. State Digests

Although West publishes digests for 47 states, digests from other publishers are available in a few states. Lawyers in states where competing digests are published usually develop a preference for one or the other, but they should be aware of both systems. No single approach to legal classification is perfectly designed for analysis of all legal problems. There are situations where one approach appears ill-suited but a different system may produce results.

Bancroft–Whitney, publisher of the official *California Reports* and *California Appellate Reports,* also publishes digests using headnotes from its reports. Older cases are covered in *McKinney's New California Digest,* and recent cases are digested in *California Digest of Official Reports, 3d Series.* The third series contains notes from *Cal.3d* |Cal. 4th?Œ and *Cal.App.3d*, as well as coverage of California federal court cases and references to the legal encyclopedias *American Jurisprudence 2d* and *California Jurisprudence 3d.*

Callaghan & Co. publishes digests for the cases of three midwestern states. *Callaghan's Illinois Digest 3d, Callaghan's Michigan Digest* and *Callaghan's Wisconsin Digest* cover state supreme and appellate court cases, as well as federal cases construing and applying state law. They also include references to treatises, law review articles, and annotations, as well as indexes and case tables. Illustration J shows a page from *Callaghan's Michigan Digest,* including an entry for the same point of law in *Fisher v. Lowe* digested by West in Illustrations C through E.

12. *Lawyers' Edition* also has a *Desk Book,* a handy volume with several useful features such as an "Index to Cases and Annotations" and a "Table of Federal Laws, Rules, and Regulations." Coverage begins with the October 1956 term, reported in 1 L.Ed.2d. The book also contains a Table of Cases with entries for "all *full* decisions (those reported with opinions)" since the October 1956 term. Its format is the same as the full Table of Cases in the digest. Because it omits the Court's first 150 years and the multitude of orders and memoranda in the larger case table, however, it is a quicker and easier place to find recent opinions. The *Desk Book* is updated with a soft-cover supplement.

Illustration J

A page from *Callaghan's Michigan Digest*

§ 175 AUTOMOBILES AND MOTOR VEHICLES

(MSA § 24.13106; MCL § 500.3106). Shinabarger v. Citizens Mut. Ins. Co., 90 Mich App 307, 282 NW2d 301.

1979 Under no-fault insurance act providing for recovery of personal protection benefits for injury arising out of ownership, operation, maintenance, or use of parked motor vehicle as motor vehicle, establishment of causal connection between injury and use of motor vehicle is sufficient to entitle insured to recovery even though such connection does not amount to proximate cause and even though independent cause exists as well, provided that injury is not result of independent cause in no way related to use of vehicle even though vehicle is sight of injury (MSA § 24.13106; MCL § 500.3106). Shinabarger v. Citizens Mut. Ins. Co., 90 Mich App 307, 282 NW2d 301.

1980 Since there was no specific exception of two-wheeled vehicles from definition of "vehicle" in property protection insurance benefits exclusion statute, definition of vehicle in statute clearly includes motorcycle (MSA § 24.13123; MCL § 500.3123). Degrandchamp v. Michigan Mut. Ins. Co., 99 Mich App 664, 299 NW2d 18.

1981 A person who seeks no-fault insurance benefits from his insurer must establish a causal connection between the use of a motor vehicle and the injury which is more than incidental and fortuitous and which is foreseeably identifiable with the normal use of the vehicle; an assault by an armed assailant upon the driver of a vehicle is not the type of conduct which is so foreseeably identifiable, and the fact that a vehicle is commercially rather than privately insured is inconsequential to the issue. Ciaramitaro v. State Farm Ins. Co., 107 Mich App 68, 308 NW2d 661.

1981 A plaintiff's injuries arose out of the operation and use of a motor vehicle as a motor vehicle, as a matter of law, where the plaintiff, a service station attendant engaged in fueling an automobile, was struck by another automobile (MSA § 24.13105; MCL § 500.3105). Gutierrez v. Dairyland Ins. Co., 110 Mich App 126, 312 NW2d 181.

1981 The term "physical contact" in the hit-and-run provision of the Motor Vehicle Accident Claims Act has been given a wider meaning than a strict interpretation would require because of the remedial nature of the act and because the possiblity of fraud is minimal; "physical contact" has been construed to include situations where no direct contact occurs, the most common circumstances where recovery is permitted being (1) where the hit-and-run vehicle strikes a second or intervening vehicle which in turn is propelled into plaintiff's vehicle, and (2) where an object is propelled into the plaintiff's vehicle by another vehicle which does not stop (MSA § 9.2812; MCL § 257.1112). Adams v. Zajac, 110 Mich App 522, 313 NW2d 347.

1981 A no-fault insurer is liable to pay benefits for accidental bodily injury arising out of and which is foreseeably identifiable with the normal ownership, operation, maintenance, or use of a motor vehicle where the injured person establishes a causal connection which is more than incidental, fortuitous, or "but for" between the use of a motor vehicle and the injury. Gajewski v. Auto-owners Ins. Co., 112 Mich App 59, 314 NW2d 799.

1983 No tort liability arises for damage to a tree caused by an automobile insured under the no-fault insurance act. Fisher v. Lowe, 122 Mich App 418, 333 NW2d 67.

1983 A plaintiff alleges a sufficient causal connection between his bodily injury and the use of a vehicle for him to maintain an action for such injury under the no-fault insurance provision pertaining to injuries arising from parked vehicles where the plaintiff alleges that he was injured while attempting to open the vehicle door with the intention of unloading the contents of the vehicle. Teman v. Transamerica Ins. Co. of Michigan, 123 Mich App 262, 333 NW2d 244.

1959 Excess clause which was contained in liability policy issued to lessor of truck, and which was in conflict with other insurance and pro rata clauses in policy issued to leasee of truck, was controlling, and would be given its full effect, to render lessor's insurer liable to full extent of policy limits for payment of claims against lessor and lessee arising from accident involving insured truck. Citizens Mut. Automobile Ins. Co. v. Liberty Mut. Ins. Co., 273 F2d 189.

1964 Operation of a crane for moving concrete from ready-mix concrete truck and pouring it into foundation of building being constructed, was an insured use under insurance policy insuring truck owner against liability for injury arising out of use of vehicle, including loading and unloading, so that policy covered injuries resulting when boom upon crane fell and injured an employee of general contractor. St. Paul Mercury Ins. Co. v. Huitt, 336 F2d 37.

Nevada is one of the three states for which West does not publish a digest, although its cases are covered in the *Pacific Digest* and the American Digest System. An attorney researching Nevada law can use the *Nevada Digest*, published by the Legislative Counsel of the State of

Nevada. This set of about fifty looseleaf volumes contains abstracts of Nevada state and federal cases and of Nevada attorney general opinions.

All of these digests are organized by alphabetically arranged topics divided into numbered sections. Cases published in *California Reports, California Appellate Reports, Illinois Appellate Court Reports,* and *Wisconsin Reports* indicate the digest classification assigned to each headnote, so researchers can go directly from a case to related material in the digest. Headnotes in *Illinois Reports, Michigan Reports, Michigan Appeals Reports,* and *Nevada Reports* do not include digest classifications.

To find state cases *by name,* one can use the Tables of Cases published as part of any of West's digests or as part of the other digest discussed above. An alternative approach is to use one of *Shepard's Case Names Citators,* which are published for over forty states. These citators are simply alphabetical listings of cases, with coverage ranging from state to state. Most cover decisions from the last thirty to sixty years. These tools are not "digests," but they perform one of the functions of a digest.

Legal research is not a uniform matter in all states. Because each state has slightly different ways of disseminating and indexing its decisions, a person practicing law or doing research in a particular state would do well to become familiar with the distinct characteristics of its publications.[13]

c. *Specialized Digests*

Any series of case reports needs some means of providing subject access to the decisions it contains, or it will be of very little use to researchers. Access to cases in the National Reporter System is provided through West's American Digest System and its jurisdictional and regional digests. Other publishers of judicial opinions use a variety of methods to provide access, but digest systems are widely used. The main advantage a classified digest has over a simply alphabetical index is its rigorous analytical framework. In theory all cases on a particular issue will receive the same classification, even if the descriptive terms used in the opinions differ widely.

Almost all of the specialized looseleaf and topical reporters mentioned in Chapter 2 provide subject access to their cases through digests of some sort. Some digests appear only in each volume of opinions as a guide to its contents, but employ a consistent classification framework so that one can find relevant cases by looking under the same classification number in every volume. Other digests are published separately, to

13. Guides to legal research in individual states are listed in Appendix A, at the end of this volume. Other tools digesting cases from particular states include the *Florida Digestive Index* and *Georgia Digestive Index,* both published by the Harrison Company. The latter set is in two units, separately covering decisions of the Georgia Supreme Court and Court of Appeals. Lawyers Co-op publishes *Florida Supplement 2d Digest* to accompany its reporter of Florida trial court and administrative decisions. Butterworth's *Dunnell Minnesota Digest* includes textual summaries of Minnesota law, making it more of a legal encyclopedia than a digest.

cover cases appearing in five or ten years' worth of reporter volumes, and some are published as cumulative sets for all reported cases.

These topical digests are of three basic types. Some are organized on an alphabetical basis similar to West's system, but with topics designed for a specialized area of law. Digests for *American Maritime Cases, Public Utilities Reports,* or the *United States Patents Quarterly* work in this way.

Instead of alphabetized digest topics, a second group of specialized reporters have one classified numerical framework for the entire body of legal doctrine. Headnotes are assigned to classified subdivisions within topics, but those topics are arranged by subject rather than alphabetically. The Bureau of National Affairs uses this approach in its digests covering cases in the *Environment Reporter* and *Labor Relations Reference Manual.* Labor law topics such as "Picketing," "Boycotts," and "Other Methods of Publicizing Disputes," for example, are grouped within the division "Economic Weapons of Labor."

The third group of specialized reporters are those which focus on specific laws or court rules and use digest arrangements based on those subject materials. Digest paragraphs are grouped by code or rule section, each of which is then divided into numbered subject subsections. The major tax looseleafs, CCH's *Standard Federal Tax Reporter* and RIA's *United States Tax Reporter,* consist largely of digest paragraphs from cases organized in this manner. To accompany the *UCC Reporting Service,* Callaghan & Co. publishes the *Uniform Commercial Code Case Digest,* organized by U.C.C. section. Lawyer's Co-op recently took over Callaghan's publication of digests arranged by rule for federal procedural and evidence rules. The *Federal Rules Digest, 3d Ed.* provides access to the *Federal Rules Service,* and the *Federal Rules of Evidence Digest* accompanies the *Federal Rules of Evidence Service.*

Finally, digests are published to accompany *American Law Reports,* the annotated reporters commonly known as *ALR*. These digests contain both headnote paragraphs from the cases printed in *ALR* and citations of relevant annotations. The purpose and scope of *ALR,* and the use of its digests, will be discussed in the next section.

3. AMERICAN LAW REPORTS

a. Overview of Annotated Reporting Systems

When the model for case reporting used by the West Publishing Company came to dominate legal publishing, it displaced another manner of handling judicial decisions. The West Company stressed a uniform, comprehensive style of reporting; its algorithm was to report and categorize everything. The old model called for a process of selection, choosing only the best cases, then providing commentary on what made the cases important. This model contrasts with the West paradigm of case reporting in two important ways. First, someone, or some group of people, is choosing which cases are important. Second, someone is providing commentary and research assistance that runs beyond the words of the judge in the case. Given the paranoid nature of American legal research, such a process is suspect. Only one survivor from this era of case reporting still thrives—the set known as *American Law Reports.*

Initially, the cases printed in *ALR* were important in their own right and often of national significance, but today they are chosen for their convenience as springboards for the extensive accompanying annotations. Lawyers' Co-operative, the publisher of *ALR,* has editors who monitor new court decisions, looking for cases that may resolve a long-standing argument, set out a new question, or explore issues in an interesting way. Once a case is selected for annotation, it is assigned to an editor who then produces a thoroughly researched survey of the particular legal issue, tracing its development and its judicial treatment in all jurisdictions. The editor starts by following the research trail provided by the headnotes accompanying the West publication of the case. After finding related cases, the editor traces them through Shepard's citators to complete the picture. A LEXIS search and research tools published by Lawyers' Co-op and others are used to find even more cases. The goal is to work through every possible twist of the issue at hand. If successful, the resulting *ALR* annotation will provide a thoroughly researched explanation of the issue raised in the case.

In a sense, this is an upside down version of West's American Digest System and Key Number methodology. Where the American Digest System has a list of topics prepared in advance and fits every case into its appropriate spot, *ALR* picks only a few cases, then produces an in-depth exploration of the issues presented. The annotations range in length, depending on the complexity of the issues covered and the frequency with which they arise in published cases, from short articles of a few pages to extensive treatments of several hundred pages. *ALR* is far from comprehensive—it is just a collection of interesting, well-annotated cases—but an annotation on a point of interest can be very helpful.

The text of an *ALR* annotation is very spare and telegraphic in style. The holdings of all the published cases on the particular issue are abstracted, and the discussion organized so that the cases are arranged to form a cohesive picture of the law. While it is rarely possible to reconcile all conflicting decisions, an annotation presents the decisions in a manner that permits a lawyer to compare their fact situations with his or her own. Do not use the text as persuasive authority. Think of the *ALR* annotation as a memo prepared by a research assistant. A great deal of drudgery has already been suffered by others so that the researcher does not have to redo it.

One reason that many people are intimidated by *ALR* is the fact that it has appeared in a variety of series. The series and their dates of publication are:

ALR (First Series)	1919 to 1948	175 volumes
ALR2d (Second Series)	1948 to 1965	100 volumes
ALR3d (Third Series)	1965 to 1980	100 volumes
ALR4th (Fourth Series)	1980 to 1992	90 volumes
ALR5th (Fifth Series)	1992 to date	Current
ALR Federal	1969 to date	Current

The first two series are so dated so as to be of little use. They are from a time when the annotations were shorter and less helpful, and the methods used to keep them current are primitive. Beginning with *ALR3d,* the publisher began to use pocket parts to keep the information up to date. *ALR Federal* represents a decision to put all federal cases in one set, and to treat only state court cases in the regular set. The fourth series of *ALR* was introduced without making significant changes or improvements to the set, but *ALR5th,* the series initiated in 1993, represents quite a change indeed.

Until *ALR5th,* the publisher represented *ALR* as a case reporter with attached annotations. The reporting of cases was so spotty, however, it could not be taken seriously as a case reporter. It had become a set driven by the content of the annotations. Recognizing this, *ALR5th* puts the cases in the back of the book and the annotations up front. Further, the editors now do a more thorough job of listing the sources consulted, including the LEXIS search that was most successful. These changes enhance *ALR* 's value as a research tool. The publisher has even gone back and compiled a separate volume of the best online searches for all the annotations in *ALR4th;* this volume is shelved with the set.

Lawyers Co-op also publishes *United States Reports, Lawyers' Edition,* a comprehensive collection of United States Supreme Court opinions discussed in Chapter Two. Each volume of the set includes a few annotations on specific legal issues addressed in some of that volume's Supreme Court cases.

b. Using ALR

As *ALR* has gone through its various series, it has produced a variety of finding aids. Among these are digests keyed to each series. The description of how each of these aids works can be found in the hard-cover edition of this text, *How to Find the Law.* The modern researcher only needs to know that the simplest way to find a relevant annotation by subject is to use the *ALR Index to Annotations.* This six-volume index covers the entire series except *ALR1st,* which has a separate index. The general index, most recently published in 1992, is kept up to date by pocket parts. A single volume, soft-cover *Quick Index* includes all major annotation references from *ALRD3d* to the present series.

The indexing style of *ALR* is quite different from the analytical set-up of the Key Number System. Some researchers find it to be quite accessible and easy to use, but others think it is obscure. Page through the index to get a feel for it, then try it for yourself.

Shepard's case citators, discussed in Chapter 3, indicate any time a case is either printed in *ALR* or mentioned in an *ALR* annotation. If the case is printed in full, the *ALR* citation is listed in parentheses as one of its parallel citations. If the case is cited or discussed in an annotation, the exact page in *ALR* is listed as citing reference. In either situation, a researcher Shepardizing a case and seeing an *ALR* citation has a good chance of finding several more related cases by examining the annotation. (Occasionally, of course, the citing annotation may turn out to be on a different point of law in the case than the one being researched.) As an essential step in the research process, Shepard's provides one of the quickest ways into *ALR*.[14]

The same kind of cross-referencing is provided by Auto-Cite, the case verification system on LEXIS, described in Chapter 3. Auto-Cite is produced by Lawyers Co-op, having started as an in-house citation system for *ALR* editors. Any time a case citation is verified on Auto-Cite, the case history is followed by a display of all *ALR* annotations citing the case or any other case listed in the history.

If one finds an Annotation that is on point, one must check to see if it has been superceded or supplemented by a subsequent Annotation. ALR will sometimes carry a series of Annotations on a topic as it develops, and the law can change quickly. The ALR system includes a unique way to check on the validity of an Annotation: "Annotation History Tables." One looks up the citation to one's Annotation in this table, and the citation to relevant new Annotations is provided. The main History Table appears at the end of the *Index to Annotations* volumes. It is supplemented in the pocket part that appears in the last index volume.

ALR is also available online as part of the LEXIS system. The full text can be searched for particular terms or phrases, although in many instances it is more effective to look for keywords only in the *titles* of annotations. Because the titles of *ALR* annotations are generally lengthy and descriptive, a title keyword search usually retrieves annotations on point. A full-text search, on the other hand, may turn up several annotations which focus on unrelated issues but include the keywords in describing the facts and holdings of the cases discussed. *ALR* can also be accessed via the online index.

American Law Reports is part of almost every law library, but is often underutilized. If the researcher can focus on what can and cannot be expected from an *ALR* annotation, the set has considerable value. When one finds an annotation on point, one has access to a tremendous

14. Annotation references in Shepard's citators for federal and regional reporters are also published separately in *Shepard's Citations for Annotations*, first published in 1989. This two-volume set duplicates the information found in the case citators, but may be handier if shelved next to *ALR*. A small section in volume two lists citations *to* annotations in court decisions.

amount of prepared research, full of useful cites and helpful leads. Do not neglect *ALR* 's power.

4. OTHER CASE–FINDING TOOLS

So far, this chapter has concentrated on materials such as digests and annotations which are designed expressly for the purpose of case finding. Because finding judicial decisions is a central part of most legal research, however, almost every research tool to be discussed in this book can serve as a case-finding tool to some extent. Other primary sources such as statutes include notes of relevant cases, to aid in interpreting and applying the terms of the primary source. Virtually every secondary source in law provides citations to cases, either to support the positions taken and the statements made in its text or to provide primary source references as part of its informational function.

These other research tools are discussed more fully in other chapters, but their importance as case finders should not be overlooked. For some research issues, digests, annotations, and computerized research are the most effective and valuable tools. For other problems, however, beginning with one of these other resources may save considerable time or may be the proper approach. To find United States Court of Appeals cases interpreting a Supreme Court holding, for example, one would use Shepard's instead of a digest or annotation. To find cases construing a legislative provision, one would turn first to an annotated code. Unfortunately, there is no simple, cut-and-dried case-finding technique that can be applied to every problem.

a. Shepard's Citations

As already discussed in Chapter 3, Shepard's case citators are used to verify the authority of a decision and to trace its subsequent judicial history and treatment. A Shepard's listing for a case also includes every subsequent published decision citing the case. Armed with one case on an issue, a researcher can usually use Shepard's to find more recent decisions on related matters. Whether a decision is cited by later courts depends on such factors as its weight as authority and the strength of its reasoning, and some published decisions may never be cited at all. Shepardizing most cases, however, provides a list of later decisions. These cases can then be examined for other authorities on which they rely, and Shepardized themselves to find still more recent cases.

As will be seen in subsequent chapters, Shepard's also publishes citators for various other legal materials, including statutes, court rules, and law review articles. Each of these citators includes references to cases discussing or mentioning the subject material. To find cases in *Shepard's Citations,* one thus does not even need to start with a case. A wide variety of primary and secondary legal authorities will do almost as well.

b. *Annotated Statutes*

Since many cases and many research problems involve the application or interpretation of statutes, the use of annotated statutory codes (to be discussed in the next chapter) is frequently the best initial case-finding approach for such problems. Following the text of each statutory section, an annotated code provides annotations containing headnote paragraphs from decisions which have applied or interpreted the section. These abstracts are composed like headnotes in West reporters; in the *United States Code Annotated* and the many state codes published by West, they are in fact identical to West's headnotes and digest entries. The annotations, like the statutes themselves, are updated regularly, usually in annual pocket parts and interim pamphlets.

Using an annotated code to find cases has the major advantage of saving research steps. In one resource are located the statutory text needed for the problem and the case abstracts in the annotations, as well as the other notes and cross-references which are usually provided in the codes.

c. *Words and Phrases*

Many cases turn on the definition or interpretation of a particular word or phrase, in a statute, a contract, or some other legal document. Case finding often involves the search for decisions containing such interpretations. To meet this need, West publishes *Words and Phrases,* a specialized digest of judicial definitions of legally significant words and phrases. *Words and Phrases* consists of ninety volumes of headnote abstracts drawn from West reporters and identical to the abstracts appearing in West digests and annotated codes. Here the abstracts are presented under the alphabetically arranged words and phrases which they define, interpret or construe. *Words and Phrases* covers all federal and state jurisdictions.

West also publishes, as part of each of its federal and state digests, a "Words and Phrases" table. These tables provide citations to cases but do not reprint headnotes. If the construction applied by a particular court is important, as it often is, the digest "Words and Phrases" may be the best place to look first. The encyclopedic *Words and Phrases* set is available for comprehensive research in all jurisdictions. In either event, the "words and phrases" approach is faster and more efficient than other tools if research concerns the judicial interpretation of a particular term. Both *Words and Phrases* and the tables in jurisdictional digests are supplemented by annual pocket parts and by tables appearing in the advance sheets and bound volumes of all West reporters.

d. *Encyclopedias and Treatises*

The two national legal encyclopedias, *Corpus Juris Secundum* and *American Jurisprudence 2d,* and the several state encyclopedias often serve as excellent and easily accessible case finders. Legal encyclopedias have two major functions: they explain and summarize basic legal doctrines, and they provide footnote citations to supporting primary authority. Even a researcher who does not need the overview provided by the text can use the footnotes to find relevant cases. Because encyclopedias are generally well-indexed and clearly written, appropriate sections are often easier to locate than they are in digests, and case citations thus easier to find.

Legal treatises perform functions similar to encyclopedias, but limit their focus to relatively specialized areas of legal doctrine. Their texts may be more interesting and opinionated than the impartial approaches taken in the encyclopedias, but like encyclopedias they use extensive footnotes to cases to support their propositions. A good treatise combines an informative text with convenient access to primary authorities. Legal encyclopedias, treatises, and the Restatements of the Law (which can also be used for finding cases) are discussed in Chapter 10.

e. Periodical Articles

Articles in legal periodicals, particularly those in academic law reviews, are often the single best place to begin researching a legal issue. A recent article on a specific topic will articulate the current status of legal doctrine, without requiring the reader to examine a pocket part or other supplement. In addition, most law review articles are packed with footnotes citing cases, statutes, regulations, other articles, and numerous other secondary sources. References to cases are usually, but not always, an important component of these footnotes. A law review article may distinguish relevant cases in far greater detail than a treatise would, with extensive quotations reprinted in the footnotes. Even law review articles that are barely readable are useful as research tools, since the footnotes should have been checked extensively for accuracy and relevance by long-suffering but ambitious law students working on the law review staff. Methods for finding relevant law review articles will be discussed in Chapter 10.

f. Looseleaf Services

One of the great research values of topical looseleaf services is their effectiveness in bringing together several forms of authority in one set of volumes, with prompt supplementation and integrated indexing approaches. For the subject it covers, a typical looseleaf provides the texts of statutes; judicial and administrative decisions, either full text or abstracted; administrative rules and regulations; and an explanatory discussion of legal developments. Many services also include a series of topical case reporter volumes, with its own set of finding aids. These finding aids, both in the looseleaf service and the reporter volumes, invariably include tables of cases and subject indexing, and sometimes also include case digests and citators. Because these finding tools are usually designed specifically for the subject field, they often provide the most efficient access to the subject covered. Looseleafs will be discussed further in Chapter 10.

C. ELECTRONIC CASE RETRIEVAL

Using printed digests and mastering the Key Number System was the dominant method for finding cases for one hundred years. But searching the massive body of American case law poses two problems that computer technology solves especially well. First, the sheer number of cases makes manipulating them in any print form a major challenge. Cases in electronic form, however, can be stored, moved, broken up, and re-assembled with great ease.

Second, paper publications impose inherent limitations upon systems built around them for sorting or finding cases. The cases are printed in one particular order, and various indexes and digests are developed to help the researcher find a specific case that meets his needs. As the body of cases becomes huge, these indexes and digests become more and more complex. Further, human editors make decisions about how to classify cases into the indexing or digesting scheme. The expertise and training of these human indexers can be of enormous help to the researcher, but the decisions that are made limit the information's accessibility. If an editor at West decides that a headnote of a case should be classified in a particular way, assigned to a particular Topic and Key Number, the case can only be found under that heading. No matter how good the indexer, the system is inherently rigid and limiting. The electronic availability of cases frees the researcher to search for words or phrases he or she thinks may appear in relevant cases. Search methods like Boolean searching and natural language queries, discussed below, allow the researcher to combine words in any number of ways to obtain a particular, complex research result that would not be possible with conventional print indexes and digests.

The problems for case retrieval posed by traditional paper publications were solved with the introduction of full-text, free-text searching in WESTLAW and LEXIS. Over the course of a generation, since LEXIS and WESTLAW became available in the 1970's, the use of full-text online systems became a viable, if not preferred, alternative for finding cases. Other forms of electronic publication also have arisen in the past decade. Most notable are the production of cases on compact disks, and the availability of the text of cases via the Internet. Doubtless, more innovations will follow.

1. WESTLAW AND LEXIS

Although LEXIS and WESTLAW offer far more than just cases, they began as case reporters and case finders, and still offer great case-finding power to the researcher. Both systems contain full texts of opinions from the federal courts and from all fifty states. Cases available online include not only those published in official reports and commercial reporters, but also "slip opinions" obtained from the courts and inaccessible through traditional printed resources. The decisions available for any particular jurisdiction are basically the same in either WESTLAW or

LEXIS, although one system may have more extensive retrospective coverage and one may have quicker access to recent opinions. The major difference in the cases appearing in the two systems is that LEXIS documents consist simply of opinions as received from the courts, while WESTLAW includes (for cases published in West reporters) the West synopses and headnotes, along with the corrected, enhanced text of the opinion.

Some aspects of computerized research have already been addressed. In Chapter 2, we discussed the extensive scope of online case databases and emphasized the speed with which new decisions are available electronically. In Chapter 3, we explained the case verification systems Insta–Cite (a component of WESTLAW) and Auto–Cite (available on LEXIS), as well as online access to *Shepard's Citations* through either system. In this section we discuss WESTLAW and LEXIS capabilities for case-finding.

a. Choosing a Database

The first decision an online researcher must make is the choice of *database* (or library and file, in LEXIS) in which to search. In both WESTLAW and LEXIS, one can search the decisions of a particular state or a particular court, or can use databases which combine the decisions either of all fifty states or of all federal courts. Whether to limit research to a particular jurisdiction depends on a variety of factors, such as the nature and purpose of the research, the amount of available time and money, and the value of precedent from other jurisdictions.

One of the more valuable aspects of online searching is that it allows the searcher to move beyond these sets of cases that have been prearranged by the publisher. In WESTLAW and LEXIS the researcher can create her own database or case reporter by using document *fields* (in WESTLAW) or *segments* (in LEXIS) in constructing a search. WESTLAW and LEXIS assign several tags, e.g. date of decision, judge who wrote the opinion, to each case loaded into their systems. A search request limited to a particular field or segment can retrieve, for example, all cases involving a specific corporation or decided after a certain date. It would be a lengthy and tedious process to find all opinions written by a particular judge using paper case reporters. Online databases can easily retrieve a complete list of a judge's opinions, and allow the researcher to combine that request with other search terms to find a judge's opinions on particular issues. In WESTLAW, one can use the "synopsis" and digest fields to search only for words appearing in the paragraphs added by West to summarize each case's facts and holding, and can thus retrieve a smaller body of cases more precisely on point. Each time a researcher searches, she is creating her own case reporter, built around her specific request.

The ability to assemble cases online in a virtually limitless number of ways is one of the major advantages electronic information has over paper case reports, which can only be collected in a set way. The smaller and more customized any system of data is, the easier it is to get good search results. The wise researcher uses as small a part of the data base as possible.

b. Boolean Searching

The advent of WESTLAW and LEXIS introduced a significant innovation for finding cases—Boolean searching capability. Boolean searching, named after the mathematician, Geoffrey Boole, allows one to search the database for any cases in which a certain word or words occur. By connecting terms with "and" and "or," one can get cases which include the terms in certain combinations. The use of proximity connectors allows the researcher to specify how close terms must be to each other. For example, one can retrieve all cases containing the words "damages" and "shrubbery," or all cases where those two words appear within five or ten words of each other. Instead of functioning as a simple concordance to every word in every opinion, the systems thus allow a unique and complex set of search criteria to be created for any research issue.

This ability to combine two or more search terms means that one can automatically limit retrieval to cases containing each of several essential elements, instead of scanning several columns or pages of a digest or an annotation for cases with particular facts. It also means that one can combine two concerns in a way not possible in most printed resources. An attorney working on the *Fisher v. Lowe* litigation, for example, might have to choose whether to research issues of tree damages or issues of no-fault insurance, since even a case directly on point would be indexed under one but not the other. Online, however, both issues can be combined in one search to retrieve any cases directly on point.

One of the biggest advantages of the WESTLAW system is that it includes the headnotes from the National Reporter System, and it allows the researcher to search by Topic and Key Numbers. This allows the researcher to combine word searches with Digest searching in an online environment. This is especially useful for researchers who are familiar with the Topic and Key Number System.

The specific methods of using Boolean searching in WESTLAW and LEXIS can best be learned through the extensive hands-on training programs and support materials developed by each system expressly for that purpose.[15] This section is not intended to teach computerized legal

15. The basic instructional materials for the two systems are *Discovering WESTLAW: The Essential Guide, 3d ed. (West, 1993)*; and *Learning LEXIS: A Handbook for Modern Legal Research* (Mead Data Central 1989). The first five chapters of William Harrington, *The Dow Jones–Irwin Lawyer's Guide to Online Data Bases* (Dow Jones–Irwin, 1987), provide an interesting and readable introduction to online research and a comparative explanation of searching procedures on both systems. Other useful references include Cary Griffith, *Griffith's Guide to Computer Assisted Legal Research*, (Anderson, 1992), Steven Emmanuel, *LEXIS for Law Students* (Emmanuel Law Outlines, 1994) and Christopher Wren & Jill Robinson Wren, *Using Computers in Legal Research: A Guide to*

research, but rather to caution the researcher that Boolean searching, despite its potential, is very difficult. For example, when framing a search request one must try to include any words or phrases that judges would use to express the concept. Because judges can be as idiosyncratic as they wish when writing opinions, it is often hard to anticipate what particular words will be used. Will a judge refer to a child as "child," "minor," "juvenile," "boy" or "girl," or by the child's proper name? There is no way to tell. For printed indexes and digests, an editor ensures that all references to a particular subject can be found in one place. A full-text database, which has no intervening editor, requires the user to search for all possible terms. Even WESTLAW, with its inclusion of the normalized language of the topic synopsis only goes so far in assisting the researcher.

The real lesson here is that one should never begin research in a subject by diving into a Boolean search. Just as it is disastrous to go into the Digest system cold, it is foolish to jump into a huge online database with an uninformed subject search. The art of framing successful search requests can be learned only through a familiarity both with the legal terminology of the subject area and the potentials of the computer system. Come to the Boolean search with jargon, specifics, and the ability to narrow the database as much as possible.

The online databases have grown so rich in content that intelligent searching is crucial. Moreover, since many LEXIS and WESTLAW users outside of the law school context pay according to use, the issue of cost must be considered. Due to financial constraints, researchers may be limited in how much they can use the systems, and must be conscious of costs incurred as research progresses. Learning Boolean searching skills while in law school, when searching is free to the student, is the best way for American lawyers to become proficient. Unfortunately, the fact that law students are not responsible for paying for the use of these systems sometimes leads to laziness and poor searching habits. Do not fall into this trap.

c. *WIN and Freestyle Searching*

WESTLAW introduced a major change in online searching when it introduced the WIN (WESTLAW is Natural) search engine. WIN allows the researcher to enter a natural language query into the system. The query is sorted by the computer for usable terms and run against the requisite database according to an algorithm which allows the system to determine relevancy. By allowing the user to type in a standard English sentence like, "What is the liability of companies that dispose of hazardous waste for accidents caused by natural disasters?" without Boolean connectors or special protocols, WIN enables even the most computer-phobic researcher to use the system. Cases are displayed in order of relevancy (as calculated by the computer), not by court hierarchy or by

LEXIS and WESTLAW (Adams & Ambrose 1994).

date. The relevance ranking algorithm thus introduces a new level of retrieval precision.

LEXIS has countered with its own natural language innovation, FREESTYLE, which permits the researcher to enter a search in plain English. Like WIN, this system is designed to offer ease of use and relevance functions.

Both WIN and FREESTYLE allow the knowledgeable user to tinker with the system, but each can be used easily by researchers with little preparation. Enhancements will continue to be added to these new and developing technologies. WIN and FREESTYLE will get better, and a whole new generation of search engines may be coming.

The vital point for the researcher to keep in mind is that just as the editors at West Publishing, or any other publisher of paper digests, intervene in the research process by editing, summarizing, and classifying information, search programs like WIN and FREESTYLE also intervene. Teams of programmers have created these electronic case-retrieval tools much in the same way as human editors create print tools. But WIN and FREESTYLE are only as good as their relevance ranking algorithms. Do not assume that because the operation is part of a computer program that it is any more valid or intelligent than a printed product. Recognize the limits that are built into them.

It is important to remember that computers can never eliminate one of the most important research steps, *reading* cases retrieved by either manual or electronic methods to determine their relevancy. One must read a case to analyze its reasoning and to ascertain the precedent on which it relies.

2. COMPACT DISK SYSTEMS

The CD–ROM, or compact disk, systems now on the market use a mix of search methods that are not unlike those discussed in connection with LEXIS and WESTLAW. Boolean searching, field limiters, and "intelligent" search engines similar to WIN and FREESTYLE will be found. The fact that data is stored locally on a compact disk makes no difference, except in cost, and the same critical criteria as to how useful the systems are should be used.

The cost element is not insignificant. When online with WESTLAW and LEXIS, one is often billed by time used, or library searched. This makes lean, well-planned searching essential. If one is using a locally stored compact disk system, no time-related charges are involved. Slower searches do not incur extra cost. This is not to say that sloppy searching is ever a good idea, but it does allow much more flexibility to the searcher who is not worried about the cost of the search.

Whether one is using an online system, a CD–ROM product or a data base on Internet, there are two questions that must be faced. One concerns the data. How extensive is the coverage? How reliable is the text? The second concerns the searching software. How does it work?

Is it easy to use? Does it sort through information that the searcher will never see? These critical standards will be crucial as more and more avenues for finding cases emerge.

D. SUMMARY

The enormous body of published decisions in American law is accessible through the varied research tools described in this chapter. Case digests, represented by the many units of the West Key-Number Digest system, can be used to find cases from any period or jurisdiction. Annotations gather cases on specific legal or factual issues. WESTLAW and LEXIS provide vast opportunities for creative and effective case research. Citators permit one to go straight from a single relevant case to other, more recent decisions. Annotated statutory codes are most useful for problems involving a statutory provision. *Words and Phrases* can be used when the search focuses on legally significant terminology. Encyclopedias and treatises provide case citations while summarizing and explaining the law. Periodical articles provide useful analyses as well as extensive references to various resources. Looseleafs focus on specific subjects and include information on any relevant developments, including cases.

The wise researcher learns all of these approaches, tests them, uses them, and develops individual preferences for particular types of problems. Flexibility, rather than rote application of a single procedure, is required for fully effective case research, since the creative use of several resources will often lead to the best and most thorough result.

Chapter 5

STATUTES

A. Introduction.
B. Pattern of Statutory Publication.
   1. Slip Laws.
   2. Session Laws.
   3. Statutory Compilations or Codes.
   4. Annotated Codes.
C. Federal Statutes.
   1. Slip Laws.
   2. Advance Session Law Services.
   3. *U.S. Statutes at Large.*
   4. Codification of Federal Statutes.
      a. *Revised Statutes.*
      b. *U.S. Code.*
      c. *U.S. Code Annotated.*
      d. *U.S. Code Service.*
   5. Electronic Sources.
D. Federal Statutory Research.
   1. Finding Statutes.
      a. Indexes.
      b. Tables.
   2. Updating Statutes.
      a. *USCA* and *USCS.*
      b. WESTLAW and LEXIS Databases.
   3. Interpreting Statutes.
      a. Judicial Decisions.
      b. Legislative History.
      c. Other Resources.
E. Other Forms of Federal Legislation.
   1. U.S. Constitution.
   2. Treaties.
   3. Interstate Compacts.
   4. Reorganization Plans.
F. State Statutes.
   1. Slip Laws and Session Laws.
   2. State Codes.
   3. Electronic Sources.
G. State Statutory Research
   1. Finding State Statutes.
   2. Updating and Interpreting State Statutes.
H. Uniform Laws and Model Acts.

A. INTRODUCTION

Statutes and other legislative forms constitute the second category of primary legal sources. Because of the focus on appellate decisions in American legal education, and on cases in the popular conception of the lawyer's work, the role of statute law in legal research tends to be underemphasized. In practice, however, statute law is central to many legal issues. Checking to see if there is a relevant statute is often the first step in approaching a research problem. Indeed, the vast majority of appellate decisions today involve the application or interpretation of statutes, rather than merely consideration of common law principles.[1]

The term "legislation" can be broadly construed to include constitutions, statutes, treaties, municipal charters and ordinances, interstate compacts, and reorganization plans. In this chapter, we focus on federal and state statute publications, although briefer discussions of the other types of legislation are included. Administrative regulations and court rules are considered "delegated legislation," but are treated separately in Chapters 8 and 9, respectively.

The federal nature of our government and legal system is important in understanding legislation. The U.S. Congress and the legislature of each of the fifty states has its own structure and procedure for the initiation and passage of legislation. Similarly, the forms of publication of statutory materials vary from jurisdiction to jurisdiction. These statutory publications, however, share some basic characteristics. By concentrating on the functional similarities of these sets, the researcher can know what to expect to find in any jurisdiction.

B. PATTERN OF STATUTORY PUBLICATION

Each of the jurisdictions in the United States issues its legislative publications according to a pattern. The names of the specific publications differ among the jurisdictions, but the generic equivalent always exists. The pattern of statutory publication is as follows:

Slip Laws
Session Laws
Code
Annotated Code

1. An interesting study of the impact on the courts of this growth of legislation is to be found in Professor Guido Calabresi's Oliver Wendell Holmes lectures, published as *A Common Law for the Age of Statutes* (Harvard University Press, 1982).

Although statutory research usually begins in an annotated code, an understanding of the earlier forms of the statute provides an essential background.

1. SLIP LAWS

"Slip laws" are separately issued pamphlets, each of which contains the text of a single legislative act. Typically, each is individually paginated, designated by a chapter or law number, and issued officially by the government. Most states do not distribute slip laws widely. Only larger research law libraries receive them. Many lawyers rarely see statutes in this initial form, but slip laws are usually the first official text of laws to be published. The federal government and a number of states post new legislative acts, in slip law form, on an electronic bulletin board accessible to the public through the Internet.

2. SESSION LAWS

The term "session laws" refers to the permanent publication, in chronological sequence, of the slip laws enacted during a legislative session. The federal government and each of the fifty states publish some form of session laws following the end of each legislative session. The session laws often come out quite slowly. Most jurisdictions also have commercial legislative publication services which provide more prompt access to new laws as they are enacted. These services, providing the texts of new laws in pamphlet form, are known as "advance session law services."

In most states, the session laws constitute the *positive law* form of legislation, *i.e.*, the authoritative, binding text of the laws, and the determinative version if questions arise from textual variations in subsequent printed versions. Other forms (such as codes) are only *prima facie* evidence of the statutory language, unless they have been designated as positive law by the legislature. Prima facie evidence means that the wording as found is presumptively valid, but can be disproven by reference to the positive law version if there is a discrepancy.

Session law publications have several common characteristics, including subject indexes for each volume and tables indicating which existing laws have been modified or repealed by newly enacted legislation. These indexes and tables cover only one year's worth of new legislation and do not cumulate. Session law volumes are important as archives of the positive law, but they are impractical as tools for most real research. Coming out so slowly they cannot be used for current research, lacking indexing beyond each individual year, they are severely limited for purposes of subject searching. Therefore another form of statute publication developed.

3. STATUTORY COMPILATIONS OR CODES

As used in this chapter, the term "code" refers to a publication of the public, general and permanent statutes of a jurisdiction in a fixed subject or topical arrangement. Statutory codes preserve the original language of the session laws more or less intact, but rearrange and group them under broad subject categories. This greatly enhances access to the text. In this process of rearranging the individual statutes, amendments are incorporated, repealed laws are deleted, and minor technical adjustments are sometimes made in the text of the laws to fit them into a functional and coherent compilation.

There is no universal subject arrangement into which statutes are organized. Jurisdictions vary considerably in the approach used. Some jurisdictions use a small number of very broad topics, others use a large number of very specific ones. It is a matter of judgment. Since the law, and the areas that it covers, change so rapidly, one might assume that jurisdictions would re-arrange the topical breakdown of codes fairly frequently. Such is not the case. Recodifying is laborious and fraught with pitfalls. In the course of re-arranging the laws there is the potential for much political wrangling as well as substantial intellectual challenges. It is more likely for a jurisdiction to issue or approve a code and then leave it untouched for years. Newly enacted statutes are just dropped into the code. Often it is left to commercial publishers to keep the code up-to-date. Sometimes such publishers even update the subject arrangements.

Statutory codes may appear in either official or unofficial editions. Official statutory codes are published or sanctioned by the government. They normally include the text of the law and brief editorial notes as to the authority and historical development of the law. Law students often encounter unofficial statutory codes, perhaps in the form of one title of a state or federal code, printed and sold as a study aid.

Despite their convenience in providing subject access, official codes have certain shortcomings. Like other official publications such as judicial reports, they are often issued very slowly. More important, their limited editorial notes are simply not adequate for most statutory research. They do not provide citations to judicial interpretations of a statute, which are important extrinsic aids in determining its meaning or legislative intent. The researcher must turn to the unofficial, annotated codes for access to this type of material.

4. ANNOTATED CODES

An annotated code reproduces the text and arrangement of the official code. It also incorporates new legislation, revisions and amendments within that structure, and deletes repealed laws. Its unique contribution to legal research is the inclusion of *annotations* after each statutory section. These include references to relevant judicial or administrative decisions, administrative code sections, encyclopedias, attorney general opinions, legislative history materials, law reviews, and treatises.

The annotated code provides more than just case *citations*. A brief abstract of each cited opinion is provided. These brief editorial descriptions allow researchers to browse the annotations to find relevant cases. Since some statutory sections have been construed in thousands of court cases, this can be an enormous time-saver.

Annotated codes play other important roles in research. They provide citations to relevant administrative rules, form books, law review articles and other sources. An annotated code will refer the researcher to other elements of the research system developed by its publisher. This will include references to relevant Topics and Key Numbers in annotated codes produced by West, and references to the Total Client Service Library in annotated codes produced by Lawyer's-Co-op. Even smaller publishers will provide cross-references. These features make the annotated code a truly integrated research tool, pulling together a variety of primary and secondary source material.

Another advantage of annotated codes is more frequent supplementation by means of pocket parts and pamphlet supplements. These features of the commercial annotated codes make them the most effective source for updating most statutory material.

A final feature of annotated codes is good indexing. Most annotated codes feature good general indexes at the end of the set. These indexes feature entries that consist of words and phrases drawn from common usage. They are often more intuitive and easy to use than the jargon driven indexes and digests built around cases. Since annotated codes do supply citations to cases, this feature can make them a good place to start a search for relevant cases.

C. FEDERAL STATUTES

The Congress passes several forms of legislative enactment. This section will concentrate on acts and joint resolutions, which are the basic forms of legislation.

Each new act is designated either as a "public law" or a "private law." Usually, private laws are passed for the specific benefit of an individual or a small group of individuals, whereas public laws are intended to be of general application.[2] The two categories are numbered, as enacted, in separate series. Although private laws are issued in a slip law form and appear in the federal session law publication (the *Statutes at Large*), most of the other publications discussed in this chapter contain only public laws.

1. SLIP LAWS

The first official form of publication of a federal law is the *slip law,* a separately paginated pamphlet text of each law, with no internal indexing. Each new act is designated by a public law number, e.g., Public

2. In this century most private laws concern special relief for individuals under the immigration laws. For more on this distinction, see Note, "Private Bills in Congress," 79 *Harv.L.Rev.* 1684 (1966).

Law 92–195. The first part of the number represents the number of the Congress which enacted the law (in this case, the 92d Congress) and the second part of the number indicates the chronological sequence of its enactment (the 195th public law enacted by that Congress).

The form of the printing is almost identical to that which appears in the *Statutes at Large,* and in recent years both the slip law and *Statutes at Large* publication include a brief summary of each law's legislative history following the text. Illustration A shows the first page of PL 92–195, as it "appears" in its *Statutes at Large* form.

The slip law is the first authoritative official text of the statute and is rebuttable as evidence of the law only by reference to the enrolled Act. When the *Statutes at Large* are published, they supersede the slip law as authority.

Slip laws are distributed rather slowly. For those with access to Internet they are available on several federal electronic bulletin boards. For a printed form of the text of recently enacted federal statutes, most researchers rely on one of the commercial services to be described next.

2. ADVANCE SESSION LAW SERVICES

The two commercial general advance session law services for federal statutes are West Publishing Company's *United States Code Congressional and Administrative News* (cited as *U.S.C.C.A.N.*) and Lawyers Co-operative Publishing Company's *Advance* pamphlets to the *United States Code Service* (*USCS*).[3] Both services issue monthly pamphlets, generally publishing new federal statutes within a month or two of enactment. In both *USCCAN* and *USCS Advance,* each page of statutory text indicates the location at which it will eventually appear upon publication in the official *Statutes at Large.*

In addition to the text of newly enacted public laws, each service publishes Presidential proclamations, executive orders, amendments to court rules, and selected administrative regulations. Both services include in their pamphlets a cumulative index and various tables that aid in locating the sections of the Code which have been affected by recent legislative, executive, or administrative action.

Advance pamphlets are designed only for temporary use, until the new material has been incorporated into *USCS,* while *USCCAN* pamphlets are cumulated at the end of each year into bound volumes. Chapter 6 will discuss how *USCCAN* when bound can aid in legislative history.

Much more timely ways to gain access to information on newly enacted federal statutes will be discussed in Section 5 below when electronic sources are discussed.

3. The *United States Code Service* is discussed below in Section C.4.b.

Illustration A

The first page of a law in the *U.S. Statutes at Large*, in a format similar to the slip law

85 STAT.] PUBLIC LAW 92-195–DEC. 15, 1971 649

Public Law 92-195

AN ACT

December 15, 1971 [S. 1116]

To require the protection, management, and control of wild free-roaming horses and burros on public lands.

Be it enacted by the Senate and House of Representatives of the United States of America in Congress assembled, That Congress finds and declares that wild free-roaming horses and burros are living symbols of the historic and pioneer spirit of the West; that they contribute to the diversity of life forms within the Nation and enrich the lives of the American people; and that these horses and burros are fast disappearing from the American scene. It is the policy of Congress that wild free-roaming horses and burros shall be protected from capture, branding, harassment, or death; and to accomplish this they are to be considered in the area where presently found, as an integral part of the natural system of the public lands.

Wild horses and burros. Protection.

SEC. 2. As used in this Act—

Definitions.

(a) "Secretary" means the Secretary of the Interior when used in connection with public lands administered by him through the Bureau of Land Management and the Secretary of Agriculture in connection with public lands administered by him through the Forest Service;

(b) "wild free-roaming horses and burros" means all unbranded and unclaimed horses and burros on public lands of the United States;

(c) "range" means the amount of land necessary to sustain an existing herd or herds of wild free-roaming horses and burros, which does not exceed their known territorial limits, and which is devoted principally but not necessarily exclusively to their welfare in keeping with the multiple-use management concept for the public lands;

(d) "herd" means one or more stallions and his mares; and

(e) "public lands" means any lands administered by the Secretary of the Interior through the Bureau of Land Management or by the Secretary of Agriculture through the Forest Service.

SEC. 3. (a) All wild free-roaming horses and burros are hereby declared to be under the jurisdiction of the Secretary for the purpose of management and protection in accordance with the provisions of this Act. The Secretary is authorized and directed to protect and manage wild free-roaming horses and burros as components of the public lands, and he may designate and maintain specific ranges on public lands as sanctuaries for their protection and preservation, where the Secretary after consultation with the wildlife agency of the State wherein any such range is proposed and with the Advisory Board established in section 7 of this Act deems such action desirable. The Secretary shall manage wild free-roaming horses and burros in a manner that is designed to achieve and maintain a thriving natural ecological balance on the public lands. He shall consider the recommendations of qualified scientists in the field of biology and ecology, some of whom shall be independent of both Federal and State agencies and may include members of the Advisory Board established in section 7 of this Act. All management activities shall be at the minimal feasible level and shall be carried out in consultation with the wildlife agency of the State wherein such lands are located in order to protect the natural ecological balance of all wildlife species which inhabit such lands, particularly endangered wildlife species. Any adjustments in forage allocations on any such lands shall take into consideration the needs of other wildlife species which inhabit such lands.

Jurisdiction; management.

3. U.S. STATUTES AT LARGE

The official, permanent session law publication for federal laws is the *United States Statutes at Large* (cited as Stat.). At the end of each annual session of Congress, the enacted public and private laws are cumulated and published in chronological order as the *Statutes at Large* for that session, along with concurrent resolutions, Presidential proclamations, and reorganization plans. In recent years, each session's compilation has comprised up to six volumes (referred to as parts); the several parts for each session bear one volume number.

A federal session law is properly cited by its Public Law number and the volume and page in which it appears in *Statutes at Large*.[4] But variations may occur. A newly enacted law may be referred to only by its Public Law number. On other occasions the name by which the Act was titled in *Statutes at Large* will be used. This can range from very well known statutes like Title IX to rather obscure ones like the Wild Burros Act. To help find a statute when one has only a name, one can consult the popular name tables that will be part of the sets discussed in subsequent sections.

The first eight volumes of the *Statutes at Large* cover legislation from 1779 to 1845. From that point the set moves forward in smaller time increments. The period of time covered in each volume varied until Volume 50 (1938) when the current pattern of one set of Statutes at Large volumes for each session of Congress began. Through volume 64 (1950–51), the full texts of newly approved treaties were also included in each volume, but that practice was discontinued when a separate series, *U.S. Treaties and Other International Agreements,* was begun in 1950.

Although the publication of current volumes of the *Statutes at Large* is slow, lagging one to two years behind the end of the session covered, they are the authoritative text of federal statutes, superseding the slip laws. The *Statutes at Large* is the positive law form of statutes, and "legal evidence of laws . . . in all the Courts of the United States."[5] The *United States Code* is only *prima facie* evidence of the laws, except for those of its titles which have been reenacted by Congress as positive law.[6]

Indexes by subject and individuals' names appear at the back of each part of a *Statutes at Large* volume.[7] These indexes facilitate access to each volume, but access to individual volumes is inadequate for most research. One cannot effectively search each session laws volume for statutes on a specific issue, and then analyze successive amendments and repeals in order to determine what laws are currently in force. Effective statutory research depends on the use of the codified versions of federal laws.

4. Session laws before 1957 are designated by chapter numbers, not Public Law numbers. Public Law numbers have been assigned to Acts of Congress since 1901, but chapter numbers remained the traditional and primary means of identification until they were discontinued at the end of the 1956 session.

5. 1 U.S.C. § 112 (1988).

6. 1 U.S.C. § 204 (1988).

7. Volumes 71 (1957) to 90 (1976) also included tables indicating which existing laws had been modified or repealed by laws published in each volume. This feature, useful for current awareness but of limited historical value, was discontinued in 1977.

4. CODIFICATION OF FEDERAL STATUTES

The most useful publications of federal laws are not those published chronologically, but those that are arranged by subject. The most important of these is the current *United States Code* in its various editions, but one earlier codification which remains a source of positive law must first be discussed.

a. Revised Statutes

There are two sets, largely of historical interest, but still valid, which are the foundation of modern federal statute law. The *Revised Statutes of the United States, Passed at the First Session of the Forty-Third Congress, 1873–'74; Embracing the Statutes of the United States, General and Permanent in Their Nature, in Force on [December 1, 1873]* ... and the *Revised Statutes* of 1876. The first represents an attempt to pass a codification of all federal statute law in the form of one statement of positive law. The whole thing was enacted as one bill. It was to be the definitive statement of all general statutes that were in force. Because of errors and disputes, in the 1873 version, the *Revised Statutes* of 1876 was passed. It redid the job, but this time it was passed as a prima facie codification. This experience was so traumatic, it took 50 years for another codification effort to be undertaken.

b. U.S. Code

After much legislative travail, a new codification effort was approved on June 30, 1926, and published as 44 Stat. Part 1 under the title: *The Code of the Laws of the United States of America of a General and Permanent Nature, in Force December 7, 1925* ... It has since been known as the *United States Code.*

Unlike the *Revised Statutes,* the new Code was not a positive law reenactment and did not repeal the prior *Statutes at Large.* It was *prima facie* evidence of the law, rebuttable by reference to the *Statutes at Large.* However, Congress subsequently began revising the titles of the Code and reenacting each into positive law as the revision is completed. So far, over forty per cent of the titles have been so reenacted, and are now legal evidence; for the rest, the *Statutes at Large* remains legal evidence and the Code is *prima facie* evidence. A list of titles at the beginning of each *U.S. Code* volume indicates which have been reenacted as positive law.[8]

The *U.S. Code* is arranged in fifty subjects, each known as a Title, and generally in alphabetical order. The breakdown of fifty subjects for

8. The distinction between titles which are positive law and titles which are *prima facie* evidence is only rarely a matter of concern, since the code text is taken from the original language of the enactment. Certain changes in form or numbering may occur in order to fit the text into the existing code framework, but these variations are not substantive. Occasional errors have been made, however, so the distinction is of potential legal effect. *See, e.g., United States Nat'l Bank v. Independent Ins. Agents, Inc.* 113 S.Ct. 2173 (1993); *Stephan v. United States,* 319 U.S. 423 (1943); *Five Flags Pipeline Co. v. Department of Transp.,* 854 F.2d 1438 (D.C.Cir.1988); *Royer's, Inc. v. United States,* 265 F.2d 615 (3d Cir.1959).

organizing federal law was created in 1926 and has not been changed since, even though some topics, like Title 34 (Navy), are now empty. This illustrates both how rare a re-arrangement of topics is and how innately conservative legal publishing tends to be.

Titles are divided into chapters and then into sections, with a continuous sequence of section numbers for each title. Citations to the Code indicate the title and section numbers, and the year of publication, e.g., 16 U.S.C. § 1311 (1988).

Following each statutory section in the *U.S. Code,* there is a parenthetical reference to its source in the *Statutes at Large,* including sources for any amendments. This reference enables one to locate the original text, which may be the positive law form, and from there to find legislative history documents relating to the law's enactment. The *Code* also includes historical notes and cross-references to related sections. Illustration B shows the *U.S. Code* page on which the codified form of PL 92–195, the Wild Burros Protection Act, shown in Illustration A begins.

The *U.S. Code* is reissued in a new edition every six years, and updated between editions by annual bound supplements. Each year's supplement incorporates material in preceding supplements, so that only the latest one need be consulted for changes since the last revision. Both *Code* and supplement are multivolume works. The 1988 edition consists of twenty-eight volumes, and its *Supplement V* fills eight volumes.

The *U.S. Code* features a number of useful research aids. These include an extensive general index, filling seven volumes in the 1988 *Code* edition, and several tables, such as a popular name table and various parallel reference tables. These features are discussed in greater detail in Section D.1, below.

The *U.S. Code* is a well-prepared and effective research tool, accompanied by thorough indexing and helpful tables. Its publication is not as tardy as some other government publications, but its latest volumes still are generally eight months to two years out of date. It also lacks citations to relevant cases. Such cases can explain the meaning of a statute, or even invalidate it. For more current coverage as well as for the notation of relevant cases it is necessary to use one of the commercial annotated editions of the Code.

Illustration B

Pages from the *United States Code*, 1988 edition

§ 1309 TITLE 16—CONSERVATION Page 1250

(Pub. L. 91-559, § 9, Dec. 19, 1970, 84 Stat. 1471.)

REFERENCES IN TEXT

The civil service laws, referred to in text, are set forth in Title 5, Government Organization and Employees. See, particularly, section 3301 et seq. of Title 5.

TERMINATION OF ADVISORY BOARDS

Advisory boards in existence on Jan. 5, 1973, to terminate not later than the expiration of the 2-year period following Jan. 5, 1973, unless, in the case of a board established by the President or an officer of the Federal Government, such board is renewed by appropriate action prior to the expiration of such 2-year period, or in the case of a board established by the Congress, its duration is otherwise provided by law. See sections 3(2) and 14 of Pub. L. 92-463, Oct. 6, 1972, 86 Stat. 770, 776, set out in the Appendix to Title 5, Government Organization and Employees.

§ 1309. Consultation with Secretary of the Interior; conformity of program with wetlands programs administered by Secretary of the Interior; consultation with and utilization of technical services of appropriate local, State, Federal, and private conservation agencies; coordination of programs

The Secretary shall consult with the Secretary of the Interior and take appropriate measures to insure that the program carried out pursuant to this chapter is in harmony with wetlands programs administered by the Secretary of the Interior. He shall also, insofar as practicable, consult with and utilize the technical and related services of appropriate local, State, Federal, and private conservation agencies to assure coordination of the program with programs of such agencies and a solid technical foundation for the program.

(Pub. L. 91-559, § 10, Dec. 19, 1970, 84 Stat. 1471.)

§ 1310. Authorization of appropriations; maximum amount of payments pursuant to agreements

There are hereby authorized to be appropriated without fiscal year limitation, such sums as may be necessary to carry out the program authorized by this chapter. In carrying out the program, in each fiscal year through the fiscal year ending September 30, 1980, the Secretary shall not enter into agreements with owners and operators which would require payments to owners or operators in any calendar year under such agreements in excess of $10,000,000. In carrying out the program, in each fiscal year after the fiscal year ending September 30, 1980, the Secretary shall not enter into agreements with owners and operators which would require payments to owners or operators in any calendar year under such agreements in excess of $30,000,000. Not more than 15 percent of the funds authorized to be appropriated in any fiscal year after the fiscal year ending September 30, 1980, may be used for agreements entered into with owners or operators in any one State.

(Pub. L. 91-559, § 11, Dec. 19, 1970, 84 Stat. 1471; Pub. L. 96-182, § 4, Jan. 2, 1980, 93 Stat. 1317.)

AMENDMENTS

1980—Pub. L. 96-182 limited restrictions on Secretary's authority to enter into agreements in excess of $10,000,000 to each fiscal year through fiscal year ending Sept. 30, 1980, and inserted restrictions relating to agreements in excess of $30,000,000 for each fiscal year after fiscal year ending Sept. 30, 1980, and that not more than 15 percent of the funds authorized to be appropriated in any fiscal year after fiscal year ending Sept. 30, 1980, may be used for agreements entered into with owners or operators in any one State.

§ 1311. Rules and regulations

The Secretary shall prescribe such regulations as he determines necessary and desirable to carry out the provisions of this chapter.

(Pub. L. 91-559, § 12, Dec. 19, 1970, 84 Stat. 1471.)

CHAPTER 30—WILD HORSES AND BURROS: PROTECTION, MANAGEMENT, AND CONTROL

CHAPTER REFERRED TO IN OTHER SECTIONS

This chapter is referred to in title 43 section 1901.

§ 1331. Congressional findings and declaration of policy

Congress finds and declares that wild free-roaming horses and burros are living symbols of the historic and pioneer spirit of the West; that they contribute to the diversity of life forms within the Nation and enrich the lives of the American people; and that these horses and burros are fast disappearing from the American scene. It is the policy of Congress that wild free-roaming horses and burros shall be protected from capture, branding, harassment, or

[G20,010]

death; and to accomplish this they are to be considered in the area where presently found, as an integral part of the natural system of the public lands.

(Pub. L. 92-195, § 1, Dec. 15, 1971, 85 Stat. 649.)

SHORT TITLE

Pub. L. 92-195, Dec. 15, 1971, 85 Stat. 649, which enacted this chapter, is popularly known as the "Wild Free-Roaming Horses and Burros Act".

§ 1332. Definitions

As used in this chapter—

(a) "Secretary" means the Secretary of the Interior when used in connection with public lands administered by him through the Bureau of Land Management and the Secretary of Agriculture in connection with public lands administered by him through the Forest Service;

(b) "wild free-roaming horses and burros" means all unbranded and unclaimed horses and burros on public lands of the United States;

(c) "range" means the amount of land necessary to sustain an existing herd or herds of wild free-roaming horses and burros, which does not exceed their known territorial limits, and which is devoted principally but not necessarily exclusively to their welfare in keeping with the multiple-use management concept for the public lands;

(d) "herd" means one or more stallions and his mares; and

(e) "public lands" means any lands administered by the Secretary of the Interior through the Bureau of Land Management or by the Secretary of Agriculture through the Forest Service.

(f) "excess animals" means wild free-roaming horses or burros (1) which have been removed from an area by the Secretary pursuant to applicable law or, (2) which must be removed from an area in order to preserve and maintain a thriving natural ecological balance and multiple-use relationship in that area.

(Pub. L. 92-195, § 2, Dec. 15, 1971, 85 Stat. 649; Pub. L. 95-514, § 14(b), Oct. 25, 1978, 92 Stat. 1810.)

AMENDMENTS

1978—Subsec. (f). Pub. L. 95-514 added subsec. (f).

§ 1333. Powers and duties of Secretary

(a) Jurisdiction; management; ranges; ecological balance objectives; scientific recommendations; forage allocation adjustments

All wild free-roaming horses and burros are hereby declared to be under the jurisdiction of the Secretary for the purpose of management and protection in accordance with the provisions of this chapter. The Secretary is authorized and directed to protect and manage wild free-roaming horses and burros as components of the public lands, and he may designate and maintain specific ranges on public lands as sanctuaries for their protection and preservation, where the Secretary after consultation with the wildlife agency of the State wherein any such range is proposed and with the Advisory Board established in section 1337 of this title deems such action desirable. The Secretary shall manage wild free-roaming horses and burros in a manner that is designed to achieve and maintain a thriving natural ecological balance on the public lands. He shall consider the recommendations of qualified scientists in the field of biology and ecology, some of whom shall be independent of both Federal and State agencies and may include members of the Advisory Board established in section 1337 of this title. All management activities shall be at the minimal feasible level and shall be carried out in consultation with the wildlife agency of the State wherein such lands are located in order to protect the natural ecological balance of all wildlife species which inhabit such lands, particularly endangered wildlife species. Any adjustments in forage allocations on any such lands shall take into consideration the needs of other wildlife species which inhabit such lands.

(b) Inventory and determinations; consultation; overpopulation; research study: submittal to Congress

(1) The Secretary shall maintain a current inventory of wild free-roaming horses and burros on given areas of the public lands. The purpose of such inventory shall be to: make determinations as to whether and where an overpopulation exists and whether action should be taken to remove excess animals; determine appropriate management levels of wild free-roaming horses and burros on these areas of the public lands; and determine whether appropriate management levels should be achieved by the removal or destruction of excess animals, or other options (such as sterilization, or natural controls on population levels). In making such determinations the Secretary shall consult with the United States Fish and Wildlife Service, wildlife agencies of the State or States wherein wild free-roaming horses and burros are located, such individuals independent of Federal and State government as have been recommended by the National Academy of Sciences, and such other individuals whom he determines have scientific expertise and special knowledge of wild horse and burro protection, wildlife management and animal husbandry as related to rangeland management.

(2) Where the Secretary determines on the basis of (i) the current inventory of lands within his jurisdiction; (ii) information contained in any land use planning completed pursuant to section 1712 of title 43; (iii) information contained in court ordered environmental impact statements as defined in section 1902 of title 43; and (iv) such additional information as becomes available to him from time to time, including that information developed in the research study mandated by this section, or in the absence of the information contained in (i-iv) above on the basis of all information currently available to him, that an overpopulation exists on a given area of the public lands and that action is necessary to remove excess animals, he shall immediately remove excess animals from the range so as to achieve appropriate management levels. Such action shall be taken, in the following order and priority, until

§ 1333 TITLE 16—CONSERVATION Page 1252

all excess animals have been removed so as to restore a thriving natural ecological balance to the range, and protect the range from the deterioration associated with overpopulation:

(A) The Secretary shall order old, sick, or lame animals to be destroyed in the most humane manner possible;

(B) The Secretary shall cause such number of additional excess wild free-roaming horses and burros to be humanely captured and removed for private maintenance and care for which he determines an adoption demand exists by qualified individuals, and for which he determines he can assure humane treatment and care (including proper transportation, feeding, and handling): *Provided*, That, not more than four animals may be adopted per year by any individual unless the Secretary determines in writing that such individual is capable of humanely caring for more than four animals, including the transportation of such animals by the adopting party; and

(C) The Secretary shall cause additional excess wild free-roaming horses and burros for which an adoption demand by qualified individuals does not exist to be destroyed in the most humane and cost efficient manner possible.

(3) For the purpose of furthering knowledge of wild horse and burro population dynamics and their interrelationship with wildlife, forage and water resources, and assisting him in making his determination as to what constitutes excess animals, the Secretary shall contract for a research study of such animals with such individuals independent of Federal and State government as may be recommended by the National Academy of Sciences for having scientific expertise and special knowledge of wild horse and burro protection, wildlife management and animal husbandry as related to rangeland management. The terms and outline of such research study shall be determined by a research design panel to be appointed by the President of the National Academy of Sciences. Such study shall be completed and submitted by the Secretary to the Senate and House of Representatives on or before January 1, 1983.

(c) Title of transferee to limited number of excess animals adopted for requisite period

Where excess animals have been transferred to a qualified individual for adoption and private maintenance pursuant to this chapter and the Secretary determines that such individual has provided humane conditions, treatment and care for such animal or animals for a period of one year, the Secretary is authorized upon application by the transferee to grant title to not more than four animals to the transferee at the end of the one-year period.

(d) Loss of status as wild free-roaming horses and burros; exclusion from coverage

Wild free-roaming horses and burros or their remains shall lose their status as wild free-roaming horses or burros and shall no longer be considered as falling within the purview of this chapter—

(1) upon passage of title pursuant to subsection (c) of this section except for the limitation of subsection (c)(1) of this section; or

(2) if they have been transferred for private maintenance or adoption pursuant to this chapter and die of natural causes before passage of title; or

(3) upon destruction by the Secretary or his designee pursuant to subsection (b) of this section; or

(4) if they die of natural causes on the public lands or on private lands where maintained thereon pursuant to section 1334 of this title and disposal is authorized by the Secretary or his designee; or

(5) upon destruction or death for purposes of or incident to the program authorized in this section; *Provided*, That no wild free-roaming horse or burro or its remains may be sold or transferred for consideration for processing into commercial products.

(Pub. L. 92–195, § 3, Dec. 15, 1971, 85 Stat. 649; Pub. L. 95–514, § 14(a), Oct. 25, 1978, 92 Stat. 1808.)

References in Text

Section 1902 of title 43, referred to in subsec. (b)(2), was in the original "section 2 of the Public Range Lands Improvement Act of 1978" (classified to 43 U.S.C. 1901) and was changed to reflect the probable intent of Congress.

Amendments

1978—Subsec. (b). Pub. L. 95–514 substituted provisions for: maintaining current inventory of wild free-roaming horses and burros; listing the purpose of the inventory and determinations to be made in consultation with persons of scientific expertise and special knowledge; immediate removal of excess animals from the range on the basis of information from various sources so as to achieve appropriate management levels; order and priority of removal; and research study to be reported to Congress for prior authorization of humane destruction of old, sick, or lame animals and capture and removal of additional excess animals for private maintenance under humane conditions and care, now incorporated in subsec. (b)(2)(A) and (B).

Subsec. (c). Pub. L. 95–514 substituted provision for grant of title to limited number of excess animals adopted for requisite period for prior authorization of humane destruction of wild free-roaming horses and burros as an act of mercy or to prevent overpopulation only when necessary to preserve and maintain the habitat in a suitable condition for continued use.

Subsec. (d). Pub. L. 95–514 substituted provisions relating to circumstances and conditions operating to take wild free-roaming horses and burros or their remains from the purview of this chapter for prior declaration that nothing in the chapter shall preclude the customary disposal of the remains of a deceased wild free-roaming horse or burro, including those in the authorized possession of private parties, and prohibition of sale for any consideration, directly or indirectly, of the remains, or any part thereof, now incorporated in cl. (5).

Termination of Advisory Boards

Advisory boards in existence on Jan. 5, 1973, to terminate not later than the expiration of the 2-year period following Jan. 5, 1973, unless, in the case of a board established by the President or an officer of the Federal Government, such board is renewed by appropriate action prior to the expiration of such 2-year period, or in the case of a board established by the

[G20,012]

c. *U.S. Code Annotated*

In 1927, the West Publishing Company began publication of an unofficial, annotated edition of the U.S. Code, entitled *United States Code Annotated* (cited as *U.S.C.A.*). This edition retains the text and organization of the *U.S.C.*, employing identical title and section numbers. In addition to providing the same research aids found in the official *Code,* such as authority references, historical notes, cross references, tables, and indexes, *USCA* offers three major advantages for researchers: it includes abstracts of judicial decisions, it provides references to secondary sources that aid in the interpretation of Code sections, and it is updated on a more frequent basis.

After each section of the Code, *USCA* cites the *Statutes at Large* origin of the text, and includes several editorial features. Where relevant, it provides references to such sources as the *Code of Federal Regulations* and legislative history materials in *U.S. Code Congressional and Administrative News* (*USCCAN*). An annotation section labeled "Library References" contains citations to West's American Digest System topics and key numbers, to the legal encyclopedia, *Corpus Juris Secundum,* and to West treatises on the statutory subject.

Following each Code section which has been interpreted or applied judicially, *USCA* provides "Notes of Decisions," consisting of abstracts of judicial decisions that have considered the particular section. These annotations are usually preceded by an alphabetical subject index, which assists in locating decisions on particular aspects of the statutory section. Because judicial interpretations are a vital part of reading and understanding statutes, these case abstracts are the most important aspect of an annotated code. They also take a great deal of space, causing the *USCA* version of the Code to occupy well over 200 volumes. Illustrations C–1 and C–2 show a code section as printed in *USCA,* followed by various research aids and notes of decisions. Note in Illustration C–2 that the chapter was held unconstitutional in a U.S. District Court decision, which was reversed by the Supreme Court.

USCA provides extensive annotations of judicial decisions not only for the fifty titles of the *U.S. Code*, but also for the provisions of the U.S. Constitution and for several major sets of court rules, such as the Federal Rules of Civil Procedure (in several volumes following Title 28) and the Federal Rules of Criminal Procedure (in several volumes following Title 18).

Access to *USCA* is provided by a multivolume general index for the entire set and individual indexes for each title. Indexes to individual titles are not updated until a volume is revised and replaced, but a new edition of the general index is issued each year in softcover volumes. The set also contains many of the same tables published in the *U.S. Code,* which are discussed below in Section D.1.b.

USCA is far more current than the official edition, and is kept up to date by several forms of supplementation. The most basic of these is the annual cumulative pocket part, which is inserted in the back of each volume and indicates any changes in the statutory text, additional annotations to judicial decisions, and later notes and references to other sources. For some volumes, a separate, cumulative softcover pamphlet, also issued annually, takes the place of the pocket part. A list in the front of each pocket part or pamphlet indicates the cut-off point for coverage of decisions from the various reporter series. Illustration C–3 shows a page from a *USCA* pocket part, providing updated coverage of cases and other materials related to the statute.

Unlike official *U.S. Code* volumes, which are replaced every six years, *USCA* volumes are generally replaced when the supplementation becomes unwieldy. Several new volumes are published each year, but parts of the set are several decades old. Every volume is up to date, though, since new statutes, amendments, and annotations are printed in its current pocket part or supplementary pamphlet. Every time a *USCA* volume is used, its supplementation *must* be checked for more recent developments.

Between annual pocket parts, other forms of supplementation are used. Legislative and judicial developments are noted in quarterly pamphlets that update the whole set. Each pamphlet is arranged by Code section, and contains both the text of new laws and notes of recent decisions. The public laws printed in each pamphlet are listed on the front cover and spine, and the reporter volumes covered are listed in a table at the front of the pamphlet. Because they are not cumulative, it is important to remember to check all available interim pamphlets.

West Publishing further updates these quarterly pamphlets in two ways. During each legislative session, the monthly advance pamphlets of *USCCAN* contain the text of newly enacted statutes in chronological order, and provide parallel tables indicating the Code sections affected by the new laws. The table entitled, "U.S. Code and U.S. Code Annotated, Sections Amended, Repealed, New, Etc.," should be checked to determine whether a statute's status has changed since the last *USCA* pamphlet.

d. *U.S. Code Service*

The second unofficial annotated federal code publication is the *United States Code Service* (cited as *U.S.C.S.*), published by Lawyers Co-operative Publishing Company. *USCS* maintains the original title and section numbering of the *U.S. Code,* but there is some variation in the text. *USCS* preserves more closely the context and language of the original *Statutes at Large* text and uses parentheticals and notes for clarification.

Why would the language of the *Statutes at Large* differ from the language in the *U.S. Code*? Newly enacted laws appear in *Statutes at Large* in the form in which they passed the Congress. They are then put into the proper place in the *U.S. Code*. When a provision is moved, its language may have to be changed to conform to the part of the *U.S. Code* in which it is being placed. This means that the actual language may differ between the two versions. There should be no substantive difference, usually just issues of grammar and form. In a wonderful example of how the competitive marketplace functions, each annotated code chooses to follow one of the versions.

Illustration C-1

The first page of a chapter in *United States Code Annotated*

CHAPTER 30—WILD HORSES AND BURROS: PROTECTION, MANAGEMENT, AND CONTROL

Cross References

Necessity of amendments to this chapter to facilitate humane adoption or disposal of wild horses and burros, see section 1901 of Title 43, Public Lands.

§ 1331. Congressional findings and declaration of policy

Congress finds and declares that wild free-roaming horses and burros are living symbols of the historic and pioneer spirit of the West; that they contribute to the diversity of life forms within the Nation and enrich the lives of the American people; and that these horses and burros are fast disappearing from the American scene. It is the policy of Congress that wild free-roaming horses and burros shall be protected from capture, branding, harassment, or death; and to accomplish this they are to be considered in the area where presently found, as an integral part of the natural system of the public lands.

(Pub.L. 92–195, § 1, Dec. 15, 1971, 85 Stat. 649.)

136

Illustration C–2

Annotations for 16 U.S.C.A. § 1331 (West 1985)

Historical Note

Short Title. Pub.L. 92–195, Dec. 15, 1971, 85 Stat. 649 [enacting this chapter] is popularly known as the Wild Free-Roaming Horses and Burros Act.

Legislative History. For legislative history and purpose of Pub.L. 92–195, see 1971 U.S. Code Cong. and Adm.News, p. 2149.

Code of Federal Regulations

Purpose and objectives, see 43 CFR 4700.0–1 et seq.

Library References

Animals ⇐2.
Game ⇐3½, 7 et seq.
Public Lands ⇐7.

C.J.S. Animals §§ 4 to 9.
C.J.S. Game §§ 7, 10 et seq.
C.J.S. Public Lands §§ 3 to 5, 41.

Notes of Decisions

Common law 1
Constitutionality 2
Jurisdiction 4
State regulation or control 3

1. Common law

Under common law, wild animals are owned by state in its sovereign capacity, in trust for benefit of people, and this sovereign ownership vested in colonial government and was passed to states. State of N.M. v. Morton, D.C.N.M.1975, 406 F.Supp. 1237, reversed on other grounds 96 S.Ct. 2285, 426 U.S. 529, 49 L.Ed.2d 34, rehearing denied 97 S.Ct. 189, 429 U.S. 873, 50 L.Ed.2d 154.

2. Constitutionality

This chapter was constitutional exercise of congressional power under property clause, U.S.C.A. Const. Art. 4, § 3, cl. 2, at least insofar as it was applied to prohibit New Mexico Livestock Board from entering upon public lands of United States and removing wild burros under New Mexico Estray Law, 1953 Comp.N.M. § 47–14–1 et seq. Kleppe v. New Mexico, N.M.1976, 96 S.Ct. 2285, 426 U.S. 529, 49 L.Ed.2d 34, rehearing denied 97 S.Ct. 189, 429 U.S. 873, 50 L.Ed.2d 154.

In absence of any evidence to support theory and in absence of any congressional findings to indicate it was in any way based on U.S.C.A. Const. Art. 1, § 8, cl. 3, this chapter could not be sustained as exercise of power granted in commerce clause. State of N.M. v. Morton, D.C.N.M.1975, 406 F.Supp. 1237, reversed on other grounds 96 S.Ct. 2285, 426 U.S. 529, 49 L.Ed.2d 34, rehearing denied 97 S.Ct. 189, 429 U.S. 873, 50 L.Ed.2d 154.

3. State regulation or control

This chapter overrides New Mexico Estray Law, 1953 Comp.N.M. § 47–14–1 et seq., insofar as it attempts to regulate federally protected animals. Kleppe v. New Mexico, N.M.1976, 96 S.Ct. 2285, 426 U.S. 529, 49 L.Ed.2d 34, rehearing denied 97 S.Ct. 189, 429 U.S. 873, 50 L.Ed.2d 154.

4. Jurisdiction

This chapter does not establish exclusive federal jurisdiction over public lands in New Mexico. Kleppe v. New Mexico, N.M.1976, 96 S.Ct. 2285, 426 U.S. 529, 49 L.Ed.2d 34, rehearing denied 97 S.Ct. 189, 429 U.S. 873, 50 L.Ed.2d 154.

§ 1332. Definitions

As used in this chapter—

(a) "Secretary" means the Secretary of the Interior when used in connection with public lands administered by him through the Bureau of Land Management and the Secretary of Agriculture in connection with public lands administered by him through the Forest Service;

(b) "wild free-roaming horses and burros" means all unbranded and unclaimed horses and burros on public lands of the United States;

(c) "range" means the amount of land necessary to sustain an existing herd or herds of wild free-roaming horses and burros, which

Illustration C–3

Pocket part supplementation for *USCA*

§ 1283. Management policies

[See main volume for text of (a) and (b)]

(c) Water pollution

The head of any agency administering a component of the national wild and scenic rivers system shall cooperate with the Administrator, Environmental Protection Agency and with the appropriate State water pollution control agencies for the purpose of eliminating or diminishing the pollution of waters of the river.

(As amended Pub.L. 99–590, Title V, § 509, Oct. 30, 1986, 100 Stat. 3337.)

1986 Amendment. Subsec. (c). Pub.L. 99–590 substituted "Administrator, Environmental Protection Agency" for "Secretary of the Interior".

§ 1286. Definitions

As used in this chapter, the term—

[See main volume for text of (a) and (b)]

(c) "Scenic easement" means the right to control the use of land (including the air space above such land) within the authorized boundaries of a component of the wild and scenic rivers system, for the purpose of protecting the natural qualities of a designated wild, scenic or recreational river area, but such control shall not affect, without the owner's consent, any regular use exercised prior to the acquisition of the easement. For any designated wild and scenic river, the appropriate Secretary shall treat the acquisition of fee title with the reservation of regular existing uses to the owner as a scenic easement for purposes of this chapter. Such an acquisition shall not constitute fee title ownership for purposes of section 1277(b) of this title.

(As amended Pub.L. 99–590, Title V, § 510, Oct. 30, 1986, 100 Stat. 3337.)

1986 Amendment. Subsec. (c). Pub.L. 99–590 added provisions relating to function of appropriate Secretary for any designated wild and scenic river with respect to acquisition of fee title.

Law Review Commentaries

Governmentally created erosion on the seashore: The Fifth Amendment washed away. Leslie M. MacRae, 89 Dick.L.Rev. 101 (1984).

§ 1287. Authorization of appropriations

Code of Federal Regulations

Land uses, see 36 CFR 251.9 et seq.

CHAPTER 30—WILD HORSES AND BURROS: PROTECTION, MANAGEMENT AND CONTROL

§ 1332. Definitions

Notes of Decisions

Takings 2
Wild free-roaming horses and burros 1

2. Takings

Damage to private lands caused by wild horses and burros protected by the Wild Free-Roaming Horses and Burros Act did not constitute a "taking," entitling private owners to compensation from the government; although grazing habits of the animals diminished value of the property in question, such reduction in value did not constitute a taking, where property owners were not deprived of all "economically viable use" of their lands. Mountain States Legal Foundation v. Hodel, C.A.10 (Wyo.) 1986, 799 F.2d 1423, certiorari denied 107 S.Ct. 1616, 94 L.Ed.2d 800.

§ 1333. Powers and duties of Secretary

Notes of Decisions

Adoption of horses and burros 9

5. Population of horses

Secretary of Interior is not required to maintain wild horse population levels on public lands at levels existing at time of enactment of Wild Free-Roaming Horses and Burros Act and holders of

Like *USCA, USCS* expands on many of the research aids published in the *U.S. Code* (authority references, historical notes, cross-references, etc.), in a section titled "History; Ancillary Laws and Directives." It then provides references to the *Code of Federal Regulations,* and under the heading "Research Guide," references to *American Law Reports* (*ALR*) annotations, the Lawyers Co-op encyclopedia, *American Jurisprudence 2d* (*Am.Jur.2d*), other Lawyers Co-op practice publications, and law review articles.

The case annotations following Code sections are located under the title, "Interpretive Notes and Decisions." They usually are preceded by a detailed topical outline and include both judicial and administrative decisions. Illustration D–2 includes these various features following 16 *U.S.C.S.* § 1331. One of the major differences between *USCA* and *USCS* lies in the manner in which cases are chosen to appear in the annotations. *USCA* follows the general West policy of comprehensive coverage. It provides abstracts of every case that even remotely touches upon the statute. *USCS* is more selective. It prints only those cases that its editors feels are truly relevant. The researcher is presented with the classic trade-off of comprehensive retrieval versus editorial assistance.

USCS has a multivolume, soft-cover general index, issued annually and periodically updated in pamphlet form, and individual title indexes. *USCS* also includes several volumes of tables providing parallel references and citations from popular names.

USCS is updated in much the same way as *USCA.* Cumulative annual pocket parts show changes in statutory text and provide additional annotations. Quarterly supplements entitled *Cumulative Later Case and Statutory Service* function as interim supplementation between the annual pocket parts. *USCS* 's monthly *Advance* pamphlets contain the text of newly enacted statutes, executive documents, court rules, and selected regulations, with tables for determining which Code sections have been affected by recent legislative or administrative action.

Also like *USCA, USCS* devotes several heavily annotated volumes to the U.S. Constitution and to major sets of court rules. The rules volumes, however, are all shelved at the end of the set, rather than after particular titles to which they relate.

There are other differences between these two commercial versions of federal statutes. *USCS,* for example, publishes the frequently amended Internal Revenue Code in several soft-cover volumes that are reissued annually. It also includes a volume of annotations on *uncodified* laws, arranged by *Statutes at Large* citation. Generally, *USCA* tends to be more comprehensive, including notes of decisions that *USCS* editors exclude as obsolete or repetitive. In another respect *USCS* is more comprehensive, because it provides notes of administrative decisions, which are not found in *USCA.* For many provisions, each edition will note some cases the other omits. At any given time, one of the competitors may also be a bit more up to date than the other.

Illustration D-1

The first page of a chapter in *United States Code Service*

CHAPTER 30. WILD HORSES AND BURROS: PROTECTION, MANAGEMENT, AND CONTROL

CROSS REFERENCES

This chapter is referred to in 43 USCS § 1901.

Auto-Cite®: Any case citation herein can be checked for form, parallel references, later history, and annotation references through the Auto-Cite computer research system.

---

§ 1331. Congressional findings and declaration of policy

Congress finds and declares that wild free-roaming horses and burros are living symbols of the historic and pioneer spirit of the West; that they contribute to the diversity of life forms within the Nation and enrich the lives of the American people; and that these horses and burros are fast disappearing from the American scene. It is the policy of Congress that

551

Illustration D–2

Continuation of text and annotations for 16 U.S.C.S. § 1331 (Law. Co-op. 1984)

16 USCS § 1331 CONSERVATION

wild free-roaming horses and burros shall be protected from capture, branding, harassment, or death; and to accomplish this they are to be considered in the area where presently found, as an integral part of the natural system of the public lands.
(Dec. 15, 1971, P. L. 92-195, § 1, 85 Stat. 649.)

HISTORY; ANCILLARY LAWS AND DIRECTIVES

Short titles:
Act Dec. 15, 1971, P. L. 92-195, 85 Stat. 649 [enacting 16 USCS §§ 1331 et seq.] is popularly known as the Wild Free-Roaming Horses and Burros Act.

CODE OF FEDERAL REGULATIONS

Range management, 36 CFR Part 222.
Prohibitions—Forest Service, Department of Agriculture, 36 CFR Part 261.
Wild free-roaming horse and burro protection, management, and control, 43 CFR Part 4700.
Law enforcement—criminal, 43 CFR Part 9260.

RESEARCH GUIDE

Am Jur:
63 Am Jur 2d, Public Lands § 30.

INTERPRETIVE NOTES AND DECISIONS

Wild Free-Roaming Horses and Burros Act (16 USCS §§ 1331 et seq.), enacted to protect all unbranded and unclaimed horses and burros on public lands of United States, is constitutional exercise of congressional power under property clause. Kleppe v New Mexico (1976) 426 US 529, 49 L Ed 2d 34, 96 S Ct 2285, reh den 429 US 873, 50 L Ed 2d 154, 97 S Ct 189.

In 1971, Congress enacted Wild Free-Roaming Horses and Burros Act (16 USCS §§ 1331–1340) to preserve primeval status of "all unbranded and unclaimed horses and burros on public lands of United States." American Horse Protection Asso. v United States Dept. of Interior (1977) 179 App DC 246, 551 F2d 432.

§ 1332. Definitions

As used in this Act [16 USCS §§ 1331 et seq.]—

(a) "Secretary" means the Secretary of the Interior when used in connection with public lands administered by him through the Bureau of Land Management and the Secretary of Agriculture in connection with public lands administered by him through the Forest Service;

(b) "wild free-roaming horses and burros" means all unbranded and unclaimed horses and burros on public lands of the United States;

(c) "range" means the amount of land necessary to sustain an existing herd or herds of wild free-roaming horses and burros, which does not exceed their known territorial limits, and which is devoted principally but not necessarily exclusively to their welfare in keeping with the multiple-use management concept for the public lands;

552

Many researchers work in libraries that subscribe to only one annotated edition of the U.S. Code. For them there is no dilemma choosing which to use. A person with access to both *USCA* and *USCS* should become somewhat familiar with each, and will probably develop a personal preference for one or the other. One edition can be used on a regular basis for most research needs, but the other may occasionally be needed for its editorial features or to ensure comprehensive coverage.

5. ELECTRONIC SOURCES

Several of the forms of federal statutory publication discussed above are available for computerized research in either WESTLAW or LEXIS, and all three versions of the U.S. Code are on CD–ROM. The online Code databases are generally up to date within a few months or less; the United States Public Laws databases are often up to date within weeks or days. The currency of these databases is indicated on scope or directory screens, and should be checked before relying on an online search for current information.

Recently enacted public laws can be found online in both WESTLAW and LEXIS. WESTLAW's US–PL database features the full text of public laws as set forth in enrolled bills passed by both houses of Congress, regardless of whether they are codified or not. A "slip copy" document (not to be confused with an official slip law) is often available within days of a law's enactment, and provides complete citation information (public law number and *Statutes at Large* citation) and legislative history references at the beginning of the document. These slip copy documents are later edited and rereleased with full editorial enhancements, including exact page references to the official *Statutes at Large* text (star paging) and, where appropriate, classifications to *USCA* titles and sections. WESTLAW also maintains an archival database (US–PL–OLD) of public laws passed in the last few years, starting with the 101st Congress, 1st Session (1989). In LEXIS, the PUBLAW file, found in the GENFED or CODES library, provides the *USCS Advance* legislative service version of United States Public Laws. It includes the full text of public laws passed since the 100th Congress, 2d Session (1988).

While neither online Public Law database includes legislative history documents, these materials are available in other databases, which will be discussed in Chapter 7. WESTLAW and LEXIS also offer the full text of pending federal bills, and bill tracking databases that provide the status of legislation introduced in the current Congress.

The text of the U.S. Code in either of its commercial annotated versions is also available online. The USC database in WESTLAW contains the statutory text, *Statutes at Large* references, and legislative history references as they appear in the *United States Code Annotated,* but does not include any of *USCA* 's annotations or other research aids. All of *USCA* 's editorial features (CFR references, notes of decisions, etc.) are available, however, in WESTLAW's USCA database. LEXIS provides access to the Code as published in the *United States Code Service,* including the history notes and references to other Lawyers Co-op publications, as well as the notes of decisions and *USCS* 's other editorial enhancements.

Both WESTLAW and LEXIS have separate databases for the Federal Rules, and LEXIS offers a separate file for the United States Constitution (USCNST).

The online researcher can retrieve a known statutory provision by searching for a particular citation, or can find statutes on a particular subject by searching for a combination of descriptive words. Because the annotations in *USCA* and *USCS* are usually more descriptive than the formal statutory language, their availability online enhances the researcher's ability to search for sections relevant to particular legal problems.

The WESTLAW and LEXIS U.S. Code databases are often most useful in situations where an issue is not adequately covered in indexes or where a combination of particular terms is important. If the interpretation of a statutory word or phrase is in issue, an online search can be used to quickly and efficiently retrieve all Code provisions using that word or phrase.

A search of the Code online retrieves only those *sections* which match the particular query. The systems treat each Code section as a separate document, so that there are over 40,000 sections or documents in a Code database. The online display of a section includes a heading indicating the title and chapter in which it belongs, but otherwise there is little immediate perspective of its place in the subject scheme. To better understand relationships between various code provisions, a searcher can view the table of contents for a particular chapter or title. In WESTLAW, the "jump" markers next to the chapter and title headings of each code section enable the researcher to view the related tables of contents. LEXIS has a separate file for the *USCS* Table of Contents; one can browse backwards and forwards through its levels of hierarchy, which descend topically from the more broad to the more specific. Both services also allow the searcher to enter commands to display other sections classified before or after a section which matches the search query, thus providing some sense of its context.

As noted earlier, the official and unofficial versions of the U.S. Code are available on CD–ROM from a number of sources. Each provides full text access to the Code's fifty titles, and can be searched in a number of ways. Updates of the CD–ROMs are issued regularly. The reliability of many of the new CD–ROM products has not yet been established. The U.S. Code is also available at several Internet sites, though the reliability and timeliness of these versions is not yet established. The wise researcher will consult with a local reference librarian to discuss which, if any, such compilations are available in any particular library. The situation is just that fluid.

D. FEDERAL STATUTORY RESEARCH

Because of the different forms of publication, research in statutory law varies considerably from that in case law. The emphasis is on regularly updated, heavily annotated, primary sources. The need for extrinsic aids to statutory interpretation, such as judicial decisions and legislative history, gives an added dimension to statutory research.

1. FINDING STATUTES

Statutory research typically begins with a search to determine whether there are statutes applicable to the particular problem or topic under consideration, and then locating the relevant statutory provisions. Sometimes, however, one has a reference to a particular law by number or popular name, and merely needs a table to locate that statute in its code form. There are various indexes and tables for these purposes.

a. Indexes

When confronted with a research problem involving legislation, the best course is to break the relevant issue down into the smallest possible components. Catchphrases and related terms from the issue can then be distilled and taken to a relevant index. The index is likely to send one directly to the relevant legislation. The searching is much more direct than case research.

The general index to the *U.S. Code* is quite thorough and extensive, and is updated in the *Code*'s cumulative annual supplements. The official index forms the basis, in fact, for the indexes in both *USCA* and *USCS*, which make only slight modifications in its entries. The major advantage offered by the indexes in the annotated codes is that they are more frequently updated. Both the *USCA* and *USCS* general index volumes are revised and reissued annually. Material in the quarterly pamphlets updating both annotated codes also is indexed. Illustration E shows a page from the general index in the *U.S. Code*.

Most of these indexes include plenty of cross-references, which are of two basic types. Cross-references between subject headings provide notice of related statutes covered elsewhere in the index. Entries for terms which are *not* used as subject headings indicate the synonymous or related terms which are used instead. A researcher who looks in the index under "Cattle" finds references to "Animals," "Beef Research and Information," and "Dairies," rather than no entry at all. Since indexers cannot foresee all possible terms a researcher might use, of course, it may sometimes be necessary to reformulate a query before finding any information. If an issue turns out not to be covered by federal statutory law, there may be no index entry to be found.

Every volume of the *Statutes at Large* has its own index, and there are also indexes for the annual volumes of *U.S. Code Congressional and Administrative News,* and cumulative indexes in each monthly issue of *USCCAN* and *USCS Advance*. The older indexes in bound volumes can be used to find laws from particular years, and the pamphlet indexes to find the latest laws passed by Congress.

Illustration E

A typical page from the General Index to the *United States Code*, 1988 edition

For online research, the *USCA* and *USCS* General Indexes are available as WESTLAW (USCA–IDX) and LEXIS (USINDX) databases, respectively. An alphabetical list of all the main index headings can be accessed; one can also retrieve a list of all the references under each main heading. Both online services have features that allow the researcher to move from an index listing to the code section to which it refers.

For access to early federal laws, one can consult the indexes to earlier editions of the *U.S. Code,* the *Revised Statutes,* or individual *Statutes at Large* volumes. Two retrospective indexes to federal law prepared by the Library of Congress are also of occasional use in historical research. These indexes cover the periods indicated in their respective titles: Middleton G. Beaman & Agnus K. McNamara, *Index Analysis of the Federal Statutes, 1789–1873* (1911), and Walter H. McClenon & Wilfred C. Gilbert, *Index to the Federal Statutes, 1874–1931* (1933).[9] These include only general, public and permanent laws.

b. Tables

A researcher often has reference to a particular statute, and does not need to use a subject index. If the reference provides a current U.S. Code citation, access to the statute is no problem. Frequently, however, the reference gives only the name of a statute or provides an outdated or *Statutes at Large* citation. Two types of tables provide assistance in these situations.

Popular name tables consist of alphabetical lists of statutes, providing citations to their session law and codified locations. For an older statute, "popular name" often means a name with which it has come to be associated over time, such as "Mann Acts" or "White–Slave Laws." Most modern statutes, on the other hand, specify short titles by which they may be cited. These names, such as "Marine Plastic Pollution Research and Control Act of 1987," are also listed in popular name tables. A person knowing only the name of an act can use these table to find its Public Law number and its citation in both the *Statutes at Large* and the Code. Most codified acts are not printed all in one place, so the table usually lists scattered sections of the Code where provisions appear.

As noted above, all three editions of the U.S. Code include popular name tables. The *U.S. Code* 's "Acts Cited by Popular Name," printed in the final text volume, is quite thorough, but not as current as those in *USCA* and *USCS.* The *USCA* table is printed in the last general index volume, which is reissued every year; the *USCS* table appears in a bound volume with other tables, updated by an annual pocket part. The *USCA* table is further updated by an "Alphabetical Table of Laws" in the front of each quarterly pamphlet, and a table near the back of each issue of *USCCAN,* which cumulates each month for the entire session of Congress. The *USCS* table is updated in the back of every monthly *Advance* pamphlet and quarterly *Cumulative Later Case and Statutory Service.* Illustration F shows a page from the *USCA* popular name table.

9. The McClenon & Gilbert index superseded George W. Scott & Middleton G. Beaman, *Index Analysis of the Federal Statutes, 1873–1907* (1908).

Illustration F

A page from the Popular Name Table in *USCA*

White Cane Safety Day Act
Pub. L. 88–628, Oct. 6, 1964, 78 Stat. 1003 (Title 36, § 169d)

White Charger Act
Pub. L. 86–616, § 10, July 12, 1960, 74 Stat. 395 (Title 10, § 3297 note)

White Earth Reservation Land Settlement Act of 1985
Pub.L. 99–264, Mar. 24, 1986, 100 Stat. 61 (Title 25, § 331 note)
Pub. L. 100–153, § 6(a), (b), Nov. 5, 1987, 101 Stat. 887 (Title 25, § 331 notes)
Pub.L. 100–212, § 4, Dec. 24, 1987, 101 Stat. 212 (Title 25, § 331 note)

White House Conference for a Drug Free America
Pub.L. 99–570, Title I, §§ 1931 to 1938, Oct. 27, 1986, 100 Stat. 3207–56 (Title 20, § 4601 note)
Pub. L. 100–138, §§ 1 to 3, Oct. 23, 1987, 101 Stat. 820, 821 (Title 20, § 4601 notes)

White House Conference on Handicapped Individuals Act
Pub. L. 93–516, title III, Dec. 7, 1974, 88 Stat. 1631 (Title 29, § 701 note)
Pub. L. 93–651, title III, Nov. 21, 1974, 89 Stat. 2–16 (Title 29, § 701 note)
Pub. L. 94–224, §§ 1, 2, Feb. 27, 1976, 90 Stat. 201 (Title 29, § 701 note)

White House Conference on Productivity Act
Pub. L. 97–367, Oct. 25, 1982, 96 Stat. 1761 (Title 15, § 2401 note)

White House Conference on Small Business Authorization Act
Pub.L. 98–276, May 8, 1984, 98 Stat. 169 (Title 15, § 631 note)

White House Police Act
Apr. 22, 1940, ch. 133, 54 Stat. 156 (See Title 3, § 203)

White Phosphorous Matches Act
Apr. 9, 1912, ch. 75, 37 Stat. 81

White Pine Blister Rust Protection Act
Apr. 26, 1940, ch. 159, 54 Stat. 168 (Title 16, § 594a)
July 1, 1978, Pub. L. 95–313, § 13(a)(2), 92 Stat. 374 (Title 16, § 594a)

White Russian Act
June 8, 1934, ch. 429, 48 Stat. 926

White-Slave Laws
Mar. 26, 1910, ch. 128, 36 Stat. 263
June 25, 1910, ch. 395, 36 Stat. 825 (See Title 18, §§ 2421–2424)

White-Slave Traffic Act
See White-Slave Laws

Whitman Mission National Historic Site
Pub. L. 87–471, May 31, 1962, 76 Stat. 90 (Title 16, § 433n)

Wholesome Meat Act
Pub. L. 90–201, Dec. 15, 1967, 81 Stat. 584 (Title 19, § 1306; Title 21, §§ 601–623, 641–645, 661, 671–680, 691)

Wholesome Poultry Products Act
Pub. L. 90–492, Aug. 18, 1968, 82 Stat. 791 (Title 21, §§ 451–461, 463–465, 467, 467a–467f, 470)

Widows' Pension Act
Apr. 19, 1908, ch. 147, 35 Stat. 64

Wilcox Air Base Act
Aug. 12, 1935, ch. 511, § 4, 49 Stat. 610 (See Title 10, § 9774)

Wild and Scenic Rivers Act
Pub. L. 90–542, Oct. 2, 1968, 82 Stat. 906 (Title 16, §§ 1271–1287)
Pub. L. 92–560, § 2, Oct. 25, 1972, 86 Stat. 1174 (Title 16, § 1274)
Pub. L. 93–279, § 1, May 10, 1974, 88 Stat. 122 (Title 16, §§ 1274, 1275, 1276, 1278, 1286, 1287)
Pub. L. 93–621, § 1, Jan. 3, 1975, 88 Stat. 2094 (Title 16, §§ 1275, 1276, 1278)
Pub. L. 94–199, §§ 3(a), 5(a), Dec. 31, 1975, 89 Stat. 1117, 1118 (Title 16, §§ 1274, 1276)
Pub. L. 94–273, § 2(11), Apr. 21, 1976, 90 Stat. 375 (Title 16, § 1287)

The *USCA* popular name table also is available online, in the WESTLAW database, USCA–POP. A search restricted to the specific popular name of an act, using the caption (CA) or citation (CI) fields, yields a listing of the enacting and amending information provided in the print version. One can also retrieve an alphabetical list of all Popular Name Acts. Similarly, the *USCS* popular name table appears in a LEXIS file (USNAME), although it is used somewhat differently. The table is presented as an alphabetical list (actually a series of documents, one for each letter of the alphabet) that can be searched or navigated in several ways.

Parallel reference tables are the other tables that allow access to statutes. These tables list one citation for a statute, typically its session law location, and provide a cross-reference to another citation where it may be found, usually as codified.

The *U.S. Code*'s Tables volumes contain various parallel conversion tables which provide references between earlier revisions and later texts, and between different forms of statutory publication. Table I covers U.S. Code titles that have been revised and renumbered since the adoption of the Code in 1926, showing where former sections of the title are incorporated into the latest edition. Table II indicates the status of sections of the *Revised Statutes of 1878* within the Code, and Table III lists the *Statutes at Large* in chronological order and indicates where each section is incorporated into the Code. Other tables cover executive orders, proclamations, reorganization plans, and internal cross-references within the Code. The *U.S. Code*'s annual bound supplements generally include updates to these tables.

The most extensive and useful parallel reference tables in federal statutory research are, like the *U.S. Code*'s Table III, from Public Law number or *Statutes at Large* citation to the U.S. Code. The *USCA* and *USCS* versions of these tables are updated in each publication's quarterly and monthly pamphlets. The newer tables add citations for new statutes and update information on older statutes that have been repealed or moved. Illustration G shows a page from the *Statutes at Large* parallel reference table in *USCS*.

Like the *U.S. Code,* the *USCA* and *USCS* include other parallel reference tables that provide access from *Revised Statutes* sections to U.S. Code sections, and explain the disposition of sections of Code titles which have been revised. The latter tables can be very handy if one has a reference to a Code section from an older case or article, but upon trying to locate the text finds either nothing at all or an unrelated provision.

The *USCS* Revised Title and Statutes-at-Large Tables are available in LEXIS files (USREVT and USSALT). At this time, WESTLAW does not include similar tables from *USCA*.

Illustration G

A typical parallel reference table in *USCS*

85 Stat — STATUTES AT LARGE — 92d Cong

Pub. L	Section	Stat. Page	USCS Title	USCS Section	Status
			1971 Dec—Cont'd		
92-184—Cont'd					
		638-642	Appn.		Unclass.
92-185	1	642	38	765	
	2	643	38	765 nt	
92-186	1-3	643	Spec.		Unclass.
92-187	1	644	5	2108	
	2	644	5	5924	
	3	644	5	7152	
92-188	1	645	38	703, 741	
	2	645	38	707	
	3	645	38	prec 701	
	4	645	38	707 nt	
92-189	1	646	25	640a nt	
	2	646	25	640a	
	3	646	25	640b	
	4	646	25	640c	
	5		25	640c-1	Added
	6		25	640c-2	Added
92-190		646	31	52b	
92-191	1	647	18	1716	
	2	647	39	3001	
	3	647	18	1716 nt	
92-192		647	Spec.		Unclass.
92-193		648	38	704	
92-194		648	5	5542	
92-195	1	649	16	1331	
	2	649	16	1332	
	3	649	16	1333	
	4	650	16	1334	
	5	650	16	1335	
	6	650	16	1336	
	7	650	16	1337	
	8	650	16	1338	
	9		16	1338a	Added
	10[9]	651	16	1339	Redes.
	11[10]	651	16	1340	Redes.
92-196		651-660	Local		Unclass.
92-197	1	660	38	411	
	2	660	38	413	
	3	661	38	414	
	4	661	38	415	
	5	662	38	417	
	6	662	38	321, 341	
	7	662	38	724	
	8	662	38	417 nt	
	9	662	38	322	
	10	662	38	411 nt	
92-198	1(a), (b)	663	38	521	
	1(c), (d), (e)	663	38	541	
	1(f)	664	38	542	
	2	664	38	503	
	3	664	38	3012	
	4	664	38	521 nt	
	5	664	38	101	

Pub. L.	Section	Stat. Page	USCS Title	USCS Section	Status
			1971 Dec—Cont'd		
92-198—Cont'd					
	6	664	38	521 nt	
92-199		664	Spec.		Unclass.
			1971 Dec. 17		
92-200	1-10	665-680	Local		Unclass.
			1971 Dec. 18		
92-201		681	Appn.		Unclass.
92-202		682-685	Appn.		Unclass.
	1-18	686, 687	Appn.		Unclass.
92-203	1	688	43	1601 nt	
	2	688	43	1601	
	3	689	43	1602	
	4	689	43	1603	
	5	690	43	1604	
	6	690	43	1605	
	7	691	43	1606	
	8	694	43	1607	
	9	694	43	1608	
	10	696	43	1609	
	11	696	43	1610	
	12	701	43	1611	
	13	702	43	1612	
	14	702	43	1613	
	15	705	43	1614	
	16	705	43	1615	
	17	706	43	1616	
	18	710	43	1617	
	19	710	43	1618	
	20	710	43	1619	
	21	713	43	1620	
	22	713	43	1621	
	23	715	43	1622	
	24	715	43	1623	
	25	715	43	1624	
	26, 27	715, 716	43	1601 nts	
	28		43	1625	Added
	29		43	1626	Added
	30		43	1627	Added
	31		43	1628	Added
92-204		716-720	Appn.		Unclass.
	301	720	10	4308 nt	
		721-726	Appn.		Unclass.
	701, 702	726	Appn.		Unclass.
	703	726	31	700	
	704	726	Appn.		Unclass.
	705	727	31	649a	
	706, 707	727	Appn.		Unclass.

182

2. UPDATING STATUTES

Just as finding decisions is not all there is to case research, finding statutes through indexes, tables, or other means is just the first step of statutory research. Before relying on a statute as authority, one must verify that it is still in force and ascertain how it has been affected by subsequent legislation and by judicial decisions.

a. USCA and USCS

One reason that annotated codes are such powerful research tools is that they serve two essential functions: they print the text of a primary authority and they provide regularly updated information on its validity and treatment. The frequent and varied supplementation for *USCA* and *USCS* has already been described. These updating materials provide the text of amendments to a statutory provision and include carefully edited, topically arranged annotations of interpretive judicial decisions. A case researcher must do a good deal of work to update a decision, but a statutory researcher finds much of the work already done by the annotated code.

b. WESTLAW and LEXIS Databases

The convenient updating features of *USCA* and *USCS*, such as frequent supplementation and extensive annotations, are available in their online formats. Online statutory research can be further updated by searching for the specific code section or general subject matter in question in the WESTLAW or LEXIS Public Laws database. This should yield recently enacted legislation directly affecting the relevant code section, and other related matter, such as new statutes or uncodified material.

WESTLAW offers a convenient "update" feature in its USC and USCA databases. When viewing a statutory section, the researcher can type "update" (or use the update "link" prompt) to obtain recent amending or repealing legislation. This "update" feature is limited at this time, however, to retrieving only editorially enhanced documents in US–PL. To find the most current "slip copy" documents affecting a particular statute, it is necessary to conduct a separate search in US–PL using descriptive terms and ci(slip), rather than relying on the "update" feature.

Finally, citations to statutes in decisions and articles can be found using the online systems by searching in full-text case or periodical databases. Such a search, using either the title or citation of a statute, will find very recent references that have yet to be covered by an annotated code.

3. INTERPRETING STATUTES

The procedures for finding and updating statutes just described constitute the basic methods of statutory research. An essential purpose of such research is to determine what Congress meant by a particular enactment. To do so, one must use resources discussed more fully in other chapters of this book. Because they are treated elsewhere, the following materials are only noted here.

a. Judicial Decisions

Judicial interpretations and constructions of ambiguous or controverted statutory language are often used to establish the meaning of a statute. Such interpretations may have been made in earlier cases dealing with the specific statute, or in cases involving other statutes containing similar provisions or language. Relevant decisions can be located through several methods, including: (1) reading the annotations in *USCA* or *USCS;* (2) Shepardizing a statutory provision; or (3) searching WESTLAW or LEXIS full-text case databases for references to a statute by citation or name. The publication of judicial decisions and procedures of case research have been discussed in Chapters 2 through 4.

b. Legislative History

To determine the meaning of a statutory provision, one can investigate the legislative documents that led to its enactment. Various versions of a bill, reports of Senate and House Committees that considered the proposed legislation, transcripts of floor debates, and other Congressional materials may all be of use in interpreting the text of a statute. These legislative history documents, and the finding aids and research procedures for their investigation, are treated in detail in Chapter 6.

c. Other Resources

Statutes are often discussed in looseleaf services, periodical articles, and treatises. Such discussions may be quite helpful in statutory research and interpretation, and often include references to cases, other statutes, legislative history materials, and regulations. Specialized finding aids of varying quality exist for each of these types of secondary material. Looseleaf services, legal periodicals, and treatises will be discussed in Chapter 10.

Attorney general opinions are an important source of persuasive statutory interpretation on the *state* level, but U.S. Attorney General opinions are not prepared or consulted on such a regular basis. They may be of occasional use, however, and are discussed in Chapter 8.

E. OTHER FORMS OF FEDERAL LEGISLATION

Statutes are not the only form of federal legislation. Most of the following additional legislative materials are discussed elsewhere, but they should be noted in this context.

1. U.S. CONSTITUTION

The federal Constitution is the basic, organic legislation of the United States, and appears in a variety of published sources. These publications, and research in constitutional law generally, are discussed in Chapter 6.

2. TREATIES

Treaties are international agreements negotiated between sovereign powers. Article VI of the Constitution provides that treaties made under the authority of the United States have the same legal authority and force as statutes. They are a special kind of federal legislation because they do not follow the usual enactment process through Congress. Under Article II, § 2, the President "shall have Power, by and with the Advice and Consent of the Senate to make treaties, provided two thirds of the Senators present concur." Treaty legislation thus arises in the executive branch but requires legislative approval to become law. Research in the law of treaties is a specialized skill. It is treated in depth in *How to Find the Law*.

3. INTERSTATE COMPACTS

The Constitution, as interpreted by the courts, authorizes agreements between the states, provided they are first approved by Congress.[10] After the compact is agreed upon by the states, it goes to Congress for authorizing legislation. When enacted, each compact thus appears in the *U.S. Statutes at Large* and in the session laws of the states which are parties to it. The Council of State Governments publishes a description of such compacts in *Interstate Compacts & Agencies,* which is revised from time to time and updated between revisions in the Council's biennial publication, the *Book of the States*.

Most interstate compacts also appear in the annotated statutory codes of the states enacting them, and are listed as cited material (by their statutory enactment) in Shepard's statutory citators. One can use either of those publications to locate cases which have applied or interpreted interstate compacts.

4. REORGANIZATION PLANS

Reorganization plans are an unusual hybrid form of legislation. They consist of Presidential proposals to reorganize executive agencies below the departmental level, submitted to Congress for approval pursuant to a general authorizing statute. Reorganization plans are treated with other Presidential lawmaking materials in Chapter 8.

F. STATE STATUTES

Statutory research on the state level is quite similar to the federal paradigm already discussed at length. This section will be more brief, and assumes familiarity with principles outlined in the preceding sections on statutory publication generally and federal statutory research.

10. Article I, § 10 provides: "No state shall, without the Consent of Congress, . . . enter into any Agreement or Compact with another State. . . ." For further information, see Frederick L. Zimmerman & Mitchell Wendell, *The Law and Use of Interstate Compacts* (1976).

1. SLIP LAWS AND SESSION LAWS

State statutes are enacted and published in a manner similar to the federal pattern. Most states publish their statutes initially in a slip law form, but some do not.[11] All states publish bound session law volumes. The titles of these publications vary from state to state (*e.g., Alaska Session Laws, California Statutes, Acts and Resolves of Massachusetts, Laws of New York*). Like the *U.S. Statutes at Large,* they all print acts chronologically and include noncumulative subject indexes and tables.

Official state session laws are usually not published until well after the end of a legislative session. In over half of the states, commercially published advance session law services, sometimes known as "legislative services," provide quicker access to current acts. These monthly or bimonthly pamphlets are generally issued by the publisher of a state's annotated code as a form of supplementation to the code. They are similar to West's *USCCAN* (but without the legislative history component) and to the *USCS Advance* pamphlets.

For online research, LEXIS provides access to the slip laws or advance legislative services of all fifty states, either in individual files for every state (e.g., OHALS), or in a group file (ALLALS). WESTLAW has similar databases for each state's recent legislation (e.g., OH–LEGIS), historical legislative services (e.g., CA–LEGIS87), and all the states' legislation combined (LEGIS–ALL). Coverage varies by state, so the scope or directory screens should be checked before relying on an online search for current information.

Both WESTLAW and LEXIS offer bill tracking for the fifty states, individually or combined. In conjunction with State Net, from Information for Public Affairs, WESTLAW also provides the full text of bills from the current legislative sessions of about twenty states, with more likely to be added in the future. LEXIS has the full text of pending legislation from several states, as well.

Increasingly states are putting newly enacted laws, and pending bills, onto electronic bulletin boards that may be accessible over the Internet. Once again, the best route for the researcher is to check with a local reference librarian for the current situation in any jurisdiction.

2. STATE CODES

State statutory compilations are published in a wide variety of forms and with varying degrees of "official" status. Code provisions in some states are reenacted as positive law, but in most states they are only *prima facie* evidence of the authoritative session laws. Some states have an official, unannotated code, regularly revised and published by the state on an annual or biennial basis. A few small states prepare their own annotated codes. Others have arrangements with commercial pub-

11. For information on the availability of state slip laws and on state legislative activity generally, see Lynn Hellebust, *State Legislative Sourcebook* (annual). Also useful, although not as current, is Mary L. Fisher, *Guide to State Legislative Materials* (4th ed., 1988).

lishers to prepare annotated codes, which are legislatively or administratively sanctioned as "official." Many states, however, rarely revise their official codification, so they become obsolete and only of historical interest.[12] In such states, the subject arrangement of an earlier official code is usually retained and updated by a commercial publisher. In most state codes, a certificate or prefatory note in the front of each volume indicates its status as authority.

At least one annotated code is published for every state, and several larger states have two annotated codes issued by competing publishers. While codes vary from state to state in frequency of updating and in editorial quality, they are the most useful and most frequently consulted versions of state statutes.

Most state codes are published in bound volumes with pocket part supplements, although several are published in pamphlets filed in looseleaf binders. In either form, both statutory provisions and annotations are updated at least once a year. Many codes are further updated by pamphlets issued between annual supplements, containing the latest amendments and case notes. Every code is accompanied by an index, and most include parallel reference tables.

In addition to noting state and federal cases applying or interpreting statutory provisions, the state codes provide various research aids. West publishes codes for more than twenty states, and includes references to relevant key numbers and *C.J.S.* sections. Lawyers Co-op publishes a few codes, which provide references to *ALR* annotations and *Am.Jur.2d.* Codes from other publishers include a wider variety of research references. The Michie Company, which publishes codes for nearly two dozen states, frequently includes references to *both Am.Jur.2d* and *C.J.S.*

3. ELECTRONIC SOURCES

WESTLAW provides access to the statutes, court rules, and constitutions of all fifty states, as set out in each state's code. Annotated and unannotated code databases are available for all states except Nebraska, for which no annotations are available. Searching in a state's annotated code database provides access to the editorial features, like case annotations and references to secondary materials, included in the print version of the code.

In LEXIS, each state's code file includes the state constitution, the current advance legislative service, and all the titles of the state code. Separate statutory tables of contents files allow the researcher to view the hierarchical structure of each state code, and to then review the desired code section.

In addition to databases for specific codes, both systems offer the ability to search at once in all state codes. Statutory language differs

12. For example, the *Consolidated Laws of New York* have not been officially reissued since 1909.

from state to state, but this is nonetheless a powerful capability for someone doing comparative statutory research or interested in finding how a particular word or phrase has been applied in other states.

The frequency of updating varies from state to state. Before relying on an online code as current, a prudent researcher would verify its status by consulting the online database directories or scope screens.

Various publishers have issued CD–ROM versions of state statutes. In some states, more than one CD–ROM edition of the code is available. Such CD–ROM publications may combine statutes, cases and commentary on a single disk. The reliability and utility of these products is still being established. Yet again, the local reference librarian is the best source for a current assessment of these developments in a particular jurisdiction.

G. STATE STATUTORY RESEARCH

1. FINDING STATE STATUTES

Almost all annotated codes include parallel reference tables comparable to those in the three versions of the U.S. Code, and every code has an extensive index. These indexes frequently occupy several volumes, and are either supplemented or reissued each year. WESTLAW includes separate databases for the general index of each state's statutes.

Only a few state codes include tables of acts by name, but comprehensive coverage of state popular name acts is provided in two forms by *Shepard's Citations.* The Shepard's citator for each state includes a "Table of Acts by Popular Names or Short Titles." These tables, which are updated in the supplementary pamphlets, generally provide citations only to codes, not session laws. In addition, *Shepard's Acts and Cases by Popular Names: Federal and State,* three volumes published in 1992 supplemented regularly by cumulative, soft-covered pamphlets, provides one alphabetical listing of statutes from throughout the country, with references to the specific state codes or session laws where the acts or provisions can be found. The nationwide *Acts and Cases by Popular Names* sometimes has more current information than the list in a state citator.[13] It is most useful in situations where the title of an act, but not the state of enactment, is known, or when similar acts from several states are sought.

Multistate statutory searches are not frequently required by practitioners, but they are quite common in scholarly research. Searching fifty state codes is very time-consuming, particularly since different indexes often treat similar subjects in very different ways. Rather than

13. For both the state listings and the general *Acts and Cases,* paperback supplements list new acts but take no notice of the recodification or moving of older acts. Such changes are only recognized when a volume is recompiled and reissued. The more current source for a particular state, then, depends on whether the state citator was published before or after the most recent revision of *Shepard's Acts and Cases by Popular Names.*

expecting a single search procedure to work for every state, one must approach each index as its own system of classifications and cross-references.

Several resources may help in multistate statutory searches. An online keyword search in the WESTLAW or LEXIS database containing the complete set of every state's statutes may retrieve most relevant documents if terminology is fairly standard. The last volume of the *Martindale–Hubbell Law Directory* contains digests of state laws on a variety of standardized subjects, and provides references to statutory primary sources. Topical looseleaf services in some subject areas reprint state laws; the *Environment Reporter,* for example, contains state laws and regulations on such issues as air pollution, mining, and waste disposal.

State laws on particular subjects are also collected or surveyed in a variety of other sources, such as treatises, law review articles, and government publications. Some of these sources provide the texts of laws, but even those that only list code citations can save a considerable amount of research time. Extensive guides to these collections and surveys of state laws have been published in recent years. Lynn Foster & Carol Boast, *Subject Compilations of State Laws: Research Guide and Annotated Bibliography* (1981) is arranged by subject, with descriptive annotations and indexes by author and publisher. It is updated by regular supplements under the title, *Subject Compilations of State Laws: An Annotated Bibliography*, authored by Cheryl Nyberg and Carol Boast for 1979–83 (1984), and by Cheryl R. Nyberg for 1983–85 (1986), 1985–88 (1989), and annually since 1991. The *National Survey of State Laws,* edited by Richard Leiter (1993) collects the texts of statutes on selected topics from all 50 states. Another guide to subject compilations is Jon S. Schultz, *Statutes Compared: A U.S., Canadian, Multinational, Research Guide to Statutes by Subject* (1991–), published in looseleaf format.

2. UPDATING AND INTERPRETING STATE STATUTES

The primary engine for updating the statutes in any state is its annotated code. The code will be kept current by pocket parts and usually by pamphlets. A common research mistake is to use only the pocket part and to stop. Check and see if the set is updated between the issuance of pocket parts, if so, be sure and use the temporary pamphlets that will be used. Check the advance session law pamphlets as well.

An increasing number of states are making new legislation available via online bulletin boards. Find out if the jurisdiction in question offers such a service. It may be the quickest and most reliable updating available.

If using LEXIS or WESTLAW, be certain of the coverage of the data base. How recently has new information been added? Are there files of new legislation that should be checked? Of course one can always run a Boolean search that consists of the statutory citation through the relevant case data base (limited to relevant dates of decision) to ascertain if any comment has been made about one's statute.

H. UNIFORM LAWS AND MODEL ACTS

For many years, one of the major aspects of the law reform movement in this country has been a drive for the enactment of uniform laws by the several states, in those fields in which uniformity would be beneficial. To this end, the National Conference of Commissioners on Uniform State Laws was formed in 1892. The Conference, consisting of representatives of each state, meets annually to draft, promulgate and promote uniform laws, which the states can then adopt as proposed, or modify, or reject, as they see fit. Over two hundred uniform laws have been approved by the Conference, of which over a hundred have been adopted by at least one state. The Uniform Commercial Code, jointly sponsored by the Conference and the American Law Institute, has been enacted at least in part by every state.[14]

All of the uniform laws which have been adopted by at least one state are compiled in an annotated set published by West called *Uniform Laws Annotated,* Master Ed., with annual pocket part or pamphlet supplementation and periodic additions. *U.L.A.* includes the Commissioners' notes on each law, explains variations in individual states' enactments, and provides references to law review commentaries and court decisions from all adopting states. The notes of decisions are in the usual West format of headnote abstracts. These annotations, reflecting the interpretations of a uniform law in states which have enacted it, are particularly important for research in states which are considering adopting a law or have recently done so.

Tables in each volume and supplementation list states which have adopted each uniform law. In addition, an annual pamphlet accompanying the set provides a directory of uniform acts, lists for each state of enacted uniform legislation, and a brief index covering all acts. Each individual act is indexed in full in the back of its volume.

The *Uniform Laws Annotated* is available in WESTLAW's ULA database, and includes notes of decisions and other editorial features offered in the print version. Another WESTLAW database, HAWKLAND, contains the Uniform Commercial Code, along with the full text of *Uniform Commercial Code Series,* a nine-volume treatise by William D. Hawkland. The UCC is the only uniform law currently available in LEXIS. The official text and comments, as they appear in *Callaghan's Uniform Commercial Code Reporting Service,* constitute a file in the UCC library. Clark Boardman Callaghan also offers a CD–ROM database of the Uniform Commercial Code, called UCCSearch.

Another important publication on uniform laws is the annual *Handbook of the National Conference of Commissioners on Uniform State Laws.* The *Handbook* contains current information about pending laws

14. Louisiana has adopted only Articles 1, 3, 4, 5, 7, 8, and 9.

under consideration by the Conference and discussions of new and proposed legislation. It is one of the few sources of the texts of uniform laws which have not yet been adopted by any state.

"Model acts" are drafted for fields where individual states are likely to modify a proposed law to meet their needs, rather than adopt it *in toto*. The National Conference has drafted some model acts, but two of the more influential model acts were developed by the American Law Institute: the Model Penal Code and the Model Business Corporation Act. Research tools for these acts include American Law Institute, *Model Penal Code and Commentaries* (6 vols., 1980–85), and *Model Business Corporation Act Annotated* (4 vols.) (3d ed. 1994).

It should be noted that neither uniform laws nor model acts have any legal effect in a state unless actually adopted by its legislature. When adopted, they appear in the session laws and annotated code. These sources are, of course, invaluable for research purposes, since only they contain the actual text *as enacted,* with whatever changes and variations were made in the form proposed by the National Conference.

I. LOCAL LAW SOURCES

Legal problems and issues are governed not only by federal and state law, but also by the laws of counties, cities, villages, and other local units. Local laws are a form of delegated legislation, based on law-making powers granted by the state legislatures, or, in the case of Washington, D.C. and other federally controlled areas, by the U.S. Congress.

Despite the trend toward greater centralization of governmental authority over the last fifty years, local laws remain important in many areas of daily life and economic activity. Housing, transportation, social welfare, education, municipal services, zoning, and environmental conditions are all heavily regulated at this level of government. Local taxation is an ever-increasing area of legal activity. Consequently, local law is a frequent subject of research. This research is often very frustrating, since local law sources in general are poorly published, inadequately indexed, and infrequently supplemented.

1. MUNICIPAL CHARTERS AND ORDINANCES

A city's *charter* is its organic law, similar in purpose to a federal or state constitution. An *ordinance* is a measure passed by its council or governing body to regulate municipal matters, and is the local equivalent of a federal or state statute. Most of the larger cities in the United States publish collections of their charter and ordinances in codes of varying quality. Very few municipal codes include annotations to case law. There has been a movement by several small private publishers to prepare codes for smaller cities and towns, and these have greatly improved access to local law in the communities served. The small size of the prospective market have kept almost all municipal material off of the on-line data bases. At this point only the New York City charter is available on WESTLAW.

In general, however, individual ordinances (if their existence is known and they can be identified) must be obtained from the Clerk's Office of the county, city, or town. In larger cities, municipal reference libraries can be very helpful, and some public libraries are useful sources of information on local law.

One of the best sources for information on municipal government is the National Institute of Municipal Law Officers. (NIMLO) NIMLO consists of professionals who work in the field of municipal law and it offers a wide range of helpful publications. Two of special use here are the *Municipal Attorney* and the *NIMLO Municipal Law Court Decisions*.

State digests, state legal encyclopedias, and local practice sets include references to court decisions on particular local law problems and may discuss local ordinances in point. General legal treatises on municipal law may be helpful for their discussion of broader issues, but are less likely to provide local references.

2. *ORDINANCE LAW ANNOTATIONS*

Besides covering ordinances in its state citators, Shepard's also publishes a digest of national scope on judicial decisions involving local ordinances, entitled *Ordinance Law Annotations* (13 vols., 1969–date). This service provides brief abstracts of decisions under broad subject headings, which are arranged alphabetically and subdivided into more specific subtopics. The set is kept up to date by annual pocket parts, and includes a two-volume table of cases arranged by state and city or county. Unlike the state citators, which provide access to decisions involving ordinances of specific localities, *Ordinance Law Annotations* allows one to survey municipal lawmaking throughout the country.

J. SUMMARY

Statutory law plays a pivotal role in the modern legal system and in legal research. Most appellate decisions involve the application or interpretation of statutes. Administrative regulations, court rules, and local laws all derive from delegations of power created by statute. The scope of judicial jurisdiction or executive authority is largely determined by legislative enactments. All legal research must therefore include the question: Is there a statute on point?

This chapter can perhaps best be summarized by the following questions applicable to every statutory research problem:

1. What statutory materials are available for the jurisdiction and what is their authority?

2. What statutory research approaches are best suited to this issue in this jurisdiction?

3. Have I found all possible sources of statutory law on this issue?

4. Is what I have found current, reflecting the latest enactments and the most recent judicial interpretations?

5. What other extrinsic aids to statutory interpretation are available on this problem?

K. ADDITIONAL READING

Jack Davies, *Legislative Law and Process in a Nutshell* (2d ed. 1986).

Colin S. Diver, "Statutory Interpretation in the Administrative State," 133 *U.Pa.L.Rev.* 549 (1985).

P. Frickey and D. Eskridge, *Cases and Materials on Legislation: Statutes and the Creation of Public Policy*, (West, 1988). This landmark work on the legislative process offers excellent insights.

"Special Issue on Legislation: Statutory and Constitutional Interpretation," 48 *U.Pitt.L.Rev.* 619 (1987).

U.S. Office of the Federal Register, *How to Find U.S. Statutes and U.S. Code Citations,* (3d rev. ed. 1977).

Chapter 6

LEGISLATIVE HISTORY

A. Introduction.
B. The Documents of the Federal Legislative Process.
   1. Congressional Bills.
   2. Hearings.
   3. Committee Reports.
   4. Congressional Debates.
   5. Presidential Approval or Veto.
   6. Other Congressional Documents.
C. Tools for Compiling a Federal Legislative History.
   1. Compiled Legislative Histories.
   2. *Congressional Information Service (CIS).*
   3. CCH *Congressional Index.*
   4. Online Legislative Research Services.
   5. *Digest of Public General Bills and Resolutions.*
   6. *Statutes at Large.*
   7. *Federal Index.*
D. Contextual Legislative History.
   1. Sources for General Context.
   2. Sources for Specialized Context.
E. State Legislative Histories.
F. Summary.
G. Additional Reading.

A. INTRODUCTION

When one finds a statute, the research process often is not complete. Statutory language can be vague or ambiguous, and determining the precise meaning of a provision can be quite a challenge. The determination of how to interpret a word or a phrase can determine the outcome of many issues.

Statutes may be difficult to interpret for several reasons. The imprecision of the English language itself is one likely culprit. It is hard to understand what a word like "reasonable" means whether it's used by a legislature or a court. The changes in circumstances caused by the passage of time can bring about entirely new applications of a statute that make it difficult to understand how its language applies. A good example of this is the attempt to apply copyright law to ever-expanding information technology. Still other problems can be caused by poor drafting on the part of the legislature. Sometimes statutes are just ineptly drawn. Finally, confusion can be introduced by a conscious decision on the part of a legislative body to reach an acceptable compromise on a controversial measure by using language ambiguous enough to be acceptable to each contending party.

One way of determining what a statute "really means" is to perform a legislative history. A traditional legislative history is the gathering together of every relevant document that was part of the passage of a piece of legislation. The idea is to find out what the legislative body thought it was doing when it passed the legislation by examining the evidence of what the legislators knew and said at the time. In the matter of federal legislation, this process leads one through a large number of documents of various types.

This method is not without controversy. Can the intent of a legislative body ever really be determined? Isn't it possible that each legislator who voted had a different intent? We know that many members of Congress never read the text of the documents that are collected as a part of the legislative history exercise. So how can such documents shed any light on Congressional intent? Such objections are being raised in prominent places. Justice Antonin Scalia of the Supreme Court is quite hostile to the use of legislative histories. He believes that one can find anything one wants to in the welter of documents surrounding the passage of legislation. He feels one should just stick to the plain language of the statute to find its meaning. But Justice Scalia's opinion remains a minority view. Legislative histories are cited more and more often in judicial opinions.

Traditional legislative history consists of three steps. First, one must identify the documents that might be relevant. Second, one must gather the documents. Third, one must analyze what is found. This Chapter will assist with the first two of these functions. Section B will review the documents generated as a part of the federal legislative process. The federal legislative process produces a rich mosaic of materials. Each type of document will be discussed in turn. Section C will discuss methods that can be used to assemble the documents. Analyzing the documents is best addressed in a course on Legislation.

To this point we have spoken of traditional legislative history, a process which uses official documents. In Section D we will talk about **contextual** legislative history. Contextual legislative history is a more active form of research that will move beyond the normal federal materials. This approach can help one to focus on certain documents, or even parts of documents, making the whole process simpler.

Section E is devoted to state legislative histories. State legislatures do not produce the same wealth of documents that the Congress does. The federal system, with fifty different state legislatures operating in fifty distinct manners, makes any systematic discussion of state tools impossible. We will look for functional commonalities that can help.

B. THE DOCUMENTS OF THE FEDERAL LEGISLATIVE PROCESS

The documents of a legislative history must be viewed in the context of the parliamentary practices which produce them. Congressional procedures are quite complex. The following brief survey of the normal stages of Congressional action is designed to place the major documents of federal legislative history in their procedural setting. More detailed information about that legislative process can be found in two brief Congressional pamphlets, *How Our Laws Are Made* and *Enactment of a Law: Procedural Steps in the Legislative Process.*[1] Illustrations A–1 and A–2 show the beginning and end of the text of a federal statute, the Foreign Intelligence Surveillance Act of 1978, as it appears in the *Statutes at Large.* The illustrations that follow in this chapter show various documents and finding tools relating to the legislative history of that law.

1. CONGRESSIONAL BILLS

The bill is the first relevant legislative document. Each bill, when introduced, is printed, assigned a bill number, and then referred to a committee of the house in which it is presented. The bill may be amended at any stage of its legislative progress and some bills are amended many times. The bill number is the key to tracing legislative actions prior to enactment and to locating many of the documents reflecting such actions. The finding tools for such research are called *status tables.* They usually list bills by number, identify documents relevant to their consideration, and frequently describe significant legislative actions taken. After enactment, similar tables arranged by public law number recapitulate the steps and documents of the legislative history of each enactment. These tables are discussed in Section C below.

Variations in the text of the bill as it is introduced, as it appears in a committee print, as amended, and as passed, may be helpful in determining its meaning. The deletion or insertion of particular language in the text implies a legislative choice and thus may reveal the intent of the legislature. Almost every printing of a bill represents a distinct step in its progress toward enactment and may ultimately be a significant document in its legislative history.

1. Willet, Edward F., *How Our Laws Are Made, (20th Edition)* H.R. Doc. No. 101–139, 101st Cong., 2d Sess. (1986) (rev. and updated); *Enactment of a Law: Procedural Steps in the Legislative Process,* S.Doc. No. 97–20, 97th Cong., 1st Sess. (1982) (rev. by R.B. Dove).

Illustration A–1

Beginning of the text of the Foreign Surveillance Act of 1978, as printed in the *U.S. Statutes at Large*

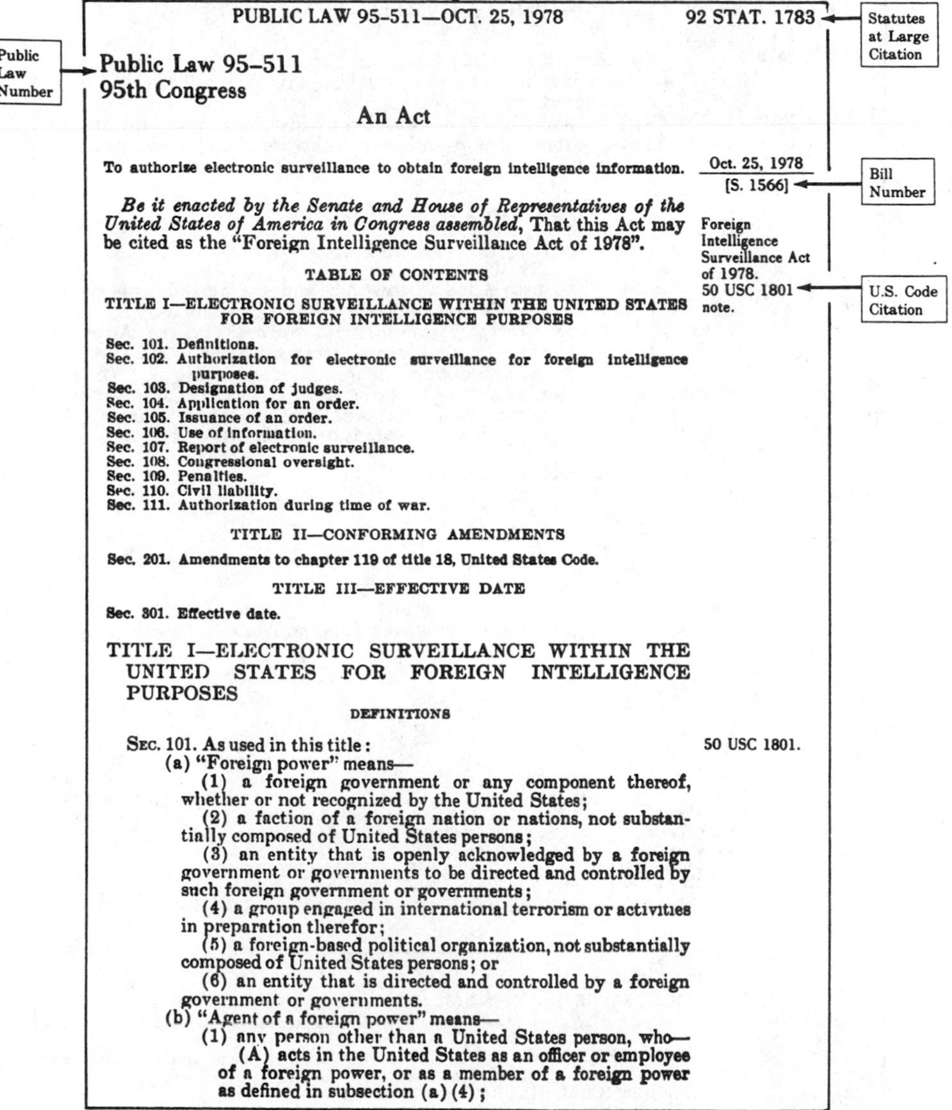

PUBLIC LAW 95-511—OCT. 25, 1978 92 STAT. 1783

Public Law 95-511
95th Congress

An Act

To authorize electronic surveillance to obtain foreign intelligence information.

Oct. 25, 1978
[S. 1566]

Be it enacted by the Senate and House of Representatives of the United States of America in Congress assembled, That this Act may be cited as the "Foreign Intelligence Surveillance Act of 1978".

Foreign Intelligence Surveillance Act of 1978. 50 USC 1801 note.

TABLE OF CONTENTS

TITLE I—ELECTRONIC SURVEILLANCE WITHIN THE UNITED STATES FOR FOREIGN INTELLIGENCE PURPOSES

Sec. 101. Definitions.
Sec. 102. Authorization for electronic surveillance for foreign intelligence purposes.
Sec. 103. Designation of judges.
Sec. 104. Application for an order.
Sec. 105. Issuance of an order.
Sec. 106. Use of information.
Sec. 107. Report of electronic surveillance.
Sec. 108. Congressional oversight.
Sec. 109. Penalties.
Sec. 110. Civil liability.
Sec. 111. Authorization during time of war.

TITLE II—CONFORMING AMENDMENTS

Sec. 201. Amendments to chapter 119 of title 18, United States Code.

TITLE III—EFFECTIVE DATE

Sec. 301. Effective date.

TITLE I—ELECTRONIC SURVEILLANCE WITHIN THE UNITED STATES FOR FOREIGN INTELLIGENCE PURPOSES

DEFINITIONS

SEC. 101. As used in this title: 50 USC 1801.
(a) "Foreign power" means—
(1) a foreign government or any component thereof, whether or not recognized by the United States;
(2) a faction of a foreign nation or nations, not substantially composed of United States persons;
(3) an entity that is openly acknowledged by a foreign government or governments to be directed and controlled by such foreign government or governments;
(4) a group engaged in international terrorism or activities in preparation therefor;
(5) a foreign-based political organization, not substantially composed of United States persons; or
(6) an entity that is directed and controlled by a foreign government or governments.
(b) "Agent of a foreign power" means—
(1) any person other than a United States person, who—
(A) acts in the United States as an officer or employee of a foreign power, or as a member of a foreign power as defined in subsection (a) (4);

Congressional bills are individually numbered in a separate series for each house and retain that number through both of the annual sessions of each Congress. A citation to a bill includes the number of the Congress and session in which it was introduced or printed, as follows: S. 1566, 95th Cong., 1st Sess. (1977). At the end of the two-year term of Congress, pending bills lose their active status and must be reintroduced if they are to be considered.

Illustration A–2

End of text and legislative history summary for Foreign Surveillance Act of 1978, in *Statutes at Large*

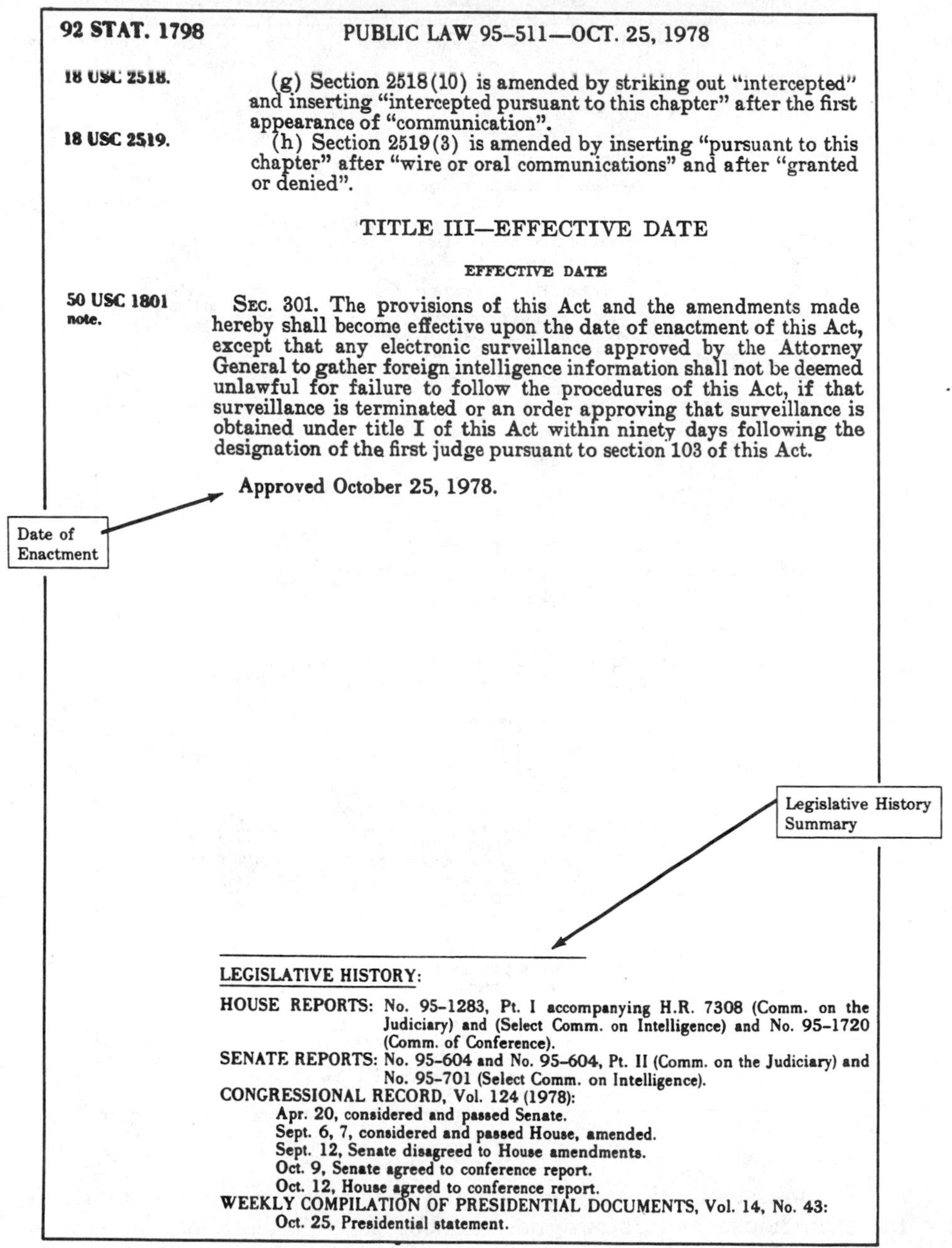

92 STAT. 1798 PUBLIC LAW 95-511—OCT. 25, 1978

18 USC 2518. (g) Section 2518(10) is amended by striking out "intercepted" and inserting "intercepted pursuant to this chapter" after the first appearance of "communication".

18 USC 2519. (h) Section 2519(3) is amended by inserting "pursuant to this chapter" after "wire or oral communications" and after "granted or denied".

TITLE III—EFFECTIVE DATE

EFFECTIVE DATE

50 USC 1801 note. SEC. 301. The provisions of this Act and the amendments made hereby shall become effective upon the date of enactment of this Act, except that any electronic surveillance approved by the Attorney General to gather foreign intelligence information shall not be deemed unlawful for failure to follow the procedures of this Act, if that surveillance is terminated or an order approving that surveillance is obtained under title I of this Act within ninety days following the designation of the first judge pursuant to section 103 of this Act.

Approved October 25, 1978.

LEGISLATIVE HISTORY:

HOUSE REPORTS: No. 95-1283, Pt. I accompanying H.R. 7308 (Comm. on the Judiciary) and (Select Comm. on Intelligence) and No. 95-1720 (Comm. of Conference).
SENATE REPORTS: No. 95-604 and No. 95-604, Pt. II (Comm. on the Judiciary) and No. 95-701 (Select Comm. on Intelligence).
CONGRESSIONAL RECORD, Vol. 124 (1978):
Apr. 20, considered and passed Senate.
Sept. 6, 7, considered and passed House, amended.
Sept. 12, Senate disagreed to House amendments.
Oct. 9, Senate agreed to conference report.
Oct. 12, House agreed to conference report.
WEEKLY COMPILATION OF PRESIDENTIAL DOCUMENTS, Vol. 14, No. 43:
Oct. 25, Presidential statement.

On occasion, a bill is transmitted to Congress by the President, along with a message. The message may provide useful context for the bill, explaining what the President hopes it will accomplish if enacted.

Such statements can be found in *Weekly Compilation of Presidential Documents*, and are sometimes reprinted by Congress. Illustration B shows such Presidential communication reprinted as a House Document.

Each session of Congress produces thousands of bills; almost no library can keep them in paper. Microfiche sets of the bills are received by libraries that have been designated as federal documents depositories. Most law school law libraries are such depositories. Copies of bills can also be obtained individually from the clerk of the House or Senate, from the legislators who sponsor them, or from the clerk of the committee considering them. The texts of a few bills also appear in the *Congressional Record,* but that is not the regular form of publication for bills. A commercial publisher, Congressional Information Service (CIS), issues Congressional bills and resolutions on microfiche beginning with the 74th Congress (1935–36). Bills are also available on line from CQ Alert and LEGI–SLATE, two data bases that provide a variety of information about Congressional activities. Both WESTLAW and LEXIS contain the full text of Congressional bills, though each service has only begun to load them quite recently, e.g. LEXIS begins with the 101st Congress. Check the coverage of these files as they may expand to cover earlier material as time passes. The full text of Congressional bills can also be reached over the Internet by tapping into the bulletin board of the House of Representatives, or the LOCIS system maintained by the Library of Congress. In early 1995 the federal government announced the creation of *Thomas,* an Internet site that provides access to a wide variety of Congressional documents, including bills. A more complete discussion of online services will be found in Section C.3 below.

Illustrations C–1 and C–2 represent the first page of different stages of bill number S. 1566, which became the Foreign Intelligence Surveillance Act of 1978. The bill was introduced by Senator Kennedy and referred to the Senate Committee on Judiciary. Illustration C–1 shows the bill after it was reported out by the Judiciary Committee with amendments, and referred to the Select Committee on Intelligence. After its passage by the Senate, the bill was introduced in the House of Representatives, as shown in Illustration C–2.

2. HEARINGS

Hearings are held by standing and special committees of the House and Senate to investigate particular problems or situations of general concern, and also to elicit the views of persons or groups interested in proposed legislation. Hearings may be designed to air a controversial situation, determine the need for new legislation, or bring before the Congress information helpful to its consideration of a pending bill. Hearings do not *have* to be held on every bill, and occasionally legislation is enacted for which hearings have not been held in one or both houses. But that is unusual and, even then, relevant hearings may be found on similar or related bills which may aid in interpreting the provisions of such an enactment.

Illustration B

Presidential communication transmitting proposed legislation, printed as a House Document

94th Congress, 2d Session - - - - - - - House Document No. 94–422

FOREIGN INTELLIGENCE SURVEILLANCE ACT OF 1976

COMMUNICATION

FROM

THE PRESIDENT OF THE UNITED STATES

TRANSMITTING

A DRAFT OF PROPOSED LEGISLATION TO AMEND TITLE 18, UNITED STATES CODE, TO AUTHORIZE APPLICATIONS FOR A COURT ORDER APPROVING THE USE OF ELECTRONIC SURVEILLANCE TO OBTAIN FOREIGN INTELLIGENCE INFORMATION

MARCH 24, 1976.—Referred to the Committee on the Judiciary and ordered to be printed

---

U.S. GOVERNMENT PRINTING OFFICE

57–011 WASHINGTON : 1976

Illustration C–1

A Senate bill after being reported out by the Judiciary Committee, with amendments, and referred to the Select Committee on Intelligence

95TH CONGRESS
1ST SESSION

S. 1566

[Report No. 95–604]

IN THE SENATE OF THE UNITED STATES

MAY 18 (legislative day, MAY 16), 1977

Mr. KENNEDY (for himself, Mr. BAYH, Mr. EASTLAND, Mr. INOUYE, Mr. McCLELLAN, Mr. MATHIAS, Mr. NELSON, Mr. THURMOND, Mr. HUDDLESTON, and Mr. GARN) introduced the following bill; which was read twice and referred by unanimous consent to the Committee on the Judiciary, and, if and when reported, then to the Select Committee on Intelligence

NOVEMBER 15 (legislative day, NOVEMBER 1), 1977

Reported by Mr. KENNEDY, with amendments

[Omit the part struck through and insert the part printed in italic]

NOVEMBER 15 (legislative day, NOVEMBER 1), 1977

Referred, by unanimous consent, to the Select Committee on Intelligence

A BILL

To amend title 18, United States Code, to authorize applications for a court order approving the use of electronic surveillance to obtain foreign intelligence information.

Be it enacted by the Senate and House of Representatives of the United States of America in Congress assembled, That this Act may be cited as the "Foreign Intelligence Surveillance Act of 1977".

SEC. 2. Title 18, United States Code, is amended by adding a new chapter after chapter 119 as follows:

II

Illustration C–2

Bill as introduced in House of Representatives after passage by the Senate

95TH CONGRESS
2D SESSION

S. 1566

IN THE HOUSE OF REPRESENTATIVES

APRIL 24, 1978

Referred to the Committee on the Judiciary

AN ACT

To amend title 18, United States Code, to authorize applications for a court order approving the use of electronic surveillance to obtain foreign intelligence information.

Be it enacted by the Senate and House of Representatives of the United States of America in Congress assembled, That this Act may be cited as the "Foreign Intelligence Surveillance Act of 1978".

SEC. 2. Title 18, United States Code, is amended by adding a new chapter after chapter 119 as follows:

I

The hearings, as published, consist of transcripts of testimony before a particular committee or subcommittee, questions by the legislators and answers by witnesses, exhibits submitted by interested individuals or organizations, and sometimes a print of the bill in question. Not every hearing which is held is published. Those that are published are listed in the *Monthly Catalog of U.S. Government Publications,* in *CIS/Index,* and in some of the status tables and legislative services described in Section C below.

Hearings relevant to the interpretation of a particular enactment may have been held and published by a session of Congress prior to the one which enacted the law in question. Sometimes relevant hearings may extend over several sessions and be published in several parts or volumes. Longer hearings sometimes contain indexes which are helpful in locating specific references.

As evidence of legislative intent, hearings rank below committee reports and the variant texts of bills. The testimony they contain may range from the helpful and objective views of disinterested experts to the partisan comments of interest groups. Although careful research can frequently turn up useful material in published hearings, this source must be used with a critical and discriminating view.

Hearings are generally identified by the number of the Congress and session in which they were held, the name of the committee which held them, the short title which appears on the cover of the published hearing, the number of the bill being discussed, and the dates covered by the hearing. Hearings are not generally published or numbered in consecutive series, but in recent years more committees have begun to employ convenient numbering arrangements for their published hearings. Illustration D shows the title page for the following Senate hearings: *Foreign Intelligence Surveillance Act of 1978: Hearings before the Subcomm. on Intelligence and the Rights of Americans of the Select Comm. on Intelligence of the United States Senate . . . on S. 1566,* 95th Cong., 2d Sess. (1978).

While hearings are indexed in the official *Monthly Catalog of U.S. Government Publications,* the most useful listings and indexes appear in the commercial publication, *CIS/Index.* Published by Congressional Information Service since 1970, *CIS/Index* has provided a comprehensive finding tool for federal legislative history (described more fully in Section D.1 below). Its annual coverage of hearings includes abstracts of testimony and indexing under the name of each witness. CIS also publishes a detailed retrospective index of hearings held from 1833 to 1969, under the title *CIS US Congressional Hearings Index* (42 vols., 1981–85). This index provides access to hearings by subject, witness name, bill number, and hearing title. For unpublished committee hearings, CIS also publishes two indexes, *CIS Index to Unpublished US Senate Committee Hearings* (5 vols., 1986), covering the period 1823 to 1964, and *CIS Index to Unpublished US House of Representatives Committee Hearings* (2

Illustration D

Senate hearings on S. 1566, the Foreign Intelligence Surveillance Act of 1978

FOREIGN INTELLIGENCE SURVEILLANCE ACT OF 1978

HEARINGS

BEFORE THE

SUBCOMMITTEE ON INTELLIGENCE AND THE RIGHTS OF AMERICANS

OF THE

SELECT COMMITTEE ON INTELLIGENCE

OF THE

UNITED STATES SENATE

NINETY-FIFTH CONGRESS

SECOND SESSION

ON

S. 1566

FOREIGN INTELLIGENCE SURVEILLANCE ACT OF 1978

JULY 19, 21, 1977 AND FEBRUARY 8, 24, 27, 1978

Printed for the use of the Select Committee on Intelligence

U.S. GOVERNMENT PRINTING OFFICE

94-628 WASHINGTON: 1978

For sale by the Superintendent of Documents, U.S. Government Printing Office
Washington, D.C. 20402
Stock Number 052-070-04477-2

vols., 1988), covering the period 1833 to 1936. The hearings covered in each of these indexes are also available from CIS in microfiche.

3. COMMITTEE REPORTS

The most important documents of legislative history are the reports of the Congressional committees of each house, and the reports of conference committees held jointly by the two houses. There are two reasons for the importance of Reports. The first is that there is a Report for almost every bill that becomes law. The House and Senate committees generally issue a report on each bill when it is sent to the whole house for consideration, or "reported out of committee." They are thus available for scrutiny. Second, since the Report accompanies the bill when it is returned to the legislative body for debate and a vote, it is presumed that each voting member has read the Report. Thus it is the one systematic, shared evidence of Congressional intent. Of course, many voting members do not actually read each report, but the fact that each one could have serves a sort of notice function.

These reports reflect the committee's proposal after the bill has been studied, hearings held, and amendments made. They frequently contain the revised text of the bill, an analysis of its content and intent, and the committee's rationale for its recommendations. Sometimes the report also includes a minority statement, if there was disagreement among the committee members. There will only be a Report for bills that make it out of committee. Most bills die quiet deaths.

If different versions of a proposed enactment have been passed by each house, a conference committee is convened, including members from each house. The conference committee reconciles the differences and produces an agreed compromise for return to both houses and final passage. The reports of these conference committees usually contain the text of the compromise bill. Conference committee reports are another very persuasive source for interpretation.

There are other materials that could be even more helpful in interpreting statutory language, such as the transcripts of committee markup sessions, in which legislation is first examined in detail, or of conference committee proceedings. Only rarely, however, are such transcripts published or generally available.[2]

Committee reports may also be issued on special investigations, studies and hearings not related to the consideration or reporting of a specific bill. Reports are issued, for example, on nominations to the executive and judicial branches.

The committee reports of each house are published as single pamphlets in separate numerical series for each session of Congress. They are most easily identified and traced by these report numbers, and their citations include the numbers of the Congress and session which issued

2. *See* Wald, "Some Observations on the Use of Legislative History in the 1981 Supreme Court Term," 68 *Iowa L.Rev.* 195, 200–203 (1983).

them, e.g., "S.Rep. No. 701, 95th Cong., 2d Sess. (1978)"; and "H.R.Rep. No. 1283, 95th Cong., 2d Sess. (1978)." Committee reports are listed and indexed in the *Monthly Catalog of U.S. Government Publications* and the *CIS/Index.* One or more committee reports on major enactments are reprinted selectively in *U.S. Code Congressional and Administrative News,* and a few appear also in the *Congressional Record.*

The reports are also published, together with House and Senate documents (another form of Congressional publication described below), in a bound series of volumes popularly called the *Serial Set.* In that form, they can also be located by the volume numbers in which they appear. A retrospective index to the Serial Set, covering the period from 1789 to 1969, is published by the Congressional Information Service under the title *CIS US Serial Set Index* (36 vols., 1975–79). Divided into twelve chronological parts, it provides access by subjects, keywords, and proper names.

Reports can also be found in full text as a part of both LEXIS and WESTLAW, though the coverage is only recent. The full run of selected Reports printed as a part of *USCCAN* are available on WESTLAW, which takes one back to 1946. This coverage is quite selective. No doubt coverage will move to earlier documents as time passes.

The following Illustrations (pages 182–185) show various committee reports on the proposed Foreign Intelligence Surveillance Act of 1978: E, Senate Report; F, House Report; G, House publication of the Conference Report; H, *USCCAN* publication of Committee Reports selectively.

Congressional publications also include "committee prints," which like the committee reports are issued generally in consecutive series for each House, with the numbering sequence beginning over in each session of Congress. Some committee prints are not numbered at all, however, and some are reissued subsequently as House or Senate reports or documents. Committee prints usually contain material prepared specifically for the use of a committee, such as studies done by the committee staff or outside experts, or compilations of statutes in particular areas. Others are statements by members of the committee or its subcommittees on a pending bill. An example of the latter type in 1978 set forth the views of members of a subcommittee of the House Committee on the Judiciary, on the House version of the proposed Foreign Intelligence Surveillance Act.

Like other Congressional documents, committee prints since 1970 are covered in the privately published *CIS/Index.* CIS has also published a comprehensive index to earlier committee prints, from 1830 to 1969, *CIS US Congressional Committee Prints Index* (5 vols., 1980).

4. CONGRESSIONAL DEBATES

Floor debate in Congress on a pending bill can occur at almost any stage of its progress, but typically it takes place after the bill has been reported out by committee. During consideration of the bill, amendments will be proposed and accepted or defeated. Arguments for and against amendments and passage are made, explanations of unclear or controversial provisions are offered, and much of the business of the legislative process is revealed in floor discussion.

Logic would seem to dictate that the spoken words of the legislators should be the most valuable of all evidence concerning legislative intent. Such is not the case. Anyone who has witnessed Congressional debate knows that many members are not present at all. Some remarks are added to the record after the fact. Thus the utility of the transcript of Congressional debate is limited.

The essential source for this form of legislative history is the *Congressional Record,* which is published daily while either house is in session. The *Congressional Record* provides a more or less verbatim transcript of the legislative debates and proceedings, subject, however, to revision of their remarks by the individual legislators.

The *Congressional Record* has been published since 1873, but it has fallen on difficult days. It has always been published in a pamphlet form called the daily edition; then at the end of the particular Congress it would be re-issued in bound volumes. The bound set would contain more items, and it would have different pagination. The required citation was to the bound set. Sadly, the bound set has not been complete since 1984. Therefore, everyone has been citing to the pages as they appear in the daily edition. Given the state of decline of government printing, this current habit may well transform into accepted practice.

Since the 80th Congress, each issue of the *Congressional Record* contains a "Daily Digest," which summarizes the day's proceedings, lists actions taken and enactments signed by the President that day, as well as useful committee information. All of the tools in the daily version suffer from the failure to provide a bound, cumulated edition.

Beginning with the 99th Congress in 1985, the *Congressional Record* can be searched through full-text computer-assisted research. Both LEXIS and WESTLAW have databases with the text of the *Record* since 1985, and it is also available on optical disk. Another online service, LEGI–SLATE, provides access to the *Record* of the current Congress in addition to other documents such as bills and committee reports. Summaries (but not full text) of *Record* material since 1981 are also searchable in the database *Congressional Record Abstracts,* available through DIALOG Information Services. CQ Washington Alert carries summaries of debates since 1983 and the full text since 1986.

Illustration E

Report of the Senate Select Committee on Intelligence on the Foreign Intelligence Surveillance Act of 1978

Calendar No. 643

95TH CONGRESS } SENATE { REPORT
2D SESSION } { No. 95–701

FOREIGN INTELLIGENCE SURVEILLANCE ACT OF 1978

MARCH 14, (legislative day, FEBRUARY 6), 1978.—Ordered to be printed

Mr. BAYH, from the Select Committee on Intelligence, submitted the following

REPORT

together with

ADDITIONAL VIEWS

[To accompany S. 1566]

The Select Committee on Intelligence, to which was referred the bill (S. 1566) to amend title 18, United States Code, to authorize applications for a court order approving the use of electronic surveillance to obtain foreign intelligence information, having considered the same, reports favorably thereon with amendments and recommends that the bill, as amended, do pass.

AMENDMENTS

On page 1, line 4, strike "1977", and insert in lieu thereof "1978".

On page 3, strike out all after line 5 through the end of line 19, and insert in lieu thereof the following:

(A) any person, other than a United States person, who—

(i) acts in the United States as an officer or employee of a foreign power; or

(ii) acts for or on behalf of a foreign power which engages in clandestine intelligence activities contrary to the interests of the United States, when the circumstances of such person's presence in the United States indicate that such person may engage in such activities in the United States, or when such person knowingly aids or abets any person in the conduct of such activities or conspires with any person knowing that such person is engaged in such activities;

Illustration F

Report of the House Permanent Select Committee on Intelligence on the Foreign Intelligence Surveillance Act of 1978

95TH CONGRESS 2d Session } HOUSE OF REPRESENTATIVES { REPORT 95-1283, Pt. I

FOREIGN INTELLIGENCE SURVEILLANCE ACT OF 1978

JUNE 8, 1978.—Ordered to be printed

Mr. BOLAND, from the Permanent Select Committee on Intelligence, submitted the following

REPORT

together with

SUPPLEMENTAL, ADDITIONAL, AND DISSENTING VIEWS

[To accompany H.R. 7308 which on November 4, 1977, was referred jointly to the Committee on the Judiciary and the Permanent Select Committee on Intelligence]

The Permanent Select Committee on Intelligence, to whom was referred the bill (H.R. 7308) to amend title 18, United States Code, to authorize applications for a court order approving the use of electronic surveillance to obtain foreign intelligence information, having considered the same, report favorably thereon with amendments and recommend that the bill as amended do pass.

AMENDMENTS

Strike all after the enacting clause and insert in lieu thereof:

That this act may be cited as the "Foreign Intelligence Surveillance Act of 1978".

TABLE OF CONTENTS

29-228

Illustration G

House of Representatives Conference Report No. 95–1720, on the Foreign Intelligence Surveillance Act of 1978

95TH CONGRESS 2d Session } HOUSE OF REPRESENTATIVES { REPORT No. 95–1720

FOREIGN INTELLIGENCE SURVEILLANCE ACT OF 1978

OCTOBER 5, 1978.—Ordered to be printed

Mr. BOLAND, from the committee of conference, submitted the following

CONFERENCE REPORT

[To accompany S. 1566]

The committee of conference on the disagreeing votes of the two Houses on the amendments of the House to the bill (S. 1566) to authorize electronic surveillance to obtain foreign intelligence information, having met, after full and free conference, have agreed to recommend and do recommend to their respective Houses as follows:

That the Senate recede from its disagreement to the amendment of the House to the text of the Senate bill, and agree to the same with an amendment as follows:

In lieu of the matter proposed to be inserted by the House amendments insert the following:

That this Act may be cited as the "Foreign Intelligence Surveillance Act of 1978".

TABLE OF CONTENTS

Illustration H

USCCAN publication of selections of committee reports on the Foreign Intelligence Surveillance Act of 1978

LEGISLATIVE HISTORY
P.L. 95–511

FOREIGN INTELLIGENCE SURVEILLANCE ACT OF 1978

P.L. 95–511, see page 92 Stat. 1783

Senate Report (Judiciary Committee) No. 95–604 (I and II), Nov. 15, 22, 1977 [To accompany S. 1566]

Senate Report (Intelligence Committee) No. 95–701, Mar. 14, 1978 [To accompany S. 1566]

House Report [Intelligence Committee) No. 95–1283, June 8, 1978 [To accompany H.R. 7308]

House Conference Report No. 95–1720, Oct. 5, 1978 [To accompany S. 1566]

Cong. Record Vol. 124 (1978)

DATES OF CONSIDERATION AND PASSAGE

Senate April 20, October 9, 1978

House September 7, October 12, 1978

The Senate bill was passed in lieu of the House bill. The Senate Reports (this page, p. 3970, p. 3973) and the House Conference Report (p. 4048) are set out.

SENATE REPORT NO. 95–604—PART 1
[page 1]

The Committee on the Judiciary, to which was referred the bill (S. 1566) to amend title 18, United States Code, to authorize applications for a court order approving the use of electronic surveillance to obtain foreign intelligence information, having considered the same, reports favorably thereon with amendments and recommends that the bill, as amended, do pass.

* * * * [page 3] * * * *

PURPOSE OF AMENDMENTS

The amendments to S. 1566 are designed to clarify and make more explicit the statutory intent, as well as to provide further safeguards for individuals subjected to electronic surveillance pursuant to this new chapter. Certain amendments are also designed to provide a detailed procedure for challenging such surveillance, and any evidence derived therefrom, during the course of a formal proceeding.

Finally, the reported bill adds an amendment to Chapter 119 of title 18, United States Code (Title III of the Omnibus Crime Control and Safe Streets Act of 1968, Public Law 90–351, section 802). This latter amendment is technical and conforming in nature and is designed to integrate certain provisions of Chapters 119 and 120. A more detailed explanation of the individual amendments is contained in the section-by-section analysis of this report.

3904

5. PRESIDENTIAL APPROVAL OR VETO

After a bill is passed by both houses of Congress, it goes to the President for approval. If the President approves a bill, it becomes law. If the President vetoes a bill, to become law it must be repassed by both houses by a two-thirds majority. The messages or statements issued when the President signs or vetoes particular enactments can shed light on legislative history. Like other Presidential messages to Congress, these documents appear in several places, including the *Congressional Record,* the *Weekly Compilation of Presidential Documents,* the *House* and *Senate Journals,* and as House and Senate Documents.

President Reagan sometimes used signing statements to convey his interpretation of disputed provisions. These statements have been included in *USCCAN* 's legislative history section beginning in 1986, although their importance in determining legislative intent is subject to dispute.[3]

6. OTHER CONGRESSIONAL DOCUMENTS

Congress publishes many documents as required by law or by special request. These *House* and *Senate Documents* are issued in numerical series which run consecutively through both sessions of each Congress. They contain special studies and reports, reprints of Presidential messages, executive agency reports and memoranda, reports of nongovernmental organizations, and a great variety of papers ordered to be printed by either house of Congress. They are listed and indexed in the *Monthly Catalog of U.S. Government Publications,* and since 1970 in the *CIS/Index.* A document is cited by the name of the house issuing it, the number of the Congress and session, and the document number. House and Senate Documents also appear in the Serial Set and can be cited to that form by volume number. The *CIS US Serial Set Index,* referred to above, provides access to House and Senate Documents, as well as House and Senate Reports, issued from 1789 to 1969 (with access to later reports and documents through the *CIS/Index*). The value of House and Senate Documents for legislative history is usually negligible, but occasionally a document will have some relevance to a pending bill. An example of such a document, a Presidential communication transmitting a draft version of proposed legislation, was shown in Illustration B earlier in this chapter.

C. TOOLS FOR COMPILING A FEDERAL LEGISLATIVE HISTORY

To compile the legislative history of a pending bill or of an enacted statute, one traces each of the actions taken by the legislature with regard to the bills which became law or which shaped the final enact-

3. *See, e.g.,* Garber & Wimmer, "Presidential Signing Statements as Interpretations of Legislative Intent: An Executive Aggrandizement of Power," 24 *Harv.J. on Legis.* 363 (1987); Greenhouse, "In Signing Bills, Reagan Tries to Write History," *N.Y. Times,* Dec. 9, 1986, at B14.

ment. Section B just identified what those documents are. The challenge for the researcher is to find the citation to the documents that she needs, and then to find the documents themselves.

The federal government has been in the information business for more than two centuries. It is not surprising that a wide variety of tools indexing and organizing legislative documents have arisen. The tools produced by the government have the advantage of being low cost, but they have the drawbacks of most government information. They are slow, often hard to use, and sometimes incomplete. The use of these tools is so difficult that legislative histories acquired a reputation for being next to impossible to do. But in recent decades several private publishers have done an excellent job of organizing legislative information. Print tools like *C.I.S.* and *Congressional Index* take the pain out of the process. Electronic versions of the information also ease the confusion of the researcher. These are the best places to pull information together. Of course, it is even better if the entire job has already been done, so Section 1 will start there.

1. COMPILED LEGISLATIVE HISTORIES

Given the frequency with which legislative histories are used, it stands to reason that many legislative histories have already been compiled. Someone has found the citation to each relevant document and assembled them. Or perhaps someone has assembled those documents or parts of documents judged to be of value. It would be horribly wasteful to ignore all of this work and to re-do it. Thus, before doing anything else, one should check to find out whether a legislative history has already been compiled.

Therefore the first step in performing a legislative history should be to check Nancy Johnson, *Compiled Legislative Histories*, published as a part of the American Association of Law Libraries Publication Series. Ms. Johnson lists, by Congress and Public Law number, all of the already compiled legislative histories that she was able to find, and provides the citation to where to find them. One only needs the Public Law number of the statute in question to gain access to this world of information. This reference tool sits at almost every law library reference desk. Checking it will take only a minute, and it might save the researcher hours of effort.

It is also worth checking with the law librarian in one's organization to see if there is a bank of existing legislative histories kept locally. Many law firms and government entities build up their own files of legislative histories. This is especially true of organizations that specialize in certain subject areas, where the same pieces of legislation are frequently encountered. Law libraries have been willing to share locally produced legislative histories. The Law Librarians' Society of the District of Columbia has prepared *The Union List of Legislative Histories*, 6th ed., (Rothman, 1991). This offers access to many such private compilations. A local librarian may also know of a relevant interest group that collects legislative histories for laws that are related to its topic. Such a group may be willing to send a complete file on the legislation in question. Never redo what has been done.

For the quick and dirty precompiled legislative history of every newly enacted federal law since 1947, check *U.S. Code Congressional and Administrative News*. *USCCAN* serves to update the *U.S. Code* by publishing the text of new laws while Congress is in session. At the end of each Session of Congress, when the pamphlets of the set are bound, an extra feature is added. The editors gather and reprint the most important sections of the most important Congressional Reports on each new piece of legislation. This is hardly comprehensive legislative history, but it is a start. *U.S. Code Congressional and Administrative News* is in almost every law library, so it is easy to find. As a convenient location for some very quick background, it is excellent.

2. CONGRESSIONAL INFORMATION SERVICE (CIS)

In 1970 *CIS* came on the scene and brought order to the chaos of Congressional publication. *CIS* breaks down the House and Senate into committees and sub-committees. Within each unit it divides publications into Hearings, Reports and Prints. Each one is listed and abstracted. *CIS* also prepares an index to all of the documents that allows access by subject, bill number and name. Literally each witness at each hearing is indexed. *CIS* is comprehensive, clear and reliable. It captures each document that is printed. The set is issued monthly in paper form, then at the end of the year appears as bound volumes. There is also a series of retrospective sets of *CIS* covering periods before 1970.

Libraries can purchase the annual updates of the *CIS* service alone as finding tools. One can also subscribe to an accompanying microfiche set that reprints in full each document abstracted in the set. The microfiche set is keyed to a unique numbering system devised by *CIS*. This unique identifying number is part of each entry in the Abstracts volume. Thus if the microfiche is available one can go directly from an index or abstract to the full text of the document.

From 1970 until 1983 the Abstracts volume of *CIS* for each Session of Congress contained a legislative history table. The table was keyed to each new Public Law. For each new law, the table listed each relevant document. This included Hearings, Reports and Prints, bill numbers, Presidential statements and debates. Thus, for any law enacted since 1970, one need only go to CIS to get a complete listing of documents.

Starting in 1984, *CIS* began to devote an entire volume to legislative history. Still keyed to each new Public Law, the set now offered both a listing of each relevant document, and an abstract of what the document covered. This helps the researcher key on what is important. For laws enacted since 1984, the process is thus even simpler. *CIS* coverage of legislative history since 1970 is also available on-line through Dialog, a part of the WESTLAW data base.

For laws enacted since 1970, *CIS* makes legislative history much simpler. Illustration I shows entries from a *CIS* index. Illustration J shows the pre–1984 legislative history listings, and Illustration K shows the post–1984 form. This is a tool that every serious researcher should get to know.

Illustration I

Index to *CIS/Index* for 1975 to 1978

Foreign economic relations — **Index of Subjects and Names**

US foreign policy effect on long-term access to Rhodesian mineral resources, 76 H461-87
US intl energy policy, 75 H381-45, 75 J841-27.3
US Intl Trade Commission programs, FY77 authorization, 76 S361-14
US Intl Trade Commission programs, FY78 authorization, 77 S361-12
"U.S.-Mexico Economic Relations: The Role of California", 78 H181-62
US oil firms' foreign ops, 76 S521-46.12
US-Saudi-Israel relations; relationship of Somalia aid to Diego Garcia naval base estab, 77 S381-1.3
US stockpiling policies and intl trade, 76 J952-23
US 200 mile fishing zone, estab, 76 S201-6.1
USDA participation in intl agric commodity negotiations, 75 S163-30
World energy supply and demand projections, 77 H962-23.1, 77 H962-27.1
World market economy system, status assessment, 77 S382-14
see also Balance of payments
see also Blockade
see also Dumping
see also East-West trade
see also Embargoes and boycotts
see also Export controls
see also Foreign assistance
see also Foreign corporations
see also Foreign trade
see also Foreign trade promotion
see also Import restrictions
see also International debts
see also International finance
see also Multinational corporations
see also Tariffs
see also Trade agreements

Foreign exchange
AF ops and maintenance programs to defray costs of dollar devaluation, FY79 approp, 78 S181-35.5
Army ops and maintenance programs to defray costs of dollar devaluation, FY78 approp reprogramming action, 78 S181-48.11
Bd for Intl Broadcasting programs, FY76 authorization, 75 H381-48
Bd for Intl Broadcasting programs to defray costs of dollar decline, supplemental approp FY78, 78 H181-92.24
Currency convertibility problems for US publications sales in Eastern Europe, 77 J891-4.6
Developing countries acceptance of economic reforms as precondition for foreign loans, 78 H241-4.1
DOD military construction and family housing programs to defray costs of dollar decline, supplemental approp FY78, 78 H181-93.5
DOD programs, supplemental approp FY78, 78 H181-26.4
Dollar decline abroad, effect on inflation, 78 S241-57.3
"Dollar Devaluation, Floating Exchange Rates and U.S. Exports", 78 H241-30.4
Dollar stabilization policies, 78 J841-25.1
Dollar's exchange rate decline, analysis, 78 S241-23.2
Domestic intl sales corporations cost-benefit analysis, seminar, 75 S252-25.1
Economic review, Oct 1978, 78 J842-22
Eurodollar market ops and impact on intl finance, 77 J842-5
European Recovery Program extension, 1949, 76 H461-83.3
Exchange rate policy and intl monetary reform, 75 H241-39, 75 H242-11, 75 J842-27
Exchange Stabilization Fund, oversight and Fed budget inclusion, 76 H261-15
Export policy oversight, 78 S241-37
Fed budget and economic overview, FY79, 78 H181-52.2
Fed Reserve Bd intervention to strengthen dollar, 77 H241-41.1
Financial instns restructuring for economic recovery, congressional study plans, 75 H242-17
First concurrent budget resolution, FY79, economic review, 78 S251-6.4
Foreign economic policy objectives, 76 H461-46.3
Foreign economic policy overview, 78 S381-1.3
Illegal African currency transfers allegedly encouraged by Overseas Private Investment Corp, 76 H461-58
IMF Articles of Agreement amendments, congressional authorization, 76 H241-35, 76 S241-69, 76 S243-24, 76 S381-33
IMF gold agreement proposal, rpt, 75 J842-38
IMF guidelines for govtl exchange rates intervention, 77 J841-18
IMF guidelines for govtl exchange rates intervention; Exchange Stabilization Fund, Fed budget inclusion, 78 S241-8
IMF intl currency devs review, 76 H241-22
Intl Communication Agency programs to defray costs of dollar decline, supplemental approp FY78, 78 H181-92.27
Intl exchange rate fluctuations, impact on inflation, 76 S361-22
Intl monetary and energy policy, 76 J841-2
Japan-US relations, background articles, 78 H782-67
Japan-US trade relations, review, 78 S381-30.1
Mexican peso devaluation impact on US Southwest, 77 J841-31
Monetary policy oversight, 78 H241-42.1, 78 H241-42.2
Multinatl corp intl financial transactions, 76 S381-26.1
Multinatl corps transactions during dollar devaluation crisis, 75 S382-24
OPEC oil price increases impact on intl economic stability, 75 H241-5.2, 75 H241-5.3
OPEC oil price peg to spec drawing rights, US economy impact, 77 H242-11
Pres Ford's economic proposals, 75 J841-20.1
Radio Free Europe/Radio Liberty facility leases renegotiation problems relating to currency fluctuations, 76 H461-32.1
State Dept programs to defray costs of dollar decline, FY78 reprogramming actions, 78 H181-92.2
State Dept programs to defray costs of dollar decline, supplemental approp FY78, 78 H181-17.7, 78 H181-92.7, 78 H181-92.8
Tax reductions and revisions, 78 S361-42.1
Trade deficits impact on dollar stability, 78 H781-12
US-held foreign currency accounts, 76 H401-38.2
"U.S.S.R.: Hard Currency Trade and Payments, 1977-78", 77 S402-16
see also Balance of payments
see also Special foreign currency programs

Foreign Gifts and Decorations Act
House of Reps members, officers, and employees acceptance of gifts from foreign govts, rules, 78 H742-1
Senate rules on Sens and employees travel at foreign govt expense, 77 S383-22

Foreign Government Investment Control Act
Foreign investment disclosure and anti-boycott proposals, 75 S241-43
Foreign investment regulation, 75 S261-68

Foreign Income Act
Taxation of Amers working abroad, 78 H783-50

Foreign Intelligence Surveillance Act
Draft text, Pres communic, 76 H520-1
Foreign intelligence electronic surveillance, judicial warrant requirements, 76 S521-40, 76 S523-32, 76 S963-8, 77 H521-26, 77 S421-1, 77 S521-52, 77 S523-43, 77 S523-44, 78 H431-3, 78 H433-3, 78 H433-5, 78 H522-12, 78 S421-3, 78 S423-1, 78 PL95-511

Foreign Investment Act
Foreign investment disclosure and anti-boycott proposals, 75 S241-43
Foreign investment in US, disclosure and regulation requirements, 75 S241-19
Foreign investment regulation, 76 H241-1.2

Foreign Investment Disclosure Act
Foreign investment disclosure and anti-boycott proposals, 75 S241-43
Foreign investment regulation, 75 S261-68, 76 H241-1.3

Foreign Investment Reporting Act
Foreign investment regulation, 75 S261-68

Foreign Investment Review Act
Foreign investment in US, info gathering and review procedures estab, 75 S261-27

Foreign Investment Study Act
Commerce Dept programs, supplemental approp FY75, 75 S181-32
Domestic and Intl Business Admin program, supplemental approp FY75, 75 H181-12.16
Foreign direct investment regulation, 75 S261-68.2
Foreign investment in US, disclosure and regulation requirements, 75 S241-19.1
Foreign investment in US, study authorization, 75 PL93-479
Foreign investment regulation, 76 H241-1.2
Foreign investments in US, Treas and Commerce Depts rpts, 76 S261-56

Foreign Investment Survey Act
US and foreign investments data collection system estab, 76 S263-20

Foreign investments
African dev problems and US aid programs, 78 H461-76.1
AID housing investment guarantee program, FY78 approp, 77 H181-77.7
Arab bank deposit implications for US banks, 76 H461-27.4
Arab-influenced US corp discriminatory practices, 76 H461-27.3

1066 CIS/Four-Year Cumulative Index — Volumes 6-9, 1975-1978

Illustration J

Cumulative legislative history summary in *CIS/Index* 1978 "Abstracts" volume

318 and related

H721-10; H721-14.
:722-2.

H721-5; H721-38;

S721-18;
:6; S721-27.
H722-2; H722-3.
!-14.
;402-5.
Vo. 95-949); H723-
ice Report).
No. 95-1140);

124 (1978):
ssed House.
ssed Senate,

nference report.
onference report.

TICLES, duty

'8. 95-2. 1 p.
'3 •Item 575.
774.
f June 30, 19[8]1, the
es on certain metal
metal, and other ar-
er purposes."
ctures of mashed or
and salt.
2165 and related

No. 95-1361).
No. 95-1243).
124 (1978):
ssed House.
ssed Senate,

n Senate amend-

:NT OF ENERGY SECURITY AND APPLICATIONS AR ENERGY ATION ACT OF

'8. 95-2. 5 p.
/3 •Item 575.
775.
s for the Department
rity programs for fis-
r purposes."
: R&D on strategic
:ations of nuclear en-

1686 and related

:; H201-25.
.4; S201-19.5;

Io. 95-1108).
nd S313-23 (No.
2693).

Congressional Record Vol. 124 (1978):
May 16, 17, considered and passed House.
Sept. 30, considered and passed Senate, amended, in lieu of S. 2693.
Oct. 11, House concurred in Senate amendment.

PL95-510 SMALL BUSINESS ACT, amendment, volunteer programs, establishment and operation.
Oct. 24, 1978. 95-2. 3 p.
• CIS/MF/3 •Item 575.
92 STAT. 1780.

"To amend the Small Business Act by transferring thereto those provisions of the Domestic Volunteer Service Act of 1973 affecting the operation of volunteer programs to assist small business, to increase the maximum allowable compensation and travel expenses for experts and consultants, and for other purposes."

Transfers statutory authority for SBA-administered Service Corps of Retired Executives and Active Corps of Executives.

Legislative history: (H.R. 13418 and related bills):
1978 CIS/Annual:
House Hearings: H721-27.
House Report: H723-7 (No. 95-1375).
Congressional Record Vol. 124 (1978):
Sept. 25, considered and passed House.
Oct. 11, considered and passed Senate.

PL95-511 FOREIGN INTELLIGENCE SURVEILLANCE ACT OF 1978.
Oct. 25, 1978. 95-2. 16 p.
• CIS/MF/3 •Item 575.
92 STAT. 1783.

"To authorize electronic surveillance to obtain foreign intelligence information."

Establishes judicial warrant requirements for executive branch use of electronic surveillance to obtain foreign intelligence information, and restricts the use of such information.

Legislative history: (S. 1566 and related bills):
1973 CIS/Annual:
Senate Hearings: S521-45.
1974 CIS/Annual:
House Hearings: H521-64.
1975 CIS/Annual:
Senate Hearings: S521-35; S521-60.
Senate Committee Print: S522-6.
1976 CIS/Annual:
House Document: H520-1.
House Hearings: H521-15; H521-16.
Senate Hearings: S521-40.
Senate Reports: S523-32 (No. 94-1035, accompanying S. 3197); S963-8 (No. 94-1161, accompanying S. 3197).
1977 CIS/Annual:
House Hearings: H401-4.4; H521-26.
Senate Hearings: S421-1; S521-52.
Senate Committee Print: S522-2.
Senate Reports: S523-43 (No. 95-604); S523-44 (No. 95-604, pt. 2).
1978 CIS/Annual:
House Hearings: H431-3.
Senate Hearings: S421-3.

House Committee Print: H522-12.
House Reports: H433-3 (No. 95-1283, pt. 1, accompanying H.R. 7308); H433-5 (No. 95-1720, Conference Report).
Senate Report: S423-1 (No. 95-701).
Congressional Record Vol. 124 (1978):
Apr. 20, considered and passed Senate.
Sept. 6, 7, considered and passed House, amended.
Sept. 12, Senate disagreed to House amendments.
Oct. 9, Senate agreed to conference report.
Oct. 12, House agreed to conference report.
Weekly Compilation of Presidential Documents Vol. 14, No. 43 (1978):
Oct. 25, Presidential statement.

PL95-512 COMPTROLLER GENERAL ANNUITY ADJUSTMENT ACT OF 1978.
Oct. 25, 1978. 95-2. 3 p.
• CIS/MF/3 •Item 575.
92 STAT. 1799.

"To provide for cost-of-living adjustments in the annuity of a retired Comptroller General, and for other purposes."

Amends Budget and Accounting Act of 1921.

Legislative history: (S. 3412 and related bill):
1978 CIS/Annual:
House Hearings: H401-31.
Senate Hearings: S401-53.
House Report: H403-10 (No. 95-1241, accompanying H.R. 12196).
Senate Report: S403-54 (No. 95-1267).
Congressional Record Vol. 124 (1978):
July 25, H.R. 12196 considered and passed House.
Oct. 9, considered and passed Senate.
Oct. 11, considered and passed House, in lieu of H.R. 12196.

PL95-513 VIETNAM VETERANS WEEK, designation authorization.
Oct. 25, 1978. 95-2. 1 p.
• CIS/MF/3 •Item 575.
92 STAT. 1802.

"Authorizing and requesting the President to designate the seven-day period beginning on May 28, 1979, as 'Vietnam Veterans Week'."

Legislative history: (H.J. Res. 1147):
Congressional Record Vol. 124 (1978):
Oct. 10, considered and passed House.
Oct. 12, considered and passed Senate.

PL95-514 PUBLIC RANGELANDS IMPROVEMENT ACT OF 1978.
Oct. 25, 1978. 95-2. 8 p.
• CIS/MF/3 •Item 575.
92 STAT. 1803.

"To improve the range conditions of the public rangelands."

Amends Federal Land Policy and Management Act of 1976 to provide for management of public grazing lands under Bureau of Land Management. Includes provisions for grazing fees and control of wild horses and burros.

Legisl
bills):
1976
Senat
Senat
pan
1978
Hous
Hous
H4
Senat
Cong
June
Sept.
am
Oct.
Oct.
Week
ment
Oct.

PL9

"To
parin
the s
other
In lie
anism
in Fe
Legis
1976
Hous
Hous
co
1977
Sena
1978
Sena
Hou
co
Sena
Cong
Sept.
Oct.
H
in

PL9

"For
Man
ters.
Also
grap
Legi
bill):
1978
Hou
M
13

JANUARY-DECEMBER 1978 Volume 9, Number 1-12

Illustration K

Legislative history entry for related Act in *CIS/Index* 1984 "Legislative Histories" volume

Public Law 98-477 **98 Stat. 2209**

Central Intelligence Agency Information Act

October 15, 1984

Public Law

1.1 **Public Law 98-477, approved Oct. 15, 1984. (H.R. 5164)**

"To amend the National Security Act of 1947 to regulate public disclosure of information held by the Central Intelligence Agency, and for other purposes."

Prohibits search, review, or release, under the Freedom of Information Act (FOIA) of CIA-designated sensitive operational information detailing intelligence sources or methods.

Authorizes search and review of designated sensitive files containing information relating to improper or illegal intelligence activities.

Authorizes search and review of designated sensitive files containing information on special activities when existence of such activities must be disclosed under the FOIA.

Authorizes judicial review of CIA designations of sensitive files.

Requires review for declassification and release of CIA information of historical value.

Requires additional CIA reports to congressional committees for oversight of FOIA processing activities.

Clarifies the relationship between the FOIA and the Privacy Act to prohibit Federal agency use of a Privacy Act exemption as grounds for denial of information otherwise accessible under FOIA provisions.

(CIS84:PL98-477 4 p.)

P.L. 98-477 Reports

98th Congress

2.1 **S. Rpt. 98-305 on S. 1324, "Intelligence Information Act of 1983," Nov. 9, 1983.**

(CIS83:S423-3 45 p.)
(Y1.1/5:98-305.)

2.2 **H. Rpt. 98-726, pt. 1 on H.R. 5164, "Central Intelligence Agency Information Act," May 1, 1984.**

(CIS84:H433-2 42 p.)
(Y1.1/8:98-726/pt.1.)

2.3 **H. Rpt. 98-726, pt. 2 on H.R. 5164, "Central Intelligence Agency Information Act," Sept. 10, 1984.**

(CIS84:H403-20 26 p.)
(Y1.1/8:98-726/pt.2.)

P.L. 98-477 Debate

130 Congressional Record
98th Congress, 2nd Session - 1984

4.1 **Sept. 17, 19, H.R. 5164 considered and passed House.**

4.2 **Sept. 28, H.R. 5164 considered and passed Senate.**

P.L. 98-477 Hearings

96th Congress

5.1 **"Freedom of Information Act: Central Intelligence Agency Exemptions," hearings before the Subcommittee on Government Information and Individual Rights, House Government Operations Committee, Feb. 20, May 29, 1980.**

(CIS81:H401-40 iii+205 p.)
(Y4.G74/7:F87/2.)

5.2 **"H.R. 6588, The National Intelligence Act of 1980," hearings before the Subcommittee on Legislation, House Select Intelligence Committee, Mar. 18, 19, 27, Apr. 15, 22, 1980.**

(CIS81:H431-2 iv+608 p.)
(Y4.In8/18:In8/2.)

97th Congress

5.3 **"Freedom of Information Act, Vol. 1," hearings before the Subcommittee on Constitution, Senate Judiciary Committee, July 15, 22, 31, Sept. 24, Oct. 15, Nov. 12, Dec. 9, 1981.**

(CIS82:S521-71 vi+1147 p. il.)
(Y4.J89/2:J-97-50/v.1.)

5.4 **"Freedom of Information Act: Appendix, Vol. 2," hearings before the Subcommittee on Constitution, Senate Judiciary Committee, July 15, 22, 31, Sept. 24, Oct. 15, Nov. 12, Dec. 9, 1981.**

(CIS82:S521-72 vi+880 p. il.)
(Y4.J89/2:J-97-50/v.2.)

5.5 **"Intelligence Reform Act of 1981," hearings before the Senate Select Intelligence Committee, July 21, 1981.**

(CIS81:S421-5 iv+90 p.)
(Y4.In8/19:In8/2.)

454 CIS/INDEX Legislative Histories JANUARY-DECEMBER 1984

3. CCH *CONGRESSIONAL INDEX*

Congressional Index, a commercial looseleaf service published since 1937 by Commerce Clearing House, is one of the most popular finding tools for legislative history. It is especially useful for gathering information about pending legislation. It is issued in two volumes for each Congress, one for the House and one for the Senate. *Congressional Index* offers many different approaches: indexes of all public general bills by subject and by sponsor; digests of each bill; a status table of actions taken on bills and resolutions; an index of enactments and vetoes; a table of companion bills; a list of reorganization plans, treaties, and nominations pending; tables of voting records of members of Congress by bill and resolution number; and a weekly report letter on major news and developments in Congress. Its status table section includes references to hearings, an important feature lacking in some other publications.

It should be noted that this service does not contain the actual text of bills, debates, reports or laws. *Congressional Index* is only a finding tool, but a most useful one, with weekly supplementation and generally good indexing.

Illustration L shows a typical page of the *Congressional Index* 's current status table of Senate bills, with a particularly informative entry for S. 1566, the bill which is the subject of the previous illustrations in this chapter.

4. ONLINE LEGISLATIVE RESEARCH SERVICES

The development of a variety of online database services has vastly improved research in legislative history. Several of these have already been described above, such as the various computer-based approaches to the *Congressional Record* and the online version of *CIS/Index.* Several of the specialized federal databases in WESTLAW and LEXIS include selective documents of legislative history of new legislation in those subject fields, with the most comprehensive coverage in federal taxation databases.

Online bill-tracking services are among the most important and timely sources for information on the status of current legislation. LEGI–SLATE is a service of the Washington Post Company covering Congressional developments and updated daily. As mentioned in earlier parts of this chapter, it includes the text of bills, committee reports, and the *Congressional Record* from the current Congress. Relevant legislation can be found by several methods, including subject, sponsor, and keyword. LEGI–SLATE tracks action on each bill day-by-day, providing information such as committee referrals, committee schedules pending, and recorded floor votes. It also lists any article discussing a bill in the

Illustration L

"Current Status of Senate Bills" table in CCH *Congressional Index*

94 10-25-78

Current Status of Senate Bills **20,507**

See also Status of Senate Bills
For digest, see "Senate Bills" Division.

1487
Reptd., amended, S. Rept. No. 95-962 .... 6/28/78
Amended on S. floor (Voice) 9/29/78
Passed S. as amended (Voice) 9/29/78
Amended to contain text of H. 8853 as passed (Voice) 10/3/78
Passed H. as amended (Voice) 10/3/78
Conferees appointed by H. 10/3/78
H. amends. rejected by S. 10/9/78
Conferees appointed by S. 10/9/78
Conf. Rept. filed, H. Rept. No. 95-1778 .... 10/12/78
Agreed to by H. (Roll-call) 10/14/78
Agreed to by S. (Voice) 10/14/78

1493
Hearing in S. 5/10/78
Reptd., amended, S. Rept. No. 95-1412 .... 10/14/78

1503
Passed S. as reptd. (Voice) 1/20/78
To H. Committee on Judiciary 1/23/78
Reptd., amended, H. Rept. No. 95-1747 .... 10/10/78
H. suspension vote postponed 10/10/78
Passed H. as reptd. (Roll-call) 10/12/78
H. amends. agreed to by S. (Voice) 10/13/78

★1509
Reptd., no amend., H. Rept. No. 95-846 .... 1/23/78
Passed H. as reptd. (Voice) 2/6/78
To President 2/8/78
Approved (P.L. 95-232) 2/17/78

1531
Hearing in H. 3/7/78

1537
Indefinitely postponed by S. 4/24/78

1546
Hearing in S. 4/5/78

1547
Amended on S. floor (Voice) 1/31/78
Text of bill incorporated into H. 7442 .... 1/31/78
Indefinitely postponed by S. 1/31/78

1556
Hearing in S. 6/15/78

1566
Reptd., amended, S. Rept. No. 95-701 .... 3/14/78
Amended on S. floor (Voice) 4/20/78
Passed S. as amended (Roll-call) 4/20/78
To H. Committee on Judiciary 4/24/78
Amended to contain text of H. 7308 as passed (Voice) 9/7/78
Passed H. as amended (Voice) 9/7/78
H. amends. rejected by S. 9/12/78
Conferees appointed by S. 9/26/78
S. amends. rejected by H. (Voice) 9/26/78
Conferees appointed by H. 9/26/78
Conf. Rept. filed, H. Rept. No. 95-1720 .... 10/5/78
Agreed to by S. (Voice) 10/9/78
Agreed to by H. (Roll-call) 10/12/78

★1568
Reptd., amended, S. Rept. No. 95-721 .... 3/23/78
Passed S. as reptd. (Voice) 4/5/78
To H. Committee on Public Works and Transportation 4/6/78
Passed H. in lieu of H. 10838 .... 5/15/78
Approved (P.L. 95-285) 5/25/78

1570
Hearing in S. (Printed) 1/19/78

★1582
Amended to contain text of H. 8009 as amended (Voice) 6/29/78
Passed H. as amended (Voice) 6/29/78
H. amends. agreed to by S. (Voice) 7/13/78
To President 7/17/78
Approved (P.L. 95-328) 7/28/78

★1585
Agreed to by H. (Roll-call) 1/24/78
To President 1/25/78
Approved (P.L. 95-225) 2/7/78

1587
Hearing in S. 3/15/78

1592
Hearing in S. 7/26/78

1613
Reptd., amended, H. Rept. No. 95-1364 .... 7/17/78
Amended to contain text of H. 9622 as passed 2/28/78 (Voice) 10/4/78
Passed H. as amended (Voice) 10/4/78
Conferees appointed by H. 10/4/78
Conferees appointed by S. 10/7/78
H. amends. rejected by S. 10/7/78

★1617
Bill title amended (voice) 2/28/78
Passed H. as amended (Voice) 2/28/78

Congressional Index — 1977-1978
014—51

Washington Post, Congressional Quarterly Weekly Report, and *National Journal.* Coverage of most Congressional action begins with the 96th Congress in 1979.

CQ Washington Alert (available on WESTLAW) is a set of data bases that offer great flexibility and coverage. The full text of Congressional bills since 1983, Reports since 1989, the Congressional Record since 1987 and a host of other useful files are available. If one has access to it, it offers a wealth of information. The data base is maintained by the Congressional Quarterly company. It is easy to use and current.

ELSS (Electronic Legislative Search System) is a bill-tracking service developed by Commerce Clearing House and covering both Congress and the state legislatures. ELSS does not include the full text of documents such as bills and reports, but provides summaries of legislation and information, updated daily. It calls for some skill to use effectively.

A service available through both WESTLAW and LEXIS is BILLCAST, which summarizes legislation in the current Congress and provides forecasts of each bill's chances of passage. A companion database, BILLCAST ARCHIVES, contains information on earlier terms, beginning with the 99th Congress in 1985.

The electronic sources mentioned above are examples. With the frequent offering of new databases and the demise of others, any description of what is available is soon outdated. The use of *current* database directories is essential for determining available resources. Two directories which are updated at least twice each year are: *The Gale Directory of Databases*, and *Directory of Online Databases* (Cuadra/Elsevier). As ever, the best method will be to ask a reference librarian what is current and useful. The librarian can also explain which data bases are available to the researcher.

5. *DIGEST OF PUBLIC GENERAL BILLS AND RESOLUTIONS*

The *Digest of Public General Bills and Resolutions* has been published since 1936 by the Congressional Research Service of the Library of Congress, and is normally issued twice during each session with occasional supplements. The final issue of the *Digest* for each session, published in two parts after its adjournment, cumulates information from the earlier issues and is invaluable for retrospective research. The *Digest* provides summaries of all bills and resolutions introduced in each session of Congress, with more detailed analyses of those bills which have been reported out of committee. There are indexes by sponsor and by subject. Separate sections of the digest provide coverage of those bills which have been enacted into law (arranged by public law number) and for all other measures receiving action (arranged by bill and resolution number). Following the summary of a bill's provisions is a list of major steps in its consideration. These lists include citations to committee reports issued on the bill, but not to hearings.

6. *STATUTES AT LARGE*

One of the simplest and most readily available places to find legislative history information for enacted laws is in the *Statutes at Large*. As shown above in Illustration A–2, at the end of the text for each law there appears a legislative history summary. This summary includes citations of reports from House, Senate, and Conference Committees, lists the dates of consideration and passage in each house, and provides references to presidential statements. It does not, however, provide references to exact *Congressional Record* pages, or to hearings and other relevant documents. This information has appeared at the end of each law only since 1975. From 1963 to 1974, it appeared at the end of each volume in a table, "Guide to Legislative History." The legislative history summaries in *Statutes at Large* are by no means complete, but they are readily available to a researcher studying the text of an act.

7. *FEDERAL INDEX*

Since 1977 *Federal Index,* issued by the National Standards Association, has provided an index to numerous government-related publications, including the *Congressional Record;* House and Senate bills, reports and hearings; the *Weekly Compilation of Presidential Documents;* the *Federal Register;* and the *Code of Federal Regulations*. It is published monthly, with annual cumulative volumes, and is also available online through DIALOG.

D. CONTEXTUAL LEGISLATIVE HISTORY

One of the reasons that doing a legislative history is such a chore is that the preliminary steps of identifying and gathering the documents can result in a huge stack of material. How is the researcher to cope with thousands of pages of material? Even the assistance of abstracts like those in *CIS* can only do so much. Flailing about in thousands of pages of Congressional documents can be the worst form of search.

That is why the idea of **context** can be such a help. Looking to secondary sources that surround the time of a new law's passage, or a bill's introduction and failure can add great insight. Contemporary accounts by knowledgeable sources help the researcher focus on what was especially controversial about the legislation. Such commentary may identify which Hearings or Reports were crucial, why one version of a bill was chosen, or what certain compromises really involved. It can identify who the relevant players were, and what groups cared about the legislation.

There are two types of context that can be of assistance. One comes from sources that monitor all legislative activity. A second comes from sources concerned with the specific issue at hand.

1. SOURCES FOR GENERAL CONTEXT

Several works on Congressional activities are published by Congressional Quarterly, Inc., including an analytical weekly magazine, a daily newsletter, and an online bill-tracking database. Each of these concentrates on what is going in the Congress—and why. CQ also publishes a variety of separate reference books relating to Congress, the most comprehensive being *Congressional Quarterly's Guide to Congress,* 4th ed. (1991).

The *Congressional Quarterly Weekly Report* offers weekly reporting of Congressional news, with summaries of major legislation and issues and cumulative indexing. *CQ Weekly Report* includes valuable analysis and background discussion of laws and legislative issues which make it popular with political scientists and many general researchers. This is the kind of context that can help the researcher sort out what to read and why.

At the end of each session a *Congressional Quarterly Almanac* volume is published, providing considerable information of permanent research value on Congressional activity during that year.

CQ also produces an online service, *Washington Alert,* which covers sessions back to 1983 and includes bill-tracking information, daily Congressional schedules, notices of new Congressional publications, and the text of *CQ Weekly Report.* The *Weekly Report* is also accessible online through LEGI–SLATE. This service is available on WESTLAW.

Another publication which watches the Congress carefully is the *National Journal.* The *National Journal* comes out monthly, and while it also covers the other branches of government, it focuses on the activities of Congress with care. Here one might find a detailed analysis of what really happened behind the scenes.

Since the *Washington Post* and the *Washington Times* are both hometown newspapers for Congress, each can be valuable for background. Checking on newspaper coverage at the time legislation was passed can give one insight and valuable leads. It is an excellent source of shortcuts in determining what Hearing was important. Each is available on-line.

2. SOURCES FOR SPECIALIZED CONTEXT

Every issue has its constituency. When doing a legislative history, or monitoring pending legislation, it is vital to identify what groups or individuals care about the issue. Are there trade groups or professional associations interested in the legislation? Are certain industries lobbying for a particular position? Have public interest groups taken a position? If so, any one of these sources could provide useful background. It may be that they have prepared background papers on the topic, they may even have done a complete legislative history already.

The general sources of legislative context discussed in Section 1 may identify such groups. If so, they should be pursued. Many such groups publish newsletters and periodicals, they may even offer on-line data bases. If one is truly lucky, one may find that they have a librarian or information officer who will help. Of course such a group may have a particular take on an issue, but if one is aware of that the work that they have done already can still be used. It would be insane to do research on legislation concerning firearms without using the resources of both the National Rifle Association and the gun control advocates.

If one cannot find a relevant group or interested party, check with a reference librarian. There are directories that can be used to find groups interested in any issue. Gale Research's *Encyclopedia of Associations* lists thousands of such groups. This multi-volume set is at most reference desks. Ask a librarian to teach one how to use it, and a world of information is suddenly available.

The work of such groups is not persuasive authority, but is can provide important background. A rule of thumb in research is to find someone who cares about the issue and use the work that they have already done.

E. STATE LEGISLATIVE HISTORIES

The use of legislative history in the interpretation of state legislation, and in statutory research at the state level generally, is no less important than in the federal area. However, the sources for state legislative history and the available research tools are much less adequate and the process is often very frustrating. In most states, it is virtually impossible to collect the necessary documents for a simple legislative history *outside* of the state capitol or its legislative library. Debates are almost never published, bills are usually available only at the legislature and during the session itself, committee reports are published in only a few states, and hearings even less often. Legislative journals are published for most states, but these rarely contain documentation explaining the decision-making process.

Many state legislatures are now covered by commercial legislative services, some of which provide status tables of pending bills. The commercial services often include document ordering options, but they can be quite expensive. In a number of states there are computer-based official or commercial information services for legislative proceedings. A growing number of states have created Internet access that allows free use of a wide range of state materials, some of which were never available in print. These usually include online access to bill tracking and bill digests, and sometimes offer information on legislative documents. For some states, however, there is no convenient method of identifying pending legislation, ascertaining its status, securing copies of documents or abstracts thereof, or tracing legislative proceedings. Recourse must be had to the legislature itself, to the legislative reference library, or to the state library.

Guide to State Legislative and Administrative Materials, 4th ed., by M.L. Fisher, has vastly improved the process of identifying what documents are available for each state, and from whom they are available. The guide provides detailed information for every state, with addresses and phone numbers of all relevant offices. It also indicates whether each state is covered by a legislative information service, in either printed or online format.

Another useful service, focusing on legislative organization and process generally rather than on specific legislative documents, is L. Hellebust, *State Legislative Sourcebook: A Resource Guide to Legislative Information in the Fifty States* (Government Research Service, annual). This looseleaf tool, first published in 1985, contains eight to ten pages of detailed information on the legislature and legislative process of each state. It also includes references to available information services.

Legal research manuals, describing legislative material, are available for a number of states (see Appendix A at the end of this book), and there are occasional periodical articles describing legislative history research in particular states.[4] The reference staff of a research law library in your state should also be consulted for details as to the local situation.

Some of the annotated state statutory compilations offer legislative session services which, like some looseleaf services with state coverage, include the text of laws enacted during the pending legislative session. These services may also provide some legislative history references, but not on a comprehensive or systematic basis. The *Legislative Reporting Service* of Commerce Clearing House, and its computer-based counterpart ELSS, referred to in Section C.3 above, offer, at considerable cost, custom-tailored information services on proposed legislation in particular subject areas.

Most states now have official or quasi-official agencies devoted to the research and recommendation of new legislation. These include independent law revision commissions, legislatively controlled councils, judicial groups, or academic bodies devoted to legislative study and drafting. The studies and proposals prepared by such agencies frequently result in enactments, although rarely in the exact form proposed. Their publications are an invaluable source of legislative history and may shed considerable light on the interpretation of the resulting enactment. Many of these studies are listed in the monthly *State Government Research Checklist*, published by the Council of State Governments.

Although the inaccessibility of legislative documents on state legislation is still an impediment to legal research, the astute researcher can often find useful material by persistent digging and the resourceful use of local libraries.

4. *See, e.g.*, O'Connor, "The Use of Connecticut Legislative History in Statutory Construction," 58 *Conn.B.J.* 422 (1984); Rhodes & Seereiter, "The Search for Intent: Aids to Statutory Interpretation in Florida—An Update," 13 *Fla.St.U.L.Rev.* 485 (1985); Allison & Hambleton, "Research in Texas Legislative History," 47 *Tex.B.J.* 314 (1984); Comment, "Legislative History in Washington," 7 *U. Puget Sound L.Rev.* 571 (1984).

F. SUMMARY

The many ambiguities in the language of our statutes derive less from the grammatical inadequacies of English prose than from the political compromises necessary to achieve a consensus for enactment. These ambiguities frequently become the focal issues of litigation in both the federal and state courts. Careful research in the documents of legislative history is necessary to ascertain the intent of the legislature in enacting the disputed provisions. Such research also provides sources for the development of arguments for or against particular interpretations.

Research into legislative history is facilitated by the use of a variety of finding tools, indexes and tables, in both official and commercial publications, as well as in an increasing number of online databases. The availability of the legislative documents themselves has been expanded by their inclusion in microfiche collections and computer-based services. Although many of these services are quite expensive the Internet is opening new vistas for the researcher. The work of the skilled researcher in federal legislative history can now be done in smaller libraries and away from large urban centers. For legislative research on the state level, the documentary sources are less adequate, but the finding tools for many states are increasing in numbers and expanding in scope.

G. ADDITIONAL READING

R. Dickerson, *The Interpretation and Application of Statutes* (Little, Brown, 1975). The standard text on statutory interpretation.

P. Frickey and D. Eskridge, *Cases and Materials on Legislation: Statutes and the Creation of Public Policy*. (West, 1988). This casebook is a wonderful analysis of the legislative process. The early chapters, particularly the explanation of the true legislative history of Title IX, is a wonderful example of contextual legislative history.

R.S. Lockwood & C.M. Hillier, *Legislative Analysis: With Emphasis on National Security Affairs* (Carolina Academic Press, 1981). A clear overview of the sources and tools of legislative history, focusing for illustrative purposes on one statutory field.

P.J. O'Rourke, Parliament of Whores (Atlantic Monthly Press, 1991). His chapter of the legislative process is an irreverent but refreshing romp. This is how bills really become law.

P.C. Schank, "An Essay on the Role of Legislative Histories in Statutory Interpretation," 80 *Law Libr. J.* 391 (1988). An argument that the concept of legislative intent is illusory, and that the use of legislative history in statutory interpretation should be limited to the elucidation of truly ambiguous provisions.

Norman Singer, Statutes and Statutory Construction (Clark Boardman Callaghan, 1992–). A looseleaf that updates the classic work by Sutherland of the same title.

Chapter 7

CONSTITUTIONAL LAW

A. INTRODUCTION

The constitution is the organic document of a political entity and of its legal system. Constitutions set the parameters for governmental action; they allocate power and responsibility among the branches of government and between the central government and its political subdivisions. In addition, they describe the fundamental rules by which the system functions, and, in some jurisdictions, they also define the basic rights of individuals. Constitutions can take any number of forms, ranging from relatively brief and general statements (the United States Constitution can be easily printed in ten pages) to quite lengthy documents of considerable specificity (the Texas constitution covers 160 pages [1]).

The Constitution of the United States defines its own primacy in our legal system. Article VI of the Constitution states: "This Constitution, and the Laws of the United States which shall be made in Pursuance thereof; ... shall be the supreme Law of the Land;...." Research in constitutional law in the United States is shaped by our concept of judicial review, which was derived in part from that clause of Article VI. This doctrine, established by Chief Justice Marshall's opinion in *Marbury v. Madison,* 5 U.S. (1 Cranch) 137 (1803), established the power of the judicial branch to review actions of the executive and legislature and to rule on their constitutionality. The power has, of course, been extensively used during various periods in our history at both the federal and state levels, and has greatly increased litigation over constitutional issues. Occasionally, it has also created political crises.

Because of the frequent judicial interpretation and application of constitutional provisions, and the vast secondary literature which has been and undoubtedly will be written on the Constitution, only a small part of constitutional law research relates to locating relevant constitutional provisions. The related historical background, judicial interpretations, legislative actions, and scholarly commentaries are a major focus of most research problems. The relationship of federal and state constitutional issues, and the conflict between federal and state jurisdiction and prerogatives introduce further complications in constitutional research. In any event, the constitutional documents of the United States and of the fifty states represent a separate and distinct literature with their own research procedures and tools.

B. THE UNITED STATES CONSTITUTION

The Constitution of the United States is usually considered the oldest constitutional document in continuous force in the world today. It provides the authority for all federal legislation (*i.e.,* acts, joint resolutions, treaties, and interstate compacts).

The text of the Constitution can be found in a variety of sources. It appears in many pamphlet editions, in standard reference works such as *Black's Law Dictionary,* and in almost all state and federal statutory compilations. Because its text is infrequently amended, obtaining a current version is not difficult. Perhaps the most easily accessible version is the one included in the *United States Code.*

Most research into problems of constitutional law requires extrinsic aids, beyond the text of the Constitution. The researcher therefore also needs access to interpretive judicial decisions and the scholarly analysis of commentators. The following sections describe the research tools

1. "Constitution of Texas 1876, Unannotated," in 1 *Vernon's Annotated Constitution of the State of Texas* 1 (1984).

available for such access—annotated editions of the Constitution, citators, digests, indexes, databases, and secondary sources.

1. ANNOTATED TEXTS

An annotated edition of the U.S. Constitution is one that provides notes of judicial decisions which have applied or interpreted its provisions. Three such "annotated" texts of the Constitution are in common use throughout the country, and many state codes include the Constitution annotated specifically with the decisions of that state's courts.

Two of the most important versions of the Constitution are part of the unofficial, annotated editions of the U.S. Code: the "Constitution" volumes of the *United States Code Annotated* (West) and of the *United States Code Service* (Lawyers Co-operative). The format and use of these sets are similar and have been described in Chapter 5, Statutes. They provide multivolume printings of the U.S. Constitution containing brief abstracts of the relevant cases decided under each clause, section, or amendment.

a. USCA

United States Code Annotated, following the traditional West approach, provides extensive coverage by including annotations to both federal *and* state decisions that concern each article or amendment of the U.S. Constitution. As a result, the text of the Constitution, when annotated in *USCA,* requires ten volumes.[2] The annotations to the due process clause of the Fourteenth Amendment alone fill two volumes. The volumes are kept up to date with cumulative annual pocket parts or supplementary pamphlets. As part of the West research system, the annotations for each clause include relevant key numbers, providing access to digests covering the Supreme Court, lower federal courts, and all state courts covered by the National Reporter System; cross-references to other West publications; and citations to periodical articles, Attorneys General opinions, and Executive Orders. The case annotations are arranged by subject, and an alphabetical index of the subjects annotated under each section is provided just before the annotations themselves. An index to the Constitution is printed at the end of the final volume, containing Amendments 14 to End. Illustration A shows the page from the bound volume of the *USCA* containing Article II, Section 4, concerning impeachment of the President and other federal officers.

b. USCS

The "Constitution" volumes of the *United States Code Service* serve many of the same functions as those of the *USCA*. The text of each

2. The *USCA* Constitution volumes were published as a "Bicentennial Edition" in 1987, after a thorough revision which eliminated annotations to many redundant and obsolete cases. The ten new volumes reduced the number of pages almost by half, replacing seventeen volumes and eleven pamphlets or pocket parts.

Illustration A

Article II, § 4 as printed in *United States Code Annotated*

Section 4. Impeachment

Section 4. The President, Vice President and all civil Officers of the United States, shall be removed from Office on Impeachment for, and Conviction of, Treason, Bribery, or other high Crimes and Misdemeanors.

CROSS REFERENCES

Effect of judgment of impeachment, see section 3, clause 7, of Art. 1.

"Former President" for purposes of retirement benefits as one whose service terminated other than by removal pursuant to this section, see 3 USCA § 102 note.

Power of impeachment by House of Representatives, see section 2, clause 5, of Art. 1.

Power of Senate to try impeachments, see section 3, clause 6, of Art. 1.

Treason, see section 3 of Art. 3.

LIBRARY REFERENCES

Encyclopedias

Impeachment as method of removal of officers, see C.J.S. United States § 62.

Law Reviews

Presidential immunity from criminal prosecution. George E. Danielson, 63 Geo.L.J. 1065 (1975).

Removal of the President: Resignation and the procedural law of impeachment. Edwin Brown Firmage and R. Collin Mangrum, 1974 Duke L.J. 1023.

Treason, bribery, or other high crimes and misdemeanors--A study of impeachment. Jerome S. Sloan and Ira E. Garr, 47 Temple L.Q. 413 (1974).

Texts and Treatises

Judicial, legislative and executive immunities, discussed generally, see Criminal Law Defenses § 204.

Texts and Treatises—Cont'd

Ultimate remedy: impeachment for high crimes and misdemeanors, see Tribe, American Constitutional Law § 4–16.

WESTLAW ELECTRONIC RESEARCH

See WESTLAW guide following the Explanation pages of this volume.

NOTES OF DECISIONS

Immunity 2
Officers of United States 1

---

1. Officers of United States

A member of Congress is not an officer of the United States in the constitutional meaning of the term as in the case of Blount, on an impeachment before the Senate in 1799, the question arose whether a senator was a civil officer of the United States within the purview of the Constitution, and the Senate decided that he was not. Member of Congress, 1882, 17 Op.Atty.Gen. 420.

2. Immunity

This clause does not imply immunity of the President from routine court process. Nixon v. Sirica, 1973, 487 F.2d 700, 159 U.S.App.D.C. 58.

section is printed, followed by annotations of court decisions arranged by subject. The *USCS* volumes also provide cross-references to *Lawyers' Edition* and *ALR* annotations, to other Lawyers Co-op publications such as *American Jurisprudence 2d* and *Federal Procedure, Lawyers Edition,* and to law review articles. *USCS* includes fewer annotations than *USCA,* so that the Constitution and its amendments, with annotations, are contained in only four volumes. There is an index at the end of the final volume. The four volumes are supplemented annually by cumulative pocket parts or supplementary pamphlets, and in the interim by *USCS* 's "Later Case and Statutory Service" pamphlets. Illustration B shows the impeachment clause as printed in the *USCS* version of the Constitution.

c. *The Library of Congress Edition*

Despite their usefulness as case finders for decisions under particular clauses of the Constitution, the *USCA* and *USCS* editions of the U.S. Constitution contain no descriptive or explanatory text. Many researchers find them too massive and cumbersome for achieving an understanding of constitutional doctrines, and turn instead to a more compact, single-volume edition which discusses the scope and development of each provision.

The Constitution of the United States of America: Analysis and Interpretation is prepared by the Congressional Research Service of the Library of Congress and published as a Senate Document.[3] This volume, edited by J.H. Killian and published in 1987, is the eighth annotated edition of the Constitution prepared under congressional direction. The first, in 1913, merely listed citations of Supreme Court cases after each provision. The work grew in scope with each edition, and adopted much of its present form with the 1953 edition, which was edited by the distinguished constitutional law scholar, Edward S. Corwin. The current edition is the third revision since 1953, and discusses Supreme Court cases decided through July 1982. A pocket part supplement, also published in 1987, updates the text with annotations of cases decided through July 1986.[4] Two subsequent supplements have been published, with the most recent providing annotations of cases through June 1990.[5]

The Library of Congress edition includes the text of the Constitution interspersed with extensive commentary, historical background, legal analysis, and summaries of judicial interpretation of each clause and amendment of the Constitution. The major constitutional decisions of the Supreme Court are discussed in detail, and the footnotes include numerous citations to other relevant cases and scholarly interpretations. Illustration C shows the page on which discussion of the impeachment clause begins.

Unlike the *USCA* and *USCS* indexes to the Constitution, which cover just its text, the Library of Congress edition's index has extensive

3. S.Doc. No. 16, 99th Cong., 1st Sess. (1987).

4. S.Doc. No. 9, 100th Cong., 1st Sess. (1987).

5. S. Doc. No. 36, 101st Cong., 2d Sess. (1990).

Illustration B

Article II, § 4 as printed in *United States Code Service*

Section 4. Removal from office.

The President, Vice President and all civil Officers of the United States, shall be removed from Office on Impeachment for, and Conviction of, Treason, Bribery, or other high Crimes and Misdemeanors.

RESEARCH GUIDE

Federal Procedure L Ed:

Government Officers and Employees, Fed Proc, L Ed, § 40:579.

Am Jur:

63A Am Jur 2d, Public Officers and Employees §§ 211-218.

Annotations:

Executive privilege with respect to Presidential papers and recordings. 19 ALR Fed 472.

Law Review Articles:

Franklin, Romanist Infamy and The American Constitutional Conception of Impeachment. 23 Buff L Rev 313.

Firmage & Mangrum, Removal of the President: Resignation and the Procedural Law of Impeachment. 1974 Duke LJ 1023.

Art II, § 4 CONSTITUTION

Rogers & Young, Public Office as a Public Trust: A Suggestion that Impeachment for High Crimes and Misdemeanors Implies a Fiduciary Standard. 63 Geo LJ 1025.

Hogan, The Impeachment Inquiry of 1974: A Personal View. 63 Geo LJ 1051.

Danielson, Presidential Immunity from Criminal Prosecution. 63 Geo LJ 1065.

Mezvinsky & Freedman, Federal Income Tax Evasion as an Impeachable Offense. 63 Geo LJ 1071.

Williams, The Historical and Constitutional Bases for the Senate's Power to Use Masters or Committees to Receive Evidence in Impeachment Trials. 50 NYU L Rev 512.

Sloan & Garr, Treason, Bribery, Or Other High Crimes and Misdemeanors—A Study of Impeachment. 47 Temp LQ 413.

INTERPRETIVE NOTES AND DECISIONS

No one has ever supposed that the effect of Art II, § 4, was to prevent removal of officers for other causes deemed sufficient by President, and no such inference could be reasonably drawn from its language. Shurtleff v United States (1903) 189 US 311, 47 L Ed 828, 23 S Ct 535.

There is no express provision respecting removals in Constitution, except as Art II, § 4, provides for removal from office by impeachment. Myers v United States (1926) 272 US 52, 71 L Ed 160, 47 S Ct 21 (ovrld on other grounds Humphrey's Exr. v United States, 295 US 602, 79 L Ed 1611, 55 S Ct 869) as stated in Kalaris v Donovan, 225 App DC 134, 697 F2d 376, cert den 462 US 1119, 77 L Ed 2d 1349, 103 S Ct 3088, reh den 463 US 1236, 77 L Ed 2d 1451, 104 S Ct 30 and (ovrld on other grounds Immigration & Naturalization Service v Chadha, 462 US 919, 77 L Ed 2d 317, 103 S Ct 2764 (superseded by statute as stated in EEOC v Westinghouse Electric Corp. (CA3 Pa) 765 F2d 389, 37 CCH EPD ¶ 35361)) as stated in United States v Woodley (CA9 Hawaii) 726 F2d 1328, different results reached on reh, en banc (CA9 Hawaii) 751 F2d 1008.

Because impeachment is available against all civil officers of United States, not merely against President, under Article II, § 4, of Constitution, contention that President is immune from judicial process cannot be based upon any immunities peculiar to President emanating by implication from fact of impeachability. Nixon v Sirica (1973) 159 App DC 58, 487 F2d 700, 19 ALR Fed 343.

Federal judges are "civil officers" within meaning of Article II, § 4. United States v Claiborne (1984, CA9 Nev) 727 F2d 842, cert den (US) 83 L Ed 2d 56, 105 S Ct 113, later proceeding (CA9 Nev) 765 F2d 784, 85-2 USTC ¶ 9821, 18 Fed Rules Evid Serv 1131.

Illustration C

Article II, § 4 as printed in the Library of Congress edition of the Constitution

which they can be held responsible must be under the general "federal question" jurisdictional statute, which, as recently amended, requires no jurisdictional amount.[27]

SECTION 4. The President, Vice President and all civil Officers of the United States, shall be removed from Office on Impeachment for, and Conviction of, Treason, Bribery, or other high Crimes and Misdemeanors.

IMPEACHMENT [1]

Few provisions of the Constitution were adopted from English practice to the degree the section on impeachment was. In England, impeachment was a device to remove from office one who abused his office or misbehaved but who was protected by the Crown.[2] It was a device which figured in the plans proposed to the Convention from the first and the arguments went to such questions as what body was to try impeachments and what grounds were to be stated as warranting impeachment.[3] The attention of

[27] *See* 28 U.S.C. § 1331. On deleting the jurisdictional amount, *see* P.L. 94-574, 90 Stat. 2721 (1976), and P.L. 96-486, 94 Stat. 2369 (1980). If such suits are brought in state courts, they can be removed to federal district courts. 28 U.S.C. § 1442(a).

[1] Impeachment is the subject of several other provisions of the Constitution. Article I, § 2, cl. 5, gives to the House of Representatives "the sole power of impeachment." Article I, § 3, cl. 6, gives to the Senate "the sole power to try all impeachments," requires that Senators be under oath or affirmation when sitting for that purpose, stipulates that the Chief Justice of the United States is to preside when the President of the United States is tried, and provides for conviction on the vote of two-thirds of the members present. Article I, § 3, cl. 7, limits the judgment after impeachment to removal from office and disqualification from future federal office holding, but allows criminal trial and conviction following impeachment. Article II, § 2, cl. 1, deprives the President of the power to pardon or reprieve in cases of impeachment. Article III, § 2, cl. 3, excepts impeachment cases from the jury trial requirement.

The word "impeachment" may be used to mean several different things. Any member of the House may "impeach" an officer of the United States by presenting a petition or memorial, which is generally referred to a committee for investigation and report. The House votes to "impeach," the meaning used in § 4, when it adopts articles of impeachment. The Senate then conducts a trial on these articles and if the accused is convicted, he has been "impeached." *See* 3 A. Hinds' *Precedents of the House of Representatives of the United States* (Washington: 1907), §§ 2469–2485, for the range of forms.

[2] 1 W. Holdsworth, *History of English Law* (London: 7th ed. 1956), 379–385; Clarke, "The Origin of Impeachment," in *Oxford Essays in Medieval History, Presented to Herbert Salter* (Oxford: 1934), 164.

[3] Simpson, "Federal Impeachments," 64 U. Pa. L. Rev. 651, 653–667 (1916).

coverage of topics addressed in its analysis, as well as an alphabetical table listing all cases discussed or noted in the text. The volume also includes the texts of proposed amendments which were not ratified; tables of Acts of Congress, state constitutional and statutory provisions, and municipal ordinances which have been held unconstitutional by the Supreme Court; and a list of Supreme Court decisions overruled by subsequent decisions.

The major shortcoming of this otherwise superb work is its infrequent revision and supplementation. Before the current 1987 edition there had been no pocket part for five years. The new volume was already five years out-of-date the day it was published; its most recent supplementation is more than four years old. Unless regular pocket part supplementation is provided, thorough updating will generally require the use of other, more current sources. Although the volume must be used with increasing caution as it ages, it remains an authoritative and useful resource for constitutional research.

d. Annotated State Statutory Codes

State courts frequently apply and interpret the United States Constitution. State laws or governmental actions are often challenged, for example, as being in conflict with the federal constitution. A state court decision is often relevant to research in constitutional issues, particularly as precedent in subsequent litigation in that state. As noted above, the annotations under the provisions of the U.S. Constitution in *USCA* and *USCS* include abstracts of state court decisions, as well as those of the federal courts. In about a dozen states, another valuable source for locating relevant cases is the annotated state code.

Almost every annotated state code contains the text of the U.S. Constitution, in addition to the constitution of that state. While every code annotates the provisions of the state constitution, only a few also annotate the U.S. Constitution. Those that do so provide a valuable service to researchers in their state, by isolating the most relevant case law from the mass of materials found in *USCA* or *USCS*. The annotations include abstracts of both state court decisions and federal cases arising in that state. References to state attorneys general opinions, law review articles, and other publications may also be provided. Notable among these state codes is the *Official Code of Georgia Annotated,* which devotes an entire volume to a thoroughly annotated U.S. Constitution.

2. SHEPARDIZING THE U.S. CONSTITUTION

References to court decisions applying and construing the provisions of the Constitution can be found in *Shepard's United States Citations* and in each of Shepard's state citators. The first volume of *Shepard's United States Citations, Statute Edition* provides references to all federal court decisions citing or discussing each constitutional clause or amendment. Supreme Court cases are listed first, followed by lower federal court decisions arranged by circuit.[6] The listings also include citations to the Constitution in federal legislation, treaties, *American Bar Association Journal* articles, and annotations in *ALR, ALR Federal,* and *Lawyers' Edition.* Because the Constitution is the subject of much interpretation and litigation, the bound volume's lists of citations under most provisions are lengthy and bewildering. Citations found in recent paperback supplements may be useful, however, in providing references to current cases that have not yet been covered in annotated editions.

Every Shepard's state citator, including those covering the District of Columbia and Puerto Rico, also includes a section listing references to the U.S. Constitution. The citations in these listings are generally limited to decisions of the particular state's courts and, in the past, state legislative acts, although some include state attorneys general opinions. Federal court decisions, even those from District Courts within the state, are *not* included. These citators can be very useful if one needs to know how a state supreme court or appellate court has applied or interpreted the federal constitution. Since only about a dozen state codes provide state annotations to the U.S. Constitution, *Shepard's* is often the quickest way to find state court decisions. Illustration D shows a typical page from *Shepard's Colorado Citations,* covering the U.S. Constitution.

3. FINDING COURT INTERPRETATIONS BY SUBJECT

Tools such as annotated texts and citators gather references to cases decided under particular constitutional provisions. If one is unsure of the relevant provision or wants a broader perspective, decisions interpreting and applying the Constitution can also be found by using any of the major case-finding methods discussed in Chapter 4.

Digests, including those in West's American Digest System, arrange headnotes of cases by subject. Although the annotated codes are more effective starting points for constitutional research, the digests can serve as an alternative approach to the same decisions. West's digests include sets covering the Supreme Court, the entire federal court system, and nearly every state court system. One of the topics West uses is "Constitutional Law," although constitutional issues are also addressed under numerous other topics. One can use the "Descriptive–Word Indexes" to find relevant sections, or approach the digest from the key numbers assigned to a known case. Because all of West's federal, regional, and state digests follow the same subject outline, it is easy to expand one's research from one jurisdiction to others or to the entire body of published case law. Unlike annotated codes or Shepard's, in which references are limited to cases citing a particular constitution, West's digests provide access to all cases with similar themes whether interpreting provisions of the U.S. Constitution or a state constitution.

6. Supreme Court decisions since 1956 which apply or interpret particular constitutional provisions are also listed in the *Lawyers' Edition Desk Book*'s "Table of Federal Laws, Rules and Regulations."

Illustration D

Citations to the U.S. Constitution in *Shepard's Colorado Citations, Statute Edition, 1994*

UNITED STATES CONSTITUTION Art. 4

Preamble
93Col418
26P2d1058

Art. 1

§ 2
Cl. 2
186Col63
525P2d466
Cl. 3
1968p274

Colorado Supreme Court decision

§ 4
172Col553
474P2d611
846P2d871
Cl. 1
172Col552
474P2d611

§ 5
172Col554
474P2d611
846P2d871
Cl. 1
172Col552
474P2d611
846P2d869

§ 6
807P2d1189
Cl. 1
810P2d207

§ 7
810P2d210
Cl. 2
195Col202
578P2d202
Cl. 3
121Col542
218P2d508

Colorado session law

§ 8
1945p756
1967p1125
101Col325
141Col291
182Col139
193Col45
198Col416
74P2d103
348P2d383
511P2d497
562P2d415
601P2d629
636P2d675
644P2d937
656P2d17
668P2d926
694P2d1288
699P2d934
715P2d1252
781P2d95
Cl. 1
106Col65
101P2d21
Cl. 3
82Col460
83Col62
93Col441
98Col437
105Col509
106Col2
113Col263
122Col330
129Col56
138Col168
140Col334
149Col263
156Col2
161Col282
179Col449
181Col363
181Col380
183Col330
193Col172
197Col495
261P3
262P915
26P2d1066
56P2d47
99P2d970
102P2d899
156P2d401
221P2d1084
266P2d1104
330P2d1111
346P2d1012
368P2d970
396P2d451
422P2d384
465P2d119
499P2d637
501P2d1050
509P2d1255
509P2d1261
517P2d841
564P2d108
593P2d1377
671P2d1306
690P2d180
698P2d253
699P2d935
715P2d1258
719P2d371
749P2d989
753P2d216
754P2d1174
763P2d1032
767P2d774
Cl. 5
699P2d934
Cl. 17
1947p895
1963p977
144Col321
186Col402
356P2d268
527P2d883

§ 9
89Col30
180Col92
183Col331
300P576
503P2d154
517P2d841
736P2d1206
757P2d1081
840P2d341
Cl. 2
138Col178
331P2d261
Cl. 3
827P2d607
834P2d238
839P2d1169
840P2d344

§ 10
83Col59
89Col30
102Col368
103Col566
105Col161
171Col559
183Col279
195Col120
196Col187
198Col556
200Col419
33CoA236
262P908
300P576
79P2d362
88P2d89
95P2d806
516P2d633
521P2d180
575P2d1296
583P2d916
609P2d107
615P2d703
618P2d1387
646P2d383
652P2d1061
684P2d183
694P2d1288
718P2d1040
728P2d365
761P2d1118
784P2d768
798P2d438
804P2d139
807P2d585
815P2d1001
818P2d265
827P2d606
834P2d192
834P2d240
840P2d341
840P2d1080
845P2d1159
Cl. 1
93Col131
93Col413
95Col297
97Col325
99Col596
101Col76
108Col265
116Col82
116Col257
121Col549
126Col553
143Col448
159Col290
184Col83
25P2d187
26P2d1056
36P2d164
49P2d1018
65P2d7
70P2d850
116P2d205
179P2d277
180P2d226
218P2d511
251P2d919
354P2d169
411P2d799
518P2d836
696P2d308
699P2d935
757P2d1079
758P2d1364
834P2d213
849P2d11
Cl. 2
93Col131
153Col539
25P2d188
387P2d48
Cl. 3
93Col131
25P2d187

Art. 2
352P2d109

§ 1
1963p1112
190Col489
549P2d777

§ 2
183Col162
516P2d629
Cl. 2
1951p849
111Col264
141P2d896

§ 3
190Col489
549P2d777

Art. 3
194Col163
198Col384
570P2d536
600P2d73
656P2d679
732P2d1205
751P2d1006

§ 1
188Col33
532P2d737
688P2d229

§ 2
92Col48
157Col439
18P2d457
403P2d219
Cl. 1
656P2d669
Cl. 3
122Col428
155Col576
222P2d615
396P2d460

§ 3
732P2d1205

Art. 4

§ 1
80Col450
85Col366
93Col187
94Col47
97Col278
104Col254
105Col412
107Col394
113Col320
113Col436
114Col32
114Col249
120Col103
120Col329
122Col52
131Col14
131Col319
136Col17
138Col2
141Col346
144Col457
145Col405
146Col10
147Col268
149Col40
169Col74
180Col146
183Col267
188Col362
192Col440
198Col238
200Col323
33CoA336
34CoA275
44CoA254
252P888
276P674
27P2d1038
49P2d428
90P2d621
98P2d1000
113P2d666
156P2d696
158P2d445
158P2d929
161P2d780
207P2d814
210P2d600
219P2d312
278P2d1020
281P2d517
314P2d296
329P2d781
348P2d264
356P2d962
359P2d363
360P2d112
363P2d1059
367P2d596
453P2d602
503P2d618
516P2d648
519P2d1223
529P2d343
534P2d1207
560P2d454
598P2d135
611P2d592
615P2d25
629P2d1077
630P2d581
637P2d364
653P2d86
660P2d517
660P2d906
709P2d83
719P2d744
739P2d912
753P2d783
757P2d1149
787P2d201
810P2d655
817P2d614

§ 2
135Col503
138Col168
156Col5
179Col449
180Col292
199Col124
199Col295
313P2d314
330P2d1111
396P2d451
501P2d1050
505P2d1
605P2d469
607P2d994
626P2d1143
687P2d450
Cl. 1
79Col508
246P1024
Cl. 2
93Col217
114Col489
121Col301
135Col504
135Col594

Continued

[G20,013] 3

In the *United States Supreme Court Digest, Lawyers' Edition* (Lawyers Co-op), it is very easy to determine which digest sections are applicable to particular constitutional provisions. The text of the Constitution is set out at the beginning of volume 17 of the set, with references after each provision to relevant digest topics and sections.

Other Lawyers Co-op reference tools also can be used to find cases. Many of the annotations in *ALR, ALR Federal,* and *Lawyers' Edition* contain extensive discussion of federal constitutional issues, including citations to state court decisions where they are relevant. As indicated above, annotations citing particular constitutional provisions are listed in *Shepard's United States Citations,* and access by subject is available in the *Index to Annotations.*

The full-text case databases of WESTLAW and LEXIS can also be very useful in finding case law under the Constitution, especially as one often needs to apply the Constitution's broad language to a particular set of circumstances. A computer search can combine the citation of a constitutional section or amendment with relevant factual or legal terms. Tips on using WESTLAW to retrieve cases are included in each of the Constitution volumes in *United States Code Annotated.*

4. SECONDARY SOURCES

Research on federal constitutional problems is often aided by the commentary and analysis of legal scholars. The extensive literature of constitutional law in such secondary sources as encyclopedias, treatises, and periodicals includes works that approach the Constitution from both historical and contemporary viewpoints. While later chapters will deal in depth with secondary sources generally, it is appropriate here to mention a few specific sources that can be of particular help to the constitutional researcher.

An excellent beginning point for analysis of constitutional issues is the *Encyclopedia of the American Constitution* (Macmillan 1986). This four-volume work, edited by Leonard W. Levy, Kenneth L. Karst and Dennis J. Mahoney, and supplemented in 1992, includes over two thousand articles, many by leading scholars. More than half of the encyclopedia discusses doctrinal concepts of constitutional law, but there are also articles on specific people, judicial decisions, statutes, and historical periods. Most articles include numerous cross-references to other articles and a short bibliography of further readings. In the final volume there are chronologies of the Constitution's birth and development, a brief glossary, and indexes by case, name, and subject.[7]

Two current texts should be noted for their broad coverage of the Constitution with a focus on current issues. Laurence H. Tribe's *American Constitutional Law* (2d ed., Foundation Press 1988) is probably the most thorough and authoritative one-volume treatment of American constitutional law. Ronald D. Rotunda & John E. Nowak, *Treatise on Constitutional Law: Substance and Procedure* (4 vols.) (2d ed., West 1992) is also an extensive analysis of constitutional issues, with an abridged hornbook version for students published as *Constitutional Law* (4th ed., West 1991).

7. Another work attempting comprehensive coverage of major concepts and cases is Ralph C. Chandler, Richard A. Enslen & Peter G. Renstrom, *The Constitutional Law Dictionary* (ABC–Clio, 2 vols., 1985–87). The first volume discusses individual rights provisions and the second covers governmental powers. A supplement to volume one was issued in 1987.

Numerous texts have been devoted to specific aspects of the Constitution and to the interpretative decisions of the Supreme Court. Among the many historical treatments of the Court and the Constitution, perhaps the most ambitious is the Oliver Wendell Holmes Devise *History of the Supreme Court of the United States* (Macmillan 1971–date). This multivolume, detailed history, with separate authors for each volume, is still incomplete; nine of its projected eleven volumes having been issued so far. Each volume covers the major constitutional issues and decisions in its respective period.

Periodical articles are a rich source of scholarly writing on the Constitution and constitutional issues. Subject access to these articles can be gained through the standard legal periodical indexes, or through one of several bibliographies published in recent years. Two of these bibliographies worth noting are Kermit L. Hall, *A Comprehensive Bibliography of American Constitutional and Legal History, 1896–1979* (5 vols.) (Kraus International 1984), with a two-volume supplement covering 1980–1987 published in 1991; and Bernard D. Reams, Jr., & Stuart D. Yoak, *The Constitution of the United States: A Guide and Bibliography to Current Scholarly Research* (Oceana 1987) (also published as volume five of *Sources and Documents of United States Constitutions, Second Series* (William F. Swindler, ed., Oceana 1982–87)).[8]

In addition to the numerous relevant articles in law reviews of general coverage, there are several periodicals specializing in constitutional issues, such as *Constitutional Commentary, Harvard Civil Rights–Civil Liberties Law Review,* and *Hastings Constitutional Law Quarterly.* The *Supreme Court Review,* published annually by the University of Chicago, includes scholarly articles on important, recent U.S. Supreme Court decisions, many of which deal with constitutional issues. The first issue of each volume of the *Harvard Law Review* usually contains an extensive analysis by its student editors of the activity of the Supreme Court in the preceding term. This survey, always prefaced by a major introductory article written by a noted scholar, is widely read and often cited. Finally, the *Yearbook of the Supreme Court Historical Society,* published annually by the Society, includes articles, usually in a popular tone, on the history of the Court and the Constitution.

C. HISTORICAL BACKGROUND OF THE FEDERAL CONSTITUTION

The events and discussions leading to the adoption of the Constitution and its amendments are preserved in a variety of reports, journals and other documents. These materials are of continuing importance as courts attempt to apply the terms of an eighteenth century document to changing modern circumstances. The significance of the framers' in-

8. Another useful bibliography is Robert J. Janosik, *The American Constitution: An Annotated Bibliography* (Salem Press 1991).

tent, however, is a subject of considerable dispute.[9]

A particularly useful guide to historical research sources on the Constitution and its amendments is Part VI, "Sources for Constitutional Provisions," of Gwendolyn B. Folsom, *Legislative History: Research for the Interpretation of Laws* (University Press of Virginia 1972; reprinted by Rothman 1979).

1. DRAFTING AND RATIFICATION

The Constitution of the United States was drafted in Philadelphia in 1787, and ratified by the states between 1787 and 1790. The Constitutional Convention was called to address deficiencies in the Articles of Confederation, which had been in force since 1781. Although the Constitutional Convention did not issue an official record of its proceedings, extensive notes were kept by James Madison and other delegates. The following sources provide useful documentary background on the drafting and adoption of the Constitution:

Max Farrand, *The Records of the Federal Convention of 1787* (3 vols.) (Yale University Press 1911) (supplement edited by J.H. Hutson, 1987, supplanting vol. 4, published in 1937). Long the standard source for documents of the constitutional convention, this set includes extensive day-by-day records including notes by major participants and the texts of various alternative plans presented.

Philip B. Kurland & Ralph Lerner, *The Founders' Constitution* (5 vols.) (University of Chicago Press 1987). This set provides references to and excerpts from primary materials illustrative of the political arguments and reasoning of the adopters of the Constitution. Following a first volume devoted to major themes leading up to the Constitution, the next three volumes are arranged by article, section, and clause of the Constitution. Volume 5 deals with the first twelve amendments.[10]

Wilbourn E. Benton, *1787: Drafting the U.S. Constitution* (2 vols.) (Texas A & M University Press 1986). Less comprehensive in scope

9. The opposing viewpoints may best be represented in speeches given in 1985 by Attorney General Edwin Meese III and Justice William Brennan, Jr. *Compare* Edwin Meese, "The Attorney General's View of the Supreme Court: Toward a Jurisprudence of Original Intent," 45 *Pub. Admin. Rev.* 701 (1985) (reprinted with minor changes as "The Supreme Court of the United States: Bulwark of a Limited Jurisdiction," 27 *S. Tex. L. Rev.* 455 (1986)), *with* William J. Brennan, Jr., "The Constitution of the United States: Contemporary Ratification," 27 *S. Tex. L. Rev.* 433 (1986). Both speeches are also printed, with others, in *The Great Debate: Interpreting Our Written Constitution* (Federalist Society 1986).

10. Two earlier, but still useful, compilations of historical documentation are: U.S. Bureau of Rolls and Library, *Documentary History of the Constitution of the United States of America, 1786–1870* (5 vols.) (U.S. Department of State 1894–1905; reprinted by Johnson Reprint 1965); and Library of Congress, Legislative Reference Service, *Documents Illustrative of the Formation of the Union of the American States* (Charles C. Tansill, ed.), H.R.Doc. No. 398, 69th Cong., 1st Sess. (1927).

A variety of documents from 1492 to 1977, including major Supreme Court decisions and other primary sources, are reprinted in *Sources and Documents of U.S. Constitutions, Second Series* (5 vols.) (William F. Swindler & Donald J. Musch, eds., Oceana 1982–87).

than *The Founders' Constitution,* this work also reproduces excerpts from participants' notes, arranged by article and section.

The Federalist, containing the essays of James Madison, John Jay and Alexander Hamilton in support of the adoption of the Constitution, has been issued in many editions since its first collected publication in 1788, and remains an indispensable work for the study of the Constitution. The full texts of *The Federalist,* as well as *Documents Illustrative of the Formation of the Union of the American States* (including the Declaration of Independence, the Articles of Confederation, and James Madison's notes on the debates in the Federal Convention of 1787), can be searched online in WESTLAW's "Bicentennial of the Constitution" (BICENT) database.

The debates concerning ratification of the federal Constitution by the state conventions are recorded in a variety of sources, including Jonathan Elliot's *Debates in the Several State Conventions on the Adoption of the Federal Constitution*, 2d ed. (5 vols.) (Elliot 1836–45; reprinted by Ayer 1987). Merrill Jensen's ambitious multivolume set, *Documentary History of the Ratification of the Constitution* (15 vols. to date) (Merrill Jensen, John P. Kaminski, & Gaspare J. Saladino, eds., State Historical Society of Wisconsin 1976–date), will be, when completed, the most comprehensive compilation of documents on the ratification of the Constitution by the states.

2. AMENDMENTS

Under the terms of Article V, amendments to the Constitution are proposed by Congress and presented to the states for ratification. The first ten amendments, which are known as the Bill of Rights, were proposed in 1789 and ratified in 1791. Although many other amendments have been suggested over the years, the Constitution has so far been amended only twenty-six times.

Information on the Bill of Rights and other proposed or enacted amendments to the federal Constitution can be found in several sources. Volume five of *The Founders' Constitution,* discussed above, covers the first twelve amendments as well as the original seven articles. The texts of major documents relating to the Bill of Rights appear in Bernard Schwartz, *The Bill of Rights: A Documentary History* (2 vols.) (Chelsea House 1971). There are also numerous documentary compilations which focus on the history of individual amendments.

A series of books providing information on amendments proposed during successive time periods all have titles beginning with the words *Proposed Amendments to the Constitution....* The first, covering the Constitution's first century, was prepared by Herman V. Ames, and published as 2 *Am.Hist.A.Ann.Rep.* (1896) and as H.R.Doc. No. 353, Pt. 2, 54th Cong., 2d Sess. (1897). Later volumes published as Senate documents cover the periods 1890–1926, S.Doc. No. 93, 69th Cong., 1st Sess. (1926); 1926–63, S.Doc. No. 163, 87th Cong., 2d Sess. (1963); and 1963–68, S.Doc. No. 38, 91st Cong., 1st Sess. (1969). The latest contribution to the series, covering 1969 to 1984, was edited by R.A. Davis and published in 1985 by the Library of Congress.

D. STATE CONSTITUTIONS

Each of the fifty states has its own constitution. These documents vary considerably in length and scope, and most address day-to-day activities of state government in a far more detailed manner than that of the U.S. Constitution. State constitutions can also be a vital tool in ensuring citizens' rights; even where the words in a state document mirror those in the federal Constitution, the judiciary of each state can interpret the terms of its own fundamental law.[11] A state constitution cannot deprive persons of federal constitutional rights, but it can guarantee additional protections not found in federal law.[12]

1. TEXTS

The texts of state constitutions are easily located in any of several sources. Each state's statutory code contains the text of the state's current constitution, along with earlier constitutions and other organic documents. Most useful are the annotated editions of the state codes, which contain *annotated* texts of the state constitution, similar to those for the U.S. Constitution in *USCA* and *USCS*. These annotated editions usually include references to historical background, attorney general opinions, and legislative history. The West state annotated codes can also be used for references, by key numbers, to the West digest system. Illustration E shows the section of the New Mexico Constitution concerning grounds for impeachment, as it appears in *New Mexico Statutes Annotated.* Note the cross-references to other constitutional provisions; annotations of cases and New Mexico Attorney General opinions; citations to law review articles; and references to *Am.Jur.2d, ALR,* and *C.J.S.*[13]

Another source for the texts of state constitutions is *Constitutions of the United States, National and State,* 2d ed. (7 vols., 1974–date), published by Oceana Publications for the Legislative Drafting Research Fund of Columbia University. This set collects the constitutions of all

11. In an influential article Justice William J. Brennan, Jr. urged the independent consideration and application of state constitutional rights. William J. Brennan, Jr., "State Constitutions and the Protection of Individual Rights," 90 *Harv. L. Rev.* 489 (1977).

12. For example, the U.S. Supreme Court has held that police are not required to inform a criminal suspect of counsel's efforts to provide legal assistance. *Moran v. Burbine,* 475 U.S. 412 (1986). Several state courts have declined to follow *Burbine* and have held that their state constitutions mandate such a duty. *See, e.g., People v. Houston,* 42 Cal.3d 595, 230 Cal.Rptr. 141, 724 P.2d 1166 (1986); *State v. Stoddard,* 206 Conn. 157, 537 A.2d 446 (1988).

13. Note also in Illustration E that Section 37 prohibits legislators from taking free railroad trips, a provision of less impact today than when the New Mexico Constitution was adopted in 1911. Many state constitutions reflect the prevailing political attitudes and concerns of the times in which they were drafted. For earlier examples, see Willi P. Adams, *The First American Constitutions: Republican Ideology and the Making of the State Constitutions of the Revolutionary Era* (Rita & Robert Kimter, trans., University of North Carolina Press 1980).

Illustration E

A page from the New Mexico Constitution, in *New Mexico Statutes Annotated*

Sec. 36. [Officers subject to impeachment.]

All state officers and judges of the district court shall be liable to impeachment for crimes, misdemeanors and malfeasance in office, but judgment in such cases shall not extend further than removal from office and disqualification to hold any office of honor, trust or profit, or to vote under the laws of this state; but such officer or judge, whether convicted or acquitted shall, nevertheless, be liable to prosecution, trial, judgment, punishment or civil action, according to law. No officer shall exercise any powers or duties of his office after notice of his impeachment is served upon him until he is acquitted.

Cross-reference. — As to power of impeachment, and exercise thereof, see N.M. Const., art. IV, § 35.

Legislators. — The impeachment route could be used to handle violation by a legislator of N.M. Const., art. IV, § 28 (relating to appointment of legislators to civil office and interests of legislators in contracts with the state or municipalities) or of art. IV, § 39 (relating to bribery or solicitation involving member of the legislature). 1965 Op. Att'y Gen. No. 65-229.

Judicial officers. — Although the supreme court, upon proper recommendation of the board of bar commissioners, could hold an individual subject to discipline, even though he was a judge, insofar as his activities and standing as a member of the bar association were concerned, recommendation by the board to the court regarding a judge's alleged dishonest, illegal or fraudulent act could not as such affect the individual's capacity as a judge during his term of office, inasmuch as the constitution provides the only method for the removal of a judicial officer. In re Board of Comm'rs of State Bar, 65 N.M. 332, 337 P.2d 400 (1959).

Officers appointed by governor are subject to removal by him, whether or not they may be impeached. State ex rel. Ulrick v. Sanchez, 32 N.M. 265, 255 P. 1077 (1926).

Comparable provisions. — Iowa Const., art. VI, § 19.

Montana Const., art. V, § 13.

Utah Const., art. VI, § 19.

Wyoming Const., art. III, § 18.

Law review. — For student symposium, "Constitutional Revision — Judicial Removal and Discipline — The California Commission Plan for New Mexico?" see 9 Nat. Resources J. 446 (1969).

Am. Jur. 2d, A.L.R. and C.J.S. references. — 46 Am. Jur. 2d Judges §§ 18, 19; 63 Am. Jur. 2d Public Officers and Employees §§ 171 to 176.

Physical or mental disability as ground for impeachment, 28 A.L.R. 777.

Power of officer as affected by pendency of impeachment proceeding, 30 A.L.R. 1149.

Offense under federal law or law of another state or country, conviction as vacating accused's holding of state or local office or as ground of removal, 20 A.L.R.2d 732.

Infamous crime, or one involving moral turpitude, constituting disqualification to hold public office, 52 A.L.R.2d 1314.

Conviction, what constitutes, within statutory or constitutional provision making conviction of crime ground of disqualification for, removal from or vacancy in, public office, 71 A.L.R.2d 593.

48 C.J.S. Judges § 27; 67 C.J.S. Officers § 68; 81A C.J.S. States §§ 94 to 101.

Sec. 37. [Railroad passes.]

It shall not be lawful for a member of the legislature to use a pass, or to purchase or receive transportation over any railroad upon terms not open to the general public; and the violation of this section shall work a forfeiture of the office.

Cross-reference. — As to prohibition against use of railroad passes by public officers, see N.M. Const., art. XX, § 14.

Purpose. — This provision was adopted for the primary purpose of eliminating graft upon the part of members of the legislature and to relieve said members of any feeling of obligation toward a railroad company by virtue of possession of a free pass. 1939-40 Op. Att'y Gen. 34.

Use of railroad passes prohibited. — There is no legislation against accepting free passes on railroads, but under this section and N.M. Const., art. XX, § 14, members of the legislature, of the state board of equalization, of the corporation commission, judges of the supreme or district courts, district attorney, county commissioner and county auditor assessor are prohibited from accepting and using passes. 1912-13 Op. Att'y Gen. 22.

Grant or receipt of free passes by motor carrier unlawful. — No carrier is required to transport any state employee or other person free of charge whether traveling on official business or not, and it is unlawful for a motor carrier which is regulated by the state to grant passes to any such person or for such person to accept them. 1937-38 Op. Att'y Gen. 160.

Prohibition inapplicable to railroad employees. — The prohibition does not apply to bona fide employees of the railroad companies or their wives, if they become legislators. 1939-40 Op. Att'y Gen. 34.

The acceptance of a pass from a railroad company by a member of the legislature who is also regularly employed by such company would not be within the contemplation of this provision of the constitution. 1937-38 Op. Att'y Gen. 56.

A railroad employee who becomes a member of the legislature does not come within the purview of this law prohibiting free passes. 1933-34 Op. Att'y Gen. 53.

A.L.R. references. — Evidence of right to free transportation on public conveyance, 3 A.L.R. 387.

Carriers, free passes to public officials or employees, 8 A.L.R. 682.

the states and territories in looseleaf volumes, kept current by regular supplements and revisions. The publisher has begun but not completed an indexing service for the set. Rather than compiling one comprehensive index for all the constitutions, as it had previously,[14] it plans to issue a series of separate subject indexes in a looseleaf binder. Only two subject indexes have been issued to date: "Fundamental Liberties and Rights: A 50–State Index" (1980), and "Laws, Legislature, Legislative Procedure: A Fifty State Index" (1982), both by Barbara F. Sachs.

State constitutions are also available online in WESTLAW or LEXIS. In WESTLAW, constitutions are simply included within each state's statutory database, but in LEXIS one can search in a file containing only a particular state's constitution or in one containing the state's constitution and statutes. Comparative research in constitutional provisions has been greatly facilitated by the ability to search all fifty state constitutions online.

The multi-volume *Book of the States,* published biennially by the Council of State Governments, also gives information about proposed state constitutional developments and revisions.

2. CASES AND SECONDARY SOURCES

Each of Shepard's state citators, in its statutory volumes or sections, covers that state's constitution. Shepard's provides references to judicial citations of constitutional provisions in that state's courts and in federal courts. It also includes citations in state session laws, law reviews, and *ALR* annotations. In addition, because proposed amendments to state constitutions are printed in the state session laws, they can also be Shepardized in the session law sections of the state citators. Many proposed amendments are not ratified, so it is useful to be able to check their status in Shepard's.

The traditional subject approaches to case-finding can also be used in research on state constitutional law. The topic "Constitutional Law" is used in West's digests for issues arising under both federal and state constitutions, and many issues of state governmental powers are digested under the topic "States." Numerous *ALR* annotations discuss matters involving state constitutional issues, and the state case law databases in WESTLAW and LEXIS can be used to find documents combining citations of constitutional provisions with other particular search terms.

Writings on state constitutional law can be found by using the standard periodical indexes or guides for particular states. Two recent bibliographies of articles and other works are the brief survey "State Constitutional Law Resources," in *Developments in State Constitutional Law* (Bradley D. McGraw, ed., West 1985), and the extensive monograph *The Constitutions of the States: A State-by-State Guide and Bibliography to Current Scholarly Research,* by Bernard D. Reams, Jr., & Stuart D. Yoak (Oceana 1988).

14. Columbia University, Legislative Drafting Research Fund, *Index Digest of State Constitutions* (2d ed., Oceana 1959, with pocket part supplementation through 1967), has been discontinued, but is still useful for earlier coverage.

3. HISTORICAL RESEARCH

Unlike the venerable and rarely amended United States Constitution, state constitutions are subject to frequent amendment and revision. The amendment process in many states has been used for quite mundane matters. The Alabama Constitution of 1901, for example, includes well over 400 amendments. Many states have had several constitutional conventions and a number of corporate revisions. Louisiana has had eleven constitutions in its history. On the other hand, nineteen states still operate under an amended version of their original constitution, and the constitutions for Massachusetts, New Hampshire and Vermont date from the eighteenth century.

The most comprehensive source for documents pertaining to state constitutions is the microfiche collection issued by Congressional Information Service, *State Constitutional Conventions, Commissions, and Amendments,* which includes documents issued from 1776 through 1978 for all fifty states. Access to the microfiche is provided by three bibliographies: Cynthia E. Browne, *State Constitutional Conventions from Independence to the Completion of the Present Union, 1776–1959: A Bibliography* (Greenwood Press 1973); Bonnie Canning, *State Constitutional Conventions, Revisions, and Amendments, 1959–1976: A Bibliography* (Greenwood Press 1977); and the two-volume *State Constitutional Conventions, Commissions, and Amendments, 1959–1978: An Annotated Bibliography* (CIS, 1981), and its successor volume covering 1979–1988 (published in 1989).

The major constitutional documents of every state, including enabling acts, acts of admission, and all enacted constitutions, are reprinted in William F. Swindler, *Sources and Documents of United States Constitutions* (10 vols.) (Oceana 1973–79). Here the past constitutions and other documents are assembled in chronological order for each state, with background notes, editorial comments on provisions of succeeding constitutions, selected bibliographies on the constitutional history of each state, and indexes.[15]

E. SUMMARY

The impact of judicial interpretation and application of constitutional provisions has had and continues to have significant effect on the development of law in the United States. It is therefore important that research problems be closely examined for possible constitutional issues.

15. Two older compilations, still valuable for research in early constitutions, are: Benjamin P. Poore, *The Federal and State Constitutions, Colonial Charters, and Other Organic Laws of the United States* (2 vols.) (Government Printing Office 1877); and Francis N. Thorpe, *The Federal and State Constitutions, Colonial Charters, and Other Organic Laws of the States, Territories and Colonies Now or Heretofore Forming the United States of America,* (7 vols.) H.R.Doc. No. 357, 59th Cong., 2d Sess. (1909).

Albert L. Sturm, *A Bibliography on State Constitutions and Constitutional Revision, 1945–1975* (Kristin Hall, ed., Citizens Conference on State Legislatures 1975), while out of date, contains useful lists of articles and other secondary sources on constitutional revision generally and in each state.

The extensive literature and research apparatus described in this chapter provides easy access to the texts of the federal and state constitutions, to relevant judicial decisions under each constitutional provision, and to secondary sources. These resources can be used to cut through the bewildering array of constitutional literature and locate further analysis and interpretation.

F. ADDITIONAL READING

Jerome A. Barron & C.Thomas Dienes, *Constitutional Law in a Nutshell* (2d ed., West 1991).

Charles L. Black, *People and the Court: Judicial Review in a Democracy* (Macmillan 1960; reprinted Greenwood Press 1977).

David P. Currie, *The Constitution of the United States: A Primer for the People* (University of Chicago Press 1988).

Michael G. Kammen, *A Machine that Would Go of Itself: The Constitution in American Culture* (Knopf 1986).

Jethro K. Lieberman, *The Enduring Constitution: An Exploration of the First Two Hundred Years* (Harper & Row 1987).

219-256

Chapter 8

ADMINISTRATIVE AND EXECUTIVE PUBLICATIONS

A. INTRODUCTION

The third source of primary authority is administrative law. Administrative law is the output of federal and state administrative bodies. These agencies are created by legislation, hence technically administrative law is subordinate to legislation. The volume and importance of administrative law, however, makes its treatment as a separate area both appropriate and necessary.

Research in administrative law can be challenging. The material is not as systematically treated as judicial opinions, nor is it as contained as legislation. There is no equivalent of the digest system or annotated codes for administrative materials. The agencies are numerous, and each has its own practices and publications. In this area the problem that federalism causes for the legal researcher is increased geometrically. Not only are there 51 jurisdictions, each jurisdiction has a full complement of administrative bodies issuing rules, regulations and decisions.

Things are made somewhat simpler by the fact that these agency publications tend to resemble the legislative and judicial documents already discussed. The forms will be familiar. Further, the federal level, which will occupy a great deal of the discussion here, has now been well organized. This is also an area where the advent of electronic information has been a real boon.

One of the biggest obstacles to successful research using administrative materials is the neophyte researcher's relative unfamiliarity with them. Many law students have little or no contact with administrative materials in law school. Even the law school course titled "Administrative Law" is traditionally about the Administrative Procedure Act, and issues of rulemaking. It touches very little on administrative agency publications. Most law students come to understand the workings of the judicial system while in law school. Most people have at least a basic appreciation of how the legislature works from a high school civics class. But many people have no understanding about how administrative agencies work. Nor is there any template which explains them all. Each is a research universe unto itself. Because this unfamiliarity can be a real barrier, the Chapter first presents some research tips that are applicable to doing research on any administrative law area.

B. RESEARCH STEPS

1. KNOW THE AGENCY

No one should carry out research using administrative materials until she gains a basic understanding of the administrative agency that regulates the area. Each agency, federal or state, has a mission that it is trying to accomplish. It sets out parameters of operation. This is crucial background. Plunging directly into compilations of regulations without understanding the context in which they were issued is the worst kind of blind research.

If one is dealing with a federal agency, this problem is easily solved. For basic background one can turn to *The United States Government Manual*. This publication of the Office of the Federal Register is a compendium of information about all three branches of government. Along with relatively brief coverage of the legislature and the Courts, there is current information about every bureau, office, agency, commission and board of the Executive Branch. The user can see what an agency is doing and why. It provides the names and telephone numbers of important agency personnel, and it lists resources that the agency offers to the public. It may turn out that there is a regional library for the agency in the researcher's area. If one does not know the name of the relevant agency, there is a subject index. This tool is normally kept at the reference desk of law libraries. Illustration A shows a sample page from the *United States Government Manual.*

A more sophisticated general guide is *The Federal Regulatory Directory* published by Congressional Quarterly. This provides much of the same information as the *United States Government Manual*, but often provides more detail. It concentrates on the large agencies, but gives summary treatment of the others. It is kept more up-to-date and, typical of privately compiled reference tools, its indexing is easier to use.

These are only the two most general and basic tools for the federal government. Other specialized directories are devoted to individual agencies and subjects. There are also services, both on-line and in paper, which track the phone numbers and addresses of relevant agency personnel. The best advice on available resources in this area is to talk with a reference librarian in the law library that one is using. Find out what the most current and available source is.

There are various guides to state agencies and publications. *The BNA Directory of State Codes and Administrative Registers* (1993) can provide good background on published sources. Virtually all of the states publish state manuals, often called "bluebooks" providing basic information about the government, its agencies and its functions. The quality of these publications vary from state to state, but they serve the same basic purpose as the *United States Government Manual.* All of these state publications are listed in *State Reference Publications: A Guide to State Bluebooks* . . . published by Government Research Services, a private publisher. If you are working with materials in your own state, a local reference librarian can quickly introduce you to the available state resources. Use whatever is available to get background.

The rule of thumb is not to begin until one has at least a rudimentary understanding of the agency or agencies regulating one's area.

2. KNOW THE LEGISLATION

Professor Dan Rodriguez of Boalt Hall Law School once gave a guest lecture in an Advanced Legal Research course on the subject of research in administrative law. He said that there are three secrets to performing good research in any administrative area. 1. Look to the underlying legislation; 2. Look to the underlying legislation; and 3. Look to the underlying legislation. This subtle hint is a point well taken. Administrative agencies are created by legislation. The underlying legislation is the foundation for all that an agency does. By reviewing the legislation itself, one can see the purposes that motivate the agency, and the rules that circumscribe its actions. The wise researcher returns to the original legislation and examines it with care. Since administrative agencies are sometimes challenged for exceeding their charge, this kind of background is essential.

Illustration A

Page from United States Government Manual

POSTAL RATE COMMISSION

1333 H Street NW., Washington, DC 20268–0001
Phone, 202–789–6800

Janet D. Steiger	*Chairman*
Maureen Drummy	*Special Assistant*
Gerald E. Cerasale	*Legal Adviser to the Chairman*
Bonnie Guiton	*Vice Chairman*
Ferrell D. Carmine	*Special Assistant*
Henry R. Folsom	*Commissioner*
(Vacancy)	*Special Assistant*
John W. Crutcher	*Commissioner*
Leonard Merewitz	*Special Assistant*
Patti Birge Tyson	*Commissioner*
W. Lawrence Graves	*Special Assistant*
Charles L. Clapp	*Chief Administrative Officer and Secretary*
David F. Stover	*General Counsel*
Stephen L. Sharfman	*Assistant General Counsel*
Robert Cohen	*Director, Office of Technical Analysis and Planning*
Charles C. McBride	*Assistant Director, Office of Technical Analysis and Planning*
Stephen A. Gold	*Director, Office of the Consumer Advocate*
Cyril J. Pittack	*Personnel Officer*

[For the Postal Rate Commission statement of organization, see the *Code of Federal Regulations,* Title 39, Part 3002]

The major responsibility of the Postal Rate Commission is to submit recommended decisions to the United States Postal Service on postage rates and fees and mail classifications. In addition, the Commission may issue advisory opinions to the Postal Service on proposed nationwide changes in postal services; initiate studies and submit recommendations for changes in the mail classification schedule; and receive, study, and issue recommended decisions or public reports to the Postal Service on complaints received from the mailing public as to postage rates, postal classifications, postal services on a substantially nationwide basis, and the closing or consolidation of small post offices.

The Postal Rate Commission is an independent agency created by chapter 36, subchapter I of the Postal Reorganization Act (84 Stat. 759; 39 U.S.C. 3601–3604), approved August 12, 1970, as amended by the Postal Reorganization Act Amendments of 1976 (90 Stat. 1303).

The Postal Rate Commission promulgates rules and regulations and establishes procedures and takes other actions necessary to carry out its functions and obligations. Acting upon requests from the United States Postal Service, or on its own initiative, the Commission recommends to the Board of Governors of the United States Postal Service changes in rates or fees in each class of mail or type of service. It submits recommended decisions on establishing or changing the mail classification schedule, and holds such hearings on the record as are required by law and are necessary to arrive at sound and fair recommendations. The Commission has appellate jurisdiction to review Postal Service determinations to close or consolidate small post offices.

Sources of Information

Rules of Practice and Procedure The Postal Rate Commission's Rules of Practice and Procedure governing the

The directories listed in Section A.1. above provide citations to the underlying legislation. It is best to read the legislation as it is printed in an annotated code. There one may find references to relevant judicial opinions and other commentary that give useful insight on how the legislation creating the agency has been interpreted.

3. INTERACTIVE RESEARCH

Administrative agencies are unlike the courts and legislature. These administrative agencies regulate behavior, make judgments, set limits. Often the agency will interpret its own rules, issue its own opinions etc. Thus monitoring the agency is not a static enterprise. One who only uses the books and pamphlets on the library shelves or the data in the on-line systems, may be missing the boat. It is necessary to interact with an agency. Many of the tools that will be discussed in the balance of this chapter provide telephone numbers and e-mail addresses, where the researcher can get feedback and help.

Use these avenues for interaction. Working on administrative materials in isolation, working out one's own theory as to what they mean, may be disastrous. The better route is to ask the people who are enforcing the rules what the rules mean. It may turn out that they do not know either, but that is important data too. Be active.

C. REGULATIONS OF FEDERAL ADMINISTRATIVE AGENCIES

The United States Congress enacts detailed legislation on a bewildering variety of subjects. Congress, however, cannot possibly provide for the multitude of possible situations which might arise under its enactments. Members of Congress are not experts in all areas of regulation, and the complexities of the legislative process are not well suited to rational consideration of detailed technical distinctions. Much of the work of creating specific rules to govern conduct is left to agencies specializing in particular activities. These agencies interpret and apply their governing statutes to create highly detailed rules, or regulations, which give specific content to the statutory intent and provide procedures for implementation and enforcement.[1]

Regulations are published by the federal government in the same two basic formats as statutes, first chronologically and later in a subject arrangement. The *Federal Register*, is issued every business day. It is the diary of the federal government concerning regulations. Every agency must print every new regulation there. The same regulations are then published in a more accessible format, arranged by issuing agency and subject, in the *Code of Federal Regulations.* CFR

1. The terms "rule" and "regulation" have the same meaning in this context. 1 C.F.R. § 1 (1989). We use "regulation" more often, since there are numerous other "rules" to be reckoned with in legal research, such as court rules or citation rules.

While the basic method of regulatory publication is analogous to that for statutes, there is little similarity between the research systems. Statutory codes are generally published in bound volumes, with amendments and annotations issued in pocket parts or supplements. Because the great volume of administrative regulations would make such a system impracticable, different methods are employed to update regulations and make current information available. Research in federal regulations has its own unique procedure, one that is different from research approaches discussed previously. The status of a *CFR* section is determined by consulting numerous finding lists for references to *Federal Register* pages. The process may sound laborious, but most of it is mechanical and quite straightforward.

1. THE *FEDERAL REGISTER*

The Federal Register is the source for all generally applicable federal rules and regulations. The Federal Register is a much more recent creation than either the sources setting out statute law or judicial opinions. Although executive and administrative agencies are as old as our government, it was not until the 1930s that their rules and regulations began to be organized. Roosevelt's New Deal caused a growth in agencies and in their output. No system was in place for publishing this new type of legal information. Hundreds of executive orders, thousands of regulations, and tens of thousands of pages of other documents of legal effect were issued with no regular method of publication. In many instances no attempt at public notice was even made.

Public pressure for reform finally came to a head when two cases concerning New Deal regulation of the oil industry reached the Supreme Court, even though they were based on a provision which had been revoked before the lawsuits were begun.[2] The ridiculousness of a system where no one knew what the law really was, accentuated by Chief Justice Hughes anger about the matter, led to the creation of a new form of publication.

The Federal Register Act[3] was designed to end this chaotic uncertainty by establishing a central repository for the publication of federal proclamations, orders, regulations, notices and other documents of general legal applicability. It initiated a new daily publication, the *Federal Register,* in which such documents must be published. The first *Federal Register* issue was published on Saturday, March 14, 1936. The *Register* 's statutory mandate is to publish the following classes of documents:

> (1) Presidential proclamations and Executive orders, except those not having general applicability and legal effect or effective only against Federal agencies or persons in their capacity as officers, agents, or employees thereof;

2. *United States v. Smith,* 293 U.S. 633 (1934) (appeal dismissed); *Panama Refining Co. v. Ryan,* 293 U.S. 388 (1935).

3. Ch. 417, 49 Stat. 500 (1935).

(2) documents or classes of documents that the President may determine from time to time have general applicability and legal effect; and

(3) documents or classes of documents that may be required so to be published by Act of Congress.

. . . [E]very document or order which prescribes a penalty has general applicability and legal effect.[4]

Publication in the *Federal Register* is deemed to provide any parties affected by a regulation with constructive notice of its contents.[5]

Despite the substantial improvements in access brought about by the Federal Register Act, the decision-making procedures used by the agencies remained unclear and arbitrary. In 1946 Congress passed the Administrative Procedure Act,[6] which gave the public the right to participate in agency rulemaking and significantly expanded the scope of the *Federal Register*. The act provided that notice of proposed rulemaking be published in the *Register*, affording the public the opportunity to comment on the proposed rules.[7] In its January 1, 1947 issue, the *Federal Register* inaugurated a new "Proposed Rule Making" section with proposed standards for grades of canned tangerine juice.[8] Further improvements in publication of notices were added by the Freedom of Information Act,[9] which requires agencies to publish organizational descriptions and policy statements,[10] and the Government in the Sunshine Act,[11] which requires agencies to publish notices of most meetings.[12]

In each issue of the *Federal Register*, material is published in the following order:

(1) Presidential documents (proclamations, executive orders, and other executive documents);

4. 44 U.S.C. § 1505(a) (1982). The Administrative Committee of the Federal Register has further defined "document having general applicability and legal effect" as "any document issued under proper authority prescribing a penalty or course of conduct, conferring a right, privilege, authority, or immunity, or imposing an obligation, and relevant or applicable to the general public, members of a class, or persons in a locality, as distinguished from named individuals or organizations." 1 C.F.R. § 1.1 (1988).

5. 44 U.S.C. § 1507 (1982). Justice Jackson sharply criticized the effects of this notice provision:

> To my mind, it is an absurdity to hold that every farmer who insures his crops knows what the Federal Register contains or even knows that there is such a publication. If he were to peruse this voluminous and dull publication as it is issued from time to time in order to make sure whether anything has been promulgated that affects his rights, he would never need crop insurance, for he would never get time to plant any crops. Nor am I convinced that a reading of technically-worded regulations would enlighten him much in any event.

Federal Crop Insurance Corp. v. Merrill, 332 U.S. 380, 387 (1947) (Jackson, J., dissenting).

6. Ch. 324, 80 Stat. 237 (1946).

7. 5 U.S.C. § 553 (1988).

8. 12 Fed.Reg. 32 (1947).

9. Act of July 4, 1966, Pub.L. No. 84–487, 80 Stat. 237.

10. 5 U.S.C. § 552(a)(1) (1988).

11. Pub.L. No. 94–409, 90 Stat. 1241 (1976).

12. 5 U.S.C. § 552(e)(3) (1988).

(2) Rules and regulations (documents having general applicability and legal effect);

(3) Proposed rules (texts of proposed regulations, as well as regulatory agendas and notices of hearings);

(4) Notices (documents not concerned with rulemaking proceedings, such as announcements of application deadlines or license revocations); and

(5) Notices of Sunshine Act meetings.

The arrangement of documents in each section of the *Register* is determined by the title of the *Code of Federal Regulations* in which the rules will appear or which they affect. Some documents are published as separate sections at the end of an issue, rather than in their appropriate place, so that issuing agencies can make additional copies available for distribution. Illustration B shows two pages of the April 22, 1992 *Federal Register* in which the National Marine Fisheries Services changes some of the fish listed as endangered under the auspices of the Endangered Species Act. (Remember Prof. Rodriguez!) . The rule amends 50 C.F.R. 221.4. The relevant section is part of series of changes made to various parts of Title 50 in this issue of the Federal Register. Immediately before the printed change is a great deal of information on why the change is being made, the name of a relevant officer of the agency, even citations to studies that were used in formulating the change. The *Federal Register* often contains such useful information. It helps put the rule into context.

Each issue of the *Federal Register* also contains a number of finding aids. There is a table of contents arranged by agency name and listing rules, proposed rules, and notices. Illustration C shows one page from the table of contents for the April 22, 1992 *Federal Register* issue, containing the endangered fish rules. Note that cross-references are provided to agency subdivisions if their regulations and notices are listed separately from the agency's.

The table of contents is followed by a list of *CFR* parts affected in that day's issue. It places all new regulations into the proper order of the CFR. Regular readers of the *Federal Register* can scan this list to see if there are any developments affecting parts of the *Code of Federal Regulations* with which they are concerned.[13]

At the end of each issue, there are finding aids covering more than that day's issue of the Register. First there is a list of telephone numbers in the Office of the Federal Register where one may obtain information and assistance on specific topics. These numbers can be used in the interactive research discussed in Section B. Following this is a table of pages and dates for each *Federal Register* issue published during the current month. This can be helpful since the *Register* is

13. To a person first confronting the *Federal Register,* it may seem absurd that anyone would regularly read "this voluminous and dull publication," to quote Justice Jackson in *Federal Crop Insurance Corp. v. Merrill, supra note 10. Lawyers dealing closely with particular agencies or specializing in specific areas of administrative law, however, would be poorly serving their clients if they were unaware of proposed changes that could affect those clients' interests. Examining each issue of the* Federal Register *is the best and most thorough way to stay informed.*

Illustration B

Federal Register pages

of the inability of the Secretary to complete the work necessary to designate critical habitat." H. Rep. No. 567, 97th Cong., 2d Sess. 19 (1982).

NMFS has determined that final listing is appropriate and necessary to the conservation of Snake River spring/summer and fall chinook salmon. The prompt listing will bring the protection of the ESA into force, including the requirement that all Federal agencies consult with NMFS to ensure their actions are not likely to jeopardize the continued existence of the species. Prompt listing will result in consultations during the planning stages of certain 1992 operations and activities, and thus promote timely and effective consideration of measures to conserve Snake River spring/summer and fall chinook salmon.

Furthermore, NMFS has concluded that critical habitat is not determinable at this time because information sufficient to perform the required analysis of the impacts of the designation is lacking. NMFS recently solicited information necessary to determine critical habitat (56 FR 51684; October 15, 1991). Designation of critical habitat requires a determination of those physical and biological features that are essential to the conservation of the species and which may require special management considerations or protection. NMFS has been reviewing scientific and biological information concerning habitat requirements of Snake River spring/summer and fall chinook salmon and has been identifying activities that may adversely impact those habitats. In addition, designation of critical habitat requires the consideration of economic information. NMFS is presently gathering and analyzing economic information needed for the designation (Tuttle 1991).

Further, management considerations and protection for spring/summer and fall chinook salmon are complicated by the possibility that these measures, if developed in isolation, may not be appropriate for Snake River sockeye salmon listed as an endangered species. Thus, NMFS is planning to propose concurrently critical habitat determinations for all listed Snake River salmon stocks.

Technical Amendment

NMFS is also issuing a technical amendment to 50 CFR 227.72(e) to clarify that the exception for incidental taking in subpart D—Threatened Marine Reptiles applies only to listed species of sea turtles, and not to listed salmon species.

Classification

The 1982 amendments to the ESA (Pub. L. 97–304) in section 4(b)(1)(A) restricted the information that may be considered when assessing species for listing. Based on this limitation of criteria for a listing decision and the opinion in *Pacific Legal Foundation* v. *Andrus*, 657 F. 2d 829 (6th Cir., 1981), these decisions are excluded from the requirements of the National Environmental Policy Act.

The Conference Report on the 1982 amendments to the ESA notes that economic considerations have no relevance to determinations regarding the status of species, and that E.O. 12291 economic analysis requirements, the Regulatory Flexibility Act, and the Paperwork Reduction Act are not applicable to the listing process. Similarly, listing actions are not subject to the requirements of E.O. 12612, or the President's Memorandum of January 28, 1992.

References

The complete citations for the references used in this document can be found in one of the following:

Columbia River Inter-Tribal Fish Commission. 1991. Lyons Ferry Fall Chinook Coded Wire Tag Analysis. Summary of presentation by Jim Berkson, dated 30 October 1991, submitted to NMFS ESA Administrative Record for fall chinook salmon.

Environmental and Technical Services Division. 1991. Factors for Decline, A Supplement to the Notice of Determination for Snake River Spring/Summer Chinook Salmon Under the Endangered Species Act. National Marine Fisheries Service. June, 1991.

Environmental and Technical Services Division. 1991. Factors for Decline, A Supplement to the Notice of Determination for Snake River Fall Chinook Salmon Under the Endangered Species Act. National Marine Fisheries Service. June, 1991.

Fish Passage Center of the Columbia Fish and Wildlife Authority. 1991. Bi-Weekly Report # 91–25. November, 1991.

Hoar, W.S. 1988. The Physiology of Smolting Salmonids, pp. 275–343. In W.S. Hoar and D.J. Randall [eds.], Fish Physiology volume 11B. The Physiology of Developing Fish. Academic Press, New York, N.Y.

Idaho Department of Fish and Game. 1991. Snake River Basin Redd Counts. Information dated 27 November 1991 submitted to NMFS ESA Administrative Record for spring/summer and fall chinook salmon.

Matthews, G.M. 1991. Personal communication on 7 November 1991.

Matthews, G.M., and R.S. Waples. 1991. Status Review for Snake River Spring and Summer Chinook Salmon. U.S. Dep. Commer., NOAA Tech. Memo. NMFS F/NWC–200.

Tuttle, M.E. 1991. Letter to Economic Technical Committee dated 19 December 1991. National Marine Fisheries Service, Environmental Technical Services Division.

U.S. Army Corps of Engineers, Walla Walla District. 1985. Comprehensive Report of Juvenile Salmonid Transportation. Walla Walla District, North Pacific Division, U.S. Army Corps of Engineers, Portland, Ore.

Vigg, S., and C.C. Burley. 1989. Developing a Predation Index and Evaluating Ways to Reduce Juvenile Salmonid Losses to Predation in the Columbia River, pp. 5–221. In Nigro, A.A. (ed.) Developing a Predation Index and Evaluating Ways to Reduce Salmonid Losses to Predation in the Columbia River Basin, 1989 Annual Progress Report, Bonneville Power Admin., Portland, Ore.

Waples, R.S., G.M. Matthews, O.W. Johnson, and R.P. Jones, Jr. 1991. Status Review Report for Snake River Fall Chinook Salmon. U.S. Dep. Commer., NOAA Tech. Memo. NMFS F/NWC–195.

Waples, R.S. In press. Pacific Salmon and the Definition of "Species" Under the Endangered Species Act. Marine Fisheries Review.

Washington Department of Fisheries. 1991a. Genetic Evaluation of the Lyons Ferry Hatchery Stock and Wild Snake River Fall Chinook. Summary by Craig Busack dated 15 May 1991 submitted to NMFS ESA Administrative Record for fall chinook salmon.

Washington Department of Fisheries. 1991b. Stock Composition of Fall Chinook at Lower Granite Dam. Letter from Larrie Lavoy dated 12 December 1991 submitted to NMFS ESA Administrative Record for fall chinook salmon.

Washington Department of Fisheries. 1991c. 1991 Fall Chinook Radio Telemetry and Spawning Surveys for the Snake River. Preliminary summary by Glenn Mendal dated 13 December 1991 submitted to NMFS ESA Administrative Record for fall chinook salmon.

List of Subjects in 50 CFR Part 227

Endangered and threatened species, Exports, Imports, Marine mammals, Transportation.

Dated: April 17, 1992.

Michael F. Tillman,

Deputy Assistant Administrator for Fisheries

For the reasons set out in the preamble, 50 CFR part 227 is amended as follows:

PART 227—THREATENED FISH AND WILDLIFE

1. The authority citation of part 227 continues to read as follows:

Authority: 16 U.S.C. 1531 *et seq.*

2. In § 227.4, new paragraphs (g) and (h) are added to read as follows:

§ 227.4 Enumeration of threatened species.

* * * * *

(g) Snake River spring/summer chinook salmon (*Oncorhynchus tshawytscha*). Includes all natural population(s) of spring/summer chinook

[G20,014]

Federal Register / Vol. 57, No. 78 / Wednesday, April 22, 1992 / Rules and Regulations 14663

salmon in the mainstream Snake River and any of the following subbasins: Tucannon River, Grande Ronde River, Imnaha River, and Salmon River.

(h) Snake River fall chinook salmon (*Oncorhynchus tshawytscha*). Includes all natural population(s) of fall chinook salmon in the mainstem Snake River and any of the following subbasins: Tucannon River, Grande Ronde River, Imnaha River, Salmon River, and Clearwater River.

3. In Subpart C, § 227.21 is revised to read as follows:

§ 227.21 Threatened salmon.

(a) *Prohibitions.* The prohibitions of section 9 of the Act (16 U.S.C. 1538) relating to endangered species apply to the threatened species of salmon listed in § 227.4 (e), (g) and (h) of this part, except as provided in paragraph (b) of this section.

(b) *Exceptions.* (1) The exceptions of section 10 of the Act (16 U.S.C. 1539) and other exceptions under the Act relating to endangered species, and the provisions of regulations issued under the Act relating to endangered species (such as 50 CFR part 222, subpart C—Endangered Fish or Wildlife Permits), also apply to the threatened species of salmon listed in § 227.4 (e), (g) and (h) of this part. This section supersedes other restrictions on the applicability of 50 CFR part 222, including, but not limited to, the restrictions specified in §§ 222.2(a) and 222.22(a).

(2) The prohibitions of paragraph (a) of this section relating to threatened species of salmon listed in § 227.4 (g) and (h) of this part do not apply to activities specified in an application for a permit for scientific purposes or to enhance the propagation or survival of the species *provided that* the application has been received by the Assistant Administrator by May 22, 1992. This exception ceases upon the Assistant Administrator's rejection of the application as insufficient, upon issuance or denial of a permit, or on December 31, 1992, whichever occurs earliest.

§ 227.72 [AMENDED]

4. In § 227.72, paragraph (e)(1) is amended by removing the words "any species listed in § 227.4" and adding, in their place, the words "any species of sea turtle listed in § 227.4 (a), (b) and (c)."

[FR Doc. 92-9370 Filed 4-21-92; 8:45 am]

BILLING CODE 3510-22-M

50 CFR Part 663

[Docket No 920403-2103]

Pacific Coast Groundfish Fishery

AGENCY: National Marine Fisheries Service (NMFS), NOAA, Commerce.

ACTION: Emergency interim rule; request for comments.

SUMMARY: The Secretary of Commerce (Secretary) issues an emergency interim rule to restrict operations in the Pacific whiting fishery. These regulations are intended to minimize the impact of the Pacific whiting fishery on Pacific salmon stocks without undue hardship to the Pacific whiting industry. This action is necessary because many Pacific salmon stocks appear to be at record low levels, and some stocks may not meet 1992 escapement goals even if no fishery were conducted.

EFFECTIVE DATES: This emergency rule is effective from April 16, 1992 at 1706 hours, e.d.t., until 2400 hours (local time) July 21, 1992, and may be extended for an additional 90 days. Comments will be accepted through May 7, 1992.

ADDRESSES: Comments on this emergency rule may be submitted to Rolland A. Schmitten, Director, Northwest Region, National Marine Fisheries Service, 7600 Sand Point Way N.E., Bin C15700, Seattle WA 98115-0070; or E. Charles Fullerton, Director, Southwest Region, National Marine Fisheries Service, 501 West Ocean Blvd., suite 4200, Long Beach, CA 90802-4213.

FOR FURTHER INFORMATION CONTACT: William L. Robinson at 206-526-6140, or Rodney R. McInnis at 310-980-4040.

SUPPLEMENTARY INFORMATION:

Background

In 1991, the Pacific whiting (whiting) fishery was completely "Americanized." The joint venture fishery (U.S. catcher vessels delivering whiting to foreign processing vessels at sea), which in the previous year had taken over 93 percent of the whiting quota, was completely displaced by a domestic at-sea catching and processing fleet. The domestic at-sea processing fleet is permitted to operate in areas that had been prohibited to foreign processing vessels south of 39° N. latitude. Those areas have been closed to foreign processing vessels due to concerns over the bycatch of salmon and rockfish and for national security reasons. In addition, domestic catcher vessels have been allowed to fish from 0-200 nautical miles (nm) offshore, whereas foreign trawl vessels could only fish seaward of 12 nm.

Whiting are found in fishable concentrations off California in the spring. The fishery follows the stock northward until it is predominantly in Canadian waters or offshore in the fall. The 1992 Pacific whiting season begins on April 15. An earlier fishery could be expected to increase effort in waters near the Cordell Bank and the Gulf of the Farallones National Marine Sanctuaries off the Coast of California, and could increase the likelihood of interception of Sacramento winter-run chinook salmon that have been listed as "threatened" under the Endangered Species Act (ESA). Chilipepper and bocaccio rockfish, which are also caught as bycatch in the whiting fishery, are found in these waters as well and used in fish meal. Otherwise, in a directed fishery for rockfish, chilipepper and bocaccio would generate a significantly higher price. In part to alleviate these concerns, an April 15 opening date was established for the whiting fishery beginning in 1992. This opening date approximates the traditional start of the fishery and was meant to maintain the historical season structure by counteracting the 1991 trend of beginning to fish for whiting early in the year and in the southernmost area of the fishery.

Although the April 15 opening date helps to reduce impacts on some salmon stocks, particularly Sacramento winter-run chinook salmon, further review of the fishery data for 1991 indicates that the bycatch of Sacramento winter run chinook and other salmon stocks, most notably Klamath River fall chinook, could be reduced further without undue hardship on the whiting fishery.

Recently completed salmon stock assessments for 1992 indicate that the abundance of Klamath River fall chinook salmon is predicted to be at a record low level and is not expected to meet the minimum escapement level or "escapement floor" of 35,000 even in the absence of all fishing. This year will mark the third consecutive year of underescapement and will thus require the Pacific Fishery Management Council (Council) to conduct a review of the depressed status of the stock to determine the cause of the stock decline and its relationship to fishing. Because of the depressed status of the Klamath River fall chinook stock, the Council is considering, for the first time, severely restrictive fishing options for the commercial and recreational salmon fisheries, one of which is a prohibition of ocean salmon fishing along a substantial portion of the Oregon and California coasts. These circumstances prompted the Council to consider further

[G20,015]

usually cited by page number, but page numbers are not listed on the spine or front cover of an issue. The date does appear in those places, so after using the table one can easily find the needed issue. Next comes a cumulative list of *CFR* parts affected during the current month. This list is updated each day to include the developments in that issue, and hence incorporates the items listed in the front of the issue. This table is an important tool for updating regulations, as will be explained in Section C.4 below. Following the table of *CFR* parts there are a list of

Illustration C

A *Federal Register* table of contents page

[G20,016]

public laws received by the Office from Congress and a weekly checklist of current *CFR* volumes.

Each year's output comprises a new volume of the *Federal Register*, with continuous pagination throughout the year. The first volume in 1936 contained 2,400 pages. The size expanded to a peak of 86,405

Illustration D

Reader aids in the *Federal Register*

Reader Aids

Federal Register
Vol. 57, No. 78
Wednesday, April 22, 1992

INFORMATION AND ASSISTANCE

Federal Register

Index, finding aids & general information	202-523-5227
Public inspection desk	523-5215
Corrections to published documents	523-5237
Document drafting information	523-5237
Machine readable documents	523-3447

Code of Federal Regulations

Index, finding aids & general information	523-5227
Printing schedules	523-3419

Laws

Public Laws Update Service (numbers, dates, etc.)	523-6641
Additional information	523-5230

Presidential Documents

Executive orders and proclamations	523-5230
Public Papers of the Presidents	523-5230
Weekly Compilation of Presidential Documents	523-5230

The United States Government Manual

General information	523-5230

Other Services

Data base and machine readable specifications	523-3447
Guide to Record Retention Requirements	523-3187
Legal staff	523-4534
Privacy Act Compilation	523-3187
Public Laws Update Service (PLUS)	523-6641
TDD for the hearing impaired	523-5229

FEDERAL REGISTER PAGES AND DATES, APRIL

10973-11260	1
11261-11424	2
11425-11552	3
11553-11670	6
11671-11904	7
11905-12176	8
12177-12402	9
12403-12694	10
12695-12862	13
12863-12988	14
12989-13266	15
13267-13622	16
13623-14320	17
14321-14474	20
14475-14636	21
14637-14790	22

CFR PARTS AFFECTED DURING APRIL

At the end of each month, the Office of the Federal Register publishes separately a List of CFR Sections Affected (LSA), which lists parts and sections affected by documents published since the revision date of each title.

1 CFR

Proposed Rules:
305 13667
425 14669

3 CFR

Proclamations:
6418 12693
6419 12863
6420 12989
6421 13265
6422 13621

Executive Orders:
12438 (Revoked by EO 12797) 11671
12543 (See EO 12801) 14319
12794 11417
12795 11421
12796 11423
12797 11671
12799 12401
12800 12985
12801 14319
12802 14321

Administrative Orders:
Presidential Determinations:
No. 92-19 of March 16, 1992 11553
No. 92-20 of April 3, 1992 13623
No. 92-21 of April 10, 1992 12865

Memorandum:
March 20, 1992 11554

4 CFR

Ch. III 14148

5 CFR

430 14637
451 14637
531 12403
536 12403
540 14637
550 12403
553 12405
735 11800
890 14323
2633 11800
2634 11800
2638 11886
2641 11673

Proposed Rules:
532 11586
735 11586
890 13667

7 CFR

2 11261
54 11425
272 11218
274 11218
276 11218
277 11218
278 11218
301 10973
318 14475
319 10974
354 14475
718 14456
719 14456
800 11427
981 10976
1240 11262
1413 .... 12406, 14325, 14326, 14456
1414 14456
1421 12406
1427 14326
1455 12410
1901 11555
1924 12991
1940 11555
1951 11555
1980 12991

Proposed Rules:
28 14492
29 14669
354 14498
1001 11276
1002 11276
1413 11588

8 CFR

3 11568
103 11568
214 .... 10978, 12177, 12179
242 11568
251 10978
258 10978
292 11568

9 CFR

91 10978
92 12190

Proposed Rules:
317 14499
320 14499
327 13053
381 14499

10 CFR

170 13625
171 13625

Proposed Rules:
20 14500
50 14514
61 14500
100 11691

11 CFR

100 11262

[G20,017]

pages in 1980, and has since subsided to under 70,000 pages for 1993. Although the texts of most final rules are arranged by subject in *CFR*, much of the other material in the *Federal Register* never appears elsewhere.[14] Proposed rules, agency policy statements, discussion of comments received, and descriptive statements on agency organization give the *Register* a permanent reference value, and most large law libraries have a complete backfile, either bound or in microfilm or microfiche editions.

Access to the *Federal Register* is provided through several different indexes, tables, and computer databases. These research techniques will be discussed in Sections C.3, Finding Regulations, and C.4, Updating and Verifying Regulations. Because most research in administrative regulations requires use of both the *Register* and the *Code of Federal Regulations*, however, we must first introduce the latter publication.

2. CODE OF FEDERAL REGULATIONS

When Congress sought to control the chaos of administrative rules through the Federal Register Act, it understood the need for a subject arrangement of regulations in force. Section 11 of the act required each agency to compile and publish in the *Register* its then current body of regulations.[15] It was not until an amendment in 1937,[16] however, that a regular form of codification was established. The first edition of the new *Code of Federal Regulations* was published in 1939, and contained regulations in force as of June 1, 1938.

The *Code* is to contain "documents of each agency of the Government having general applicability and legal effect, . . . relied upon by the agency as authority for, or . . . invoked or used by it in the discharge of, its activities or functions." [17] The regulations are codified in a subject arrangement of fifty titles somewhat similar to those employed for federal statutes in the *United States Code*. For example, 26 U.S.C. is the Internal Revenue Code and 26 C.F.R. contains tax regulations, and Title 7 of each code is concerned with agriculture. The titles do not always match, however. Education statutes are in 20 U.S.C. but corresponding regulations are in 34 C.F.R.; Title 40 of *CFR*, dealing with protection of the environment, has no direct statutory counterpart. The real difference lies in the fact that instead of truly grouping administrative rules together by subject, the *CFR* groups the agencies together by subject. This keeps all of one agency's rules and regulations together. Regulations on a single topic, such as tobacco, may be spread through several agencies, hence several titles of the *CFR*.

14. In *Wiggins Bros., Inc. v. Department of Energy*, 667 F.2d 77 (Temp.Emer.App. 1981), *cert. denied*, 456 U.S. 905 (1982), the court reversed a district court ruling that excluded consideration of *Federal Register* material not published in *CFR* in construing an agency regulation. The court held that the agency's failure to include a preamble in the codified regulation did not mean that the preamble should be disregarded.

15. Ch. 417, § 11, 49 Stat. 500, 503 (1935).

16. Act of June 19, 1937, ch. 369, 50 Stat. 304.

17. 44 U.S.C. § 1510(a) (1982).

Each title is divided into *chapters*, each of which is devoted to the regulations of a particular agency. Chapters are numbered with Roman numerals,[18] and sometimes are divided into subchapters designated by capital letters. In the back of every *CFR* volume there is an alphabetical list of federal agencies indicating the *CFR* title and chapter of each agency's regulations.

The regulations of a particular agency are divided into *parts*, each of which consists of a body of regulations on a particular topic or agency function. (Each *Federal Register* issue, you may recall, includes lists of *CFR* parts affected in that issue and during that month.) Parts are further divided into *sections*, the basic unit of the code. A section "ideally consists of a short, simple presentation of one proposition." [19] The citation identifying a *CFR* section shows the title, the part and the section (but not the chapter), so that 1 C.F.R. § 1.1 is title 1, part 1, section 1.

Before 1967 the CFR appeared in various cumulations. Since that date it has been totally republished in paperbound pamphlets each year. This schedule of annual republication of the whole set is very ambitious. The colors of the volume covers change each year, so annual editions can be readily distinguished from each other. The cover of each volume of the CFR explains exactly what it covers. Illustration E shows the cover of Title 50, Parts 200 to 599 for 1993. Note how it states that it represents all the rules as of October 1, 1993.

The current code consists of about two hundred volumes. Rather than reissue the entire set at one time, the Office of the Federal Register revises the set on a quarterly basis. Titles 1–16 contain regulations in force as of January 1 of the cover year; titles 17–27 as of April 1; titles 28–41 as of July 1; and titles 42–50 as of October 1. Because one year's edition gradually supplants the previous year's, a current *CFR* set almost always consists of volumes of two or more colors. The republication schedule is a goal that is not always met. Be sure and check the cover for the dates of coverage.

The table of contents for each title lists its chapters; that for each chapter, its parts; and for each part, its sections. In addition, at the beginning of each part the agency provides notes showing the statutory or executive authority under which the regulations in that part are issued. This *authority note* is followed by a *source note*, providing the citation and date of the *Federal Register* in which the part was last published in full. Illustration F shows the beginning of 50 C.F.R. 227, with authority and source notes following the table of sections. If an individual section is based on a different authority a separate authority or source note follows that section. Illustration G shows the following page where the remainder of 227.4 is printed.

18. Chapters in Title 41, Public Contracts and Property Management, and Title 48, Federal Acquisition Regulations System, are designated by Arabic, not Roman, numeral.

19. Office of the Federal Register, *Document Drafting Handbook* 2 (rev. ed. 1986).

Illustration E

Cover of 50 CFR

code of federal regulations

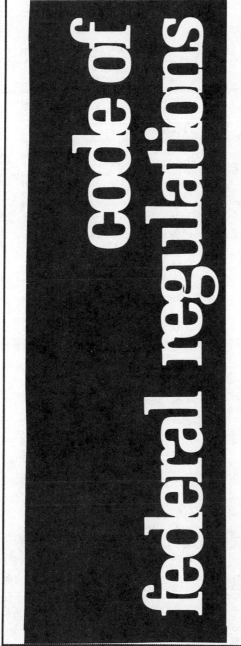

Wildlife and Fisheries

1 DAY ONLY

50

PARTS 200 TO 599

Revised as of October 1, 1993

[G20,018]

Illustration F

The Beginning of 50 CFR 227

PART 227—THREATENED FISH AND WILDLIFE

Subpart A—General Provisions

AUTHORITY: 16 U.S.C. 1531 *et seq.*

SOURCE: 43 FR 32809, July 28, 1978, unless otherwise noted.

EDITORIAL NOTE: For a document relating to adoption of alternative scientific testing protocol for evaluating TEDs see 55 FR 41092, Oct. 9, 1990.

Subpart A—General Provisions

§ 227.1 Purpose.

The regulations contained in this part identify the species, subspecies, or any other group of fish and wildlife of the same species or smaller taxa in common spatial arrangement that interbreed when mature, under the jurisdiction of the Secretary of Commerce which have been determined to be threatened species under the Endangered Species Act of 1973 and provide for the conservation of such species by establishing rules and procedures to govern activities involving the species.

§ 227.2 Scope.

(a) The regulations contained in this part apply only to the threatened species enumerated in § 227.4.

(b) The provision of this part are in addition to, and not in lieu of other regulations of parts 217 through 222 and part 225 of this chapter II which prescribe additional restrictions or conditions governing threatened species.

(c) Certain of the threatened fish or wildlife listed in 50 CFR 17.11 and enumerated in 50 CFR 227.4 are included in Appendix I or II to the Convention on International Trade in Endangered Species of Wild Fauna and Flora. The importation, exportation, and reexportation of such species are subject to additional regulations provided in part 23, chapter I (title 50).

§ 227.3 Definitions.

In addition to the definitions contained in the Act, and in parts 217 and 225 of this chapter, and unless the context otherwise requires, in this part 227:

(a) *Act* means the Endangered Species Act of 1973, as amended, 16 U.S.C. 1531 through 1547;

(b) *Assistant Administrator* means the Assistant Administrator for Fisheries, National Oceanic and Atmospheric Administration, Department of Commerce, or his authorized delegate. The Assistant Administrator for Fisheries is in charge of the National Marine Fisheries Service;

(c) *Ongoing project(s)* means an activity for scientific purposes or to enhance the propagation or survival of such species which are not conducted in the course of a commercial activity initiated before the listing of the effected species;

(d) *Plastron* means the ventral part of the shell of a sea turtle consisting typically of nine symmetrically placed bones overlaid by horny plates; and

(e) *Sea turtle(s)* means those sea turtle species enumerated in § 227.4 and any part(s), product(s), egg(s) or offspring thereof, or the dead body or part(s) thereof.

§ 227.4 Enumeration of threatened species.

The species listed as threatened under the Act which are under the ju-

[G20,019]

Illustration G

50 CFR 227.4

§ 227.1 50 CFR Ch. II (10–1–93 Edition)

PART 227—THREATENED FISH AND WILDLIFE

Subpart A—General Provisions

Subpart B—Threatened Marine Mammals

Subpart C—Threatened Marine and Anadromous Fish

Subpart C—[Reserved]

Subpart D—Threatened Marine Reptiles

AUTHORITY: 16 U.S.C. 1531 *et seq.*

SOURCE: 43 FR 32809, July 28, 1978, unless otherwise noted.

EDITORIAL NOTE: For a document relating to adoption of alternative scientific testing protocol for evaluating TEDs see 55 FR 41092, Oct. 9, 1990.

Subpart A—General Provisions

§ 227.1 Purpose.

The regulations contained in this part identify the species, subspecies, or any other group of fish and wildlife of the same species or smaller taxa in common spatial arrangement that interbreed when mature, under the jurisdiction of the Secretary of Commerce which have been determined to be threatened species under the Endangered Species Act of 1973 and provide for the conservation of such species by establishing rules and procedures to govern activities involving the species.

§ 227.2 Scope.

(a) The regulations contained in this part apply only to the threatened species enumerated in § 227.4.

(b) The provision of this part are in addition to, and not in lieu of other regulations of parts 217 through 222 and part 225 of this chapter II which prescribe additional restrictions or conditions governing threatened species.

(c) Certain of the threatened fish or wildlife listed in 50 CFR 17.11 and enumerated in 50 CFR 227.4 are included in Appendix I or II to the Convention on International Trade in Endangered Species of Wild Fauna and Flora. The importation, exportation, and reexportation of such species are subject to additional regulations provided in part 23, chapter I (title 50).

§ 227.3 Definitions.

In addition to the definitions contained in the Act, and in parts 217 and 225 of this chapter, and unless the context otherwise requires, in this part 227:

(a) *Act* means the Endangered Species Act of 1973, as amended, 16 U.S.C. 1531 through 1547;

(b) *Assistant Administrator* means the Assistant Administrator for Fisheries, National Oceanic and Atmospheric Administration, Department of Commerce, or his authorized delegate. The Assistant Administrator for Fisheries is in charge of the National Marine Fisheries Service;

(c) *Ongoing project(s)* means an activity for scientific purposes or to enhance the propagation or survival of such species which are not conducted in the course of a commercial activity initiated before the listing of the effected species;

(d) *Plastron* means the ventral part of the shell of a sea turtle consisting typically of nine symmetrically placed bones overlaid by horny plates; and

(e) *Sea turtle(s)* means those sea turtle species enumerated in § 227.4 and any part(s), product(s), egg(s) or offspring thereof, or the dead body or part(s) thereof.

§ 227.4 Enumeration of threatened species.

The species listed as threatened under the Act which are under the ju-

[G20,020]

risdiction of the Secretary of Commerce are:

(a) Green sea turtle (*Chelonia mydas*) except for those populations listed under 50 CFR 222.23(a).[1]

(b) Loggerhead sea turtle (*Caretta caretta*).[1]

(c) Pacific ridley sea turtle (*Lepidochelys olivacea*) except for those populations listed under 50 CFR 222.23(a).[1]

The effective date of the listing of the species in paragraphs (a), (b), and (c) of this section is September 6, 1978.

(d) Guadalupe fur seal (*Arctocephalus townsendi*).

(e) Sacramento River winter-run chinook salmon (*Oncorhynchus tschawytscha*).

(f) Steller (northern) sea lion (*Eumetopias jubatus*).

(g) Snake River spring/summer chinook salmon (*Oncorhynchus tshawytscha*). Includes all natural population(s) of spring/summer chinook salmon in the mainstream Snake River and any of the following subbasins: Tucannon River, Grande Ronde River, Imnaha River, and Salmon River.

(h) Snake River fall chinook salmon (*Oncorhynchus tshawytscha*). Includes all natural population(s) of fall chinook salmon in the mainstem Snake River and any of the following subbasins: Tucannon River, Grande Ronde River, Imnaha River, Salmon River, and Clearwater River.

[43 FR 32809, July 18, 1978, as amended at 45 FR 29055, May 1, 1980; 50 FR 51258, Dec. 16, 1985; 55 FR 46523, Nov. 5, 1990; 55 FR 49210, Nov. 26, 1990; 57 FR 14662, Apr. 22, 1992]

Subpart B—Threatened Marine Mammals

§227.11 Guadalupe fur seal.

(a) *Prohibitions.* The prohibitions of section 9 of the Act (16 U.S.C. 1538) relating to endangered species apply to the Guadalupe fur seal except as provided in paragraph (b) of this section.

(b) *Exceptions.* (1) The Assistant Administrator may issue permits authorizing activities which would otherwise be prohibited under paragraph (a) of this section in accordance with the subject to the provisions of part 222 subpart C—Endangered Fish or Wildlife Permits.

(2) Any Federal, State or local government official, employee, or designated agent may, in the course of official duties, take a stranded Guadalupe fur seal without a permit if such taking:

(i) Is accomplished in a humane manner;

(ii) Is for the protection or welfare of the animal, is for the protection of the public health or welfare, or is for the salvage or disposal of a dead specimen;

(iii) Includes steps designed to ensure the return of the animal to its natural habitat, if feasible; and

(iv) Is reported within 30 days to the Director, Southwest Region, National Marine Fisheries Service, 300 S. Ferry Street, Terminal Island, CA 90731.

(3) Any animal or specimen taken under paragraph (b)(2) of this section may only be retained, disposed of, or salvaged in accordance with directions from the Director, Southwest Region.

[50 FR 51258, Dec. 16, 1985]

§227.12 Steller sea lion.

(a) *Prohibitions*—(1) *No discharge of firearms.* Except as provided in paragraph (b) of this section, no person subject to the jurisdiction of the United States may discharge a firearm at or within 100 yards (91.4 meters) of a Steller sea lion. A firearm is any weapon, such as a pistol or rifle, capable of firing a missile using an explosive charge as a propellant.

(2) *No approach in buffer areas.* Except as provided in paragraph (b) of this section:

(i) No owner or operator of a vessel may allow the vessel to approach within 3 nautical miles (5.5 kilometers) of a Steller sea lion rookery site listed in paragraph (a)(3) of this section;

(ii) No person may approach on land not privately owned within one-half statutory miles (0.8 kilometers) or within sight of a Steller sea lion rookery site listed in paragraph (a)(3) of

[1] Department of Commerce, National Oceanic and Atmospheric Administration, National Marine Fisheries Service, jurisdiction for sea turtles is limited to turtles while in the water.

[G20,021]

In addition to the regulations which form the main contents of the code, Title 3 consists of the texts of proclamations, executive orders and

other presidential documents. These materials will be separately described below in Section E.

Among the *CFR* volumes revised and reissued each year is an "Index and Finding Aids" volume. This volume is just one of several indexes and means of access to the *Code of Federal Regulations,* and will be discussed in the next section.

3. FINDING REGULATIONS

There are several methods of finding federal agency regulations. Both the *Federal Register* and the *Code of Federal Regulations* have indexes prepared by the Office of the Federal Register and by commercial publishing companies. Both are available in full text on WESTLAW and LEXIS where Boolean searching can be especially helpful.

Ordinarily research into the regulations of a federal agency begins with the *Code of Federal Regulations,* rather than the daily *Federal Register.* Since the CFR pulls all the regulations together into one place, especially since it is updated on an annual basis, it is the logical starting place.

If one knows the name of the agency one is interested in the list of agencies and the location of their rules in the back of each volume can point out where to look. Given Section B's emphasis on starting research with context, the researcher should at least know the name of the agency.

For more specific searches, the *Code* is accompanied by an annually revised volume entitled *Index and Finding Aids,* most of which consists of an index of subjects and agencies. The index provides references to *parts,* rather than sections, so it is not always as specific as would be desired. It also covers a very broad area in relatively terse fashion, so it is not very specific and is sometimes difficult to use. Of course one who is following research suggestions set out in Section B would already know an agency, and should come to the set with full citation in hand. Starting a new search in any subject index is a bad idea.

For those who do need a subject index, there are two commercial annual indexes of the *CFR.* Congressional Information Service has published an *Index to the Code of Federal Regulations* since 1981. In four annual volumes, it provides very detailed indexing of the *CFR* by subject and by geographic location. As in the official index, however, its entries refer to parts rather than to specific sections. Unlike many commercial publications which appear much more quickly than official works, this index is published rather slowly. The index for one year's *CFR* edition generally does not appear until the following autumn.

The *United States Code Service* (USCS) publishes a one volume paperbound index of *CFR* materials. It is a reprint of the *CFR's* Finding Aids volume. It is shelved as part of the *USCS* set.

The *Federal Register* also has both official and commercial indexes. The government's *Federal Register Index,* is published monthly, and consists of a consolidation of the entries in each issue's table of contents. Entries are arranged by agency, not by subject. Within each agency's listing, rules, proposed rules and notices are listed alphabetically by subject. Each month's index cumulates those earlier in the year, so the January–February index replaces the January index, and the January–December index serves as the final annual index. A table of *Federal Register* pages and dates, similar to that in each daily issue, appears in the back of each index for the months covered. The index usually does not appear until several weeks after its period of coverage ends.

A much more thorough and current index to the *Register* has been published since 1984 by Congressional Information Service. Its *CIS Federal Register Index* is published weekly, within two or three weeks of the period covered. The weekly issues are cumulated periodically, until the publication of permanent bound semiannual volumes. The index provides thorough coverage of all *Federal Register* documents except Sunshine Act notices, and is divided into four sections: a calendar of effective dates and comment deadlines, and indexes by subjects and names, by *CFR* section numbers affected, and by agency docket numbers. The subject and name index provides access by numerous methods, including general policy area, specific subject matter, agency name, authorizing legislation, and affected industries, organizations, corporations, individuals, or geographic areas.

An increasingly important means of access to both the *Code of Federal Regulations* and the *Federal Register* is provided by full-text coverage in both WESTLAW and LEXIS. *Federal Register* issues since the summer of 1980 are searchable on both systems, and each new issue is available online within a week of its publication. On LEXIS the *Register* is in the FEDREG file of the GENFED library, and on WESTLAW it is in the FR database. The current edition of the *Code of Federal Regulations* is also available online, in the CFR file on LEXIS and the CFR database on WESTLAW. Both systems also have databases, such as CFR86, containing previous years' editions of *CFR*. LEXIS also has a combined file of both *Register* and *Code,* called ALLREG. WESTLAW has combined files in six major topical areas including tax, bankruptcy & securities (e.g., FSEC-CODREG). Boolean searching can be especially effective for some searches in these data bases. When one is doing research in federal administrative regulations, one often has the name of a very specific product or topic. If one wanted to find regulations on the "Guadalupe fur seal" (50 CFR 227.4(d)) a Boolean search would be just the ticket. The CFR and the Federal Register appear at various Internet sites as well. Reliability and timeliness remain a challenge with these sources so they must be used with care.

Often one has a statute or presidential document and would like to find regulations promulgated under its authority or related to it. A "Parallel Table of Authorities and Rules" in the *Index and Finding Aids* volume provides access. It lists every statute and presidential document cited by an agency as authority for its rules, taken from the rulemaking authority citation in *CFR*. The table consists of separate sections for *United States Code* sections, *Statutes at Large* pages, public law numbers, and presidential documents. Authority citations are provided by the agencies, and may follow different formats; the same statute may be cited by code section by one agency and by public law number by another agency. The table does not reconcile inconsistencies, so it may be necessary to check more than one section to find all references to a statute. The table in the *Index and Finding Aids* volume is current as of January 1st of each year. During the course of the year, both additions to and removals from the list are printed in the monthly pamphlet *LSA: List of CFR Sections Affected.* These monthly lists cumulate until the next annual edition.

One of the simplest ways to find relevant regulations may be to use a looseleaf service or other resource which collects and reprints agency regulations in a particular subject area. If relevant regulations are already collected, there may be no need to search through indexes or computer databases. Topical looseleaf services focusing on the work of particular agencies (such as the Internal Revenue Service or the National Labor Relations Board) provide currently supplemented and well annotated texts of both substantive and procedural regulations of their subject agencies. Appendix B is designed to help locate relevant citations by agency. Locations of rules and decisions for federal agencies, with citation to official, unofficial and online sources, is provided.

In addition, procedural regulations of over two dozen agencies are printed in the "Administrative Rules of Procedure" volume of *United States Code Service.* Like the rest of *USCS,* the administrative rules volumes include annotations of interpretive agency and court decisions and references to relevant forms, *ALR* annotations, and other research tools, and are updated by annual pocket parts and interim supplements. Pike and Fischer's *Administrative Law, Second Series, Deskbook* also contains the texts of eight major agencies' procedural regulations under the Administrative Procedure Act.

4. UPDATING AND VERIFYING REGULATIONS

Even though the *Code of Federal Regulations* is reissued every year, at some point during the year each volume will be up to a year or more out of date. Administrative regulations change frequently, and researchers must be able to determine their current status. To make sure that a *CFR* section is still current, and to find any new or proposed rules affecting it, there is a straightforward routine to be followed. It consists of several steps, different and often simpler than the ways cases and statutes are updated.

The first step in updating a *CFR* section is to check for references in a monthly pamphlet entitled *LSA: List of CFR Sections Affected.* Like the daily and monthly lists in each issue of the *Federal Register, LSA* indicates *Register* pages of any new or proposed rules affecting the *Code.* Under each *CFR* title, there are separate listings for final actions and for proposed rules. Except for proposed rules, references are to exact sections and include a descriptive word or phrase indicating the nature of the change, such as "amended," "removed," or "revised." Illustra-

tion H shows a page from the November, 1994 *LSA* indicating that a change has been made in 50 *CFR* 227.4. The *LSA* volumes physically resemble the *CFR* volumes and are normally shelved at the end of the set.

The coverage of *LSA* reflects changes back to the last revision of each title. Because *CFR* volumes are updated as of four different dates during the year, this means that the dates covered for each title will vary. Fortunately, the cover of each issue of the *LSA* lists exactly what it covers. Because *LSA* cumulates every month, it is not necessary to examine more than the most recent pamphlet to find out about changes since the latest *CFR* revision.

The second step in updating sends us back to the *Federal Register*. Because the latest *LSA* pamphlet does not bring a search completely up to date, a similar list must be consulted in the last *Federal Register* issue of each month not covered in the pamphlet. This list is by part rather than section. A researcher in late October who has examined a September *LSA* pamphlet need only check the "List of CFR Parts Affected in October" in the latest available *Federal Register* issue to be assured that no changes in the regulation have been promulgated.

Finally, updating takes us beyond administrative materials to judicial decisions. There is a chance that the regulation has been challenged in court or interpreted in litigation. *CFR,* however, does not include annotations to decisions construing or applying regulations, and no publisher issues a comprehensive annotated set of federal regulations. In specialized areas, looseleaf services include annotations to regulations. Appenidx B can assist in this search. *Shepard's Code of Federal Regulations Citations,* however, is the best source for checking for judicial treatment of regulations. It includes citations of regulations in federal courts since about 1949, in state courts and selected law reviews since 1977, and in *ALR* annotations. Abbreviations similar to those used in Shepard's statutory citators are used to indicate, for example, when a regulation has been found constitutional (C), valid (Va), void or invalid (V), or void or invalid in part (Vp). A page from this citator is shown in Illustration I, indicating the effect of *Sierra Club v. E.P.A.,* 719 F.2d 436 (D.C.Cir.1983) on various subsections of 40 C.F.R. § 51.1. *Shepard's Code of Federal Regulations Citations* also covers presidential proclamations, executive orders, and reorganization plans, as will be discussed below in section D. Several of the topical Shepard's units include coverage of regulations in their subject areas. Some, such as *Shepard's Federal Tax Citations,* include citations to regulations in topical reporters, such as *American Federal Tax Reports,* but coverage unfortunately does not extend to administrative agency decisions applying or interpreting regulations.

Illustration H-1

An *LSA* page, showing *CFR* sections affected

SEPTEMBER 1994 169

CHANGES OCTOBER 1, 1993 THROUGH SEPTEMBER 30, 1994

Chapter II—National Marine Fisheries Service, National Oceanic and Atmospheric Administration, Department of Commerce (Parts 200—299)

204.1 (b) table amended (OMB numbers) **59401**
Regulation at 58 FR 33567 confirmed 13894
(b) table amended (OMB numbers); eff. 7-27-94 through 10-31-94 39303
(b) table amended (OMB numbers) 43781
(b) table amended (OMB numbers); eff. 10-6-94 46134
215 Harvest quotas **58297**
215.32 (b) revised 35474
216 Temporary regulations 8142
Finding of conformance 15655
216.3 Amended 16145, 35865
216.4 (b)(1) through (h) removed; (b) introductory text revised **65134**
216.15 (f) added **58297**
216.24 (a)(1), (b)(1)(iii) heading and (v) amended; (d)(2)(vii)(C)(*1*) introductory text and (*i*)(*D*) revised **63539**
(d)(2)(viii) introductory text, (A) introductory text, (B), (C) and (E) amended **63540**
(e)(3)(i)(A)(*1*) revised 16145
(e) heading and (9) revised 30306
Note amended; eff. 6-17-94 through 9-1-95 31165
(e)(1) redesignated as (e)(1)(i); (e)(1)(ii) added 35865
216.110—216.113 (Subpart I) Removed **65134**
217 Temporary regulations ... 23169, 29545
217.12 Amended **54067**
Amended; interim 10586
222.23 (a) amended 450, 31095
(a) amended; interim; eff. 8-18-94 to 5-26-95 42532
226.13 Added 28805
226.22 Added **68551**
226 Table 3 and Figure 5 added **68552**
Figures 6, 7 and 8 added 28805
Table 2 amended 30716
227 Temporary regulations ... 23169, 29545
227.4 (e) removed; (f), (g) and (h) redesignated as (e), (f) and (g) 450
(f) and (g) removed; interim; eff. 8-18-94 to 5-26-95 42532
227.12 (a)(3) Table 1 amended **53139**
(a)(3) illustration revised **53141**
(a)(3) corrected **58594**
227.21 (Subpart C) (a), (b)(1) and (2) amended 450
Section removed; interim; eff. 8-18-94 to 5-26-95 42532
227.72 (e)(4)(ii) and (iii) redesignated as (e)(4)(iii) and (iv); new (e)(4)(iv) introductory text revised; new (e)(4)(ii) added **54067**
(e)(5) heading and (i) revised **54068**
(e)(4)(i)(G)(*2*) redesignated as (e)(4)(i)(G)(*2*)(*i*); (e)(4)(i)(G)(*2*)(*ii*) added 25829
(e)(4)(i)(I) added; (e)(4)(iv)(A) revised; interim 33449
(e)(3)(i) and (ii)(B) revised 33699
227 Figures 10 and 11 added **54069**
Figure 12a added 25830
Figure 12b added 25831
228.51—228.57 (Subpart F) Added; eff. 3-3-94 through 3-3-99 5126
229 Regulation at 54 FR 21921 eff. date extended to 4-1-94 .... **51789**
Regulation at 54 FR 21921 eff. date extended to 5-1-94 17048
Added; eff. 6-17-94 through 9-1-95 31165
Heading correctly added 34899
229.1 (b) amended **51789**
(b) amended 17049
242 Policy statement 28922, 36063
282.2 Regulation at 58 FR 33567 confirmed and amended 13894
282.3 Regulation at 58 FR 33567 confirmed 13894
282.5 Regulation at 58 FR 33567 confirmed 13894
282.6 Regulation at 58 FR 33567 confirmed 13894
282.8 Regulation at 58 FR 33568 confirmed 13894
282.9 Regulation at 58 FR 33568 confirmed 13894
282.14 Regulation at 58 FR 33568 confirmed 13894
282.15 Regulation at 58 FR 33568 confirmed 13894
285 Harvest quotas **53434**

NOTE: Boldface page numbers indicate 1993 changes.

[G20,022]

Illustration H-2

A page from the Federal Register

designated concurrently with the listing of a species. NMFS published a final rule designating critical habitat for Sacramento River winter-run chinook salmon on June 16, 1993. The designated critical habitat includes: the Sacramento River from Keswick Dam (RM 302) to Chipps Island (RM 0) at the westward margin of the Sacramento-San Joaquin Delta, all waters from Chipps Island westward to Carquinez Bridge, all waters of San Pablo Bay, and all waters in San Francisco Bay north of the San Francisco/Oakland Bay Bridge. The final rule also identifies those physical and biological features of the habitat that are essential to the conservation of winter-run chinook salmon.

List of Subjects

50 CFR Part 222

Administrative practice and procedure, Endangered and threatened species, Exports, Imports, Reporting and recordkeeping requirements, Transportation.

50 CFR Part 227

Endangered and threatened species, Exports, Imports, Marine mammals, Transportation.

Dated: December 14, 1993.

Nancy Foster,

Deputy Assistant Administrator for Fisheries, National Marine Fisheries Service.

For the reasons set forth in the preamble, 50 CFR parts 222 and 227 are amended as follows:

PART 222—ENDANGERED FISH OR WILDLIFE

1. The authority citation for part 222 continues to read as follows:

Authority: 16 U.S.C. 1531–1543.

§ 222.23 [Amended]

2. In § 222.23, paragraph (a) is amended by adding the phrase "Sacramento River winter-run chinook salmon (*Oncorhynchus tshawytscha*);" immediately after the phrase "Snake River sockeye salmon (*Oncorhynchus nerka*)" in the second sentence.

PART 227—THREATENED FISH AND WILDLIFE

3. The authority citation for part 227 continues to read as follows:

Authority: 16 U.S.C. 1531 *et seq.*

§ 227.4 [Amended]

4. In § 227.4, paragraph (e) is removed and paragraphs (f) through (h) are redesignated paragraphs (e) through (g) respectively.

§ 227.21 [Amended]

5. In § 227.21, paragraphs (a) and (b)(1), the phrase "(e), (g) and (h)" is removed, and the phrase "(f) and (g)" is added in its place; in paragraph (b)(2), the phrase "(g) and (h)" is removed and the phrase "(f) and (g)" is added in its place.

[FR Doc. 93–31089 Filed 12–28–93; 4:17 pm]

BILLING CODE 3510–22–P [G20,023]

Occasionally a researcher will have a citation to a *CFR* section no longer appearing in the current code. The section or its part might have been repealed or simply transferred to another location in the code. In order that one can determine just what has happened to missing sections, each *CFR* volume contains a list of all changes occurring in its contents since January 1, 1973. These changes are listed by year, at the back of the volume. The entries are the same as those appearing in *LSA* pamphlets, but are limited to the sections in each particular volume. Changes in the entire code before 1973 are listed in separate, hardbound volumes, entitled *List of CFR Sections Affected, 1949–1963, 1964–1972 and 1973–1985.*

5. SUMMARY: USING THE FEDERAL REGISTER SYSTEM

The Federal Court has said that attorneys "may be presumed to understand how to use the Federal Register system." [20] This presumption can be satisfied by a familiarity with the standard means of finding and verifying the status of agency regulations. A basic search for current regulations ordinarily covers the following steps:

(a) Using the general index to the *Code of Federal Regulations* or one of the commercial indexes to the code, or searching the CFR

20. *National Federation of Federal Employees v. Devine,* 591 F.Supp. 166, 169–70 (D.D.C.1984). At issue was whether a supplemental *CFR* volume had to be published when the 1984 edition of Title Five included Office of Personnel Management regulations which had been barred by Congress and declared void before ever taking effect. While noting that a *Federal Register* notice was sufficient to apprise attorneys of what regulations were in force, the court held that a supplemental volume was necessary "to assure that less sophisticated users of the Code are able to have ready access to the regulations currently in effect. Nonattorney users of the Code cannot be expected to be able to engage in legal research such as that done by an attorney." *Id.* at 170.

Illustration I

A page from *Shepard's Code of Federal Regulations Citations*

CODE OF FEDERAL REGULATIONS TITLE 40

§§50.4 to 50.10
539F2d986 △1976
564F2d1274 △1977
590F2d1058 *1977

§§50.4 to 50.7
696F2d152 *1982
696F2d172 *1980

§50.4
427US251 *1975
49LE480 *1975
96SC2523 *1975
480F2d974 *1972
572F2d1153 *1976
572F2d1290 *1976
621F2d800 *1976
659F2d1242 *1980
684F2d1010 △1982
696F2d157 *1981
715F2d326 *1982
739F2d1075 *1982
352FS706 △1972
364FS241 △1973
445FS1072 △1975
483FS1008 *1979
49ChL363 *1981
69VaL617 *1971
89YLJ1493 *1979

§50.4(a)
752F2d1447 *1983

§50.4(b)
659F2d1240 *1980
696F2d152 *1982
752F2d1447 *1983

§50.5
427US251 *1975
49LE480 *1975
96SC2523 *1975
480F2d974 *1972
572F2d1153 *1976
572F2d1290 *1976
621F2d800 *1976
659F2d1242 *1980
696F2d157 *1981
739F2d1075 *1982
752F2d1447 *1983
352FS706 △1972
364FS241 △1973
445FS1072 △1975
89YLJ1493 *1979

§50.6
Va655F2d322 *1979

696F2d163 *1982
364FS241 △1973
445FS1072 △1975
466FS1335 △1979
NM
681P2d732 *1982
690P2d452 *1982
46LCP(3)84 *1982

§50.7
696F2d163 *1982
364FS241 △1973
445FS1072 △1975
466FS1335 △1979
34PaC565 △1978
Pa
384A2d283 △1978
49ChL363 *1981
46LCP(3)84 *1982

§§50.8 to 50.11
C540F2d1130 *1975
383FS142 △1974

§50.8
504F2d654 △1974
598F2d1167 △1979
361FS1398 △1972
400FS559 *1972
427FS1351 △1977
445FS1072 △1975
552FS678 *1981

§50.9
499F2d294 *1973
504F2d654 △1974
759F2d551 *1984
364FS241 △1973
400FS559 *1972
445FS1072 △1975
387Mas388 *1981
Mass
439NE804 *1981
129PaL1063 *1980

§50.9(a)
Va665F2d1181 *1980

§50.10
659F2d1248 *1980
400FS559 *1972
445FS1072 △1975

§50.11
480F2d974 *1972
Va655F2d323 *1979

400FS559 *1972
445FS1072 △1975
30CLA777 *1982

§50.12
705F2d512 *1982
84CR595 *1983

Part 51
421US67 *1974
426US169 *1975
43LE739 *1974
48LE560 *1975
95SC1476 *1974
96SC2008 *1975
477F2d502 △1973
489F2d396 *1972
499F2d293 △1974
500F2d252 △1974
508F2d744 △1975
547F2d130 △1976
621F2d263 △1980
Vp636F2d351 *1978
659F2d1240 *1980

682F2d629 △1982
490FS1146 △1980
46LCP(3)181 *1980
73NwL440 *1977
AEn§10.10
SII§7.27

§51.1
Vp719F2d442 *1982

§51.1(n)
481F2d169 *1972
489F2d394 *1972
507F2d918 △1974
73NwL398 *1977

§51.1(p)
426US181 *1975
48LE566 *1975
96SC2013 *1975
535F2d1322 *1975

§51.1(q)
FRCI§13.14

§51.1(ff)
Va719F2d460 △1983

§51.1(gg)
Va719F2d464 △1983

§51.1(hh)
V719F2d451 △1983

§51.1(ii)(2)
Vp719F2d467 △1983

§51.1(ii)(2)(ii)
C719F2d443 △1983

§51.1(ii)(3)
V719F2d443 △1983

§51.1(jj)
Va719F2d443 △1983

§51.1(kk)
719F2d443 △1983

§51.2
30CLA761 *1981

§51.2(b)
427US266 *1975
49LE488 *1975
96SC2530 *1975
481F2d169 *1972
500F2d252 △1974
504F2d676 △1974
352FS706 △1972
424FS1219 *1975
450FS808 *1975
460FS1316 *1975

§51.2(d)
427US266 *1975
49LE488 *1975
96SC2530 *1975
481F2d169 *1972
500F2d252 △1974
504F2d676 △1974
515F2d216 *1972
424FS1219 *1975
450FS808 *1975
460FS1316 *1975

§51.3
478F2d880 △1973
682F2d642 △1982
FRCI§6.04

§51.3(a)
659F2d1243 *1980

§51.3(b)(1)(iii)
499F2d293 △1974

§51.3(b)(2)
478F2d880 △1973

* followed by a year refers to the CFR edition, if cited. If not cited,
△ followed by a year indicates the date of the citing reference

977

database on either LEXIS or WESTLAW, to determine the titles and sections of relevant regulations.

(b) Examining the text of the regulations in the latest revised edition of its *Code* volume.

(c) Inspecting the latest monthly pamphlet of *LSA: List of CFR Sections Affected* to determine whether the relevant sections have been affected by later changes. The latest *LSA* pamphlet includes all changes from the current *CFR* edition through the end of the month indicated on its cover.

(d) Examining the cumulative "List of CFR Parts Affected" in the most recent issue of the *Federal Register.* This list updates *LSA* and indicates all changes published during the current month. (Depending on how current the latest *LSA* pamphlet is, it may also be necessary to check the final issue of the previous month.)

(e) Checking the citations found in steps (c) and (d) in the *Register* itself to evaluate the substance of the changes.

(f) Using *Shepard's Code of Federal Regulations Citations* to determine whether the current status of the regulation has been affected by any court decisions.

There are ways to save some of these steps. A looseleaf service reprinting regulations in a particular subject area should frequently update and cumulate *CFR* changes appearing in the *Federal Register,* so that its subject arrangement of regulations would be more current than the latest *CFR* edition. A LEXIS or WESTLAW search in the *Federal Register* database for citations of particular *CFR* parts would retrieve changes and proposed changes and eliminate the need to examine *LSA* or the *Register* 's lists of *CFR* parts affected.

D. DECISIONS OF FEDERAL ADMINISTRATIVE AGENCIES

Among the functions of most administrative agencies is the exercise of quasi-judicial power in determining cases and questions arising under their statutes and regulations. These adjudications usually involve a fact-finding process and the application of agency regulations to particular situations or problems. Agency decisions may follow lengthy formal hearings or consist of rulings on specific submitted inquiries.

As administrative agencies grew during the 1930's and assumed more decision-making authority, they came under increasing attack as to their fairness, efficiency, and procedural methods. In 1939 President Roosevelt asked the Attorney General to appoint a committee to study agency procedures, and in 1941 the extensive final report of the Attorney General's Committee on Administrative Procedure was submitted to

Congress.[21] The pressure for reform culminated in enactment of the Administrative Procedure Act in 1946.[22] The Act strengthened procedural safeguards, established minimum standards to ensure fairer hearings, and provided a framework for judicial review of agency action.

Under the Administrative Procedure Act, most agency hearings are conducted by an administrative law judge, who has a role very similar to that of a trial judge and issues the initial decision of the agency. That decision can be appealed to a higher authority within the agency, such as the secretary of the department or the commission, and review of a final agency decision can generally be sought in federal court. The statutes creating and empowering most major agencies provide that actions for review be brought in the United States Court of Appeals.[23]

Most federal agencies write formal opinions to justify or explain their decisions, and these are often published in both official and unofficial sources. Such opinions are very much like those issued by courts, both in form and method of publication. An agency decision can be an important document in interpreting a regulation or statute, or in applying regulations to particular facts. Although most agencies do not consider themselves strictly bound by their prior decisions under the doctrine of stare decisis, the decisions do have considerable precedential value for attorneys practicing before an agency or appealing an agency decision. Whenever one is working in an area within the cognizance of a federal agency, that agency's decisions are an important primary legal source.

1. OFFICIAL REPORTS

Over two dozen federal agencies, including all the major regulatory commissions, publish official reports of their decisions, in a form very similar to official court reports. Most decisions are first published in various preliminary forms such as releases, printed slip decisions, and advance pamphlets. Usually these are cumulated after a considerable time lag into permanent bound volumes in numbered series. As time passes, agencies are producing official documents in microform or compact disk formats as well as paper. There is great variation.

When official reports are published, they almost always contain tables of cases and other aids to provide access to their contents. Some contain tables of statutes or regulations cited, and most have indexes of some sort, although their quality and depth vary widely. *Federal Trade Commission Reports* has a very brief index in each volume, while *Decisions of the Employees' Compensation Appeals Board* has an extensive digest with lengthy descriptive entries. Just as lawyers in each

21. *Administrative Procedure in Government Agencies: Report of the Committee on Administrative Procedure, Appointed by the Attorney General, at the Request of the President, to Investigate the Need for Procedural Reform in Various Administrative Tribunals and to Suggest Improvements Therein,* S.Doc. No. 8, 77th Cong., 1st Sess. (1941).

22. Ch. 324, 80 Stat. 237 (1946).

23. The model for these provisions is the Federal Trade Commission Act of 1914, ch. 311, § 5, 38 Stat. 717, 720 (current version at 15 U.S.C. § 45(c) (1982)).

state must familiarize themselves with the resources of their jurisdiction, those practicing before a particular agency need to learn the resources it offers.

2. UNOFFICIAL SOURCES

An increasing number of agency decisions are available online in WESTLAW and LEXIS. Recent decisions of most major regulatory commissions are included in topical databases. This is the most centralized place to find administrative decisions. New agencies are continually being added to the systems, and older materials to existing databases. When beginning research in a specialized area, it is often worthwhile to determine whether there is a suitable topical database or library and, if so, to learn about its contents. Illustration J shows a menu page from WESTLAW, introducing the user to resources available in Environmental law.

In addition to the various official reports, the decisions of many agencies are also published commercially, either in looseleaf services or in numbered series of bound volumes. Looseleaf editions have several advantages over the official reports. They are issued much more quickly, are better indexed, and are often supplemented by editorial discussion or integrated into other relevant source materials. A more extensive discussion of looseleafs is contained in Chapter 10. Appendix B provides citations to these sources by a relevant agency.

Illustration J

Page from WESTLAW menu screen

```
____WESTLAW DIRECTORY WELCOME SCREEN___________________________P1______
  ____ENVIRONMENTAL LAW DATABASES                              P374_____

          FEDERAL DATABASES                           FEDERAL DATABASES
        ADMINISTRATIVE LAW                                CASE LAW
FENV-EPA     E.P.A. Decisions                    FENV-CS     Federal Cases
 FENV-FIFRA   Fed. Insecticide, Fungicide          FENV-SCT    Supreme Court
              & Rodenticide Act Dec.               FENV-CTA    Courts of Appeals
 FENV-RCRA    Fed. Resource Conservation           FENV-DCT    District Court
              & Recovery Act Decisions
 FENV-TSCA    Federal Toxic Substance               COMBINED FEDERAL &
              Control Act Decisions                   STATE DATABASES
FENV-GCM     E.P.A. Gen. Counsel Memo.           ENV-CS-ALL  Environmental Law
FENV-NR      News Releases
FENV-ORW     Ocean Res. & Wildlife Rptr
OSHA-INSPCT  OSHA Inspection and
              Enforcement Reports

If you wish to:
   Select a database, type its identifier, e.g., FENV-GCM and press ENTER
   View information about a database, type SCOPE followed by its identifier
     and press ENTER
   View the Index to Environmental Law Databases, type P373 and press ENTER
                                                                  [G20,034]
```

3. FINDING AGENCY DECISIONS

One doing research that touches on the decisions of federal administrative agencies should either possess expertise in the area or at least understand its context. Each agency is a whole new story, and it is often a complicated story. The best bet is a loose leaf service. Most administrative subject areas are covered by a loose leaf service or text that helps define and sort information. The topical data bases on LEXIS and WESTLAW are helpful since they pull together administrative cases, rules and documents. But one very much needs to know the ropes. Talk to a senior lawyer or a librarian to get a feel for how the information in a specific topic area is used.

Some administrative decisions can be found by using standard legal research tools. In its topical citators, Shepard's includes agency citations of federal court cases. A researcher who has found a relevant Court of Appeals case, for example, can use *Shepard's Federal Energy Law Citations* to find citations to it in *F.E.R.C. Reports* and *N.R.C. Issuances*. Shepard's does *not* include agency citations of statutory provisions, but *United States Code Service* includes administrative decisions among its case annotations. Illustration K shows a page of *USCS* with numerous annotations from *Agriculture Decisions*. Finally, scholarly secondary sources such as law review articles will frequently combine discussion of agency and court decisions, providing both citations and commentary.

4. UPDATING AND VERIFYING AGENCY DECISIONS

Precedent may not have a determinative role in administrative adjudication, but it is always important to know if a decision has been overturned in judicial review or disapproved by a later agency decision. Although methods of finding agency decisions are not as standard and readily accessible as case-finding methods, updating techniques are becoming increasingly uniform.

Most major agencies receive coverage in one of Shepard's specialized citators or in *Shepard's United States Administrative Citations,* which consists of a compilation of citations to decisions and orders of a dozen federal administrative departments, courts, boards and commissions. *Administrative Citations* indicates when decisions of agencies such as the Federal Communications Commission or the Interstate Commerce Commission have been cited in later agency reports, in federal court opinions, and in selected law reviews. Signal references like those used in Shepard's court citators indicate the precedential effect of later agency and court decisions. In addition, the set provides cross-references between several series of official agency reports and commercial looseleaf services. Parallel citations for FCC decisions, for example, are provided in *Public Utilities Reports* and *Radio Regulation*. *Shepard's U.S. Administrative Citations* can be searched in print or online through LEXIS.

Some agencies, such as the Federal Energy Regulatory Commission, are covered both in *Shepard's U.S. Administrative Citations* and in a topical citator, such as *Shepard's Federal Energy Law Citations*. Several agencies, however, are covered only in specialized citators. *Decisions and Orders of the National Labor Relations Board* appears in *Shepard's*

Federal Labor Law Citations, for example, and *Administrative Decisions under Immigration and Nationality Laws* is covered in *Shepard's Immigration and Naturalization Citations.* In the specialized citators, administrative decisions appear both as cited and citing material; one can find later court and agency citations of an agency decision, as well as agency citations of judicial decisions. The major topical citators, in the labor, patents, and tax fields, are included in the online versions of Shepard's available through WESTLAW and LEXIS.

For some agencies there are other tools besides Shepard's for updating and verifying decisions. *Decisions and Orders of the National Labor Relations Board* and several Internal Revenue Service publications are covered by Auto–Cite, the citation verification system available through LEXIS. Selected other administrative decisions are also included, if they are published in one of the several looseleaf reporters within Auto–Cite's coverage. One can use Auto–Cite to verify a Federal Trade Commission decision, for example, only if it is published in the CCH *Trade Cases.*

It is important to keep in mind when working with administrative materials, whether decisions or regulations, that agency actions are reviewable by the courts. Judicial decisions may set standards and determine limitations on administrative action. Many of the most important procedural safeguards of agency rulemaking and adjudication have resulted from decisions of the Supreme Court and the U.S. Courts of Appeals. Methods of access and updating discussed in this chapter focus specifically on the regulations and decisions of the agencies themselves, but should not be used to the exclusion of case-finding techniques discussed in earlier chapters. Substantive and procedural areas can be researched through digests or *ALR* annotations, and case databases on LEXIS or WESTLAW can be searched for references to a specific administrative regulation or decision.

E. PRESIDENTIAL DOCUMENTS

Thus far we have discussed the regulations and decisions of administrative agencies, which are part of the executive branch of the federal government and operate under the supervision of the President. In addition, the President has the power to veto legislation passed by Congress and the duty to enforce enacted laws. The President also has a wide-ranging lawmaking authority in his or her own right, as the nation's agent of foreign relations and its military commander. In fulfilling these roles and functions, the President issues executive orders, proclamations, and other documents of legal effect.

Illustration K

A *USCS* page, including annotations of administrative decisions

AGRICULTURAL ADJUSTMENT 7 USCS § 608c

CODE OF FEDERAL REGULATIONS

This section is no longer cited as authority for:
7 CFR Part 909, 951, 952, 954–957, 1071, 1073, 1104, 1135, 140–1199, 1202–1206, 1208–1260.

RESEARCH GUIDE

Annotations:

Propriety of Federal District Court's enforcement, or injunction against violation, of agriculture order, regulation, or agreement under 7 USCS § 608a(6). 74 ALR Fed 276.

INTERPRETIVE NOTES AND DECISIONS

10.5. Confidentiality of information

1. Constitutionality

Practice of compensating prune producers for sale of reserve prunes at end of year when reserve is liquidated and fact that price is set by administrative committee under authority of Secretary of Agriculture is authorized by authority of executive branch in exercise of its powers under Commerce Clause, to regulate prices when Congress so mandates; price fixing is not taking without just compensation since producers do receive just, although perhaps not ideal, compensation and price is set by committee which is elected to represent interests of producers as well as of industry in general. Prune Bargaining Asso. v Butz (1975, ND Cal) 444 F Supp 785, affd (CA9 Cal) 571 F2d 1132, cert den 439 US 833, 58 L Ed 2d 128, 99 S Ct 113.

2. Handler defined, generally [7 USCS § 608c(1)]

Interim relief cannot be granted where under terms of Marketing Order, term "handler" is synonymous with "shipper", meaning any person who ships fresh tomatoes produced in production area in current of commerce within regulated area or between any point in regulated area and any point outside thereof, and petitioner has failed to allege facts showing that under these terms it is "handler" subject to order. Re M & R Tomato Distributors, Inc. (1982) 41 Ag Dec 33.

3. —Milk handler

Dairy co-operative is handler within meaning of 7 USCS § 608c and must therefore take administrative route to contest order of Secretary where, by its own admission, co-operative is association of milk producers that transports, processes, and distributes milk for sale to public. United States v United Dairy Farmers Cooperative Asso. (1979, CA3 Pa) 611 F2d 488.

5. Notice and hearing on proposed order [7 USCS § 608c(3)]

Produce handlers can challenge unlawful agency action under Agricultural Adjustment Act (7 USCS §§ 601 et seq.) to ensure that Act's objectives will not be frustrated; however, power granted to producers by Act to protect their interests demonstrates lessened need to rely on handlers, and when Secretary is acting within his designated powers, producers' sole opportunities for protest are hearing on proposed order and opportunity to vote on its approval; and thus judicial review is precluded to orange growers seeking to compel Secretary to terminate federal marketing order under which handling of oranges in that area is regulated by administrative committee which determines percentage of total crop that may be made available for commercial shipment by handlers, where it is not alleged that Secretary acted outside his statutory authority. Pescosolido v Block (1985, CA9 Cal) 765 F2d 827.

6. Findings and issuance of order [7 USCS § 608c(4)]

Nothing in Agricultural Marketing Agreement Act prohibits employee of Department of Agriculture from acting as both investigator and decision maker; milk marketing order promulgated pursuant to 7 USCS § 608c was not invalid because same Department of Agriculture employee who met with representatives of dairy co-operative before hearing and helped draft proposed order also helped Secretary of Agriculture write his final decision. Marketing Assistance Program, Inc. v Bergland (1977) 183 App DC 357, 562 F2d 1305.

7. Termination and suspension of orders [7 USCS § 608c(16)]

District Court did not have mandamus jurisdiction over action by orange farmers seeking to compel Secretary to terminate federal marketing order, under which handling of oranges in geographic area is regulated by administrative committee which determines, among other things, percentage of total crop that may be made available for commercial shipment by handlers, thereby precluding farmers from marketing all oranges that they grow, since (1) mandamus would essentially permit farmers to seek reopening of proceedings they brought pursuant to 7 USCS §§ 601 et seq. that have been finally concluded, (2) permitting attack would allow future plaintiffs continually to protest validity of order even after statutory procedures have been followed merely by claiming change of circumstance and (3) § 608c(16)(B) provides adequate alternative remedy in form of vote of simple majority of affected producers, which will effectively terminate order. Pescosolido v Block (1985, CA9 Cal) 765 F2d 827.

8. Amendments of orders [7 USCS § 608c(17)]

Findings and evidence are required under 7 USCS § 608c(17) only when Secretary promulgates order or makes change in order, not when Secretary merely continues in effect provision that has previously been validly promulgated; provisions of Agriculture Adjustment Act (7 USCS §§ 601 et seq.) applicable to issuance of orders are equally applicable to issuance of amendments to orders, thus before order can be amended, Secretary must make discretionary finding that amendment will tend to effectuate declared policy of Act. Re Oaktree Farm Dairy, Inc. (1979) 38 Ag Dec 113.

10.5. Confidentiality of information

Orange handlers are not entitled to injunction enjoining United States from releasing list of names and addresses of orange growers in several states, which list was generated by government in connection with grower referendum under 7 USCS § 608c(19), since (1) § 608c does not provide for any confidentiality of information gained under section, (2) disclosure would not violate § 608d, in that list was not prepared to determine if handlers were in compliance with marketing orders, but was compiled for referendum purposes only and (3) even if list was compiled pursuant to § 608d, release is still permissible under § 608d(2), in that list qualifies as "general statement" which does not identify information furnished by any particular person; further, list is not exempt from disclosure under any statutory exemptions of Freedom of Information Act (5 USCS § 552(b)). Ivanhoe Citrus Asso. v Handley (1985, DC Dist Col) 612 F Supp 1560.

11. Generally

Congressional mandate that Secretary shall prescribe different terms in certain circumstances cannot be transposed into antithesis, that is, that Secretary shall prescribe uniform provisions in absence of such circumstances. Re Oaktree Farm Dairy, Inc. (1979) 38 Ag Dec 113.

12. Classification, generally

14. —Miscellaneous

Order provisions which require handlers to account for butterfat and skim milk separately and to pay for overages and shrinkages of butterfat and skim milk at applicable class prices are in accordance with law. Re Moser Farms Dairy, Inc. (1982) 41 Ag Dec 7.

15. Minimum prices

Secretary complied with 7 USCS § 608c(18) which provides that before he may modify minimum price which handlers must pay to producers under 7 USCS § 608c(5)(A) he must fix reasonable prices based upon hearing record which considers prices of feed, available

[See "Caution" on p. 3 for §§ affected by P.L.'s 100-202 & 203] 19

1. EXECUTIVE ORDERS AND PROCLAMATIONS

Two basic forms of executive fiat are used to perform presidential functions pursuant to statutory authority or inherent powers. These are *executive orders* and *proclamations.* Proclamations are general announcements of policy issued to the nation as a whole, and are commonly associated with ceremonial occasions such as observance of National Bowling Week, 1987,[24] or National Skiing Day, 1988.[25] A few substantive proclamations deal with trade policy or tariff issues. Executive orders cover a wide range of issues and are generally issued to government officials. The two types of document have substantially the same legal effect.[26]

Executive orders and proclamations are effective upon publication in the *Federal Register.* The Office of the Federal Register assigns a number to each, in separate series for orders and proclamations. This number is the official and permanent means of identifying the document. Presidential documents are the first items appearing in each *Register* issue, in a larger typeface and more legible format than any of the other material. Their titles are listed under the alphabetical heading "Presidential Documents" in the table of contents and in the monthly indexes, and their numbers are listed in the tables of *CFR* parts affected in the particular issue and for the month. They are also listed by number in the monthly pamphlet *LSA: List of CFR Sections Affected.*

At the end of each year executive orders and proclamations are compiled and published in Title 3 of the *Code of Federal Regulations,* which becomes the standard source for these documents. Because each annual edition of Title 3 is a unique set of documents rather than an updated codification, older volumes remain part of the current *CFR* set.[27] Documents from the years 1936 to 1975 have been recompiled into multiyear hardcover editions.[28]

All executive orders and proclamations published in the *Federal Register* are also published in the *U.S. Code Congressional and Administrative News* and *USCS Advance. USCCAN* bound volumes have reprinted all orders and proclamations since 1943. In both monthly pamphlets and bound volumes of *USCCAN,* Table 7 lists proclamations and Table 8 executive orders, and the index lists documents both by subject and under the headings "executive orders" and "proclamations."

Proclamations back to 1846, but *not* executive orders, are printed in *Statutes at Large.* Some proclamations and orders issued under the specific authority of a statute are also published in the *United States Code* (and its annotated editions, *USCA* and *USCS*), following the text of the authorizing section.

Proclamations and executive orders are also available on LEXIS and WESTLAW. LEXIS has all presidential documents since January 20,

24. Proclamation No. 5596, 3 C.F.R. § 1 (1987).

25. Proclamation No. 5756, 3 C.F.R. § 185 (1987).

26. For an historical overview of the development of the use of these presidential documents, see House Committee on Government Operations, 85th Cong., 1st Sess., *Executive Orders and Proclamations: A Study of a Use of Presidential Powers* (Comm. Print 1957).

27. Beginning with the 1985 compilation, the Title 3 pamphlet has had a white cover to distinguish it from other *CFR* volumes and to inhibit the tendency to discard it upon receipt of the new year's edition.

28. There is also a two-volume set, *Proclamations and Executive Orders: Herbert Hoover, March 4, 1929 to March 4, 1933,* compiling pre-*Federal Register* documents for one president.

1981, and WESTLAW has executive orders dating back to 1936 and other presidential documents since 1984.

The Office of the Federal Register publishes a useful volume, *Codification of Presidential Proclamations and Executive Orders,* which arranges proclamations and orders by subject in fifty titles similar to those in *CFR*. It contains executive orders and proclamations of general applicability and continuing effect issued from January 20, 1961 to January 20, 1989, with amendments incorporated into the texts of documents. Orders and proclamations are printed in numerical order within each of the fifty titles. The volume also includes valuable disposition tables, listing all proclamations and orders issued from 1961 to 1985 and indicating their current status. Amendments and revocations are listed, as well as the title and page locations of documents included in the codification.

Judicial and law review citations to proclamations and executive orders are included in the coverage of *Shepard's Code of Federal Regulations Citations.* Presidential documents receive treatment similar to regulations, with symbols indicating the effect of court decisions on the documents' validity.

2. OTHER PRESIDENTIAL DOCUMENTS

While executive orders and proclamations are the most usual forms of presidential documents, the President does issue a variety of other documents of legal effect. The President issues administrative orders, transmits messages to Congress, and makes executive agreements with other countries. While these documents may be less common than executive orders and proclamations, some familiarity with them is often necessary.

Administrative orders: A variety of other documents are printed in the *Federal Register* along with executive orders and proclamations, but not included in either numbered series. These documents, such as memoranda, notices, letters, and presidential determinations, are treated similarly to orders and proclamations. They are included in the table of contents and indexes under "Presidential documents," and are cited by date under Title 3 in the lists of *CFR* parts affected and in *LSA*. They are also reprinted in the annual cumulation of 3 C.F.R. in a separate section following executive orders. Table 3 in each annual volume lists these documents by date. Unlike proclamations and executive orders, however, they are generally not reprinted in *USCCAN,* and because there is no standardized numbering system they are not covered in Shepard's citators.

Reorganization plans: A reorganization plan consists of a presidential proposal for changes in the form of agencies, and can abolish or transfer agency functions. Until recently a plan became law automatically unless either chamber of Congress passed a resolution disapproving it, and so was a powerful means of executive action. In 1983, however, the Supreme Court found such one-house legislative vetoes to be unconstitutional,[29] and a reorganization plan must now be approved by both houses of Congress to take effect.[30] Perhaps because it is no longer as efficient a device, the reorganization plan has fallen into disuse.

Reorganization plans are designated by year and plan number within that year, and published in several places. Upon taking effect they appear in the *Federal Register,* in Title 3 of *CFR,* in the *Statutes at Large,* and unofficially in *USCCAN.*[31] They are also published in Title 5 of the *United States Code,* following the particular Reorganization Act under which they were authorized. *USCA* and *USCS* include notes, presidential messages, and executive orders relating to the plans, and are therefore often the most useful research sources. Reorganization plans, like proclamations and executive orders, can be traced in *Shepard's Code of Federal Regulations Citations.* They can also be traced in *Shepard's United States Citations* under their *Statutes at Large* or *U.S. Code* citations.

Messages to Congress: Communications to Congress by the President are typically made in the form of presidential messages. They may propose new legislation, explain vetoes, transmit reports or other documents, or convey information about the state of national affairs or some matter of concern. Most messages are printed as Congressional documents. They are also printed and indexed in the *Congressional Record* and in the House and Senate journals. A few important ones appear in *USCCAN.* These documents have some value in developing legislative histories of particular statutes.

Presidential statements upon signing legislation into law may also have some relevance in legislative history research. These signing statements, which since 1986 are printed in *USCCAN,* are discussed in Chapter 6, Legislative History.

Executive agreements: The President makes executive agreements with other countries, under the authority to conduct foreign affairs. Unlike treaties, they do not require the advice and consent of the Senate. In recent years, more and more diplomatic arrangements have been made through these convenient methods. Because their purposes and publication methods are basically the same as treaties, the two forms of international agreements are discussed in detail in *How to Find the Law.*

3. COMPILATIONS OF PRESIDENTIAL PAPERS

The most comprehensive source for current presidential documents is the *Weekly Compilation of Presidential Documents,* which has been published by the Office of the Federal Register since 1965. The *Weekly Compilation* includes nominations, announcements, and transcripts of speeches and press conferences, as well as orders, proclamations, and

29. *Immigration and Naturalization Service v. Chadha,* 462 U.S. 919 (1983).

30. Reorganization Act Amendments of 1984, 5 U.S.C. § 906 (1988).

31. When submitted to Congress, reorganization plans are printed in the *Congressional Record* and in the House and Senate documents series. These are the best sources for plans that have not passed Congress.

other legally significant documents. Each weekly issue contains an index to all material in the current quarter, and there are cumulated annual indexes.

An annual volume, *Public Papers of the President,* has since the beginning of the Carter presidency cumulated all material in the *Weekly Compilation* in a final, bound format. Earlier, somewhat more selective *Public Papers* volumes have been published for Presidents Hoover, Truman, Eisenhower, Kennedy, Johnson, Nixon, and Ford.[32] The official set contains only annual indexes, but the commercially published *Cumulated Indexes to the Public Papers of the Presidents of the United States* (K.T.O. Press, 1977–79; Kraus International, since 1979) provides single-volume coverage of each administration.

The papers of earlier presidents are available in various forms. Congress created a Joint Committee on Printing in 1895,[33] and one of its first projects was a comprehensive collection of presidential papers. The resulting ten-volume set, *A Compilation of the Messages and Papers of the Presidents, 1789–1897,* was edited by James D. Richardson and published in 1896–97. The Bureau of National Literature and Art reissued the set in numerous later editions, supplementing it into the 1920's.

F. UNPUBLISHED INFORMATION

While the focus of this book is material that is generally published or available, the government has a vast store of additional documentation that it does not publish, such as internal records, data collected on individuals, and staff studies. The Freedom of Information Act [34] and the Privacy Act [35] have dramatically expanded access to government files. Although government resistance to applications and suits under the acts has increased since their passage, these laws have been quite effective in opening new areas of fact-finding for those involved in legal research.

Several books explain the procedures for gaining access to government records under these laws. They discuss the history and interpretation of the acts, explain procedures for filing requests and suing to compel disclosure, and provide the citations of relevant regulations and sample forms. Among these are:

J.D. Franklin & R.F. Bouchard, *Guidebook to the Freedom of Information and Privacy Acts,* 2d ed. (Clark Boardman, 1987).

Freedom of Information Act Guide and Privacy Act Overview. (Government Printing Office, 1992)

32. While Franklin D. Roosevelt's papers have not been included in the official series, they have been edited by S.I. Rosenman and commercially published as *The Public Papers and Addresses of Franklin D. Roosevelt,* (Random House, 13 vols., 1938–50).

33. Act of January 12, 1895, ch. 23, 28 Stat. 601.

34. 5 U.S.C. § 552 (1988).

35. 5 U.S.C. § 552a (1988).

J.T. O'Reilly, *Federal Information Disclosure: Procedures, Forms and the Law* 2d Edition (Shepard's/McGraw–Hill, 2 vols., 1990–date).

A concise handbook on the acts is *A Citizen's Guide on Using the Freedom of Information Act and the Privacy Act of 1974 to Request Government Records,* H.R.Rep. No. 199, 100th Cong., 1st Sess. (1987). The guide includes sample request forms, but does not cover procedures for filing suit after denial of a request.

G. STATE ADMINISTRATIVE MATERIALS

State administrative publications receive only brief treatment in this chapter for two reasons. First, because the availability of these materials varies widely from state to state, any discussion must necessarily be quite general. Second, state administrative documents tend to emulate the patterns of federal administrative publication, so a person familiar with federal research can usually adapt readily to a particular state's materials.

The regulatory bodies of the various states affect their citizens no less profoundly than does the federal bureaucracy. State agencies set and enforce public health and housing standards, fix and regulate utility rates and practices, govern labor and business activities, and perform many other functions. Unfortunately problems of access and control are not always met with sufficient resources or interest to make administrative materials regularly available.

Many states have administrative codes and registers similar to the *CFR* and *Federal Register,* but some states publish neither. Some states publish decisions of selected agencies, or issue other documents of legal significance. A large part of the process of doing state administrative research is determining just what publications exist for a particular state. *BNA's Directory of State Administrative Codes and Registers* (1992) is helpful for getting a feel for local practice. Another place to learn about the situation in individual states is a state-specific legal research guide. Appendix A, at the end of this volume, lists available guides.

For a survey of the officers, agencies, functions, practices and statistics in all the states, *The Book of the States* (Council of State Governments, biennial) is very helpful. A thorough reference tool on state governmental operations, it includes legal, political and statistical information from every state. The *Municipal Year Book* (International City Management Association, annual) performs a similar function for governments on a local level.

Names and addresses of state administrative personnel are available in the *National Directory of State Agencies* (National Standards Association, annual) or *State Administrative Officials Classed by Function* (Council of State Governments, annual).

1. REGULATIONS

The availability of state rules and regulations has improved considerably in recent years. In 1965 only fourteen states published administrative codes.[36] Forty states and the District of Columbia now publish subject compilations of administrative regulations, more or less resembling *CFR*. Many of these are issued in a looseleaf format with periodic updating. Some of these codes are very easily accessible, but the arrangement and indexing of others can be cumbersome and confusing even to experienced users.

In California a private publisher, Barclays, purchased the rights to the Administrative Code. The company cleaned up what had been a grossly messy administrative code. They provided a good index, and put the entire code on-line. Using on-demand printing technology, they supply a subscribers with whatever parts of the code they wish to purchase. This wonderful streamlining came at a cost to consumers, as the Code went from relatively inexpensive to being fairly costly. Most judge the trade to be a fair one. Barclay's and other companies are now trying to get rights to the Codes in other states. As they do, one can expect to see improved information at a higher cost. This process of privatizing state information could represent a trend.

WESTLAW and LEXIS each contain the text of ten state administrative codes at the time that this book is written. Because the data bases do not contain precisely the same states, thirteen states are covered between the two. This number will expand as time passes. Searching for state administrative materials in a full text setting has the same potential advantages already discussed in the federal setting.

2. DECISIONS

Some state agencies publish official reports of their decisions, similar to those of federal bodies. The most common are the reports of state tax commissioners, public utility commissions, banking commissions, insurance commissions, and labor agencies. Advance sheets are quite rare, although some agencies issue their decisions *only* in separate slip form. Occasionally state administrative decisions may be found in specialized subject reporters and looseleaf services, and a growing number of state agency decisions are included on WESTLAW and LEXIS.

State attorney general opinions are often an important resource in interpreting and applying statutory provisions. These opinions are similar in form and purpose to those of the United States Attorney General, but in most states they are used much more frequently.[37] They are typically published in annual or biennial volumes by the state (with a considerable time lag), and are also available currently on microfiche from Hein. For several states, Shepard's citators include attorney

36. Cohen, "Publication of State Administrative Regulations—Reform in Slow Motion," 14 *Buffalo L.Rev.* 410, 421 (1965).

37. State attorney general practices are surveyed in Heiser, "The Opinion Writing Function of Attorneys General," 18 *Idaho L.Rev.* 9 (1982).

general opinions as citing material, so one can find opinions discussing particular cases or statutes. Many of the annotated state codes also include references to relevant opinions. Both LEXIS and WESTLAW have databases containing state attorney general opinions, with coverage in most states beginning in 1977.

3. OTHER DOCUMENTS

Like the federal government, state governments publish a variety of documents such as reports, studies, and periodicals. A few states issue periodic lists of recent publications, and some issue annual catalogs. The most complete source for all states is the *Monthly Checklist of State Publications,* which since 1910 has recorded state documents received at the Library of Congress. Publications are listed by state and indexed by subject. This publication was slated for discontinuance in 1995, but librarians are staging a last ditch effort to keep it alive.

H. SUMMARY

The development of administrative agencies on both federal and state levels has added a massive literature of administrative regulations and decisions to the essential resources of legal research. With the growth of the executive branch generally, the legal documentation flowing from the exercise of Presidential powers has further enlarged the range of these materials. The increased sophistication of indexing and access aids in the *Federal Register* and the *Code of Federal Regulations,* commercial publications of administrative documents such as looseleaf services, and online access through WESTLAW and LEXIS have made these materials easily available to the researcher. Even state regulations and decisions are now more accessible through the proliferation of state administrative codes and registers, and their partial coverage in looseleafs and databases. What had been a wilderness of confusion and frustration has blossomed into a fertile field for the astute researcher.

I. ADDITIONAL READING

Alfred Aman and William Mayton, Administrative Law. (West Publishing, 1993). This is the Horn Book on administrative law.

K.F. Warren, *Administrative Law in the Political System,* 2d ed. (West, 1988).

Chapter 9

COURT RULES AND PRACTICE

A. INTRODUCTION

While much of legal literature focuses on substantive rights, an equally important aspect of the law deals with the processes under which parties come before courts to settle disputes. These processes are the focus of law school classes on civil procedure and of the burgeoning body of material on court rules and practice. Neither substance nor procedure would serve much purpose without the other. As Roscoe Pound succinctly explained: "Procedure is the means; full, equal and exact enforcement of substantive law is the end." [1]

For centuries the rules governing court proceedings were developed piecemeal through case law, eventually creating the arcane and formalis-

1. Roscoe Pound, "The Etiquette of Justice," 3 *Proc. Neb. St. B.A.* 231, 231 (1909).

tic pleading rituals of the Court of Chancery in Dickens' *Bleak House*. Reforms within the past century have considerably changed court procedures, making them simpler and more flexible.[2] In any area of thought shaped by lawyers and judges, however, there are bound to be unforeseen complexities and differences of interpretation. Rules that may appear straightforward must be applied in light of the large body of case law that has developed. An extensive secondary literature also exists to guide litigants through the intricate maze of court proceedings, and formbooks provide the proper format for pleadings and other court documents. This chapter surveys the sources available for finding the texts of court rules and discovering the judicial and secondary reference materials that can aid one's passage through the courts. Much of this chapter is devoted to sets that may play little role in the law school curriculum, though they may shed light on courses like Civil Procedure. But these tools are the bread and butter of anyone who works in the area of litigation.

B. COURT RULES

Court rules regulate the conduct of business before the courts. They range from purely formal details, such as the format to be followed in preparing a brief, to matters of substantial importance, such as grounds for appeal, time limitations, and the types of motions and appeals which will be heard. Court rules may specify or limit available remedies, and may thus affect rights in significant ways.

Each jurisdiction has its own requirements and procedures for the promulgation of court rules. Some involve action by special conferences of judges; others require action or approval by the highest court of the jurisdiction. Some court rules are statutory and are created by legislatures, while some require a combination of judicial action and legislative approval. While courts are traditionally considered to have inherent power to control the conduct of their affairs, court rules are generally promulgated under authority granted by the legislature and are considered a form of delegated legislation.

Federal procedure is discussed here first for two reasons. Not only does it affect more people than the procedure of any individual state, but its forms and methods of publication have been very influential on the states. An increasing number of states have chosen to model their procedural rules on those established for the federal courts in the past half-century.

1. FEDERAL RULES

Since its first session, Congress has expressly given the federal

2. "The practically universal trend of reform has been in favor of less binding and strict rules of form enforced upon the litigants and their counsel and with a large measure of discretion accorded to the trial judge in directing the course of a particular lawsuit." Charles E. Clark, "The Handmaid of Justice," 23 *Wash. U. L.Q.* 297, 308 (1938).

courts power to make rules governing their procedures.[3] It took until well into the twentieth century, however, for the Supreme Court to promulgate extensive general rules of procedure for the federal courts. The Federal Rules of Civil Procedure, adopted by the Supreme Court in December 1937 and effective September 16, 1938,[4] successfully modernized federal civil practice. The Federal Rules of Criminal Procedure followed on March 21, 1946.[5]

The new criminal rules governed proceedings both before and after trial, but appeals in civil cases continued to be handled differently in each circuit. In 1966, Congress empowered the Supreme Court to prescribe rules for the Courts of Appeals in civil actions.[6] The Federal Rules of Appellate Procedure, governing both civil and criminal proceedings, took effect on July 1, 1968.[7]

The last of the four major sets of rules governing federal court proceedings had a rather different origin. In 1972, the Supreme Court submitted proposed Federal Rules of Evidence to Congress, which passed a law preventing them from taking effect until expressly approved.[8] One problem was that the proposed rules covering evidentiary privileges were seen as substantive rather than procedural in nature, and thus outside the scope of the Court's rulemaking authority.[9] Congress adopted its own amended version of the rules, which became law on July 1, 1975.[10]

3. Section 17 of the Judiciary Act of 1789 gave the new federal courts the power "to make and establish all necessary rules for the orderly conducting [of] business in the said courts, provided such rules are not repugnant to the laws of the United States." Ch. 20, § 17, 1 Stat. 73, 83. The Supreme Court's first rules, at its first meeting in February 1790, dealt mostly with qualification of attorneys who wished to practice before it. Appointment of Justices 2 U.S. (2 Dall.) 399 (1790). A rule five years later ordered that "the Gentlemen of the Bar be notified, that the Court will hereafter expect to be furnished with a statement of the material points of the Case, from the Counsel on each side of a Cause." 3 U.S. (3 Dall.) 120 (1795).

Today, the Supreme Court and all courts created by Congress are empowered under 28 U.S.C. § 2071 (1988) to establish rules governing the conduct of their business. The Supreme Court has the power to prescribe general rules of practice and procedure for cases in the federal district courts and courts of appeal. 28 U.S.C. § 2072 (1988), *as amended by* Act of Dec. 1, 1990, 18 U.S.C.A. § 2072 (Law. Co-op).

4. 308 U.S. 645 (1938). The Supreme Court acted under a 1934 Act of Congress that had given it the authority to combine equity and law into one federal civil procedure, and to make and publish rules governing federal actions. Act of June 19, 1934, ch. 651, 48 Stat. 1064. Previously, the Supreme Court had promulgated its first set of procedural rules in equity in 1822, 20 U.S.(7 Wheat.) v (1822), but had not issued general rules for actions at law.

5. 327 U.S. 821 (1946). Congress had given the Supreme Court authority to promulgate rules governing criminal appeals in 1933, Act of Feb. 24, 1933, ch. 119, 47 Stat. 904, as amended by Act of Mar. 8, 1934, ch. 49, 48 Stat. 399; in 1940 it passed a law providing for rules with respect to criminal trial court proceedings, Act of June 29, 1940, ch. 445, 54 Stat. 688.

6. Act of Nov. 6, 1966, Pub. L. No. 89–773, 80 Stat. 1323.

7. 389 U.S. 1063 (1968).

8. Act of Mar. 30, 1973, Pub.L. No. 93–12, 87 Stat. 9.

9. The then-governing statutory provision contained the same language as the current provision, 28 U.S.C. § 2072 (1988), specifying that rules promulgated by the Supreme Court "shall not abridge, enlarge or modify any substantive right." *See* Arthur J. Goldberg, "The Supreme Court, Congress, and Rules of Evidence," 5 *Seton Hall L.Rev.* 667 (1974).

10. Act of Jan. 2, 1975, Pub.L. No. 93–595, § 2(a)(1), 88 Stat. 1926, 1948.

In 1988, Congress enacted the Judicial Improvements and Access to Justice Act,[11] and consolidated the Supreme Court's authority to promulgate "general rules of practice and procedure and rules of evidence for cases in the United States district courts (including proceedings before magistrates thereof) and courts of appeal." [12] As a result of this consolidation, scattered sections of the U.S. Code which previously had given the Court power to prescribe rules of procedure and evidence were repealed.[13] The Court's authority to promulgate rules is now concentrated in Sections 2072–2075 of 28 U.S.C.

In addition to the four major sets of federal rules, the Supreme Court also has issued rules for more limited circumstances. For example, rules governing bankruptcy proceedings were first promulgated under the authority of the Bankruptcy Act of 1898,[14] and have undergone several revisions and changes. The current Federal Rules of Bankruptcy Procedure were promulgated by the Supreme Court in 1983.[15]

An important resource in applying federal court rules is the accompanying commentary by the Advisory Committee that drafted the original rules or a later committee that drafted and proposed an amendment.[16] These notes usually consist of a few paragraphs discussing the history of procedure under prior law and the purpose of the new rule or amendment, and provide a sort of "legislative history" analogous to congressional committee reports. Advisory Committee notes are often an invaluable first step in interpreting rule provisions. In most versions of the major sets of rules, these important notes are printed immediately following the text of each rule.

Finally, in addition to the sets of rules applying to the federal courts in general, there are rules governing proceedings in particular courts. The Supreme Court and specialized courts such as the Claims Court have their own sets of rules, and individual Courts of Appeals and District Courts promulgate supplementary rules for local practice. Any federal court can establish local rules for the conduct of its business, as long as they are not inconsistent with Acts of Congress or rules pre-

11. Act of Nov. 19, 1988, Pub. L. No. 100–702, 102 Stat. 4642 (codified as amended in scattered sections of 28 U.S.C.). The part of the act dealing with court rules (the Rules Enabling Act) can be found at §§ 401–407, 102 Stat. 4648–4652.

12. 28 U.S.C. § 2072(a) (1988).

13. Before being repealed by the 1988 Act, 28 U.S.C. § 2072 had provided for rules of civil procedure; § 2076 had governed rules of evidence; and 18 U.S.C. §§ 3771–3772 had provided for rules of criminal procedure.

14. Ch. 541, § 30, 30 Stat. 544, 554. This section was repealed in 1964, when Supreme Court rulemaking power in bankruptcy was brought into conformity with its power to make other court rules. Act of Oct. 3, 1964, Pub.L. No. 88–623, § 1, 78 Stat. 1001, 1001 (codified as amended at 28 U.S.C. § 2075 (1988)).

15. 461 U.S. 977 (1983).

16. Under a 1958 Act, a permanent Committee on Rules of Practice and Procedure of the Judicial Conference of the United States studies the federal rules on a continuous basis and recommends changes as necessary. Act of July 11, 1958, Pub. L. No. 85–513, 72 Stat. 356 (codified as amended at 28 U.S.C. § 331 (1988)).

scribed by the Supreme Court.[17] These local rules are important.

These various rules governing federal court proceedings are rarely far from hand in any law library. They can be found in online databases and in numerous publications, both unannotated and annotated. The sheer number of resources about to be described may be bewildering at first, but different versions serve different purposes. The proper source to use depends on the research needs in a particular situation. Sometimes one just needs to consult the text of a set of rules, but often it is necessary to have references to judicial decisions or expert commentary. Table 1 lists the locations of rules in the tools discussed below.

a. Unannotated Texts

(1) Major Rules

A variety of resources contain the texts of federal court rules. The *United States Code* publishes both the rules and Advisory Committee notes for the major sets of rules. An appendix to Title 28, Judiciary and Judicial Procedure, contains the Federal Rules of Civil Procedure, Appellate Procedure, and Evidence, as well as rules governing proceedings in the Supreme Court and several specialized courts.[18] The Federal Rules of Criminal Procedure appear in an appendix to Title 18, Crimes and Criminal Procedure. The official *U.S. Code,* however, is always at least two or three years out of date when it is published, so it cannot be relied upon for more recent developments or changes.

Several commercially published sources also contain the texts of the major rules, updated on a more timely basis. For example, Lawyers Cooperative publishes annually the text and Advisory Committee notes for all major rules in the "National Volume" of its *Federal Procedure Rules Service,* with updates provided in a cumulative pocket part issued quarterly.[19]

Two other references, previously published by Callaghan but now under the Lawyers Co-op imprint, also include the major federal rules. The "Finding Aids" volume of *Federal Rules Service* contains the Rules of Civil Procedure and Appellate Procedure; the Rules of Evidence can be found in the corresponding volume of *Federal Evidence Rules Service.*[20] The *Cyclopedia of Federal Procedure*, Volume 16A, "Rules," (3d

17. 28 U.S.C. § 2071 (1988). The Judicial Conference reviews for consistency with federal law rules prescribed under this provision by courts other than the Supreme Court and the district courts, and is empowered to modify or abrogate any rule found to be inconsistent. 28 U.S.C § 331 (1988). The Supreme Court may also exercise its inherent supervisory power to ensure that local rules are consistent with principles of right and justice. *See, e.g., Frazier v. Heebe,* 482 U.S. 641 (1987), *on remand,* 825 F.2d 89 (5th Cir.1987) (prohibiting Eastern District of Louisiana from requiring that a member of its bar live or maintain an office in Louisiana).

18. Bankruptcy Rules and Official Forms are in an appendix to Title 11, Bankruptcy.

19. This volume also includes research references to the publisher's encyclopedia, *Federal Procedure, Lawyers Edition* (to be discussed below in Section D).

20. These very useful resources for research on judicial decisions relating to the rules will be discussed below in Section C.

ed. 1990) contains the text of the major rules, but does not include Advisory Committee notes.

Many law students first encounter the Federal Rules of Civil Procedure in one of several available soft-cover editions that usually contain the other major rules as well. For example, West's *Federal Rules of Civil Procedure* (1993–94 Educational Edition) includes the texts of the Rules of Civil Procedure, Appellate Procedure, and Evidence, along with the text of Title 28 of the U.S. Code.[21] Foundation Press publishes a similar volume aimed at law students, *The Judicial Code and Rules of Procedure in the Federal Courts,* which includes the Rules of Criminal Procedure.

(2) Local Court Rules

While not as widely applicable as the major sets of rules discussed above, rules for specific federal courts can be just as important in the day-to-day practice of law. For example, the Rules of the United States Supreme Court can be found in the *U.S. Code* and several of the other sources discussed above, as well as in Commerce Clearing House's looseleaf *Supreme Court Bulletin.*

The rules of individual lower federal courts are not quite as widely published as rules promulgated by the Supreme Court. The most comprehensive source for all circuit and district court civil practice rules is "Federal Local Court Rules," a set of updated looseleaf volumes now published by Lawyers Co-op as an adjunct to its *Federal Rules Service.* Most of the set consists of rules for individual U.S. District Courts, arranged by state; the third volume includes rules and internal operating procedures for the Courts of Appeals.

The rules of individual courts are also available in several other places. For example, eleven separate "Circuit Volumes," corresponding to the eleven numbered U.S. Courts of Appeals, are published as part of *Federal Procedure Rules Service.* Each volume contains the rules of its circuit and of each district within the circuit. Rules for the District of Columbia Circuit appear in the Third and Fourth Circuit volumes, and Federal Circuit rules are in the Second, Third and Fourth Circuit volumes. The "Rules" volume of the *Cyclopedia of Federal Procedure* also includes rules of the federal circuit, but not district, courts.

The handiest source for rules of the district courts in a particular state, and of the circuit within which that state lies, will frequently be a state court rules pamphlet published by West or Michie. These pamphlets, published for over thirty states to accompany annotated state codes, contain rules of both state and federal courts, and will be discussed further in the "state rules" section, below.

21. West also publishes annually the soft-covered *Federal Civil Judicial Procedure and Rules* and *Federal Criminal Code and Rules.* As the titles indicate, these books contain the texts of relevant statutes as well as numerous sets of court rules.

Table 1

Published and online locations of various sets of federal court rules

Annotated Editions

	United States Code Annotated	*United States Code Service*	*Supreme Court Digest, L.Ed.*	*Moore's Rules Pamphlets*
Federal Rules of Civil Procedure	Title 28 Appendix	Rules volumes	Vol. 18	Vol. 1
Federal Rules of Criminal Procedure	Title 18 Appendix	Rules volumes	Vol. 19	Vol. 3
Federal Rules of Appellate Procedure	Title 28 Appendix	Rules volumes	Vol. 17	Vol. 1 (unannotated)
Federal Rules of Evidence	Title 28 Appendix	Title 28 Appendix	Vol. 20	Vol. 2
Bankruptcy Rules and Official Forms	Title 11 Appendix	Rules volumes	Vol. 17	
Rules of the Supreme Court of the U.S.	Title 28 Appendix	Rules volumes	Vol. 17	Vol. 1 (unannotated)
Rules of individual U.S. Courts of Appeals	Title 28 Appendix	Rules volumes	Vol. 21	
Rules for the Trial of Misdemeanors before U.S. Magistrates	Title 18 Appendix	Rules volumes	Vol. 19	Vol. 3
Rules Governing Sections 2254 and 2255 (habeas corpus) Proceedings	Title 28 following §§ 2254, 2255	Rules volumes	Vol. 19	Vol. 3
Rules of the Judicial Panel on Multidistrict Litigation	Title 28 following § 1407	Rules volumes	Vol. 22	
Rules of the U.S. Claims Court	Title 28 Appendix	Rules volumes	Vol. 22	
Rules of the U.S. Court of International Trade	Title 28 Appendix	Rules volumes	Vol. 22	
Rules of the U.S. Tax Court	Title 26 following § 7453	Rules volumes	Vol. 22	
Rules of the U.S. Court of Military Appeals	Title 10 following § 867	Rules volumes	Vol. 22	

Table 1 (Continued)

Unannotated Editions

United States Code	*Federal Procedure Rules Service*	*Cyclopedia of Federal Procedure*
Title 28 Appendix	National volume	Vol. 16A
Title 18 Appendix	National volume	Vol. 16A
Title 28 Appendix	National volume	Vol. 16A
Title 28 Appendix	National volume	Vol. 16A
Title 11 Appendix		
Title 28 Appendix	National volume	Vol. 16A
	Individual circuit volumes	Vol. 16A
Title 18 Appendix	National volume	Vol. 16A
Following Title 28 §§ 2254, 2255	National volume	Vol. 16A
Following Title 28 § 1407	National volume	
Title 28 Appendix	3d & 4th Circuit volumes	Vol. 16A
Title 28 Appendix	Second Circuit volume	
Title 26 Appendix		
Title 10 Appendix		

b. Annotated Texts

Annotated editions of the federal rules contain not only Advisory Committee comments but headnotes of relevant cases. Both commercially published annotated versions of the U.S. Code provide comprehensive coverage of rules.

The *United States Code Annotated* and *United States Code Service* treat the rules in similar fashion to statutes and provide extensive annotations of relevant decisions. In *USCA,* the eighty-six Federal Rules of Civil Procedure fill ten volumes, and in *USCS* they occupy almost eight volumes. The rules are located in the sets in different places: *USCA* includes the rules at the same place they appear in the *U.S. Code,* following the code titles to which they are most closely related (for example, the Federal Rules of Civil Procedure, Appellate Procedure, and Evidence follow Title 28, Judiciary and Judicial Procedure, while the Federal Rules of Criminal Procedure appear in a volume after Title 18, Crimes and Criminal Procedure). *USCS* publishes several unnumbered "Court Rules" volumes, which are generally shelved at the end of the set. The one exception is the Federal Rules of Evidence; because they were enacted by Congress, *USCS* prints them as an appendix volume to Title 28. Both *USCA* and *USCS* also include annotated editions of the rules of the Supreme Court, of the thirteen individual circuits, and of specialized federal courts. Like the rest of the sets, the volumes of court rules are updated by annual pocket parts and by interim pamphlets.

As it does with statutes, *USCA* includes extensive cross-references to related material such as other federal rules, the publisher's treatise

Federal Practice and Procedure, and *West's Federal Forms* (discussed below in Sections D.1 and E, respectively). The notes to each section also provide relevant digest key numbers and *C.J.S.* section numbers. The bulk of each volume consists of case headnotes, arranged by subject after each rule. Illustration A shows the *USCA* version of Federal Rules of Evidence, Rule 802, concerning the admissibility of hearsay.

USCS provides the same rules text and Advisory Committee notes, along with cross-references to other rules and statutes and to its publisher's other works. These references include Lawyers Co-op's federal practice encyclopedia, *Federal Procedure, Lawyers' Edition,* as well as *Am.Jur.2d* and annotations in *ALR* and *U.S. Supreme Court Reports, Lawyers' Edition.* The notes following some rules also include references to other Lawyers Co-op texts and to law review articles. Illustrations B–1 and B–2 show Rule 802 of the Federal Rules of Evidence as it appears in *USCS.*

Federal rules are also available online in both LEXIS and WESTLAW. LEXIS has individual files in its GENFED library containing the four major sets of rules (Civil Procedure, Criminal Procedure, Appellate Procedure, and Evidence), as published in *USCS.* Historical notes and Advisory Committee comments are included as well as texts. Also available are the rules for several federal courts, including the U.S. Supreme Court, the U.S. Tax Court, the U.S. Claims Court, and the eleven circuit courts. A group file, RULES, combines these individual files with other specialized federal rules. WESTLAW's USCA (and USC) database includes the texts of rules printed in *USCA*, along with annotations. A separate database of federal rules (US–RULES) contains the four major sets of rules and the Bankruptcy Rules as they appear in the *U.S. Code* or an appendix to the *Code.* WESTLAW also provides numerous specialized sets of rules in their related topical areas.

Finally, multivolume treatises on the federal rules, such as *Federal Practice and Procedure* and *Moore's Federal Practice* (to be discussed below in Section D), can also be considered annotated editions of the rules. They are frequently arranged by rule number, and include the rule texts and Advisory Committee notes as well as extensive analyses of interpretive cases.[22]

2. STATE RULES

The publication of state court rules vary from state to state. In states where legislative acts determine court procedures, these "rules" appear as part of the state's statutory code. In states where rules are promulgated by the judiciary alone, until recently they often appeared

22. Three of the major sets of rules are published by Clark Boardman in shorter, one-volume, looseleaf format editions that are updated annually. For each rule, the text and Advisory Committee notes are accompanied by "practice comments" discussing the rule and its application. The volumes are: Thomas A. Coyne, *Federal Rules of Civil Procedure* (2d ed., 1994–date); Michelle G. Hermann, *Federal Rules of Criminal Procedure* (2d ed., 1980–date); and Paul F. Rothstein, *Federal Rules of Evidence* (2d ed., 1978–date).

Illustrations A-1 and A-2

Federal Rules of Evidence, Rule 802, in *USCA*

565. Affirmance

Even if, in antitrust suit brought by beer wholesaler against brewer and an authorized distributor, the testimony of several wholesalers was wrongfully excluded by the district court, such statements, either singularly or cumulatively, would not have altered the outcome reached by the court of appeals and, therefore, the district court's judgment would be affirmed without deciding the correctness of its application of the James test for the introduction of testimony by a coconspirator. Mendelovitz v. Adolph Coors Co., C.A.Tex. 1982, 693 F.2d 570.

Rule 802. Hearsay Rule

Hearsay is not admissible except as provided by these rules or by other rules prescribed by the Supreme Court pursuant to statutory authority or by Act of Congress.

(Pub.L. 93–595, § 1, Jan. 2, 1975, 88 Stat. 1939.)

Notes of Advisory Committee on Proposed Rules

The provision excepting from the operation of the rule hearsay which is made admissible by other rules adopted by the Supreme Court or by Act of Congress continues the admissibility thereunder of hearsay which would not qualify under these Evidence Rules. The following examples illustrate the working of the exception:

Federal Rules of Civil Procedure

Rule 4(g): proof of service by affidavit.

Rule 32: admissibility of depositions.

Rule 43(e): affidavits when motion based on facts not appearing of record.

Rule 56: affidavits in summary judgment proceedings.

Rule 65(b): showing by affidavit for temporary restraining order.

Federal Rules of Criminal Procedure

Rule 4(a): affidavits to show grounds for issuing warrants.

Rule 12(b)(4): affidavits to determine issues of fact in connection with motions.

Acts of Congress

10 U.S.C. § 7730: affidavits of unavailable witnesses in actions for damages caused by vessel in naval service, or towage or salvage of same, when taking of testimony or bringing of action delayed or stayed on security grounds.

29 U.S.C. § 161(4): affidavit as proof of service in NLRB proceedings.

38 U.S.C. § 5206: affidavit as proof of posting notice of sale of unclaimed property by Veterans Administration.

Cross References

Affidavits—
- Proof of posting notice of sale of unclaimed property by Veterans' Administration, see section 5206 of Title 38, Veterans' Benefits.
- Proof of service in National Labor Relations Board proceedings, see section 161 of Title 29, Labor.
- Unavailable witnesses in actions for damages caused by vessel in naval service, or towage or salvage of same, when taking of testimony or bringing of action delayed or stayed on security grounds, see section 7730 of Title 10, Armed Forces.

Federal Rules of Civil Procedure

Affidavits—
- Motion on facts not appearing of record, see rule 43, this title.
- Process, proof of service, see rule 4.
- Summary judgment proceedings, see rule 56.
- Temporary restraining order, see rule 65.

Depositions, admissibility of in court proceedings, see rule 32.

Federal Rules of Criminal Procedure

Affidavits—
- Motions, determination of issues of fact on, see rule 12, Title 18, Crimes and Criminal Procedure.
- Warrants, issuance upon showing grounds, see rule 4.

[G20,024]

HEARSAY **Rule 803**

Federal Practice and Procedure

Admissible or inadmissible evidence, see Wright & Graham: Evidence § 5191 et seq.
Character evidence not admissible, see Wright & Graham: Evidence § 5231 et seq.
Recognition of usual exceptions to hearsay rule, see Wright & Miller: Civil § 2407.
Scope of these rules, see Wright & Graham: Evidence § 5011 et seq.

West's Federal Practice Manual

Hearing procedure and hearsay, see § 10956.

Library References

Criminal Law ⚿419(1).
Evidence ⚿314(1).
United States Magistrates ⚿5.

C.J.S. Criminal Law § 718 et seq.
C.J.S. Evidence § 192 et seq.
C.J.S. United States Commissioners § 3.

Notes of Decisions

---

1. Constitutional rights—Generally

Legislation, or rules with the force and effect of legislation, may change common law standards for the admission of hearsay evidence so long as the confrontation clause of U.S.C.A. Const.Amend. 6, or any other relevant constitutional provision is not offended. U.S. v. Lynch, 1974, 499 F.2d 1011, 165 U.S. App.D.C. 6.

2. —— Fourteenth Amendment

The hearsay evidence rule, with all its subtleties, anomalies and ramifications, will not be read into U.S.C.A. Const.Amend. 14. Stein v. People of State of N.Y., N.Y.1953, 73 S.Ct. 1077, 346 U.S. 156, 97 L.Ed. 1522, rehearing denied 74 S.Ct. 13, 346 U.S. 842, 98 L.Ed. 362.

3. Summary judgment

Plaintiff's statement that his employees denied knowledge of alleged violations of section 2021 of Title 7 governing disqualification from food stamp program would not be admissible at trial, and therefore was not considered on summary judgment motion. Yaghnam v. U.S., D.C.Colo.1981, 526 F.Supp. 554.

Rule 803. Hearsay Exceptions; Availability of Declarant Immaterial

The following are not excluded by the hearsay rule, even though the declarant is available as a witness:

(1) Present sense impression

A statement describing or explaining an event or condition made while the declarant was perceiving the event or condition, or immediately thereafter.

(2) Excited utterance

A statement relating to a startling event or condition made while the declarant was under the stress of excitement caused by the event or condition.

(3) Then existing mental, emotional, or physical condition

A statement of the declarant's then existing state of mind, emotion, sensation, or physical condition (such as intent, plan, motive, design, mental feeling, pain, and bodily health), but not including a statement of memory or belief to prove the fact remembered or believed unless it

only in elusive pamphlets or in the state reports.[23] Increasingly, however, publishers of annotated codes recognize the importance of court rules

23. A few states provide for official publication of their court rules on a regularly updated basis, either as part of codes of administrative regulations or separately. For example, volumes 22(A)–22(C) of the *Official Compilation of Codes, Rules and Regulations of the State of New York* consist of court rules, and the Administrative Code Editor for Iowa publishes the looseleaf *Iowa Court Rules*.

Illustrations B–1 and B–2

Rule 802 in *USCS*

Rule 802 FEDERAL RULES OF EVIDENCE

Rule 802. Hearsay Rule

Hearsay is not admissible except as provided by these rules or by other rules prescribed by the Supreme Court pursuant to statutory authority or by Act of Congress.

(Jan. 2, 1975, P. L. 93-595, § 1, 88 Stat. 1939.)

HISTORY; ANCILLARY LAWS AND DIRECTIVES

Other provisions:

Notes of Advisory Committee on Rules. The provision excepting from the operation of the rule hearsay which is made admissible by other rules adopted by the Supreme Court or by Act of Congress continues the admissibility thereunder of hearsay which would not qualify under these Evidence Rules. The following examples illustrate the working of the exception:

FEDERAL RULES OF CIVIL PROCEDURE

Rule 4(g): proof of service by affidavit.

Rule 32: admissibility of depositions.

Rule 43(e): affidavits when motion based on facts not appearing of record.

Rule 56: affidavits in summary judgment proceedings.

Rule 65(b): showing by affidavit for temporary restraining order.

FEDERAL RULES OF CRIMINAL PROCEDURE

Rule 4(a): affidavits to show grounds for issuing warrants.

Rule 12(b)(4): affidavits to determine issues of fact in connection with motions.

CROSS REFERENCES

Accused's right to confront witnesses, USCS Constitution, Amendment 6.
Agricultural certificates, 7 USCS §§ 54, 79(d), 94, 511f, 1622(h).
Immigration records, 8 USCS §§ 1284(b), 1360(d), 1439(b), 1440(c), 1441(a).
Maritime matters, 10 USCS § 7730.
Banking documents, 12 USCS § 1464(j).
State prosecution for destruction of property, 15 USCS § 1281(c).
Copyright records, 17 USCS § 410(c).
Extradition proceedings, 18 USCS § 3190.
Competency and incompetency, 18 USCS §§ 4244, 4245.
Foreign trade and commerce, 19 USCS §§ 1402(b), 1509(b).
Forfeiture proceedings, 19 USCS § 1615.
Lading vessels, 19 USCS § 1708.
FDA proceedings, 21 USCS § 371.
District Courts, 28 USCS § 753(b).
Court of International Trade, 28 USCS § 2635(b)(1).
Workers' compensation proceedings, 33 USCS § 923(a).
Veterans, 38 USCS § 5206.
Bills of health for foreign vessels, 42 USCS § 269(b).
Social Security and Medicare, 42 USCS § 405(c)(3).
Destitute seamen, 46 USCS § 11104.
Maritime forfeiture judgments, 46 USCS Appx § 837.

[G20,026]

782

Carriage of goods by sea, 46 USCS Appx § 1303.
FCC, 47 USCS § 412.
Railroads, 49 USCS § 10303.
Service of process, USCS Rules of Civil Procedure, Rule 4(g).
Depositions, USCS Rules of Civil Procedure, Rule 32.
Motions and affidavits, USCS Rules of Civil Procedure, Rule 43.
Summary judgment motion, USCS Rules of Civil Procedure, Rule 56
New trial motion, USCS Rules of Civil Procedure, Rule 59.
Relief from judgment motion, USCS Rules of Civil Procedure, Rule 60.
Temporary restraining orders, USCS Rules of Civil Procedure, Rule 65(b).
Arrest warrants and probable cause, USCS Rules of Criminal Procedure, Rule 4(a).
Pretrial motions, USCS Rules of Criminal Procedure, Rule 12.
Depositions, USCS Rules of Criminal Procedure, Rule 15.
Posttrial motions, USCS Rules of Criminal Procedure, Rule 33.

RESEARCH GUIDE

Federal Procedure L Ed:
Evidence, Fed Proc, L Ed §§ 33:87, 217, 218, 223-225, 227, 228.
Witnesses, Fed Proc, L Ed § 80:43.

Am Jur:
5 Am Jur 2d, Appeal and Error § 737.
29 Am Jur 2d, Evidence §§ 493–497, 1094.
32B Am Jur 2d, Federal Rules of Evidence §§ 77, 195, 196, 200–202, 204, 356.

Am Jur Proof of Facts:
Dead Man's Statutes, 39 Am Jur Proof of Facts 2d, p. 91.

Forms:
1 Federal Procedural Forms L Ed, Actions in District Court § 1:1967.

Annotations:
Admissibility of sound recordings as evidence in federal criminal trial. 10 L Ed 2d 1169.
Exception to hearsay rule, under Rule 803(3) of Federal Rules of Evidence, with respect to statement of declarant's mental, emotional, or physical condition. 75 ALR Fed 170.
Treatises, periodicals, or pamphlets as exception to hearsay rule under Rule 803 (18) of the Federal Rules of Evidence. 64 ALR Fed 971.
What information is of type "reasonably relied upon by experts" within Rule 703, Federal Rules of Evidence, permitting expert opinion based on information not admissible in evidence. 49 ALR Fed 363.
Admissibility of statement under Rule 801(d)(2)(B) of Federal Rules of Evidence, providing that statement is not hearsay if party-opponent has manifested his adoption or belief in its truth. 48 ALR Fed 721.
Who qualifies as "widow" or "widower" under § 216 of the Social Security Act (42 USCS § 416), pertaining to survivor's benefits, where two or more alleged spouses survive decedent. 31 ALR Fed 300.
Admissibility in evidence of sound recording as affected by hearsay and best evidence rules. 58 ALR3d 598. [G20,027]

and include them within their scope of coverage. Even when court rules are not legislative in nature, they receive the same treatment as statutes and are published in a fully annotated, regularly supplemented format.

For many state codes, the rules volumes are published in a softcover format and reissued annually.

In many states, court rules are also issued in annual, *unannotated* pamphlets designed for ready desktop reference. The West Publishing Company publishes such pamphlets for virtually every state in which it publishes an annotated code, and for several other states as well. Each state has competing publishers performing the same task. As noted earlier, these rules pamphlets are valuable sources not only for state court rules but for the rules of federal courts sitting in that state. In some states, annotated editions of court rules are also published separately as part of practice treatises.

Many state court rules are available online through WESTLAW or LEXIS, usually in a state's code or statute database. WESTLAW also often provides a separate rules database (for example, IL–RULES).

To learn about available sources for state court rules other than statutory compilations, it may help to consult Betsy Reidinger & Virginia T. Lemmon, "Sources of Rules of State Courts," 82 *Law Libr. J.* 761 (1990), or one of the state legal research guides listed in Appendix A. Once the set of rules is in hand, pinpointing applicable provisions depends on the quality of organization and indexing. A steadily increasing number of states, however, have rules modeled on the various federal rules, particularly the Federal Rules of Civil Procedure and the Federal Rules of Evidence. A researcher who knows the relevant rules provision in federal court can easily check the comparable provision in another state.

For civil matters, one can use the Federal Rules of Civil Procedure numbers to find relevant state provisions even if the state rules bear no relation to the Federal Rules. Each Circuit Volume of Lawyers Co-op's *Federal Procedure Rules Service* includes a "Comparator," which correlates the provisions of the Federal Rules of Civil Procedure to the court rules or statutory provisions for each state within the circuit.[24]

Several works provide rule-by-rule comparisons of federal and state evidence provisions. Two useful references are: Gregory P. Joseph & Stephen A. Saltzburg, *Evidence in America: The Federal Rules in the States* (4 vols.) (Michie 1987–date); and the "State Correlation Tables" in *Federal Rules of Evidence Service* (Law. Co-op/Callaghan), "Finding Aids" volume.

C. UPDATING AND INTERPRETING RULES

1. FINDING AMENDMENTS TO FEDERAL RULES

It is important that practitioners be aware of and be able to find proposed and recent amendments to rules. For the major rules sets, the

24. The civil procedural systems of all fifty states and the District of Columbia were surveyed in John B. Oakley & Arthur F. Coon, "The Federal Rules in the State Courts: A Survey of State Court Systems of Civil Procedure," 61 *Wash. L. Rev.* 1367 (1986).

Supreme Court submits newly adopted amendments to Congress. The texts of the amendments, accompanied by Judicial Conference Advisory Committee notes, are printed by Congress as House Documents. The same material is reproduced in full in advance sheets for West's *Supreme Court Reporter, Federal Reporter, Federal Supplement,* and *Federal Rules Decisions,* with its inclusion prominently noted on the pamphlet covers. Any attorney monitoring the advance sheets for current case developments should thus be on notice of any prospective change in the rules. The advance sheets for the *Federal Reporter* also include amendments to the rules of individual Courts of Appeals. The monthly pamphlets for *U.S. Code Congressional and Administrative News* and *United States Code Service Advance* contain not only all these amendments, but those for other federal courts and administrative tribunals as well.

2. JUDICIAL INTERPRETATIONS OF RULES

While annotated editions of rules provide references to judicial decisions, there are other tools for finding cases construing and applying court rules. Some of these tools have already been introduced in earlier chapters, but their specific focus on court rules is discussed at greater length here.

a. Citators

The "statutes" unit of all jurisdictional Shepard's citators can be used to determine the current status and judicial treatment of federal and state court rules. *Shepard's United States Citations, Statute Edition,* provides coverage of every set of federal rules listed in Table 1 above (except U.S. Court of Military Appeals rules, which are in *Shepard's Military Justice Citations*). It also includes citations to the rules of several other specialized courts and of individual United States Court of Appeals and District Courts. Since annotated editions of very few district court rules are published, this may be the only way to find interpretive cases.

For the four major sets of federal rules, one can use *Shepard's Federal Rules Citations* to find changes in rules and both federal and state citing cases. This citator covers only the Federal Rules of Civil Procedure, Criminal Procedure, Evidence, and Appellate Procedure. For these rules, however, it provides citations in *both* federal and state courts. In addition, *Federal Rules Citations* reprints the portions of individual state citators covering state rule provisions similar to each federal rule. Researchers can thus learn how courts in different jurisdictions have interpreted identical or similar provisions, and perhaps find cases useful as persuasive authority. Law review citations to federal rules are *not* included, but coverage of citing material for state rules is identical to that in the state Shepard's volume and does include selected periodicals. Illustration C shows a page from this publication containing citations to Rule 802 of the Federal Rules of Evidence and to several state provisions based on Rules 801 and 802.

Illustration C

Coverage of federal and state rules in *Shepard's Federal Rules Citations*

Art. 8
Rule 801

FEDERAL RULES OF EVIDENCE

Subsec. 1
59MqL230
Subsec. 3
69Wis2d107
74Wis2d36
84Wis2d372
91Wis2d250
97Wis2d420
106Wis2d379
110Wis2d433
113Wis2d288
113Wis2d650
114Wis2d11
115Wis2d597
116Wis2d79
119Wis2d427
129Wis2d178
130Wis2d236
230NW2d140
245NW2d690
267NW2d344
280NW2d270
294NW2d34
316NW2d383
328NW2d899
335NW2d615
335NW2d899
337NW2d461
340NW2d914
341NW2d648
351NW2d765
384NW2d706
387NW2d102
Subsec. 4
Cir. 7
691F2d846
114Wis2d10
337NW2d461
Subd. a
75Wis2d633
84Wis2d386
87Wis2d302
87Wis2d547
92Wis2d379
114Wis2d10
118Wis2d78
250NW2d306
267NW2d344
274NW2d671
275NW2d186
277NW2d737
284NW2d919
337NW2d461
346NW2d324
¶ 1
Cir. 7
691F2d844
74Wis2d425
83Wis2d392
84Wis2d179
87Wis2d541
96Wis2d381
97Wis2d421
99Wis2d443
119Wis2d247
247NW2d81
265NW2d299
267NW2d859
275NW2d181
291NW2d843
294NW2d34
299NW2d465
349NW2d697
26CLA968
84YLJ33

¶ 2
75Wis2d672
92Wis2d378
97Wis2d422
114Wis2d9
116Wis2d77
118Wis2d77
250NW2d321
284NW2d921
294NW2d34
337NW2d460
341NW2d647
346NW2d323
¶ 3
84Wis2d372
267NW2d338
Subd. b
103Wis2d157
307NW2d620
¶ 1
74Wis2d27
74Wis2d425
85Wis2d742
93Wis2d219
97Wis2d421
110Wis2d433
121Wis2d256
245NW2d687
247NW2d81
271NW2d403
286NW2d593
294NW2d34
328NW2d899
358NW2d833
¶ 2
113Wis2d650
335NW2d615
¶ 3
82Wis2d790
264NW2d262
¶ 4
Cir. 7
503F2d655
82Wis2d790
108Wis2d545
264NW2d263
322NW2d521
¶ 5
69Wis2d109
76Wis2d506
85Wis2d598
85Wis2d725
97Wis2d420
103Wis2d157
110Wis2d433
119Wis2d427
120Wis2d619
230NW2d140
251NW2d801
271NW2d387
271NW2d403
294NW2d34
307NW2d614
328NW2d899
351NW2d765
357NW2d15

Wyoming Rules of Evidence 1978 As Amended 1985

Rule 801
632P2d128
679P2d1001
Subd. a
632P2d128
¶ 1
692P2d931
Subd. b
632P2d128
Subd. c
628P2d535
632P2d128
694P2d129
713P2d785
Subd. d
¶ 1
Cl. A
592P2d1145
26CLA968
Cl. B
592P2d1145
640P2d104
679P2d1001
¶ 2
599P2d540
656P2d546
Cl. A
692P2d931
Cl. C
592P2d1145
Cl. D
701P2d562
Cl. E
601P2d1001
649P2d674
711P2d418

FEDERAL

Rule 802
Cir. D.C.
475F2d957
595F2d756
693F2d188
421FS571
562FS203
Cir. 1
605F2d1217
638F2d278
699F2d35
477FS1208
526FS1318
Cir. 2
560F2d46
575F2d347
582F2d225
582F2d680
669F2d84
702F2d314
718F2d46
439FS1129
509FS1319
521FS53
530FS252
90FRD384
28BRW451
31BRW370
Cir. 3
579F2d751
581F2d345
651F2d195
723F2d287
738F2d597
747F2d132
758F2d951
436FS705
443FS1111
448FS822
456FS127
456FS143
481FS550
505FS1144
577FS848
578FS824
615FS1017
Cir. 4
591F2d1350
634F2d738
642F2d730
682F2d1060
691F2d677
714F2d339
740F2d1334
457FS141
468FS1271
495FS561
580FS954
Cir. 5
548F2d1196
559F2d294
563F2d1252
572F2d488
590F2d1348
592F2d836
611F2d569
628F2d418
630F2d265
632F2d556
640F2d552
641F2d351
650F2d90
650F2d815
694F2d1356
695F2d89
731F2d1230
742F2d875
748F2d248
750F2d1258
495FS421
515FS1020
551FS304
572FS558
84FRD69
98FRD6
106FRD331
Cir. 6
588F2d552
623F2d1148
686F2d396
689F2d1268
695F2d217
752F2d228
761F2d309
434FS85
446FS284
470FS264
470FS1266
486FS234
492FS468
512FS1052
519FS1103
542FS548
614FS654
44BRW682
46BRW593
Cir. 7
509F2d78
553F2d1051
582F2d1128
607F2d780
733F2d455
568FS1283
570FS1126
75FRD351
Cir. 8
541F2d196
544F2d941
551F2d1136
581F2d1304
414FS495
545FS150
580FS898
611FS1076
613FS531
Cir. 9
551F2d1169
594F2d1257
667F2d1299
680F2d619
684F2d1315
693F2d1293
713F2d499
731F2d623
732F2d1422
736F2d490
745F2d1259
538FS249
6BRW413
Cir. 10
558F2d569
596F2d943
692F2d697
744F2d723
399FS631
508FS903
521FS1149
526FS556
575FS723
Cir. 11
703F2d1230
711F2d1532
737F2d940
744F2d1523
755F2d859
759F2d1501
762F2d909
47BRW618
CtCl
608F2d510
553FS1062
Colo
654P2d317
670P2d1257
DC
154ADC373
193ADC371
224ADC73
Fla
420So2d934
Mass
20MaA928
479NE2d196
Tex
682SW2d685
31ARF318n
48ARF453n
48ARF722n
MFP§7.16

Alaska Rules of Evidence 1979

Rule 802
608P2d764
682P2d1119
707P2d925

Arizona Rules of Evidence 1977

Rule 802
124Az169
124Az311
127Az78
127Az452
130Az6
132Az298
133Az224
134Az320
144Az558
145Az549
146Az120
147Az545
602P2d833
603P2d937
618P2d248
622P2d11
633P2d415
645P2d813
650P2d1206
656P2d609
698P2d1277
703P2d493
704P2d250
711P2d1219
1977AzS367

Arkansas Uniform Rules of Evidence 1976 as Amended 1979

Rule 802
Cir. 8
697F2d208
280Ark303
280Ark352
6AkA235
640SW2d810
657SW2d540
658SW2d378

Colorado Rules of Evidence 1980 as Amended 1984

Rule 802
646P2d359
651P2d462
654P2d317
660P2d29
663P2d1057
670P2d1255
677P2d1378
685P2d183
701P2d884
703P2d611
703P2d1333
704P2d879
709P2d974
709P2d1391
712P2d1021
721P2d704
723P2d749
9CoL1781
50CUR296

Delaware Uniform Rules of Evidence 1980 as Amended 1981

Rule 802
466A2d369

Florida Statutes 1983

90.802
7FlS2d179
415So2d128
418So2d274
420So2d933
423So2d513
429So2d813
429So2d1220
440So2d479
442So2d357
460So2d976
462So2d559
468So2d428
477So2d27
483So2d867
31MiL990
38MiL607

Hawaii Rules of Evidence

Rule 802
66Haw259
3HA278
5HA53
6AHA9963
649P2d1178
659P2d748
678P2d17
712P2d1143

Idaho Rules of Evidence 1985

Rule 802
714P2d81

Iowa Rules of Evidence 1983 as Amended 1985

Rule 802
356NW2d539
383NW2d67
386NW2d535

Louisiana Revised Statutes Annotated (as Amended by Replacement Volumes to 1983) and Supplement, 1983

15:434
1984No563
236La881
243La460
244La787
249La861
255La690
258La1
258La103
258La1094
109So2d454

Continued

430

[G20,028]

Coverage of state court rules is contained in full in each of Shepard's state citators. Changes in rules are noted, as well as citations in federal and state court decisions, selected law reviews, annotations, and (in some states) attorney general opinions.

b. Reporters and Digests

While standard case reporters such as official reports and the components of the National Reporter System include many decisions dealing with the application of court rules, there are also specialized reporters for cases decided under the federal rules. West's *Federal Rules Decisions* (cited as F.R.D.) began publication in 1940 as an offshoot of the *Federal Supplement,* and provides the texts of U.S. District Court decisions that construe the Federal Rules of Civil Procedure and Criminal Procedure. Cases appearing in *F.R.D.* are not included in the *Federal Supplement. F.R.D.* is by no means an exclusive source of procedural opinions, however, since many *F.Supp.* opinions also involve procedural issues and since neither Supreme Court nor Courts of Appeals decisions are included. *Federal Rules Decisions* is just an additional component of West's National Reporter System,[25] sharing coverage of the U.S. District Courts with the voluminous *Federal Supplement.* It differs from most reporters in that it includes not just cases but also relevant articles, speeches, and the proceedings of judicial conferences.

Like other West reporters, *Federal Rules Decisions* appears first in advance sheets which then cumulate into bound volumes. Each volume and advance sheet includes West's standard editorial features, such as tables of cases and key number digests. A notable feature is the list of federal court rules cited in *any* National Reporter System unit during the volume or advance sheet's period of coverage. This list covers specialized rules, the Federal Rules of Evidence, and the Federal Rules of Appellate Procedure as well as civil and criminal rules. It is a particularly valuable feature in recent advance sheets, where the comprehensive list of current cases may provide more up-to-date coverage than the latest Shepard's pamphlet. Illustration D shows a page from this list in a recent *Federal Rules Decisions* volume, including citing references to Rule 802 of the Federal Rules of Evidence.

Federal Rules Service (cited as Fed. R. Serv.) is a competing commercial reporter for decisions construing federal rules. It has been published since 1939 by Callaghan & Co. and since 1991 by Lawyers Co-op, and is now in its third series. *Federal Rules Service* provides the texts of court decisions interpreting the Federal Rules of Civil Procedure and the Federal Rules of Appellate Procedure. Cases are published first in looseleaf format and then in bound volumes. The looseleaf cases are accompanied by current case and digest tables and a "Current Material

25. As part of the National Reporter System, decisions appearing in *Federal Rules Decisions* are digested in West's *Federal Practice Digest* and other digests discussed in Chapter 4.

Illustration D

List of rules cited, in a *Federal Rules Decisions* volume

STATUTES AND RULES

FEDERAL RULES OF CRIMINAL PROCEDURE—Continued

Rule		
8(b)	150 F.R.D.	696
11	3 F.3d	129
11	3 F.3d	609
11	4 F.3d	679
11	4 F.3d	1567
11	5 F.3d	365
11(d)	5 F.3d	365
11(e)(1)(C)	4 F.3d	70
12	3 F.3d	1234
12(b)(1)	5 F.3d	474
12(b)(2)	4 F.3d	647
12(b)(2)	829 F.Supp.	555
12(b)(4)	831 F.Supp.	755
12(c)	831 F.Supp.	755
12(d)(2)	828 F.Supp.	1489
12(e)	831 F.Supp.	755
12(f)	5 F.3d	474
12(f)	829 F.Supp.	555
14	150 F.R.D.	696
16	2 F.3d	1441
16	828 F.Supp.	1489
16	831 F.Supp.	755
16(a)(1)(C)	828 F.Supp.	1489
16(a)(2)	828 F.Supp.	1489
16(d)(1)	831 F.Supp.	755
16(d)(2)	831 F.Supp.	755
20	830 F.Supp.	960
29	3 F.3d	673
29	4 F.3d	792
29	4 F.3d	1026
29	830 F.Supp.	394
30	3 F.3d	976
32	4 F.3d	549
32(c)(3)(A)	5 F.3d	331
32(c)(3)(B)	5 F.3d	331
32(c)(3)(D) [1982 Ed.]	3 F.3d	775
32(c)(3)(D)	3 F.3d	827
32(c)(3)(D)	4 F.3d	70
32(c)(3)(D)	5 F.3d	331
32(c)(3)(D)	829 F.Supp.	265
32(d)	4 F.3d	1567
32(d)	829 F.Supp.	620
33	4 F.3d	115
33	4 F.3d	1567
33	829 F.Supp.	88
33	830 F.Supp.	90
35(c)	5 F.3d	262
36	5 F.3d	262
41	3 F.3d	300
41(c)	3 F.3d	300
41(e)	3 F.3d	1355
41(e)	830 F.Supp.	270
45(a)	831 F.Supp.	771
52(a)	150 F.R.D.	696
52(b)	3 F.3d	525
52(b)	3 F.3d	976
52(b)	4 F.3d	70
52(b)	4 F.3d	560
52(b)	4 F.3d	1573
57	150 F.R.D.	696
58(g)(1)	831 F.Supp.	771
58(g)(2)	831 F.Supp.	771

FEDERAL RULES OF EVIDENCE

Rule		
103(a)(2)	3 F.3d	868
104(b)	859 P.2d	156
105	859 P.2d	156
106	150 F.R.D.	548
201	830 F.Supp.	536
401	4 F.3d	1481
401–403	4 F.3d	864
402	3 F.3d	342
402	828 F.Supp.	1114
402	859 P.2d	156
403	3 F.3d	17
403	3 F.3d	342
403	3 F.3d	456
403	3 F.3d	502
403	3 F.3d	673
403	4 F.3d	658
403	4 F.3d	1006
403	4 F.3d	1481
403 note	859 P.2d	156
404(b)	2 F.3d	1368
404(b)	2 F.3d	1551
404(b)	3 F.3d	300
404(b)	3 F.3d	673
404(b)	3 F.3d	1201
404(b)	4 F.3d	1006
404(b)	828 F.Supp.	1048
404(b)	830 F.Supp.	596
404(b)	859 P.2d	156
406	435 S.E.2d	545
408	831 F.Supp.	691
408	150 F.R.D.	25
410	158 B.R.	687
501	830 F.Supp.	80
501	150 F.R.D.	465
501	150 F.R.D.	634
601	829 F.Supp.	1290
604	830 F.Supp.	223
606	3 F.3d	1201
606(b)	5 F.3d	1
606(b)	858 P.2d	322
606 note	5 F.3d	1
607	4 F.3d	1424
608(b)	3 F.3d	769
608(b)	4 F.3d	1481
608(b)	5 F.3d	288
609	3 F.3d	769
609	4 F.3d	1481
609(a)	829 F.Supp.	1319
609(b)	2 F.3d	1441
611(b)	3 F.3d	232
611(c)	3 F.3d	342
611(c)	4 F.3d	47
611 note	3 F.3d	342
613(b)	4 F.3d	1424
701	4 F.3d	1153
701	829 F.Supp.	1237
702	3 F.3d	769
702	3 F.3d	1191
702	4 F.3d	891
702	5 F.3d	119
702	829 F.Supp.	1237
702	829 F.Supp.	1290
702	150 F.R.D.	165
703	2 F.3d	1200
704(b)	3 F.3d	827
704(b)	4 F.3d	1573
705	2 F.3d	1200
706	830 F.Supp.	686
801	3 F.3d	342
801	828 F.Supp.	1048
801(c)	4 F.3d	2
801(c)	830 F.Supp.	1223
801(c)	150 F.R.D.	495
801(d)(1)(B)	3 F.3d	342
801(d)(2)	4 F.3d	2
801(d)(2)	828 F.Supp.	1114
801(d)(2)	830 F.Supp.	1223
801(d)(2)	830 F.Supp.	1343
801(d)(2)(D)	829 F.Supp.	1438
801(d)(2)(E)	3 F.3d	456
801(d)(2)(E)	4 F.3d	904
802	830 F.Supp.	1223
802	831 F.Supp.	341
803(4)	630 A.2d	202
803(5)	4 F.3d	1424
803(6)	4 F.3d	796
803(6)	828 F.Supp.	1114
803(6)	830 F.Supp.	1343
803(6)	158 B.R.	979
803(8)	830 F.Supp.	1343
803(17)	4 F.3d	1006
803(24)	4 F.3d	796
803(24)	150 F.R.D.	548
804(b)(1)	4 F.3d	276
804(b)(3)	830 F.Supp.	774
804(b)(3)	150 F.R.D.	548
804(b)(5)	4 F.3d	436
804 note	4 F.3d	276

[G20,029]

LI

Highlights" pamphlet, summarizing the holdings of important recent cases.

Federal Rules Service includes cases from all levels of the federal court system, not just district courts. Most of the decisions also appear in one of West's reporters, but some are not published anywhere but *Fed. R. Serv.* Each case is given one or more headnotes assigned to specific rules and numbered subject subdivisions within each rule, and these headnotes are arranged numerically in the accompanying *Federal Rules Digest.* A "Finding Aids" volume includes cumulative tables of cases and the outline of the publisher's classification system for each rule, known as the "Federal Index" or "Findex." The second edition of the *Federal Rules Digest* covers the years 1938–54, and the current third edition covers cases from 1954 to date. Because the digest is arranged by rule, and within rule by subject, its purpose is similar to that of the case annotations in *USCA* or *USCS:* a comprehensive collection of headnotes for cases decided under each provision.

In 1979, Callaghan began a separate reporting service for the new evidence rules, the *Federal Rules of Evidence Service,* providing similar coverage of evidentiary issues. As with the *Federal Rules Service,* most cases are also published in one of the West federal reporters, although a few appear only in *Fed. Rules Evid. Serv.* The service, now published by Lawyers Co-op, is accompanied by the *Federal Rules of Evidence Digest,* which arranges the case headnotes by subject within each rule. Illustration E shows a page of the digest covering the Federal Rules of Evidence provision on hearsay. A "Finding Aids" volume includes the text of the rules, a table of cases, the "Findex" or digest classification system, and state correlation tables providing information on state rules of evidence based on or similar to the Federal Rules. In addition to recent cases, the "Current Material" volume contains finding aids and a monthly "Current Material Highlights."

3. SECONDARY SOURCES

The general secondary sources in legal literature, such as law review articles and encyclopedias, contain a great deal of information on procedural matters. There are also numerous specialized resources dealing specifically with the intricacies of court rules and practice.

a. Federal Practice

The technical nature of the various federal rules and their importance in legal practice has led to the development of a number of excellent commentaries on the rules. These include two comprehensive treatises by distinguished scholars in the fields of federal courts and procedure: *Federal Practice and Procedure* and *Moore's Federal Practice.*

Federal Practice and Procedure (30 vols. to date) (West 1969–date) is an extensive treatment of federal procedural and jurisdictional issues. The set consists of four components covering the Federal Rules of Criminal Procedure, the Federal Rules of Civil Procedure, jurisdiction and related matters, and the Federal Rules of Evidence (still in prog-

Illustration E

A page from *Federal Rules of Evidence Digest*

need not be satisfied if a coconspirator statement offered for its truth satisfies another hearsay exception. Such a rule would undermine the purpose of Rule 801(d)(2)(E). The government's additional argument, that the statement was admissible against the objecting defendant employee because declarations of intention are admissible against a nondeclarant when they are linked with independent evidence that corroborates the declaration, was slightly more persuasive but irrelevant since the government offered no corroborative evidence. However, the court's error in failing to issue an instruction directing that the statement be used only against its declarant was harmless in light of the substantial evidence tending to show that the objecting defendant must have known of the illegal nature of the charged scheme. United States v. Johnson, 32 Fed Rules Evid Serv 735; 927 F2d 999 (CA7 1991).

802 HEARSAY RULE

802.1 Hearsay not admissible—general rule

US Ct App In a mail fraud conspiracy prosecution of a police lieutenant arising from allegations that he had bought an advance copy of and answers to a civil service examination, the district court did not abuse its discretion in excluding defendant's resume and other evidence of commendations that he had received in military service and as a police officer. Even assuming that the commendations could be considered character evidence under Rule 404(a)(1), the traits that they purported to show (bravery, attention to duty, community spirit) were not pertinent to the charged crimes. Moreover, the evidence was classic hearsay and inadmissible for that reason as well. In addition, given the copious quantity of character evidence offered and admitted at trial, the commendations were excludable as cumulative under Rule 403. United States v. Nazzaro, 29 Fed Rules Evid Serv 201; 889 F2d 1158 (CA1, 1989).

US Ct App In a multi-count narcotics conspiracy prosecution, the district court properly excluded as hearsay the complaint that had been filed against defendant following his arrest, which defendant claimed revealed inconsistencies between the information in the complaint and the testimony of the officers who had arrested him as part of a raid on an apartment, because the officer who had filed the complaint was not one of the officers who had first entered the apartment. In filling out the report, the officer had only recounted the descriptions that had been given to him by the other officers on the scene. Further, the officers who had participated in the raid, as well as the agent who had sworn to the complaint, testified at trial and were available for cross-examination. United States v. Torres, 30 Fed Rules Evid Serv 113; 901 F2d 205 (CA2 1990).

[G20,030]

ress). The volumes covering the rules sets are organized by rule. The entire set is commonly referred to as "*Wright & Miller*," after two of its principal authors, Professors Charles Alan Wright of the University of Texas and Arthur R. Miller of Harvard Law School.[26]

For each rule, *Federal Practice and Procedure* provides extensive discussion of its history, purpose, and application generally and in specific situations. The text includes copious footnotes to cases and other materials. The set is updated by annual pocket parts, and second edition volumes have since 1982 been supplanting original volumes. There is one index covering the civil and jurisdictional components, but the other parts are separately indexed.

The other major treatise, *Moore's Federal Practice* (13 vols.) (2d ed., Matthew Bender 1948–date), is published in a looseleaf format, revised annually by replacement pages and supplements. The set is named after its primary author, Professor James William Moore of Yale Law School, who has had numerous coauthors at different times and on various volumes. Like *Federal Practice and Procedure, Moore's* devotes several volumes to a rule-by-rule analysis of the Federal Rules of Civil Procedure, with other volumes focusing on other matters such as jurisdiction, the Federal Rules of Criminal Procedure, the Federal Rules of Evidence, and Supreme Court practice. The set includes a detailed three-volume index and one volume listing statutes and rules cited.[27]

Two other multivolume treatments of federal practice are organized not by specific rule but more generally, by subject. Lawyers Cooperative publishes an encyclopedia similar in format to its *Am.Jur.2d* but designed specifically for federal practice: *Federal Procedure, Lawyers' Edition* (40 vols.) (1982–date). It consists of eighty alphabetically arranged chapters, some of which focus on procedural issues (Access to District Courts, New Trial) and some on topical areas of federal law (Atomic Energy, Job Discrimination). The chapters deal with civil, criminal and administrative practice, and include checklists, synopses of law review articles, and texts of relevant statutes. The text also includes references to *Federal Procedural Forms, Lawyers' Edition* and other units of the publisher's Total Client–Service Library. The set is updated by annual pocket parts, and includes a three-volume index and a table of statutes, rules and regulations cited.

Lawyers Co-op recently assumed publication of another comprehensive work, *Cyclopedia of Federal Procedure* (17 vols.) (3d ed., Lawyers Co-op/Callaghan 1951–date). The *Cyclopedia* is arranged topically rath-

26. In actuality, each component is the work of a different set of authors. The criminal volumes are written by Wright alone; the civil volumes by Wright, Miller, Mary K. Kane, and Richard L. Marcus; the jurisdiction volumes by Wright, Miller, Edward H. Cooper, and Eugene Gressman; and the evidence volumes by Wright, Kenneth W. Graham, Jr., Victor J. Gold, and Michael H. Graham.

27. A similar but less voluminous work is also available from the same publisher. James W. Moore, Allan D. Vestal & Phillip B. Kurland, *Moore's Manual: Federal Practice and Procedure* (3 vols.) (1962–date) is arranged by subject rather than by rule, but contains much of the same text as the larger work. Each section in the *Manual* provides cross-references to more comprehensive treatment in *Moore's Federal Practice*.

er than alphabetically; it is divided into five parts (courts and jurisdiction; civil trial practice; criminal procedure; appeal and review; and particular actions and proceedings) and organized topically within each part. Like most of the other works described in this section, its text summarizes the ruling law and its footnotes provide extensive references to cases. Both text and footnotes are updated in annual pocket parts. In addition to an index, the set includes volumes containing the texts of relevant statutes and court rules, as mentioned earlier.

A number of works focus on the Federal Rules of Evidence. One of the principal drafters of the rules, Judge Jack B. Weinstein, has written with Margaret A. Berger a multi-volume treatise explaining the intent and application of each provision, *Weinstein's Evidence: Commentary on Rules of Evidence for the United States Courts and Magistrates* (7 vols.) (Matthew Bender 1975–date). It includes both a subject index and an author/title index (of works cited in the text), as well as tables of cases and of statutes and rules. A similar multivolume rule-by-rule analysis is Christopher B. Mueller & Laird C. Kirkpatrick, *Federal Evidence* (5 vols.) (2d ed., Law. Co-op 1994–date), which is the revised edition of the treatise of the same name, authored by David W. Louisell and Mueller.[28] Each of these works is updated annually or more frequently.

Procedural guides for particular courts are also published. One work designed specifically for attorneys practicing before the United States Supreme Court is Robert L. Stern, et. al., *Supreme Court Practice,* (7th ed., Bureau of National Affairs 1993). The book includes extensive discussions of the Court's policies and procedures, and also contains forms, checklists and Supreme Court Building floor plans.

b. State-Specific Materials

State practice manuals and procedural aids, containing such material as the text of court rules, commentaries on the rules, annotations of court decisions, and model forms keyed to the rules, are published for virtually every state. Some of the larger states have two or more competing publications of this kind. The best of these are updated regularly, either with looseleaf filings, pocket part supplements, or complete annual revisions. They provide useful, current information regarding the local rules of practice, and are essential tools for the lawyer's daily work.

West and several other publishers offer multi-volume sets on practice in particular states. Some of these are commentaries on procedural rules, while others are series of individual subject treatises in a uniform format, with legal forms and practice checklists. Usually, these works are regularly updated by either pocket parts or looseleaf supplements.

Another source for practical information on state practice is through continuing legal education materials. Many states publish materials

28. Less comprehensive but handier treatments include Michael H. Graham, *Handbook of Federal Evidence* (3d ed., West 1991), and Stephen A. Saltzburg & Michael M. Martin, *Federal Rules of Evidence Manual* (2 vols.) (5th ed., Michie 1990).

from their C.L.E. programs, often in a looseleaf format. These books often provide clear, step-by-step assistance for practitioners in a particular jurisdiction. They are usually updated or replaced periodically, although not always as frequently as works from major commercial publishers.

One of the easiest ways to learn about available treatises, practice manuals, and C.L.E. materials in a particular state is to consult a reference librarian. He can provide leads to what sets and C.L.E. providers are currently most acceptable in the jurisdiction.

c. *General Works*

Procedural manuals and treatises published for a general national audience can also be of immense practical value, although they are related to no specific procedural rules. Among these are the practice adjuncts to *American Jurisprudence*, such as *Am.Jur. Trials* and *Am. Jur. Proof of Facts*. Both of these multi-volume sets contain articles on specific issues in litigation, and contain numerous cross-references to other products in Lawyers Co-op's "Total Client–Service Library."

The first six volumes of *Am.Jur. Trials* constitute an extensive treatise on general aspects of trial preparation and procedure. Ensuing volumes, which are issued periodically, consist of "Model Trials." Individual articles in each volume describe unique aspects of specific types of litigation, on issues from compensation for multiple sclerosis to defective automobile door latches. There are more than forty volumes of "Model Trials," and the set has a two-volume index.

Am.Jur. Proof of Facts, now in its third series, contains articles on specific evidentiary issues, and provides sample interrogatories and examinations. Individual articles describe the elements of proof required for establishing particular facts in judicial proceedings, and outline useful procedures. A three-volume index covers all three series.

A similar collection of articles on trial practice in very specific areas is *Causes of Action* (Shepard's, 1983–date), which includes extensive references to law review articles, legal encyclopedias, digests, and annotations. Works such as these may be little used in academic research, but they are important time-saving resources for practicing lawyers.

D. PRACTICE FORMS

Many writings must follow certain conventions to have legal significance or to have a desired effect. This is true not only of documents such as contracts and wills, but also of forms used in court practice such as briefs or pleadings. The publication of model forms has evolved and is today a major component of legal literature. Forms are included as part of many procedural treatises, and are published separately in comprehensive collections. Some jurisdictions even have prescribed official forms that must be used for certain pleadings or motions.

For federal practice, several multi-volume collections of forms are published in conjunction with the practice treatises described in the preceding sections. Some are arranged by rule, some by subject, all provide useful cross-references to other sources. Table 2 lists practice sets and their companion form books.

Table 2

Federal Practice treatises and form books

Practice Treatise	Form Book	Arrangement
Federal Practice & Procedure (Wright & Miller)	*West's Federal Forms*	by rule
Moore's Federal Practice	*Bender's Federal Practice Forms*	by rule
Moore's Manual	*Federal Practice Forms*	by rule
Federal Procedure, Lawyers' Edition	*Federal Procedural Forms, Lawyers' Edition*	by subject
Federal Local Court Rules	*Federal Local Court Forms*	by court

Legal forms are an essential part of most state practice manuals discussed above. In addition, many states have separate, commercially published collections of forms. Some states have officially promulgated forms, such as *California Judicial Council Forms,* published annually as an adjunct to *West's Annotated California Codes.*

Although not keyed to the practice of any particular jurisdiction, general formbooks can still be very useful in preparing for litigation. *American Jurisprudence Pleading and Practice Forms,* rev. ed.(Law. Co-op 1967–date) is an extensive collection of forms for such matters as complaints, motions, and orders. Its forms are accompanied by explanatory text, case annotations, and cross-references to other Lawyers Co-op publications, as well as tables providing statutory and rules references for each jurisdiction. It is arranged alphabetically by subject, and has a two-volume index. Other series are designed for specific stages of litigation, such as *Bender's Forms of Discovery* (16 vols.) (1963–date), which includes ten volumes of sample interrogatories by subject. Practice forms appear as well in many specialized treatises and manuals.

E. MODEL JURY INSTRUCTIONS

Publications of jury instructions are an important aid to both practicing trial lawyers and judges. Before a jury is sent out to weigh the evidence, the judge instructs its members on the applicable law. Proposed instructions are frequently drafted and submitted to the judge by opposing counsel, and the outcome of a case may turn on which instructions are chosen. Collected examples of jury instructions have been published since the late nineteenth century.[29]

29. Frederick Sackett, *Instructions and Requests for Instructions from the Court to the Jury in Jury Trials* (Jameson & Morse 1881). A book published the previous year concluded with an example of an instruction *not* to be followed. It began: "Gentlemen of the Jury: The investigation of guilt and the punishment of crime are a painful,

Cases have frequently been overturned on appeal due to inadequate or erroneous instructions. To reduce the chances of error, many states have prepared standardized, approved instructions to be used in common situations. These instructions are known by various designations, including *model, pattern,* or *approved* jury instructions. The first published set of these instructions was in California, *Book of Approved Jury Instructions,* in 1938. By now there are model instructions for practically every state.[30] In some states model jury instructions are used by judges only as guides, but in others the instructions must be read verbatim if applicable. Some sets of model instructions are promulgated by the state supreme courts, while others are unofficial products of bar or judicial associations.

For the federal courts there is no general set of approved instructions, although some sets of pattern instructions have been published for individual circuits. There are, however, two sets of commercially published, unofficial instructions covering both criminal and civil cases: Edward J. Devitt, Charles B. Blackmar, Michael A. Wolff, & Kevin F. O'Malley, *Federal Jury Practice and Instructions* (3 vols.) (4th ed., West 1987–date) is an authoritative work with explanatory comments and notes of relevant cases; Leonard B. Sand et al., *Modern Federal Jury Instructions* (4 vols.) (Matthew Bender 1985–date) is a looseleaf work, consisting of sample instructions, comments, and case notes.

F. SUMMARY

Access to court rules, both federal and state, is available in a variety of sources. The most useful forms of publication are those which provide commentary and citations to court decisions interpreting and applying the rules. The extensive literature of practice manuals and formbooks is closely related to court rules. These materials describe the procedures to be followed in litigation and usually include the texts of rules as well as forms, commentary, and annotations to court decisions. They are an essential component of the working library of every practitioner.

The literature of court rules and practice is sometimes seen as dry and overly concerned with technical minutiae. This is a valid criticism, particularly when rules prescribe rigid and formalistic processes to be followed in all cases. Even so, a lawyer must be familiar with governing rules and procedures in order to avoid compromising clients' interests. As Justice Hugo Black complained thirty-five years ago: "Judicial statis-

but a highly important duty. God has so ordered it, and we worms of the dust must recognize what He has ordered." Seymour D. Thompson, *Charging the Jury: A Monograph* 176 (W.H. Stevenson 1880).

30. Recent, comprehensive listings of published jury instructions, arranged by state, are: Cheryl R. Nyberg & Carol Boast, "Jury Instructions: A Bibliography Part I: Civil Jury Instructions," *Legal Reference Services Q.*, Spring/Summer 1986, at 5; and Cheryl R. Nyberg, Jane Williams & Carol Boast, "Jury Instructions: A Bibliography Part II: Criminal Jury Instructions," *Legal Reference Services Q.*, Fall/Winter 1986, at 3.

tics would show, I fear, an unfortunately large number of meritorious cases lost due to inadvertent failure of lawyers to conform to procedural prescriptions having little if any relevancy to substantial justice."[31] Simplification and flexible application of rules, however, can allow them to achieve the salutary purpose Justice Black enunciated: "The principal function of procedural rules should be to serve as useful guides to help, not hinder, persons who have a legal right to bring their problems before the courts."[32]

31. Order Adopting Revised Rules of the Supreme Court of the United States, 346 U.S. 945, 946 (1954) (Black, J., dissenting).

32. *Id.*

Chapter 10

SECONDARY AUTHORITY

A. INTRODUCTION

To this point, primary sources of legal material have been the focus. The emphasis has been on cases, statutes and administrative materials, and tools used to find them. But there are other forms of legal information. Any material that is not a primary source is called a secondary source, but that broad term is hardly descriptive of the variety of publications that are available. Some secondary source materials have grown up around the process of legal education. They are materials seldom found outside an academic law library, though they may offer assistance to a practitioner. These will become quite familiar to the law student as she progresses through her three years. We will describe them here so that they may be placed in the proper context. Such tools are often useful beyond their role as study aids.

Other types of material have grown up to support the specialized practice of law as it is done in the real world. There is a great chasm between legal research as done in law school and as it is done in the real world. Specialized sets have grown up that are designed to make research easier and faster for practitioners. Some of them are beyond the budget of the typical academic law library. In any case, such sets would not see much use in the law school setting. A few will be mentioned here as examples.

Some of the materials discussed in this chapter, for example loose leaf services and legal periodicals, have been the subject of complete chapters in traditional research books. They will continue to merit such treatment in the hard cover version of this work, *How To Find The Law*. Recognizing that this book is one that serves as an introduction, the treatment here is more summary.

B. BOOKS ENCOUNTERED IN LAW SCHOOL

1. HORNBOOKS

Hornbooks grew out of the case book method of teaching in law school. Recall from Chapter 1 that Dean Langdell believed that the best way to learn about law was to read cases and let the points emerge. Langdell's first casebook contained **nothing** but cases. Times have changed, and the modern casebook contains a lot more than just edited cases. In spite of the changes, though, most casebooks are still filled with questions and conundrums, not answers.

This casebook method is linked to the use of the Socratic teaching method in law schools. When employing the Socratic method, a professor teaches by posing questions. Even when asked a question by a student, the professor may answer with a question. There are no "right" answers, each answer is questioned. This process, so archly portrayed in the movie, *The Paper Chase*, is designed to force one to think like a lawyer. It can also produce great anxiety in the student who wants to know the correct answer to a question. Students feel a need to know what the answer to a question is, not just each of the possible answers. Simple answers to legal questions that baldly laid out the rule became known as "Black Letter" law. Such treatment was and still is much scorned by legal academics as overly simplistic. But the demands by students for such a treatment created a market.

The first response was the development of Hornbooks. Hornbooks are texts that address the major questions in a particular legal field, invariably a field that was the focus of a law school course. These texts are authored by one or more law school professors who teach in the field. The authors lay out legal principles in a simple, straightforward manner.

A Hornbook makes it a point to discuss important cases, often cases that are covered in a law school course on the subject. Except now the case is explained and put in context. The Hornbook will have an index and a Table of Cases. The latter is an alphabetic listing of each case that is discussed in the text. This allows pin point location of the discussion of a confusing case. Where appropriate there is also a Table of Statutes discussed. Hornbook indexing is usually pretty low level, and except in rare cases, they are not kept up-to-date.

As time passed, some Hornbooks assumed a role far beyond that of a study aid. Probably the first Hornbook to break out of the mold was William Prosser's, *The Law of Torts*. Prosser was a giant in the field of Torts and his book not only described what the law was, it laid out what the law ought to be. It wove all of the cases into a readable, sensible fabric and had profound effect on the development of tort law. Prosser's book was cited thousands of times in the courts. Prosser has been dead for decades, but his book lives on a version revised by four other scholars. It is not uncommon for famous books to be carried on after the death of the original author.

Prosser's *The Law of Torts* is a classic, but there were other Hornbooks that took on a life of their own beyond assisting students. Today Hornbooks occupy a somewhat ambiguous position. A Hornbook can be pedestrian or influential. Some can be cited as persuasive authority in a brief to a court, but to use others in a such a manner would be foolish. As the potential stature of the books has grown, their simplicity and "Black Letter" tone have faded. Some Hornbooks are now quite complex, having moved a long way from simple statements of the black letter law.

Several publishers produce series of Hornbooks. The most established are the West Hornbook series (the hard copy version of this book is a member of that series) and the Foundation Press University Textbook Series. Little, Brown and Bobbs–Merrill also have entries in the market. One of the most frequently asked questions in law librarians is, "What Hornbook should I buy?" There is no easy answer. For the law student the best idea to ask the professor in the relevant course. He or she may find one book's approach more useful. For general research the best course is to ask the reference librarian in one's law library. Hornbooks rise and fall in stature, and their influence varies from place to place, so the counsel of an expert is advised.

2. NUTSHELLS

As Hornbooks became more and more complicated in content, the need for a simple, straightforward discussion of legal topics re-opened. The void was filled by West Publishing's Nutshell series. A Nutshell is a paperback volume, inexpensive by lawbook standards and written in an even more simplified manner. Each volume in the Nutshell series focuses on a topic, sometimes a quite specific topic. The treatment is general and the text is usually readable. The author does not buttress each point with citations as he would if he were writing a scholarly work. Nutshells are rarely cited by the courts, so they remain a student tool, although a practitioner venturing into a new subject area can find helpful background in them. A rule of thumb for researchers is that one should not begin a subject search until one has at least the sophistication of the Nutshell in that area. Nutshells can point one toward important cases and introduce one to crucial terminology, both key elements in any search.

Most Nutshells have a section entitled "Table of Cases" that allow one to see if a particular case is discussed within the text. The indexing is primitive. There is no supplementation, though Nutshells on hot topics may be revised with some frequency. It is always a good idea to check the copyright date on the reverse of the Nutshells's title page.

3. OUTLINES

Study outlines for law school courses have proliferated in recent years. Outlines provide a very straightforward approach to a specific legal topic that is the subject of a law school course. Outlines may even be keyed to a particular textbook in a particular course. Outlining a law school course is a practice commonly urged upon students, either alone or as a part of a study group. Thus the form is well known. Several of the best known outline series, Gilberts and Emmanuels, grew from the notes of one student. Others grew out of an outline prepared by a particularly great study group. Because the Outline form requires condensation of often confusing material, it inevitably runs the risk of oversimplifying. For all of that they are quite helpful, though they are still frowned upon by some professors. A wide variety of study aids are now available in electronic form. This market is just developing and changes will be quick.

Some of the companies that offer the bar review courses that prepare recent law school graduates to take the state bar now sell variations of their bar review outlines to students for use in preparing for law school exams. Bar review outlines are often of quite high quality, though the titles vary and some courses are far better than others.

How to know what outline to use? Once again, checking with professors and reference librarians, as well as students who have taken a particular professor may be the best method. There is a great deal of money to be made in this market so competition is quite keen and new products appear frequently. Outlines can never be thought of as persuasive authority; they are the least sophisticated of the black letter law tools.

C. DICTIONARIES

In the first Chapter the problem of legal jargon was discussed as one of the impediments to research in the law. Words that are used in common discourse, words like "liability" or "reasonable," may take on a special meaning when used in the law, other words, for example "renvoi", are unique to law. A substantial part of the law school experience lies in learning legal vocabulary. A correspondingly large part of legal research concerns the interpretation and manipulation of language. Many of the indexes and digests that we have introduced are dependent on legal jargon. It is crucial to be as precise as possible in one's use of terms.

This problem has been recognized for centuries. Dictionaries are one of the oldest forms of legal research tool. The modern versions offer a broad coverage of possible research needs. One should take care to consult dictionaries frequently. There are three ways of looking up words in the law.

1. LEGAL DICTIONARIES

Traditional legal dictionaries function much like any dictionary. A legal dictionary is an alphabetic arrangement of legal words and phrases with a definition provided for each. The difference is that in a legal dictionary, each definition is cited to a source. Complying with the law's requirement for authority, a citation backs up each assertion of meaning. These citations are to judicial opinions where possible.

The best known legal dictionary is *Black's Law Dictionary*. *Ballentine's Law Dictionary* is found in many collections as well. These two are massive single volume works, and are expensive. Students are well advised to use them at the law library, at least until one determines that a purchase of one of them is necessary. There is a large variety of paperback legal dictionaries that come onto the market. Some are keyed to specific subject fields. Paperback dictionaries should be used with care. The critical question is who compiled the dictionary and why should you rely on that person or persons expertise.

2. *WORDS AND PHRASES*

West Publishing publishes the set *Words and Phrases Judicially Defined*. When the editors at West prepare the text of cases for the National Reporter System, they note when the judge defines any word or phrase in the text of the opinion. A citation to each such definition is listed in a table in the front of each advance sheet listing any such citations. The citations are collected into *Words and Phrases*. The set currently consists of 75 volumes which are kept up-to-date with annual pocket parts. Entries are arranged in alphabetical order. The set covers all jurisdictions and lists each time a court defines a term. Thus some terms may have dozens of definitions listed while others will have none at all.

The set is an odd one, seldom used by many researchers, but on occasion it can provide an interesting entry into a research system via a specific term.

3. LEXIS AND WESTLAW

WESTLAW and LEXIS are full text data bases, containing each word of each document. Therefore if one wishes to find how a particular word has been used, or if a word or phrase has been defined, one can simply pull each use from the data base. In the case of an exotic word, this might yield useful references. In most cases, such a search will simply dump a huge mass of gibberish onto the researcher. But wise uses can be made of these systems. If one can limit the term's usage to a particular court, or to a particular time period, perhaps even to a specific judge, one may be able to find even more relevant information. At this juncture the traditional style of dictionary searching and the intelligent use of boolean operators merge.

D. LEGAL ENCYCLOPEDIA AND RESTATEMENTS

The common law, with its thousands of cases and its unavoidable lack of clarity quite naturally has lead to the production of tools that try to explain it all. From the late 17th Century through the early part of the 20th Century, great legal scholars labored to produce treatises that covered entire legal topics. Often filling many volumes, these works relied upon the eminence of the author for their authority and many defined whole fields. This monumental treatise form has declined in recent decades. The researcher will still find versions of many of these old warhorses on the shelves, but they now resemble reference tools, kept up to date by editorial staffs. They are used almost as encyclopedia, they are rarely read from beginning to end. In part this is due to the proliferation of cases and the breakdown of law into separate specialties. Simply put, no one could write a credible treatise covering **every** aspect of a field like Contracts today. Today's legal information is presented in sets that lack the intellectual ambition (or presumption) of the old treatises. They are simpler, and do not qualify as persuasive authority. Two types worth discussing are encyclopedia and Restatements.

1. LEGAL ENCYLOPEDIA

The most imposing sets are legal encyclopedia. Not unrelated in basis to the Hornbooks and Nutshells discussed in Section B, these multi-volume sets are grander attempts to encompass everything. A legal encyclopedia arrays significant legal topics in alphabetical order, and attempts to discuss each relevant issue. It is inevitable that in trying to describe everything they fall quite short of precisely describing anything. The most curious are the national legal encyclopedia. Given the federal nature of the United States, no one set could possibly describe everything. Only a fool cites to legal encyclopedia as persuasive authority.

But for all of their flaws, legal encyclopedia have virtues. They can provide useful background, they can inform the researcher of the landmark cases in an area, they acquaint one with the important jargon. Perhaps best for the legal researcher, the modern legal encyclopedia places one into a research universe. It will provide citations to relevant cases, hints for other places to look for information. If one is using a West product, relevant Topics and Key numbers are provided. If using a Lawyer's Cooperative product, the reference will be to the Total Client Service Library. Each is the gateway to many related sources.

There are two national legal encyclopedia: *Corpus Juris Secundum* and *AmJur 2d*.

a. Corpus Juris Secundum (CJS)

This huge set is bound in dark blue volumes and is published by the West Publishing Company. It consists of an alphabetic arrangement of legal terms and topics. The discussion is often terse. CJS provides the user with relevant Topics and Key Numbers as reference points into the West digests and through them into the National Reporter System, as well as citations to relevant cases. The set is kept up to date with pocket parts. In some cases, volumes have been split into two parts. This is done when the supplementation of a volume grows too large, leading to the necessary insertion of an entirely new volume into the set.

This set was constructed with the West philosophy as underpinning. The original intent was to cite the researcher to every relevant case on the topic being discussed. This goal has been abandoned as unrealistic, but *CJS* still cites to many, many cases. Pages filled with only a bit of text and great dollops of footnotes are normal. *CJS* is rather dated, and the pocket parts are extremely important in some volumes. Always check the copyright date of the volume that is being used. Pocket parts can only do so much.

CJS has a multi-volume general index at the end, and a separate index for each major topic. The index is easy to use, and this set is popular with non-lawyers. One could actually think of *CJS* as a case finding tool since the index leads one to discussion with cases and entry points into the Key Number System. Occasionally this makes it a great place to start when looking for that one good case.

b. AmJur 2d

This set was begun in the 1970s and is more open-textured attempt at describing the law. The narrative is often more clearly presented than in *CJS*. Writing clearly and simply means that sometimes the set is not as precise as one might want. It is also kept up to date with pocket parts. It too has a general index at the end as well as topic indexes. Because the set is produced by the Lawyers–Co-operative Company, the user receives citations to other elements of that company's Total Client Service Library. This consists of various practice sets, form books and primary sources that are linked into a research system. Find one useful source and one is immediately linked to others. The major components of the Total Client Service Library are:

ALR and ALR Federal

AmJur Forms

AmJur Pleading and Practice Forms

AmJur Trials

Proof of Facts

Federal Procedure

AmJur 2d has a New Topics binder at the end of the set in which entirely new topics can be introduced. This solves the problem of how to fit an entirely new topic into the existing alphabetical arrangement without reconfiguring the whole set.

AmJur 2d also contains a volume called the AmJur Deskbook. This one volume compilation of facts and figures that are of use to legal researchers. A surprising number of answers to questions like "What is the address of the Secretary of State of Wyoming?" can be answered in the Deskbook.

c. *State Legal Encyclopedia*

A number of states have a state legal encyclopedia. Some are done by West or Lawyer's-Co-operative, and not surprisingly these follow the format of the national sets, including entries into each company's research system. A few states have encyclopedia produced by other publishers. But each can be used for background and research leads. A state encyclopedia has the advantage of being able to focus on the unique nature of a state's legal system. This can result in a more coherent focus on legal questions. But be forewarned, state legal encyclopedia are viewed with disdain in many quarters, and should never be relied on as persuasive authority. They can still be the starting places for research and sources for basic background, but should be handled with care.

2. RESTATEMENTS

The Restatements represent an attempt to bring order to the development of the common law. The Restatement movement sprang from the dismay of leaders of the Bar in the early years of this century. They were upset by the proliferation of contradictory cases that were appearing. How could the common law grow if poorly drafted decisions were appearing in great droves? How to focus attention on the really important cases in a legal system that had chosen comprehensive publication? In part this dilemma is the product of the West Publishing Company's decision to publish everything.

The American Law Institute, an offshoot of the American Bar Association, was set up in part to deal with this problem. Restatements of the law in specific fields began when the ALI commissioned a reporter, a major figure in the field, to prepare a systematic summary of the best cases. The roster of these Reporters constitutes a list of great legal thinkers of the early part of the 20th Century. Consider the implications of being asked to summarize an entire field like Contracts or Torts. The Reporter's work was reviewed by different levels within the ALI and was eventually voted on by the whole body. The ALI is comprised of lawyers, legal scholars and judges. Membership in it is an honor. There was a great deal of back and forth as the various review committees made suggestions as to changes. The process took decades.

In the end the first series of Restatements was born. They stated general principles and used anonymous cases as examples. The hope was that the Restatements would come to be viewed as authoritative. No one would ever have to go back to the original cases. No actual case names were used in the first series of Restatements for that reason.

The Restatements did prove to be quite influential, and were cited by the courts with great frequency, but in the end, they became just another research source. Indeed, as the importance of the common law has faded in this era of legislation and administrative activity, the Restatements have become even less central. But new editions of the Restatements continue to appear, these days including the citations to cases used. In line with the modern trend toward specialization in the law, they are taking on narrower topics. Restatements can be used as persuasive authority, but only with care.

E. LAW REVIEWS

Law Reviews are peculiar institutions. They have long been the dominant form of publication for law professors and other legal scholars, and they are the repository of much of the best contemporary legal scholarship. What makes them so distinctive is that they are student-edited. Rather than having panels of editors drawn from the ranks of distinguished professionals, the editorial choices as to what gets published is made by groups of third year law students. These same students edit the articles.

This strange situation arises because law reviews are seen as part of the law school pedagogical process. Those students lucky enough to serve on a law review get extensive experience with the process of legal writing and argumentation. (Membership on a law review is also an excellent ornament for the resume.) Debates rage from time to time about the value of law reviews, and the faculties at some prestigious law schools may look down upon the form, but the primacy of place of the law school law review can hardly be challenged.

Law reviews come in two types. The most common is the law review that bears the name of its school of origin: the *Harvard Law Review*, the *Yale Law Journal*, etc., can be thought of as generic law reviews. Such reviews have no particular subject focus, they publish articles on various subjects. One finds an article about the First Amendment next to another on Corporate Securities. The one thing all such articles have in common is a "law review" style. Law review articles consist of a closely analyzed, heavily footnoted, very technically written exploration of a topic. Each assertion made by the author must be rooted in authority. It is not unusual to find a sixty page law review article with 500 footnotes.

Such a law review article may be citable as *persuasive* authority. Persuasive authority is authority that does not state the law, but instead states what the law should be. It can be used to convince a court to move into a new area or to change an old one. The power of any persuasive authority in the form of a law review article is determined by both the prestige of the article's author and the prestige of the law review in which the article appears. Any article by a famous figure like Lawrence Tribe will carry power. Any article in the *Harvard Law Review,* by far the most widely read and influential law review, will carry power. Thus an article by someone like Lawrence Tribe in the *Harvard Law Review* is the best cite of all. Of course sometimes the only help one find to bolster an argument comes in the form of an article by an unknown assistant professor in an obscure law review. Such an article can still be used, but understand that it is a slimmer reed to lean on.

Even if an article is not useful as persuasive authority, it can serve a second function as a mother lode of research sources. The author, and the students who served as the editors of the article, will cite to every possibly relevant source in the footnotes. Large numbers of footnotes are thought of as crucial, and every relevant legal and non-legal document will be cited. The footnotes are pure gold to the researcher interested in the topic. The author of this text reads the footnotes of a law review article first. Even if the text is useless, the footnotes are often rich. Besides, the accepted "law review" style of writing also dooms most interesting speculation to the footnotes. But interesting or not, the combined labor of the author and the student editors will introduce the researcher to a universe of legal information.

Law reviews may also contain student comments and student notes. These are articles written by students. Generally this diminishes their value as persuasive authority, but such student pieces can provide the same level of research assistance.

The second form of law review is the subject specialty review. Such reviews focus on a particular field: e.g. *Ecology Law Quarterly.* They are often started by students with an interest in exploring one special topic. They also serve the purpose of allowing more students to gain experience as law review editors.

Many law schools have a generic review and one or more subject specialty reviews. In the 1994–1995 school year the law school at Boalt Hall, the University of California at Berkeley, had nine law reviews. This is a bit extreme, but it shows the proliferation of law reviews. The *California Law Review* served as the generic review, and there were eight other specialty reviews. In large measure the specialty reviews follow law review style—heavy footnoting and careful discussion. Specialty reviews are generally less prestigious than the generic reviews, though some have attained significant status.

One of the best things about law review articles is that they are easy to find by topic. One can find law review articles in a number of ways. The print indexes to legal periodicals are arranged by topic and author, by cases discussed and by statutes. They are kept current by paper supplements. Online and compact disk based systems make searching even easier by putting all of the information in one place (no more looking through annual indexes) and offering searching alternatives. In the optical disk index the coverage of periodicals and newspapers is quite good.

The H.W. Wilson Company produces the *Index to Legal Periodicals and Books.* This is the oldest index to legal periodicals, dating back to 1908. Only in 1993 was the "and Books" added to its title, and most people use it for periodicals. It now features a joint author/title list, though its format has varied over the years. It also has tables that allow one to search for articles that have focused on a specific case or statute. The Index comes out in paper issues, and cumulates into annual and sometimes tri-ennial volumes. Since H.W. Wilson has published a variety of periodical indexes for years, it is part of the research system in many libraries. Wilson also produces a compact disk version of its legal indexing called *Wilsondisk.* It offers the convenience of electronic information, but the disk is not widely in use yet. *Index to Legal Periodicals* is also online via LEXIS and WESTLAW.

The Information Access Company (IAC) produces *Current Law Index,* (CLI), a paper index of legal periodicals and books. It began in 1980, so its historical coverage is much more limited. It uses the subject headings developed by the Library of Congress, which are much more specific than those used in the *Index to Legal Periodicals.* It also covers a wider range of periodicals and newspapers, as well as some books. CLI comes out twelve times a year and then is republished in annual volumes. There is an online version of CLI called Legal Resources Index that is available on LEXIS and WESTLAW.

IAC also produces an optical disk based system called *LegalTrac.* This system takes the information from the CLI data base, augments it with coverage of many more sources, and puts it onto a disk that is sold to law libraries. The set can be configured in different ways locally, but it usually runs over a personal computer and is attached to a printer. With the use of special software one can do Boolean searching. The system is menu driven and is very simple to use. Unfortunately this system is quite expensive, and some libraries have not been able to afford it.

Because both WESTLAW and LEXIS publish the full text of many law reviews and, in the case of WESTLAW, full text articles selected from many more, one can use Boolean searching techniques to locate articles. One can search for relevant law review articles by using key words and phrases, in combination. The language of law review authors is as difficult to predict as that of judges, but in those cases where one is seeking a very specific term, case name or citation, this method can be a real short cut.

F. PRACTICE MATERIALS

The practice of law is about solving real problems. This is a very different enterprise than the labors of the law school to make one think like a lawyer. The tools that have developed to serve lawyers in the real world reflect the needs and interests of lawyers in the real world. Such tools are often more focused on a particular topic and are much more likely to offer advice and direction to the busy professional. The tools used in legal education must carefully weigh all arguments, with the researcher urged to go back to the beginning of the problem and review all sources in a blissful paranoid compulsive exercise. By contrast, the practicing lawyer often wants help and a short cut. Whether she is in a large corporate law firm with her hours being billed by the minute serving a client who demands efficiency, or in a public interest practice with a massive overload of files and no time for anything but the basics, the modern lawyer needs help. Each research problem is a matter of available time and resources. These are the principles that inform the discussion of the tools described below.

1. LOOSE LEAF SERVICES

The term loose leaf service can be applied to any set of books that are issued in loose leaf binders. This format allows information to be added to the original publication. Indeed, the binder format allows the substitution of new pages for old, producing a book in which the process of revision never ends.

The first loose leaf services tracked federal administrative agencies. The traditional legal information system, based on court reports, did not cover these prolific agencies well. Agencies produces many documents that would never fall into the National Reporter System. Lawyers who worked in the very specialized subject areas covered by the administrative agencies needed specialized indexing. They both understood and needed the use of jargon particular to the field. They also put a premium on timeliness. Information was needed quickly.

Loose leaf services filled these needs. The loose leaf publishers could assemble panels of specialists, devoted to the subject area being covered. They could follow developments closely and issue new releases of information with great frequency, even daily. The new information could be put directly into the binder. The loose leaf publishers could create multiple indexes. One especially useful variation was the printing of cases, statutes, administrative rules and regulations, practice forms, practice tips and much more, all in the same set. Some of these loose leaf services are truly universes of information.

The Commerce Clearinghouse (CCH) is a major loose leaf publisher known for its practice sets. CCH products are often rich in detail and structurally complex, with layers of indexes and frequent supplementation. The Bureau of National Affairs (BNA) is another major publisher in the area. BNA sets are often more narrowly focused, and tend to be additive, i.e., new information is added at the end of the binder. CCH and BNA are established publishers, but there are many others. This is a field that lends itself to small companies operating in specialized areas.

There are two survival tips to keep in mind when using loose leaf services. The first is to be sure that one is using the correct loose leaf service. It is likely that the first time a law student will encounter a need to use a loose leaf service will be in practice. Loose leaf services are quintessential practice tools. Many legal fields may be served by several loose leaf sets produced by competing publishers, but there may be one intellectually dominant loose leaf service, i.e., one loose leaf service that everyone uses. If everyone working in a certain area views one loose leaf set as authoritative, that is the one to use. To determine what set is dominant, ask lawyers who work in the area or check with the law librarian in the organization. This first step is crucial.

The second survival tip is to **read the directions**. Each loose leaf service will have a section on how to use it. In the larger sets this section may be a dozen pages long. Reading this will explain the algorithm that the editors of the set used to put the set together. The "How To Use This Set" section will explain the information included in the set, the lay out, the indexing and the various aids. Spend the twenty minutes needed to read this section and any loose leaf service can be yours. There is an axiom that as a set gains more tools to help its user, as it strives to be more current, the set becomes less intuitive to use. Thus as the publisher works to make it easier to use, it grows harder to approach without guidance. The more that the set tries to help the user, the more the user needs to read the "How To" section.

Loose leaf services have always offered expertise, good indexing, integration of materials and timely delivery. These are all functions that can be delivered equally well, perhaps better, by electric information. At the very least, loose leaf services were always hard to maintain. Finding someone to reliably file the flimsy sheets of paper into the binders is a challenge to every library. Thus, many loose leaf services are now appearing on compact disks and as a part of WESTLAW and LEXIS. As such they will function exactly the same, though hypertext links may make them even more useful. As always, innovations designed to make the researchers life easier will only make it more difficult if one does not read the directions.

2. LEGAL NEWSPAPERS AND JOURNALS

Legal newspapers have long been a part of the lawyers universe. Each metropolitan area had a legal newspaper that listed court dockets, published legal notices etc. In the 1970s this universe was changed when several publishers recognized that there was a market for legal newspapers that carried stories about legal issues, law firms and practice. This idea proved quite perspicacious, and some think that it changed the way law is practiced profoundly. Though there were a number of players who participated in this change, it was Steve Brill who truly led the change.

Legal newspapers now provide coverage of hot issues, big cases, professional developments and often the text of recent cases. Because they are published with great frequency, they are timely, able to spread both news of new legal developments and gossip, quickly. Some of them print copies of decisions in paper form before any other source. Find the legal newspaper that is read by lawyers in the area where one is practicing and one has entry to a deep pocket of information.

There are three national legal newspapers. Two weeklies; The *National Law Journal* and the *Legal Times* of Washington, combine coverage of national stories with practice tips and some primary source materials. The latter obviously has a Washington, D.C. focus, hence cover federal agencies in more depth. A third national paper is the *American Lawyer*. This is a monthly that has long feature articles often prepared by investigative reporters. It tracks hot issues and provides good background.

American Lawyer is indexed in *CLI*. Other legal newspapers make no appearances in the print indexes to periodicals. All three national papers are part of the Legal Resources data base on WESTLAW and LEXIS. LegalTrac covers the national and regional legal newspapers. Legal newspapers are topical, of the moment current awareness tools. In the time compressed universe of the modern lawyer this makes them potentially very useful.

3. FORM BOOKS AND PRACTICE SETS

For the practicing lawyer, form books frequently are a way of life. These tools supply forms that are approved by the courts in the relevant jurisdiction, and aid the lawyer in doing her business. Form books also contain practice tips that can assist the practitioner in focussing on issues related to the issue at hand.

There are some national form book sets, the most elaborately articulated being the elements of the Total Client Service Library already dealt with in an earlier section. For the average lawyer, however, form books are local in scope. Each state, indeed each court, may prefer a certain set of forms. This is a *Tinkerbell* phenomenon. One wants to use the set that everyone believes in. The researcher should find out what set is preferred in her specialty or jurisdiction. Ask an experienced lawyer or law librarian for guidance. Once a set is located, the standard questions should be applied to analyzing it. Is it a part of larger research system? Does it provide references into other sets? How is it kept up to date? Remember that form books and are not primary source material. Always recall that the authority of such materials only goes so far as the quality of the set. Use them with a healthy inquisitiveness.

Forms are increasingly appearing as floppy disk or compact disk programs. In states like California there are dozens of firms fighting for the market. Only time will tell as to what sets will win a significant market, and survive. Compatibility with an organization's internal information system will decide which format is most convenient in many cases. Forms are being included on some state disks that also have cases and legislation on them. No matter the format, the same questions posed at the end of the preceding paragraph should be applied.

Practice sets are functionally distinct from form books, but in practice the two are often combined. Some loose leaf sets that dominate a practice area are really combinations of a practice book, a form book and perhaps learned commentary. What we mean here by practice set are multi-volume sets geared to day-to-day legal activity. Practice sets are produced by private publishers and continuing legal education bodies, and give practical advice on dealing with legal practice. Most states have a practice set that is dominant. If there is such a set, lawyers and judges view it as reliable and correct. At the national level there are a number of sets designed for practice. The two best known national practice sets are built around the Federal Rules of Civil Procedure and are discussed at length in Chapter 9.

The growing number of lawyers who need assistance has brought many organizations into the business of providing practice aids. Such concerns may be national in scope, or they may be quite small. The two oldest and best known continuing legal education providers are Practicing Law Institute (PLI) and California Continuing Education of the Bar (CEB). These two traditional providers of continuing legal education materials issue a variety of publications. Some are no more than outlines of seminars, others are quite substantial texts, often with forms attached. Each now has plenty of competition.

Local companies are producing products in a wide range of media. Interactive video, satellite conferencing and compact disk programs are only the edge of the technological innovation that will be seen in years to come. There is substantial money to be made in the continuing education field, this means innovation will follow. Checking with an experienced lawyer or law librarian would be the best way to assess what is accepted locally.

G. LEGAL DIRECTORIES

Finding information about a person can often be crucial to the legal research task. There are a wide variety of tools that list biographical and directory information for individuals. A good reference librarian can find information about almost anyone. Presented here are the standard sources for finding names and basic information about lawyers and judges.

1. *MARTINDALE-HUBBELL LAW DIRECTORY*

There are 1,000,000 lawyers in the United States. The problem of how to find one has brought forth a series of answers. The traditional tool for finding information on a lawyer or firm is *Martindale-Hubbell Law Directory*. This annual set is built around a state by state listing of attorneys, but lists by specialty are now a part of it as well. Any lawyer can be listed in the set by simply filling in a form. One also can pay for a display advertisement that prints much more information. In the basic listing one finds the name, address, legal education and telephone number of any lawyer. The display advertisements, listed by firm and by city include more information. Because Martindale–Hubbell has become the standard set, most lawyers choose to list in it. It is a primary source of information for law students interviewing for jobs. Here is where one can find out about the partner who is interviewing at one's school.

Martindale–Hubbell contains many other features, including useful summaries of state and foreign laws. The heart of the set remains its listings. It is updated annually. In recent years the Reed/Elsevier Company has purchased the set and has begun to retool it. To date this has meant changing its printed form, offering new types of listings and offering compact disk versions. Since Reed/Elsevier purchased LEXIS/NEXIS in 1994 more changes are likely.

2. WESTLAW LEGAL DIRECTORY

This element of the WESTLAW data base lists information about law firms, lawyers, law schools and legal organizations. It is updated frequently, and is especially useful in job hunting. In part because West has made part of the data base available for free use on Internet, it is growing rapidly. Success for a directory flows from its acceptance. WESTLAW Legal Directory may be on the way. Check current WESTLAW materials for coverage and availability.

3. *WHO'S WHO IN AMERICAN LAW*

This segment of the Marquis Who's Who family of products covers men and women who have distinguished themselves in American law. Marquis is the most respected of the general biographical directory publishers. *Who's Who in American Law* is a good place to find background on judges, prominent lawyers and politicians. In such directories, the information that appears is produced by the person listed, so that one finds both long and short entries and veracity is never guaranteed.

H. CONCLUSION

Secondary sources contain a world of information. Using them intelligently can save an enormous amount of time. As long as one understands what one is doing, and is careful about the distinction between persuasive and binding authority, research background, and good citations, one can prosper using them. New formats should not throw one. To date none has altered the functional workings of any of the tools. The same old caveats and blessings apply.

Chapter 11

RESEARCH STRATEGIES

A. INTRODUCTION

Legal research takes many forms. Some research involves only a simple look-up. Perhaps you will be called upon to find a statute, or perform a single run through Insta–Cite to confirm a citation's validity. This chapter is not about that type of research. This chapter concerns the integrated research process. By this we mean the situation where one begins with a complex problem, sorts it, and searches for an answer. What follows is an attempt to help you approach such problems. There is no one *right* way to carry out such research, each problem has its own dynamic. And as you become a more experienced researcher, you will develop your own rules and methods for approaching research. The following chapter contains a set of generic guidelines that should fit most situations. They can help you until you develop your own system.

B. THE NATURE OF THE SEARCH

Before approaching the question of strategy, one must recognize that there are two different kinds of searches. The first type of search is the incremental search, the second is the fresh search. The incremental search occurs when the searcher already has data or expertise or both concerning the problem when she starts. A searcher may already have in hand a case, a statute, a rule, or perhaps a quite intricate set of materials. The searcher may be a specialist in a subject area, already deeply familiar with the legal information that describes it. For such a searcher, the need is to find out if what she has is correct, up-to-date or subject to new attack. In the second kind of search, the researcher knows very little about the topic. This type of search must be constructed from the ground up. Because the fresh search is so much more difficult, and because it is so much more frequently encountered by newer researchers, it will be dealt with first.

1. THE FRESH SEARCH

a. Defining the Question.

When approaching a complex research problem in an area where one has little or no expertise, one must define the question with care. Defining the question can concern the subject matter of the search or the kind of materials one should use to find an answer. It must also include an anticipation of what kind of answer lies at the end of the process. Experienced researchers know that once one understands a question with precision, the search becomes much easier.

The researcher embarking on a fresh search should answer a list of questions. What is the exact topic of the search? Can it be refined? What is the context of the answer? Will the information be used by a lawyer or a client? Does the requesting party want an answer to a query or a set of alternatives? Does the source of the question want you to find a case, a statute, a regulation, some secondary authority or a relevant form? Is the problem a federal one or a state one? Without a full understanding of questions like these, no real progress can be made.

The source of the research question may be a problem here. If the researcher is a lawyer in solo practice, it might be crucial to determine the relevant facts of a problem by interviewing the client. If one is a lawyer in a large firm, the problem may come from a senior associate or partner. If one works for the government a problem may come from a supervisor. There are other variations, but consider those three. In each case, the person who is framing the problem may possess only partial or confused knowledge of it. The client may have trouble expressing himself. He may have only a fuzzy grasp of the facts involved. The senior lawyer may be uncertain of what he is asking. If he is busy he may not explain the problem as clearly as he might. If he is uncertain about much of the problem, he may mask his ignorance by being brusque, hoping that you will solve everything. In the government situation, your supervisor could have received the assignment after it has passed through many hands. If he does not understand the question, he may be unwilling to expose the fact that he does not know more himself.

It is beyond the scope of this book to help you with interviewing your client, or dealing with the politics of your boss. Learning to extract as much information as possible is a difficult skill to teach. The bottom line though is that you have to determine what their expectation is. What type of answer do they want? If they cannot tell you that, it is important to have it acknowledged at the start.

Thus the researcher sometimes begins with only a fraction of the information needed about the question. Given the fact that you may be beginning at something of a deficit, it is vital to lay out exactly what you do know and what you think that you are looking for. No search should ever be begun until you have a clear goal in mind. (Being finished does not count as a goal). Far too often the researcher wants to charge into the library, fling books about, and leap from data base to data base. With 3,000,000 cases and 750,000 statutory sections out there one can do a lot of flailing. Stop and invest time now. Write out the question, be explicit about what one expects to find. Understand what information is missing from the question and compensate where possible.

b. Understanding the Territory

Once one has a feel for the question, one must look at the topic that is covered. In a fresh search this often means unknown territory. Before one can conduct a search within the literature of a topic, one must have a baseline familiarity with it. Legal tools are organized around concepts and jargon. If you don't know the buzz words, you may never be able to find anything. Some areas are dominated by a statute or a set of regulations, and all information may be organized around these lodestars. Or an area may be based in a common law topic where judicial opinions developed over decades form the information base. It could be that one multi-volume loose leaf service dominates the area and is used by everyone. Maybe the topic of your search is one that is in great turmoil, with several competing theories of how to handle matters within it currently doing battle. The researcher must know these things before seriously beginning.

If the topic is one of legal doctrine, one should acquire enough background to feel comfortable. This level of background can be attained by use of the relevant Nutshell, a current law review article or a perhaps a law school outline. Needed expertise may reside in a research pathfinder that has been published or one that is maintained within your law firm or legal organization's local information structure. Someone may have passed this way before. Needed background might best come from a meeting with a senior lawyer or supervisor. In a face to face meeting, an experienced researcher can impart more background about a topic than any text. A few minutes with a human being at this point is better that days spent laying siege to indexes.

How much background is needed? The rule of thumb is that one should have a grasp of a new topic that is roughly equal to the familiarity one would have if one had taken a law school course in the relevant topic. Put another way, one should have the sophistication to read the Nutshell on the topic with ease. Purists might scoff that this is not enough expertise, but lawyers in practice have to learn new topics all the time. Efficiency in research, i.e. doing just as much as is needed, is often the highest virtue.

Until such familiarity is gained, one should stay away from the large data bases like WESTLAW, LEXIS and the Topic and Key Number System. These tools are massive information universes. They can help you if you know what you are doing, but they are no place to learn about the background of a topic. One comes to them with information in hand. One needs to know jargon, conceptual framework and background or one is just stumbling through a jungle of pages. To attempt an online search without it is a waste of time and money.

A word must be added about research in non-legal areas. Much of the real research work of the attorney is about non-legal matters. Whether a lawyer works in litigation or primarily in transactions, lawyers are constantly being called upon to master the intricacies of new subject areas. The same need for background applies. In the bound version of this book, *How to Find the Law,* an entire chapter is devoted to working with non-legal materials. The best rule of thumb is to learn the concepts and the jargon that is needed by getting the right background, by locating the Tinkerbell in the factual area. Once again, a few minutes spent with an experienced librarian is a good way to start.

Having reached this point, the fresh search becomes the same as an incremental search. The researcher should now have sufficient familiarity with the topic and its literature to proceed. The following sections apply to all searches.

2. THE INCREMENTAL SEARCH

a. Creating a Research Plan

Before beginning any research **write down** a research plan. The emphasis is added for a reason. Writing down a research plan is essential.

The first issue to be considered in creating your research plan is resources. How much is the question worth in terms of time and money? Not knowing this is a dealbreaker. In the real world time is money and money is everything. (This is true in public sector as well as the private.) One of the most frequent complaints made by senior lawyers about recent law school graduates is that they do not know how to budget time. To budget, you must know what is available. Therefore the foundation question is how much time are you supposed to spend on the problem?

The next question is how much in the way of resources can you expend? In the world of electronic information, the available funds are a defining element. Will you be authorized to use WESTLAW, LEXIS, AUTO–CITE or Insta–Cite? Does your organization subscribe to compact disks that you must use in lieu of online services? Can you use high cost but time sensitive services like the Shepards daily fax service? How should you balance the equation between saving your time and spending money on resources? In some situations your time is irrelevant. Law school is like that. Your professors can give you endless conflicting assignments that can only be completed if food and interpersonal relationships are mostly abandoned as concepts. But in the real world your time may be in demand. There may be competing priorities. How much is that worth in terms of resources? Find out before you act. Put it in the plan.

Once the resource questions are sorted out, prepare the guts of the plan. Point toward your deadline. Allocate your time and then list what steps your research will take. It is imperative that you list which research tools you expect to use. This allows you to plan realistically. Just as important is the need to list out search terms that you will use in indexes. Think them through before the rough and tumble of the search begins. Also, write out likely searches for use with electronic information. Of course such lists will have to be modified as your research progresses, but you must have a base to work from as you go. Make notes of new ideas as you get them. This will save time and pain later.

Look at your list to see if you will have access to everything that you need. Will you have to leave the library or office in which you normally work? Do you need a loose leaf service, data base or compact disk that is not available to you? A good first step is to go over the tools you plan to use and terms that you plan to employ with a law librarian. She can give you tips and new ideas. As a general matter, you should be aware of the information resources of your organization. Take a look at them sometime when you are not in the middle of a research crisis. Increasingly organizations are developing internal information files, files that may save the work of the past, or draw upon the work of other specialists. Sit down with the librarian and find this out. You will also find that the librarian is a part of a network of librarians. She often can get to information sources that you cannot. She may also know about individuals or groups that can help you. As discussed in Chapter 6 finding someone who cares about the issue can save you time. List people or organizations that may already have done some of your work for you.

You will have to vary from this plan, but it will guide you. The budget element is the one to watch. A research job done adequately on time and budget is infinitely better than one done perfectly but completed three days late at a cost no one can pay. A good friend in a very big law firm tells us that what he misses most about law school is the opportunity to do as much research as he would like on a complicated problem. In practice he can only do as much as the client will pay for.

The most important thing is to write down the plan before beginning. We suggest that every plan contain at least the following:

1. Deadline for project

2. Time that should be spent on the project
3. Amount of resources that can be used
4. Steps Anticipated in Research Process
5. Research tools to be used
6. Likely Search Terms
7. Possible Boolean search terms
8. People who can help.

b. *Looking at a Legal Information Tool*

Now that you are embarked on the search, the focus shifts to the tools that you will use. If you are already familiar with a subject area, you probably have mastery of the jargon and concepts that are at play. You are something of a personal expert on the topic. Such familiarity should never induce complacency. Each day, each hour, new cases are being decided, new statutes are being enacted, new rules are appearing. New fact situations are pushing and pulling at the most settled of doctrines. One must keep up, keep open and never stop looking. Perhaps it is an unfortunate metaphor in a book for law students, but legal research is a bit like a shark, it has to keep moving or it will die.

But whether one is new to a topic or an experienced hand, one must be efficient. You will have to get the most possible out of every tool that you use. To do this you must understand how to use each legal information tool. This applies to books, loose leaf services and electronic information. Look for the functions that the tool serves, how it is designed. In today's rich information environment, you must understand the research tool as well as the topic.

Listed below are some general pieces of advice on evaluating research tools. They are a necessary part of every research process, but they are especially critical for the incremental researcher.

(1) Structure

The most common mistake that one can make in using any research tool is to use it blindly. Far too often people search intuitively, trying a generic method, or guessing at how to exploit a book. It is a very common human trait to try to search by the "seat of one's pants." It can even be contended that when the legal research universe consisted largely of cases and the finding tools built around them, and when the data base of cases was small, that such a method was the workable. The information environment of the 1990s, with oceans of information being produced and highly sophisticated information tools being built by various vendors is very different. In this world, a researcher can never take information for granted. Legal research has become a much more active process.

The first time that one uses any research tool, one should sit down with it and look critically at it. What features does it have? How is it put together? When was it compiled? When was it last updated? What is the publisher trying to tell you? Is there a section that explains how to use it? If it's electronic information, have you looked at the user's manual? If it's a compact disk, do you understand both the composition of the data base and the search engine that is being used? Books on research like this one can attempt to describe what certain sets contain, but the researcher will never make any sense of the tool until he sits down to use the tool. Hold the work in your hands, or look at it on the terminal, and be sure that you understand it. Skip this step and the work is lost. The dumbest kind of research is "A to B" research where the person using a tool only knows how to look up one thing in one way. Invest the minutes to scope out the set. If the structure seems too difficult or obscure, then ask for help from the nearest reference librarian. Listen and learn now and you will look like a star later.

(2) Timeliness

One of the most salient questions to ask about a research tool today is how timely it is. Getting current information is a matter of economics. In the information world of today, one can get information almost instantaneously, if one can pay for it. It is important to understand the worth of a research problem in terms of both time and money, so that one can calculate the equation of how much resources can be spent on the search in comparison with how current the information must be to be valuable.

Take a federal statute as an example. Is the *U.S. Code*, the official compilation that is updated annually and republished every six years quick enough? Or is the *U.S. Code Annotated* or *U.S. Code Service*, privately printed with compilations more aggressively updated by pocket parts, pamphlets and legislative services enough? Or does the problem call for calling one of the long distance numbers shown in the *Federal Register's* Finding Aids section that will allow one to check on current legislation? Or should one also be checking with the relevant committees in the House and Senate to see what changes are coming? Does one need to know what happened this morning or what is scheduled to happen tomorrow morning? Any and all of this can be found. The question is how current the information has to be to meet the researcher's needs. If the resources can pay for it, it can be found. You must make an informed calculation whether it is worth it in this particular case.

Knowing the costs is not enough. One must be certain to exhaust the full extent of the timeliness built into the tool. Check the copyright date of any book that you use. Given production schedules the information is probably a year older than that date. Check when the pocket part or pamphlet supplement that keeps the set up-to-date was issued. If one is using an on-line system, inquire when the data base was last updated, and what the coverage is. Such facts are crucial. Until recently surprisingly few people recognized that Shepards citators generally were six months behind. The wise researcher always knew.

The advantage in updating goes to those who can use technology. Some publishers even have telefacsimile services that will fax materials to the user on a daily basis, or who will download information into a local e-mail system. But the less wealthy researcher can still accomplish a great deal by using the telephone. Call the numbers listed in publications, often 800 numbers, to update information. Many sets now offer this feature. Call the federal government or the state government to update primary sources. Local reference librarians have the relevant telephone numbers. Substitute creativity for cost and one can still produce results.

(3) Research Links

Every research tool is part of a larger research universe. A source may cite to cases, statutes, regulations, other works, other sets, other authors. Think of each research tool as the center of a great cross-hatching of information. Most of the citations referenced are obvious, but the deeper connections are sometimes the most useful. If the tool is produced by a major publisher, there will be built in links to other products of that publisher. Sometimes a researcher will sniff at such references, seeing them as mere puffing of products. They are that, but they may also be useful research references. Each can be exploited by the researcher to find more information. Each leads to a new location. Many legal publishers have created a cross-referenced set of publications that can save the researcher time. These are not persuasive authority, but they can represent considerable spade work already done. With experience one may find that one set of books, or the works of one publisher's system, is superior. But at the beginning of one's research career, especially when one is working in the relatively rich and varied environment of a law school library, it is worthwhile to try them all.

C. FINISHING AND ECONOMICS

The great zen koan of legal research is "When is legal research complete?" Can one ever read every relevant document? Can one ever follow every trail through Shepards to its end? If one Shepardizes every case found and then Shepardizes every case found by Shepardizing those cases, and then Shepardizes those, will one slip into an M. C. Escher spiral? Can one every really be up-to-date? As soon as the ink on one's laser printer is dry things are changing. The law will not stand still. It seems that real closure is never reached. When can one stop?

The simplest answer is that one stops when the deadline arrives. In the real world reality intervenes. That is why the section on creating a research plan emphasizes cost so much. If one has budgeted one's time, one comes to a natural end. When they are pounding on your door demanding the answer you are done. But beyond hitting the wall, how can one know when the job is really done?

One way to know that research is complete is to return to the original question and the original research plan. Is the question answered? Have you checked everything on your list? Another way is to look at the information that further research is producing. Are you running into the same citations? Frequently an area will be filled with unresolved questions and uncertainties. Are you being circled back to the same dilemmas? You should apply the law of diminishing returns. Are you getting back very little that is new for your investment of time? This probably means that you are on top of the field.

As a way to check yourself, you can consult an "end source." An end source is one of the last documents in the research stream, i.e. one of the most recent. For example, read the latest judicial opinion on the topic. Are you comfortably informed about all the issues raised and the sources cited? If the problem is in a legislative area, do you know why the latest legislation was passed and what areas are currently in dispute? If one is working in a regulatory area, do you know who issued the relevant regulations and why? Can you identify the Tinkerbell set, the set that everyone believes to be the most authoritative, in the topic area? If you can answer these questions, you understand the dynamics of the issue. You must of course continue to update as time passes. But if you truly understand the issues in an end source document, you are done.

As a last check, return to the original economic equation. Be certain that you have carried both your updating and your level of detail to the point required by the economics of the problem.

D. CONCLUSION

Legal research is a means to an end. No one ever made a living just knowing how to use research tools. One must be able to take the product of legal research and analyze it. The real joy of being a lawyer is to be able to use one's own intelligence, to take the sources and create an answer out of them. The point of this Chapter, and this book, is to make sure that you can find all the sources that you need. A good researcher can gather in all of the relevant sources so that the really good part can begin. The required first step to good lawyering is good research. Good luck.

Appendix A

STATE LEGAL RESEARCH GUIDES AND BIBLIOGRAPHIES

While state legal research generally follows the patterns discussed in this book, the legal system and bibliographic resources of a particular state may cause specialized problems or may offer shortcuts not available elsewhere. A general treatise such as this cannot fully treat the many special characteristics of legal research in each state. There are, however, an increasing number of guides and manuals available for particular states. Some of these are major, detailed treatments, while many are brief pamphlets prepared for American Association of Law Libraries (AALL) meetings. In addition to the following separately published works, articles in bar journals and law reviews sometimes provide valuable information on research strategies in particular jurisdictions.

Alabama H. Johnson, *Guide to Alabama State Documents and Selected Law-Related Materials* (AALL, 1993).

Alaska A. Ruzicka, *Alaska Legal and Law-Related Publications: A Guide for Law Librarians* (AALL, 1984).

Arizona Kathy Shimpock-Vieweg, *Arizona Legal Research Guide* (Hein 1992).

Richard Teenstra, Susan Armstrong & Beth Schneider, *Survey of Arizona State Legal and Law-Related Documents* (AALL, 1986).

Arkansas L. Foster, *Arkansas Legal Bibliography: Documents and Selected Commercial Titles* (AALL, 1988).

California D. Martin, *California Law Guide* (3rd Ed.) (Butterworths 1995).

Locating the Law: A Handbook for Non-Law Librarians (Karla Castetter, ed.) (2d ed., Southern California Association of Law Libraries, 1989).

Colorado	Gary Alexander et al., *Colorado Legal Resources: An Annotated Bibliography* (AALL, 1987).
Connecticut	Shirley R. Bysiewicz, *Sources of Connecticut Law* (Butterworth, 1987).
	L. Cheeseman, *The Connecticut Legal Research Handbook* (Conn. Law Book Co., 1992).
District of Columbia	L. Chanin, et al. *Legal Research in the District of Columbia* (Hein, 1995).
Florida	Mark E. Kaplan, Gail G. Reinertsen & Richard L. Brown, *Guide to Florida Legal Research* (3d ed., Florida Bar, Continuing Legal Education, 1992).
	N. Martin, *Florida Legal Research and Source Book* (D & S Publishers 1989).
	C.A. Roehrenbeck, *Florida Legislative Histories: A Practical Guide to Their Preparation and Use* (D & S Publishers, 1986).
	Guide to Florida Legislative Publications & Information Resources (Edward J. Tribble & Connie J. Beane, eds.) (3d ed., Capitol, 1990).
Georgia	L. Chanin and S. Cassidy, *Guide to Georgia Legal Research and Legal History* (Harrison, 1990).
Hawaii	Richard F. Kahle, Jr., *How to Research Constitutional, Legislative and Statutory History in Hawaii* (Hawaii Legislative Reference Bureau, 1986).
Idaho	Patricia A. Cervenka, John Madden, Jim Carlson, *Idaho Law–Related State Documents: An Annotated Bibliography* (AALL, 1989).
Illinois	Cheryl R. Nyberg, Joyce Olin & Peter Young, *Illinois State Documents: A Selective Annotated Bibliography for Law Librarians* (AALL, 1986).
	Laurel Wendt, *Illinois Legal Research Manual* (Butterworth, 1989).
Indiana	Linda K. Fariss & Keith A. Buckley, *An Introduction to Indiana State Publications for the Law Librarian* (AALL, 1986).
Iowa	A. Secrest, *Iowa Legal Documents Bibliography* (AALL, 1990).
Kansas	Fritz Snyder, *A Guide to Kansas Legal Research* (Kansas Bar Association, 1986).
	Martin E. Wisnecki, *Kansas State Documents for Law Libraries: Publications Related to Law and State Government* (AALL, 1986).

Kentucky	W. Gilmer, Jr., *Guide to Kentucky Legal Research 2d: A State Bibliography* (State Law Library, 1985).
Louisiana	Win–Shin S. Chiang, *Louisiana Legal Research* (2d ed., Butterworth, 1990).
	Charlotte Corneil & Madeline Hebert, *Louisiana Legal Documents and Related Publications: A Selected Annotated Bibliography* (AALL, 1984).
Maine	William W. Wells, Jr., *Maine Legal Research Guide* (Tower Publishing, 1989).
Maryland	L. Chanin, et al. *Legal Research in the District of Columbia,* Maryland and Virginia (Hein, 1995).
	Lynda C. Davis, *An Introduction to Maryland State Publications for the Law Librarian* (AALL, 1986).
Massachusetts	Margaret Botsford et al., *Handbook of Legal Research in Massachusetts* (Margaret Botsford & Ruth G. Matz, eds.) (Massachusetts Continuing Legal Education, 1988).
	Leo McAuliffe & Susan Z. Steinway, *Massachusetts* (AALL, 1985).
Michigan	R. Beer, *Michigan Legal Literature* 2d Ed. (Hein, 1991).
Minnesota	Marsha L. Baum & Mary A. Nelson, *Guide to Minnesota State Documents and Selected Law–Related Materials* (AALL, 1986).
	Arlette M. Soderberg & Barbara L. Golden, *Minnesota Legal Research Guide* (Hein, 1985).
Mississippi	Ben Cole, *Mississippi Legal Documents and Related Publications: A Selected Annotated Bibliography* (AALL, 1987).
Missouri	M. Nelson, *Guide to Missouri State Documents and Law Related Materials* (AALL, 1991).
Montana	S. Jordan, *Bibliography of Selective Legal and Law Related Montana Documents* (AALL, 1990).
Nebraska	Mitchell J. Fontenot, Brian D. Striman & Sally H. Wise, *Nebraska State Documents Bibliography* (AALL, 1988).
	Paul F. Hill, *Nebraska Legal Research and Reference Manual* (Butterworth, 1983).
Nevada	Katherine Henderson, *Nevada State Documents Bibliography, Part I: Legal Publications and Related Material* (AALL, 1984).

New Jersey	Cameron Allen, *A Guide to New Jersey Legal Bibliography and Legal History* (Rothman, 1984).
	Paul Axel–Lute, *New Jersey Legal Research Handbook* (Harold Suretsky, ed.) (New Jersey Institute for Continuing Legal Education, 1985).
	Christina M. Senezak, *New Jersey State Publications: A Guide for Law Librarians* (AALL, 1986).
New Mexico	Patricia D. Wagner & Mary Woodward, *Guide to New Mexico State Publications* (2d ed., AALL, 1991).
New York	Robert A. Carter, *Legislative Intent in New York State: Materials, Cases and Annotated Bibliography* (New York State Library, 1981).
	Robert A. Carter, *New York State Constitution: Sources of Legislative Intent* (Rothman, 1988).
	Susan L. Dow & Karen L. Spencer, *New York Legal Documents: A Selective Annotated Bibliography* (AALL, 1985).
	Ellen M. Gibson, *New York Legal Research Guide* (Hein, 1988).
North Carolina	J. McKnight, *North Carolina Legal Research Guide* (Rothman, 1994).
	Thomas M. Steele & Donna Tarleton, *Survey of North Carolina State Legal and Law–Related Documents* (AALL, 1988).
North Dakota	*For All Intents and Purposes: Essentials in Researching Legislative Histories* (North Dakota Legislative Council, 1981).
Ohio	Christine A. Corcos, *Ohio State Legal Documents and Related Publications: A Selected, Annotated Bibliography* (AALL, 1987).
	David M. Gold, *A Guide to Legislative History in Ohio* (Ohio Legislative Service Commission, 1985).
	Ohio Legal Resources—An Annotated Bibliography and Guide (2d ed., Ohio Regional Association of Law Libraries and Ohio Library Association, 1984).
	S. Schaefgen & M.K. Putnam, *Ohio Legal Research: Effective Approaches and Techniques* (Professional Education Systems, 1988).
Oklahoma	Christine A. Corcos, *Oklahoma Legal and Law–Related Documents and Publications: A Selected Bibliography* (AALL, 1983).

Oregon	Lesley A. Buhman et al., *Bibliography of Law Related Oregon Documents* (AALL, 1986).
Pennsylvania	Joel Fishman, *Bibliography of Pennsylvania* (Pennsylvania Legal Resources Institute, 1993).
	Joel Fishman, *An Introduction to Pennsylvania State Publications for the Law Librarian* (AALL, 1986).
Rhode Island	C. McConaghy, *Selective Bibliography for the State of Rhode Island* (AALL, 1993).
South Carolina	P. Benson, *A Guide to South Carolina Legal Research and Citation* (S. Carolina Bar, C.L.E. 1991).
South Dakota	Delores A. Jorgensen, *South Dakota Legal Documents: A Selective Bibliography* (AALL, 1988).
	Delores A. Jorgensen, *South Dakota Legal Research Guide* (Hein, 1988).
Tennessee	D. Cheryn Picquet & Reba A. Best, *Law and Government Publications of the State of Tennessee: A Bibliographic Guide* (AALL, 1988).
Texas	Malinda Allison & Kay Schlueter, *Texas State Documents for Law Libraries* (AALL, 1986).
	A Reference Guide to Texas Law and Legal History: Sources and Documentation (Karl T. Gruben & James E. Hambleton, eds.) (2d ed., Butterworth, 1987).
	P. Permenter & S.F. Ratliff, *Guide to Texas Legislative History* (Legislative Reference Library, 1986).
Vermont	V. Wise, *A Bibliographical Guide to the Vermont Legal System* 2d Ed. (AALL, 1991).
Virginia	L. Chanin et al., *Legal Research in the District of Columbia, Maryland and Virginia* (Hein, 1995).
	A Guide to Legal Research in Virginia (J.D. Eure, ed.) (Virginia Law Foundation, 1989).
Washington	M. Cerjan, *Washington Legal Researchers Deskbook 1994* (Washington Law School Foundation, 1994).
West Virginia	S. Stemple, *West Virginia Legal Bibliography* (AALL, 1990).
Wisconsin	R.A. Danner, *Legal Research in Wisconsin* (University of Wisconsin, Extension Law Department, 1980).
	Janet Oberla, *An Introduction to Wisconsin State Documents and Law Related Materials* (AALL, 1987).

Wyoming	Nancy S. Greene, *Wyoming State Legal Documents: An Annotated Bibliography* (AALL, 1985).

Appendix B

SOURCES OF FEDERAL REGULATORY AGENCY RULES, REGULATIONS AND ADJUDICATIONS[1]

1. Prepared by Terry L. Swanlund, Reference Librarian, Harvard Law School Library.

AGENCY	RULES AND REGULATIONS		ADJUDICATIONS, INTERPRETATIONS AND OPINIONS	
	Official	Commercial*	Official	Commercial
Agriculture, Department of	7, 9, 36, 48 CFR various parts		*Agriculture Decisions*	
Commodity Futures Trading Commission	17 CFR Parts 1–199	*Commodity Futures Law Reports* (CCH); *Securities Regulation and Law Report* (BNA) L,W; FEDSEC/CFR (LEXIS); FSEC–CFR (WESTLAW)	Available for inspection at CFTC offices, Washington, D.C.	*CFTC Administrative Reporter* (WSB); *Commodity Futures Law Reports* (CCH); FEDSEC/CFTC (LEXIS); FSEC–CFTC (WESTLAW)
Comptroller of the Currency (Department of the Treasury)	12 CFR Parts 1–199	*Federal Banking Law Reports* (CCH); BANKNG/REGS (LEXIS); FFIN–CFR (WESTLAW)	Office of the Comptroller of the Currency Interpretive Letters in *OCC Quarterly Journal* L,W (selected)	*Federal Banking Law Reports* (CCH); BANKNG/OCCIL (LEXIS); FFIN–OCCIL (WESTLAW)
Consumer Product Safety Commission	16 CFR Parts 1000–1799	*Consumer Product Safety Guide* (CCH); *Product Safety & Liability Reporter* (BNA); Reams & Ferguson, *Federal Consumer Protection: Laws, Rules and Regulations* (Oceana); TRADE/CFR (LEXIS)	Advisory Opinions available for inspection at CPSC Public Reference Room, Washington, D.C.	*Consumer Product Safety Guide* (CCH) (digests); TRADE/CONSUM (LEXIS)
Energy, Department of (DOE)	10 CFR Parts 200–1099	*Federal Energy Guidelines: Energy Management* (DOE/CCH); ENERGY/CFR (LEXIS); FEN–CFR	Economic Regulatory Administration Opinions and Orders and Office of Hearings and Appeals	ENERGY/FERC (LEXIS); FEN–FERC (WESTLAW)

		(WESTLAW)	Decisions and Orders in *Federal Energy Guidelines: Energy Management* (DOE/CCH)	
Environmental Protection Agency	40 CFR Parts 1–762	*Chemical Regulation Reporter* (BNA) [L,W]; *Environment Reporter* (BNA) [L,W]; ENVIRN/CFR (LEXIS); FENV–CFR (WESTLAW)	Appeals Board decisions, General Counsel Memoranda obtainable from EPA Library (Public Information Reference Unit), Washington, D.C.	*Environmental Law Reporter* (ELI) [L,W] (Appeals Board decisions); ENVIRN/EPAAPP, EPAGCO & ALLEPA (LEXIS); FENV–EPA & FENV–GCM (WESTLAW)
Equal Employment Opportunity Commission	29 CFR Parts 1600–1612	*Employment Practices Guide* (CCH); LABOR/CFR (LEXIS); FLB–CFR (WESTLAW)	*Equal Employment Opportunity Commission Decisions—Federal Sector*	*Employment Practices Guide* (CCH); *Fair Employment Practices* (BNA); LABOR/EEOC (LEXIS); FLB–EEOC (WESTLAW)
Federal Aviation Administration (Department of Transportation)	14 CFR Parts 1–199	*Aviation Law Reports* (CCH) (selected); TRANS/CFR (LEXIS); FTRAN–CFR (WESTLAW)		TRANS/DOTAV (LEXIS); FTRAN–DOT (WESTLAW)
Federal Communications Commission	47 CFR Parts 0–199	*FCC Rulemaking Reporter* (CCH); *Radio Regulation* (Pike & Fischer); FEDCOM/CFR (LEXIS); FCOM–CFR (WESTLAW)	*Federal Communications Commission Record*	*Radio Regulation* (Pike & Fischer); FEDCOM/FCC (LEXIS); FCOM–FCC (WESTLAW)

* The latest edition of the entire CFR is available online in GENFED/CFR (LEXIS) and CFR (WESTLAW).

L,W. Publication available online in LEXIS (L) and/or WESTLAW (W).

AGENCY	RULES AND REGULATIONS		ADJUDICATIONS, INTERPRETATIONS AND OPINIONS	
	Official	**Commercial***	**Official**	**Commercial**
Federal Deposit Insurance Corporation	12 CFR Parts 300–353	*Federal Banking Law Reports* (CCH); BANKNG/REGS (LEXIS); FFIN–CFR (WESTLAW)	FDIC Enforcement Decisions and FDIC Interpretive Letters (selectively released)	*FDIC Enforcement Decisions* (PH); BANKNG/FDIC (LEXIS); FFIN–FDIC, FDICED and FDICIL (WESTLAW)
Federal Election Commission	11 CFR Parts 1–9099	*Federal Election Campaign Financing Guide* (CCH)	Advisory opinions—full text available from Public Records Office, FEC, digests in *Federal Election Commission Record*	*Federal Election Campaign Financing Guide* (CCH); CMPGN/FECOPN (LEXIS); FEC (WESTLAW)
Federal Energy Regulatory Commission (Department of Energy)	18 CFR Parts 1–399	*Federal Energy Guidelines: FERC Statutes & Regulations* (FERC/CCH); *Utilities Law Reports* (CCH); ENERGY/CFR (LEXIS); FEN–CFR (WESTLAW)	*Federal Energy Guidelines: FERC Reports*	*Utilities Law Reports* (CCH); ENERGY/FERC (LEXIS); FEN–FERC and FEN–FERCGC (WESTLAW)
Federal Labor Relations Authority	5 CFR Parts 2411–2430	*Federal Labor Relations Reporter* (LRP); LABOR/CFR (LEXIS); FLB–CFR (WESTLAW)	*Decisions of the Federal Labor Relations Authority*	*Federal Labor Relations Reporter* (LRP); *Government Employee Relations Report* (BNA) (digests); LABOR/FLRA (LEXIS); FLB–FLRA (WESTLAW)

Federal Reserve System Board of Governors	12 CFR Parts 220–269b	*Federal Banking Law Reports* (CCH); BANKNG/REGS (LEXIS); FFIN–CFR (WESTLAW)	*Federal Reserve Bulletin; Federal Reserve Regulatory Service*	*Federal Banking Law Reports* (CCH); BANKNG/FEDRB and FRRS (LEXIS); FFIN–FRB and FRRS (WESTLAW)
Federal Service Impasses Panel (Federal Labor Relations Authority)	5 CFR Parts 2470–2472	LABOR/CFR (LEXIS); FLB–CFR (WESTLAW)	Federal Service Impasses Panel Releases	LABOR/FSIP (LEXIS); FLB–FSIP (WESTLAW)
Federal Trade Commission	16 CFR Parts 0–999	*Trade Regulation Reports* (CCH); TRADE/CFR (LEXIS); FATR–CFR (WESTLAW)	*Federal Trade Commission Decisions*	*Trade Regulation Reports* (CCH); TRADE/FTC (LEXIS); FATR–FTC (WESTLAW)
Food and Drug Administration (Department of Health and Human Services)	21 CFR Parts 1–1299	*Food Drug Cosmetic Law Reports* (CCH) (selected); *Medical Devices Reporter* (CCH) (selected); HEALTH/CFR (LEXIS); FHTH–CFR (WESTLAW)	FDA Orders in *Federal Register*	*Food Drug Cosmetic Law Reports* (CCH) (selected FDA order); *Medical Devices Reporter* (CCH) (summaries of selected FDA regulatory letters); FHTH–FDA (WESTLAW)
Health Care Financing Administration (Department of Health and Human Services)	42 CFR Parts 400–498	*Medicare and Medicaid Guide* (CCH); HEALTH/CFR (LEXIS); FHTH–CFR (WESTLAW)		

* The latest edition of the entire CFR is available online in GENFED/CFR (LEXIS) and CFR (WESTLAW).

L,W. Publication available online in LEXIS (L) and/or WESTLAW (W).

AGENCY	RULES AND REGULATIONS		ADJUDICATIONS, INTERPRETATIONS AND OPINIONS	
	Official	Commercial*	Official	Commercial
Immigration and Naturalization Service, Board of Immigration Appeals (Department of Justice)	8 CFR Parts 1–499	*Federal Immigration Law Reporter* (WSB); *Immigration Law and Procedure Reporter* (Bender); *Interpreter Releases* (Fed.Pub.) (selected); IMMIG/CFR (LEXIS); FIM–CFR (WESTLAW)	*Administrative Decisions under Immigration and Nationality Laws of the United States*	*Federal Immigration Law Reporter* (WSB) (summaries and selected full texts); *Immigration Law and Procedure Reporter* (Bender) (selected full texts); *Hein's Interim Decisions Service; Interpreter Releases* (Fed.Pub.) (selected digests); IMMIG/ADMIN (LEXIS); FIM–BIA (WESTLAW)
Interior Board of Indian Appeals (Department of the Interior)	43 CFR Parts 4.310–4.340		*Decisions of the Interior Board of Indian Appeals*	*Indian Law Reporter* (headnotes and selected full texts); ENVIRN/IBIA (LEXIS); IBIA (WESTLAW)
Interior, Department of	25, 41, 43, 48 CFR various parts		*Decisions of the Department of the Interior*	ENERGY/INTDEC and ENVIRN/INTDEC (LEXIS)
Internal Revenue Service (Department of the Treasury)	26 CFR Parts 1–602	*Federal Tax Coordinator* (RIA)[L]; *Standard Federal Tax Reporter* (CCH)[W]; FEDTAX/REGS (LEXIS); FTX-CFR (WESTLAW)	Actions on Decisions; General Counsel Memoranda; Private Letter Rulings; Revenue Rulings (in *Internal Revenue Bulletin/Cumulative*	*IRS Letter Rulings Reports* (CCH); *IRS Positions* (CCH) (AODs, GCMs and TMs); *Pension Reporter* (BNA)[L,W] (selected GCMs, PLRs and TAMs); FEDTAX/RELS

			Bulletin[L,W]); Technical Advice Memoranda; Technical Memoranda	(LEXIS); FTX–RELS (WESTLAW)
International Trade Commission	19 CFR Parts 200–212	*International Trade Reporter* (BNA) [L,W] ITRADE/CFR (LEXIS); FINT–CFR (WESTLAW)	U.S. International Trade Commission Investigations	*United States Patents Quarterly* (BNA)[W] (selected full texts); ITRADE/ITC (LEXIS); FINT–ITC (WESTLAW)
Interstate Commerce Commission	49 CFR Parts 1000–1332	*Federal Carriers Reports* (CCH); TRANS/CFR (LEXIS); FTRAN–CFR (WESTLAW)	*Interstate Commerce Commission Reports*	*Federal Carriers Reports* (CCH) (digests and selected full texts); TRANS/ICC (LEXIS); FTRAN–ICC (WESTLAW)
Justice, Department of	28 CFR Parts 0–71		*Opinions of the Attorney General of the United States; Opinions of the Office of Legal Counsel of the U.S. Department of Justice;* Antitrust Division Business Review Letters	GENFED/USAG (LEXIS) (Attorney General Opinions); USAG (Attorney General and OLC Opinions) and FATR BRL (Business Review Letters) (WESTLAW)
Labor Department Office of Administrative Law Judges	29 CFR Part 18	LABOR/CFR (LEXIS); FLB–CFR (WESTLAW)	*Decisions of the Office of Administrative Law Judges and Office of Administrative Appeals*	

* The latest edition of the entire CFR is available online in GENFED/CFR (LEXIS) and CFR (WESTLAW).

L,W. Publication available online in LEXIS (L) and/or WESTLAW (W).

AGENCY	RULES AND REGULATIONS		ADJUDICATIONS, INTERPRETATIONS AND OPINIONS	
	Official	**Commercial***	**Official**	**Commercial**
Merit Systems Protection Board	5 CFR Parts 1200–1261	*Federal Merit Systems Reporter* (LRP); LABOR/CFR (LEXIS); FLB–CFR (WESTLAW)	*Decisions of the United States Merit Systems Protection Board*	*Federal Merit Systems Reporter* (LRP); *U.S. Merit Systems Protection Board Reporter* (West); LABOR/MSPB (LEXIS); FLB–MSPB (WESTLAW)
Mine Safety and Health Administration (Department of Labor) and Federal Mine Safety and Health Review Commission	30 CFR Parts 1–199 29 CFR Parts 2700–2706	*Employment Safety and Health Guide* (CCH) (selected); *Mine Safety and Health Reporter* (BNA)	*Federal Mine Safety and Health Review Commission Decisions*	*Employment Safety and Health Guide* (CCH); *Mine Safety and Health Reporter* (BNA); FLB–FMSHRC (WESTLAW)
National Labor Relations Board	29 CFR Parts 100–103	*Labor Law Reports* (CCH); *Labor Relations Reporter: Labor Relations Expediter* (BNA); LABOR/CFR (LEXIS); FLB–CFR (WESTLAW)	*Decisions and Orders of the National Labor Relations Board*	*Labor Law Reports* (CCH); *Labor Relations Reference Manual* (BNA)[L] (digests and full texts); LABOR/NLRB (LEXIS); FLB–NLRB (WESTLAW)
National Transportation Safety Board	49 CFR Parts 800–850	*Aviation Law Reports* (CCH); TRANS/CFR (LEXIS); FTRAN–CFR (WESTLAW)	*National Transportation Safety Board Decisions*	*Aviation Law Reports* (CCH) (selected); TRANS/NTSB (LEXIS); FTRAN–NTSB (WESTLAW)
Nuclear Regulatory Commission	10 CFR Parts 0–199	*Nuclear Regulation Reports* (CCH); ENERGY/	*Nuclear Regulatory Commission Issuances*	Nuclear Regulation Reports (CCH); ENERGY/NRC

		CFR (LEXIS); FEN–CFR (WESTLAW)		(LEXIS); FEN–NRC (issuances) and FEN–NRCEA (summaries and records of NRC Office of Enforcement Actions) (WESTLAW)
Occupational Safety and Health Administration (Department of Labor) and Occupational Safety and Health Review Commission	29 CFR Parts 1900–1990 29 CFR Parts 2200–2400	*Employment Safety and Health Guide* (CCH); *Noise Regulation Reporter* (BNA) (selected); *Occupational Safety & Health Reporter* (BNA); LABOR/CFR (LEXIS); FLB–CFR (WESTLAW)	*Occupational Safety and Health Review Commission Reports*	*Occupational Safety & Health Cases* (BNA); *Occuapational Safety and Health Decisions* (CCH) LABOR/OSAHRC (LEXIS); FLB–OSRC (WESTLAW)
Office of Thrift Supervision	12 CFR Parts 500–599	*BNA's Banking Report* L,W; *Federal Banking Law Reports* (CCH); BANKNG/REGS (LEXIS); FFIN–CFR (WESTLAW)		*Federal Banking Law Reports* (CCH); BANKNG/OTSDD (LEXIS); FFIN–OTS (WESTLAW)
Patent and Trademark Office (Department of Commerce)	37 CFR Parts 1–150	PATENT/CFR (LEXIS) and TRDMRK/CFR; FIP–CFR (WESTLAW)	Decisions of the Commissioner of Patents and Trademarks; Decisions of the Board of Patent Appeals and Interferences; Trademark Trial and Appeal Board Decisions	*United States Patents Quarterly* (BNA)W; PATENT/PTO, COMMR, PATAPP, AND TRDMRK/TTAB (LEXIS); FIP–PTO (WESTLAW)

***** The latest edition of the entire CFR is available online in GENFED/CFR (LEXIS) and CFR (WESTLAW).

L,W. Publication available online in LEXIS (L) and/or WESTLAW (W).

AGENCY	RULES AND REGULATIONS		ADJUDICATIONS, INTERPRETATIONS AND OPINIONS	
	Official	**Commercial***	**Official**	**Commercial**
Pension and Welfare Benefits Administration (Department of Labor)	29 CFR Parts 2509–2580	*Pension Plan Guide* (CCH); LABOR/CFR and PENBEN/CFR (LEXIS); FLB-CFR and FPEN/CFR (WESTLAW)	Pension and Welfare Benefits Administration (ERISA) Opinion Letters	*Pension Plan Guide* (CCH) (selected summaries); LABOR/ERISA and PENBEN/ERISA (LEXIS); FPEN–ERISA (WESTLAW)
Pension Benefit Guaranty Corporation	29 CFR Parts 2601–2677	*Pension Plan Guide* (CCH); LABOR/CFR and PENBEN/CFR (LEXIS); FLB–CFR and FPEN/CFR (WESTLAW)	*Pension Benefit Guaranty Corporation Opinion Letters*	*Pension Plan Guide* (CCH) (selected summaries); LABOR/PBGC and PENBEN/PBGC (LEXIS); FPEN–PBGC (WESTLAW)
Securities and Exchange Commission	17 CFR Parts 200–301	*Federal Securities Law Reports* (CCH); *Federal Securities Laws* (CCH); *Securities Regulation* (PH); FEDSEC/CFR (LEXIS); FSEC–CFR (WESTLAW)	*SEC Docket* (SEC/CCH) (formerly Securities and Exchange Commission Decisions and Reports); Interpretive Releases (in Federal Register); No–Action Letters	*Federal Securities Law Reports* (CCH) (Adjudicative Decisions, Interpretive Releases, selected No–Action Letters); *Securities Regulation* (PH) (Adjudicative Decisions, selected full texts or digests; No–Action Letters, selected summaries); FEDSEC/SECREL and NOACT (LEXIS); FSEC–DISP, FSEC–RELS and FSEC–NAL (WESTLAW)
Small Business Administration	13 CFR Parts 101–144	FGC–CFR (WESTLAW)	SBA Office of Hearings and Appeals Decisions (SBA Public Files)	PUBCON/SBA (LEXIS); FGC–SBA (WESTLAW)

Social Security Administration (Department of Health and Human Services)	20 CFR Parts 400–499	*Medicare and Medicaid Guide* (CCH); *Unemployment Insurance Reports* (CCH); *West's Social Security Reporting Service: Regulations;* LABOR/CFR (LEXIS); FGB–CFR (WESTLAW)	*Social Security Rulings*	*Unemployment Insurance Reports* (CCH) (selected summaries); *West's Social Security Reporting Service: Rulings;* LABOR/SSRULE (LEXIS); FGB–SSR (WESTLAW)

*** The latest edition of the entire CFR is available online in GENFED/CFR (LEXIS) and CFR (WESTLAW).**

L,W. Publication available online in LEXIS (L) and/or WESTLAW (W).

Name Index

References are to pages

References are to pages

Title Index

References are to pages

Boldface references are to illustrations

Boldface references are to Illustrations

Boldface references are to illustrations

Boldface references are to illustrations

Boldface references are to illustrations

†